THE LEAGUE DOESN'T LIE

THE LEAGUE DOESN'T LIE

The 606 Book of
Football Lists

Written by
Jo Tongue, Simon Poole and Paolo Hewitt

Compiled by
Jo Tongue

Researched by
Jamie King

Foreword by
Robbie Savage

BOOKS

This book is published to accompany the radio series entitled *Radio 5 live 606*.
Produced for the BBC by Somethin' Else.
Series Producer: Jo Tongue

1 3 5 7 9 10 8 6 4 2

First published in 2012 by BBC Books, an imprint of Ebury Publishing.
A Random House Group Company.

The Random House Group Limited Reg. No. 954009

Addresses for companies within the Random House Group can be found at
www.randomhouse.co.uk

A CIP catalogue record for this book is available from the British Library.

ISBN 978 1 849 90472 8

The Random House Group Limited supports The Forest Stewardship Council® (FSC®),
the leading international forest certification organisation. Our books carrying the FSC label
are printed on FSC® certified paper. FSC is the only forest certification scheme endorsed by
the leading environmental organisations, including Greenpeace. Our paper procurement
policy can be found at www.randomhouse.co.uk/environment

Commissioning editor: Albert DePetrillo
Editor: Nicholas Payne
Project editor: Steve Tribe
Production: Phil Spencer

Printed and bound by CPI Group (UK) Ltd, Croydon, CR0 4YY

To buy books by your favourite authors and register for offers,
visit www.randomhouse.co.uk

While every effort has been made to ensure information is correct at the time of going to
press, we would like to apologise should there have been any errors or omissions.

CONTENTS

FOREWORD

Listening to **606** driving back from Bournemouth nearly 20 years ago in my dad's brown Cortina, after I'd scored for Crewe, remains one of my most cherished memories. It's part of the infrastructure of a footballing day: watch or play a game, jump in the car and tune in to Radio 5 live as you drive home dreaming about a cup of a tea and a hot dinner.

Sometimes I'd be screaming at the radio in disagreement, sometimes I'd laugh out loud and often I'd learn something new – and nothing's changed now I present it! It's an honour and a privilege to present the show, and each week a new debate sets us all off.

The beauty of **606** is that there is always a discussion to be had. Often with me it turns into an argument, but it does at least start as a discussion. I love the differing opinions of football fans up and down the country and I love how there are people out there, like me, who will just not back down!

Opinions drive the show and this book is packed full of them – 13 entertaining chapters, to be precise. There are issues that come up for debate on **606** time and time again and we've touched on many of them in here: referees, international managers, best ever players... there's plenty to choose from.

We talk a lot about being the best in *The League Doesn't Lie* – the best ever manager, the best player ever. Everyone has their own opinion on what makes someone the best, but for me it's talent combined with hard work. There's no point having just one or the other – to be the best, you need to have and want to utilise both.

The best ever manager I played for was Martin O'Neill. He was as honest as they come. His man management was second to none and I would have run all day for him. He took me aside once when I was having a hard time. I wasn't the most technically gifted player, nor the most talented, but I had a big heart and I worked hard. He asked me what I would rather have, all the ability in the world with no effort, heart or desire, or to be me? That has stayed with me ever since.

I could debate the greats all night, but the best player ever for me was Maradona. I never tired of watching him but it was in Mexico 1986 he entranced me, and the rest of the world, with his skill, flair and passion. As well as being the best player in the tournament, the Argentine won the Golden Ball scoring five goals in Mexico but it was his second against England, which, for me was the best goal in football ever. He then led Napoli to their only two Championships in Serie A. He was as talented as they come, and as passionate as they come, and he led teams. He inspired them. And that for me, makes him the best ever.

One of my favourite lists in *The League Doesn't Lie* is the 'Best Chants'. Football humour is second to none. We often sat in the dressing room and laughed about chants we had heard during matches. Because of my good looks and finely groomed long blond hair, away fans often chanted to me, 'Where's your caravan? Where's your caravan?' My reply was always, 'In Monaco, next to my boat.'

I'm pleased to see I made some of the lists – although worst-dressed players and most divisive pundits weren't really where I was hoping to pop up. Had I had it my, way there'd have been some top hair, top tan, top teeth in football lists, but also a top passion list. Despite my reputation, I'm proud of what I have achieved in my career and the fact that I've played at the highest level is something not everyone can say.

Now I'm working in the media, I feel really lucky to visit new grounds and watch games from different viewpoints. My favourite commentary position is in the Etihad. I'll be honest and say that while I love the press box with its perfect vantage point and good seating, the most impressive thing at the Etihad is the food. It's amazing and the pies at half time are second to none, and even beat those at Wigan.

And in terms of commentary positions, I now have a fear of Villa Park. For that I'm blaming the Villa captain and legend Stilyan Petrov. He managed to whack me in the nose during one of my first commentary games for 5 live with Darren Fletcher. To this day, I can't say for certain that it was an accident on his part, but I do have to say – good shot, sir!

Everyone sees things through different eyes and your personal experiences shape those opinions. I know some of you will already be disagreeing with my best manager and best ever player choices and that is why I love **606**, and the premise behind this book. We've all got our own opinions and our own reasons for them. It's purely opinion-led, and all I ask is that you embrace the often-inflammatory subject matter you'll encounter in the next few pages. If you don't, give me a call on **606** and we'll reignite the debate. I'll be ready for you.

I hope you enjoy the book and look forward to carrying on the debate soon on the UK's biggest football phone-in – **606**.

Robbie Savage

ACKNOWLEDGEMENTS

With thanks to Steve Ackerman, Andrew Bontiff, Liam Bradford, Chris Burrows, Jack Davenport, Daniel Garvey, Phil Harris, Jon Holmes, Louise Gwilliam, Matthew King, Sean Livesey, David McGuire, Rudy Noriega, Huw Owen, Rhian Roberts, Lyndsey Sinclair, Nishil Solanki, Jonathan Wall and Jon Moran.

And thanks to the team who make **606** happen week in, week out... Mark Chapman, Darren Fletcher, Alan Green, Jason Roberts and Robbie Savage.

PLAYERS

Best ever players

The eternal argument – who is the best player ever? Apart from yourself, of course. This argument has raged in pubs and homes since time immemorial. There are leading contenders for the prize and, in **606**'s mind, they are the following people.

10. Ronaldo
The Brazilian goal-scorer played for, most notably, Real Madrid, as well as Barcelona, Inter Milan and AC Milan, and wherever he was he scored goals! During the 2006 World Cup, he became the highest goal-scorer in the tournament's history with 15 goals.

9. Franz Beckenbauer
The ex-Germany and Bayern Munich player is seen as one of the greatest ever defenders, and rightly so. He basically invented the attacking sweeper role, but there was no question that this defender should be allowed to push into the opposition half, because his skill and steel have rarely been employed to such effect.

8. Zico
Brazilian Zico is one of the best dribblers and finishers to have ever graced a football pitch and was up there with the best players in the world in the early 1980s. The former Flamengo playmaker was also known for his curling free kicks. After retiring, he was appointed Brazilian Sports Minister.

7. Marco Van Basten
The former Ajax and AC Milan striker won the FIFA World Player of the Year in 1992 and was one of the greatest Dutch players ever.

6. George Best
George Best was best known for his time at Manchester United, where he played 470 times and scored 179 goals. He also played 37 times for his country, Northern Ireland, scoring nine goals. His lifestyle and popularity made him more of a pop star than a footballer but his skill alone puts him in our list. He is famous for his quote 'I spent a lot of money on booze, birds and fast cars. The rest I just squandered.' He helped Manchester United win the First Division title in 1965 and 1967; he also won the European Cup with them in 1968. His role in that tournament gave him the title of European Footballer of the Year.

5. Johan Cruyff

Former Ajax, Barcelona and Netherlands international forward, who was voted European Player of the Century in 1999. His memorable drawback of the ball with the inside of his feet is now standard practice known as the Cruyff Turn. At the time, it was awe-inspiring.

4. Zinedine Zidane

Former French, Real Madrid and Juventus midfielder Zidane won numerous awards such as Ballon d'Or 1998 and World Player of the Year three times.

3. Lionel Messi

Still in his early 20s, Lionel Messi has broken many records and is still setting new ones. He is the all-time top scorer for Barcelona in one season, scoring an incredible 72 goals in all competitions. His playing nature has people comparing him to Diego Maradona, but many think he is better. The jury is still out but if we rewrite this book in ten years' time, we'll expect to see him at number one.

2. Diego Maradona

The former Napoli and Barcelona Argentinian attacking midfielder steered the then trophy-less Napoli to an incredible two League titles and a UEFA Cup. He also played in four World Cup Finals for Argentina (1982, 1986, 1990 and 1994), winning one of them.

1. Pelé

The former Santos, New York Cosmos and Brazil forward has a goal-scoring record ratio that will not be beaten for quite some time. 'I was born for soccer, just as Beethoven was born for music.' We just can't disagree.

#Best Tweeters

Technology has allowed the space between player and fan to considerably shorten. You still won't get within a hundred yards of your footballing heroes, but at least Twitter allows you to see the football brain at full throttle, filled with imagination, tolerance and great insight. Here are ten of the best examples.

10. Robin Van Persie @Persie_Official
An essential follow. Van Persie hosts Twitter quizzes and tweets pictures of a sleeping Theo Walcott and other behind-the-scenes photos.

9. Michael Owen @themichaelowen
'About to embark on the biggest challenge of my life'
Michael Owen is a notoriously mundane tweeter, tweeting about horses and hair products and keeping the bench warm. He even tweeted about starting a 1,000-piece jigsaw. It's good to know he's keeping busy.

8. Jack Wilshere @jackwilshere
'Inconsistent refereeing needs to stop. It's killing the game. If Diaby is sent off, what's the difference between that and Kevin Nolan's challenge on our keeper!?? #Joke'
   Arsenal midfielder Jack Wilshere tweets on a range of topics from Britain's Got Talent to family life and, of course, football. The above tweet nearly landed the midfielder in a spot of trouble after criticising referee Phil Dowd for sending off teammate Abou Diaby in the 4-4 draw with Newcastle.

7. Robbie Savage @Robbiesavage8
Where do you begin? The constant filling of our timelines or the numerous 'wars' he has had with Rio Ferdinand, Darren Gough or Stan Collymore. No day is complete without a tweet from Sav. The ET picture he sent to Rio Ferdinand still makes us chuckle.

6. Rio Ferdinand @rioferdy5
Rio Ferdinand has sent some classic tweets in his time, but some highlights have been the insulting 'lookalike' pictures he sends to Robbie Savage. Favourites include an Afghan hound, Ja Ja Binks and Worzel Gummidge.

5. Joey Barton @joey7Barton

'TOWIE firm don't mess with big boys, u and ur shallow, fake, pretentious lifestyles. In a year u'll be opening sh***y poundshops if ur lucky.'

Was Joey 'well jel' of *The Only Way Is Essex*? Probably not. But he is known for losing his cool on the pitch and started a war with the TOWIE cast in November 2011.

4. Ryan Babel @RyanBabel

'And they call him one of the best referees? That's a joke. SMH'

After Liverpool felt they were unfairly treated in a game against Man Utd, Babel decided to do a bit of colouring in and post a picture of the referee Howard Webb in a Manchester United top on his Twitter feed. That cost Babel a cool £10,000.

3. Carlton Cole

'Immigration has surrounded the Wembley premises! I knew it was a trap! Hahahaha. The only way to get out safely is to wear an England jersey and paint your face w/ the St George's flag!'

England were playing Ghana at Wembley and Cole decided to tweet what he thought was a joke... He later deleted the tweet but not before the FA had spotted it and fined him £20,000 for improper conduct.

2. Wayne Rooney @waynerooney

'Hi all there's my head. It will take a few months to grow. Still a bit bloody too. But that's all normal. #hairwego.'

In June 2011, Wanye Rooney tweeted confirmation that he had had a hair transplant.

1. Darren Bent @darrenbent

'Do I wanna go to Hull City. No. Do I wanna go to Stoke. No. Do I wanna go to Sunderland. Yes. So stop ******* around Levy'

In July 2009, Spurs striker Darren Bent took to Twitter to have a swipe at Tottenham chairman Daniel Levy.

Iconic centre-halves

They are the rock of the team, the wall, the insurmountable barrier that forwards have to pit their wits against every week. They are also surprisingly skilful, and their commitment to the cause can often rally the team and turn its fortunes around. No wonder that the ten named below are amongst the most loved by their respective fans.

10. Nemanja Vidic

The Serbian has built a reputation as a no-nonsense defender in an imperious spell at Manchester United. He moved to Old Trafford in 2006 from Spartak Moscow for a fee of around £7m, and has won the Premier League in each of his first three full seasons with the club (2006/7, 2007/8 and 2008/9). He lifted the Champions League trophy in 2008 and was named as United's full-time captain at the start of the 2010/11 season. Unusually for a defender, he has received personal accolades as well, being named Player of the Year twice (in 2008/9 and 2010/11) and the PFA Players' Player of the Year in 2008/9. He captained his country before retiring in 2011, and was part of the famed defence that conceded just one goal in 10 World Cup 2006 qualifying games.

9. Alessandro Nesta

The Italian centre-back was seen as the natural successor to Franco Baresi and enjoyed a hugely decorated career. He played for almost ten years with Lazio, in which time he won the Serie A title once and the Coppa Italia twice. With his beloved Lazio in financial turmoil, he moved to Milan in 2002 for a huge fee of €31m, where he went on to win two more Serie A titles, two Champions League medals and another Coppa Italia. Nesta won 78 caps for his country, and the pinnacle of his international career came in 2006 when Italy lifted the World Cup. He was named Serie A Defender of the Year four years in a row from 2000 to 2003.

8. Fabio Cannavaro

Nicknamed 'Muro di Berlino' ('Berlin Wall') by Italian supporters, Cannavaro is a perfect example of a centre-half making the most of what he has. His diminutive stature (he stands at 5'9") did not stop him being named FIFA World Player of the Year in 2006, the year that he captained his country to World Cup victory. He played for a host of Italian clubs, including Napoli, Parma, Inter and Juventus before making a move to Spain in 2006 to play under Fabio Capello at Real Madrid. He won his first League title in the 2006/7 season, quickly followed by his second La Liga in 2008. Cannavaro moved back to Juventus for a single season in 2009/10 before finishing his career in Dubai with Al-Ahli.

7. Franco Baresi

Affectionately known as Piscinin ('little one'), Baresi is commonly mentioned as the finest defender of all time, and played only for Italian giants AC Milan during a 20-year career. The sweeper was initially rejected by Milan's rivals Inter but went on to play over 700 games for the Rossonneri. He won six Serie A League titles and three European Cups (although he was suspended for the 1994 final). He is famous for being part of one of the hardest defences in European club history, lining up alongside Paolo Maldini, Alessandro Costacurta and Mauro Tassotti. Baresi's famous number 6 jersey was retired in his honour by AC Milan after the defender hung up his boots in 1997. His international career was less successful, as he was often overlooked by Italian coach Enzo Bearzot in favour of Juventus' defensive trio of Cabrini, Gentile and Scirea. He was part of the World Cup-winning squad in 1982, but did not play as he was understudy to Gaetano Scirea.

6. Carles Puyol

A Barcelona and Spain legend who has won every major honour going, Puyol has been the gritty and determined worker in consecutive teams full of artists. Puyol made his first-team debut for Barca in 1999 under Louis van Gaal and has since gone on to win 18 major trophies for the club (most notably five La Ligas and three Champions League titles), captaining the Catalans since 2004. He has also enjoyed huge success with the Spanish national team, winning Euro 2008 and the World Cup in 2010. Spanish fans will surely never forget his bullet diving header that won the World Cup semi-final against Germany.

5. Jaap Stam

The huge Dutchman only played three seasons at Manchester United, but will be best remembered as the heart of the defence that won the famous treble in 1999. He was the most expensive defender in history when United paid PSV Eindhoven £10.6m for his services in 1998. United won the League title in each of Stam's three seasons at the club, as well as winning the FA Cup and Champions League in 1999. After Stam made controversial comments in his autobiography, Alex Ferguson decided to sell the Dutch stopper to Lazio for £16.5m and replaced him with the ageing Laurent Blanc. Ferguson admitted that 'in playing terms, it was a mistake.' Stam went on to play for Milan, before finishing his career at Ajax in his native Holland.

4. Marcel Desailly

Born in Ghana but raised in France, Desailly struck an imposing figure on the football pitch. He started his professional career in the late 1980s as a product of the famed FC Nantes youth programme, and played alongside a young Didier Deschamps. He later reunited with Deschamps at Marseille, where he won the Champions League in 1993, which earned him a big-money move to Italian giants AC Milan. While at Milan, he won two League titles and the Champions League for the second year running in 1994, scoring in the famous 4-0 demolition of Barcelona. With the national team, Desailly was an important part of the 1998 World Cup-winning side, in spite of being sent off in the final. He also was an integral part of the French side that won Euro 2000, and was named captain of his country after the tournament. Desailly moved to Chelsea in 1998, where he captained the side before moving on to finish his career in Qatar.

3. Tony Adams

A one-team man who played for Arsenal for nearly 20 years, Adams enjoyed huge success throughout a turbulent career. He won four League titles, three FA Cups, two League Cups and a UEFA Cup Winners' Cup trophy under various managers. Adams was made captain of Arsenal at the age of just 21 and went on to captain the side for 14 years until his retirement in 2002. He was well known for being part of the well-disciplined Arsenal defence under George Graham who would use the offside trap to great effect, alongside Lee Dixon, Nigel Winterburn and Steve Bould. His uncharacteristic last-minute spurt of energy and superb left-footed strike capped a 4-0 win against Everton in 1998, which sealed the Premier League title of that year. 'Mr Arsenal' will forever be remembered as a no-nonsense defender by the Gunners faithful.

2. Franz Beckenbauer

'Der Kaiser' is generally regarded as the greatest German footballer of all time and, thanks to his playing style and comfort with the ball, is often credited with having invented the role of the modern sweeper. He played 103 times for his country, and played in three successive World Cup tournaments. In 1966, he lost in the final to England but his performance in the 1970 semi-final will go down in footballing folklore. He played some of the match against Italy with his arm in a sling after fracturing his clavicle. West Germany went on to lose 'the Game of the Century' 4-3 after extra time. Beckenbauer was the first captain to lift the new FIFA World Cup Trophy in 1974 after leading his side to victory over the 'total football' of Johan Cruyff's Holland. This meant that West Germany became the first national team to hold both the Euro and World Cup titles simultaneously (after West Germany had won Euro 1972). He played over 400 games for Bayern Munich and also turned out for the New York Cosmos and Hamburg. Beckenbauer went on to manage West Germany in their 1990 World Cup triumph, becoming the first man to have won the trophy as captain and as a coach. He also managed Marseille to the Ligue 1 title and Bayern Munich to the Bundesliga.

1. Bobby Moore

Perhaps the most iconic English defender of all time, Moore was England's World Cup-winning captain and was regarded as one of the gentlemen of his era. Moore captained West Ham for more than ten years, making well over 500 appearances for his first club. He lifted the FA Cup in 1964 and the UEFA Cup Winners' Cup in 1965. Pelé (who Moore called 'the most complete player I've ever played against') described Moore thus:

'He defended like a lord, he would take the ball always hard, always fair.

He was a gentleman and an incredible footballer.'

The photo of Moore and Pelé swapping shirts after a World Cup match in 1970 is largely thought of as one of the most iconic sporting images of all time.

Moore's life was tragically cut short by bowel cancer in 1993, and the Bobby Moore Fund was set up in his honour to raise money for sufferers of the disease. West Ham have retired the number 6 shirt that Moore donned throughout his career and there is a statue of him outside the new Wembley stadium.

Best foreign import

They do things differently over there, don't they? But they still produce amazing players. As money poured into the game, clubs could suddenly afford to widen their horizons and trawl the world for great talent. Here are ten players who've had an amazing impact on modern football.

10. Dwight Yorke
With the most recognisable smile in football, the Trinidad and Tobago striker lit up the Premier League with Aston Villa before going on to win numerous honours at Manchester United, forming a lethal striker partnership with Andrew Cole.

9. David Ginola
Ginola arrived in England in 1995, signing for Newcastle United, and was an immediate hit among the Geordie supporters. He left the North East for North London in 1997 and later won the League Cup for Spurs, as well as being named PFA Players' Player of the Year and FWA Footballer of the Year in 1999. His great looks and charm simply added to his allure.

8. Paolo Di Canio
The eccentric Italian's best days came at Upton Park, and his name is still chanted around the ground. As well as producing magical moments, Di Canio was never far from controversial incidents, including his push on referee Paul Alcock in 1998, for which he received an 11-match ban.

7. Patrick Viera
At Arsenal, Viera won three Premier League titles, captained the 'Invincible' squad that went the whole League campaign unbeaten, and lifted the FA Cup four times.

6. Peter Schmeichel
The Great Dane was a formidable presence between the sticks for Manchester United and is still regarded as the finest keeper to play in the Premier League. Ferguson always claimed that Schmeichel was worth an extra ten points a season to United.

5. Gianfranco Zola
The Little Italian is adored by fans up and down the country for his brilliance

but nowhere more so than at Chelsea, where he spent five glorious years. His legacy was secured when he was voted Chelsea's greatest ever player and the number 25 shirt was retired in his honour.

4. Dennis Bergkamp

The ice-cool Dutchman was signed to Arsenal in 1995 by Bruce Rioch from Inter Milan. He instantly struck up a partnership with Ian Wright and, when Arsène Wenger joined the club in 1996, Bergkamp hit the form that keeps him a legend in Arsenal and Premier League fans' eyes to this day. In the 2005/6 season Arsenal honoured him with a special 'Dennis Bergkamp Day' in their League encounter against West Brom, in which he appropriately scored.

3. Cristiano Ronaldo

He will undoubtedly go down as one of the greatest players of all time. Signed as a gangly teenager from Sporting Lisbon in 2003, the Portuguese winger emerged as a pivotal member of Manchester United's team. He enjoyed his most prolific season in 2007/8, scoring 42 goals in 49 matches as United won the Premier League title and the UEFA Champions League. He was voted World and European Footballer of the Year after that campaign.

2. Thierry Henry

After a poor season in Italy for Juventus, Henry was rescued by his former boss Arsène Wenger for a fee of around £11 million. Initially playing as a winger, Henry grew to become the League's most clinical forward, going on to become the club's record all time goal-scorer. The knee-high socks, gloves and colourful boots were as elaborate as his dazzling goals for the Gunners. Henry had charisma and character, and led from the front.

1. Eric Cantona

The charismatic Frenchman enjoyed a triumphant time at Manchester United. Eric Cantona was quite simply the biggest enigma to play in the Premier League. In his day he was unplayable: he would produce sublime examples of skill, and he always possessed the confidence to perform on the big stage. At 30 years of age, Cantona decided to call time on his career, going out at the top. Cantona is still a legend at Old Trafford, and his name can often be heard ringing round the Stretford End.

Best partnerships in football

They say love and marriage go together like a horse and carriage. But what about in more important areas of life such as the football field – what partnerships have really shone there? Here are ten couples forever bound by their mutual ability to really work at the relationship and never take each other for granted...

10. Alfredo Di Stéfano and Ferenc Puskás (Real Madrid)

Two absolute greats in the history of the game, they were part of the original Galacticos at Real Madrid, in a period when the club won five consecutive European Cups. The pair came together when Hungarian Puskás was signed for Madrid in 1958 after a two-year UEFA ban. He was 31 by then, but was still as bright and adept as ever, grabbing four hat-tricks in his first season in La Liga. In their time together, the pair shared a remarkable goal-scoring record in all competitions. Puskás scored 211 goals in 216 appearances, with Di Stéfano grabbing 147 goals in 212 games. Together at Madrid, they won the European Cup twice (with Puskás scoring seven in the two finals), La Liga four times in a row between 1961 and 1964, the Intercontinental Cup and the Spanish Cup.

Fans of Los Blancos will forever remember the final of their fifth consecutive European Cup triumph in 1960. Madrid hammered Eintracht Frankfurt 7-3 in an incredible match at Hampden Park. Puskás scored four goals, Di Stéfano three.

9. Xavi Hernández and Andrés Iniesta (Barcelona)

The Barcelona side of the 2000s will go down in footballing history as one of the greats, and the heartbeat of that side has been Xavi and Iniesta. The pair first played together in the 2002/3 season when Iniesta was promoted from the B team. Iniesta was hardly an ever-present in the 2003/4 season when Barca finished runners-up to Valencia, but it was the 2004/5 season when things began to change. Iniesta and Xavi played nearly every League game alongside superstars Eto'o, Ronaldinho and Deco, and the Catalan club lifted the title, repeating the feat in 2005/6.

Their list of joint-honours is quite remarkable. They have won the Champions League together three times (2005/6, 2008/9 and 2010/11), shared five La Liga titles, two Copa Del Reys, a World Cup, a European Championship, two FIFA Club World Cups and two UEFA Super Cups. They have played nearly 700 League games between them, amassing a joint-total of nearly 200 international caps.

8. Emilio Butrageño and Hugo Sánchez (Real Madrid)

This partnership is a perfect example of 'opposites attract'. Butrageño (nicknamed the Vulture by Madrid fans) was a quiet and very slight striker who rose through the youth ranks at Madrid. Sánchez was a bold, brash no-nonsense Mexican striker signed from city rivals Atletico. It was widely reported that the pair did not get on at all, but this in no way hindered their on-pitch relationship, which helped their club flourish in the late 1980s. The pair were first brought together in 1985 when Sanchez moved to Real, and Los Blancos went on to record five straight League victories. This culminated in the 1989/90 season where Real Madrid scored a frankly ridiculous 107 League goals. Sánchez grabbed 38 in 35 games, famously all scored with a single touch, and Butrageño added another 10. Sanchez moved back home to Mexico in 1992, while Butrageño helped to mentor another product of the Real youth team, Raúl González, before leaving in 1995.

7. Emmanuel Petit and Patrick Vieira (Arsenal)

A partnership with its roots in France was nurtured in North London. The centre-midfield pairing was born in 1997, when Arsène Wenger signed Emmanuel Petit from his former side Monaco. The pair complimented each other perfectly, with Petit's defensive nous (Wenger switched him from centre-back to defensive-midfield) adding to Vieira's raw power and energetic bursts from midfield. They won the Premier League and FA Cup double in their first season together (1997/8) and went on to play together in France's World Cup and European Championship triumphs of 1998 and 2000.

6. Tony Adams and Steve Bould (Arsenal)

This legendary defensive partnership came about after Arsenal signed Bould from Stoke in 1988. The back four of Dixon, Winterburn, Bould and Adams were famed for their disciplined use of the offside trap under George Graham and the pair won three League championships (1988/9, 1990/1 and 1997/8). In their title-winning season of 1990/1, the Arsenal backline conceded just 18 goals, one of the best defensive records in top-flight history. The partnership was broken when Bould left for Sunderland in 1999.

5. Steve Bruce and Gary Pallister (Manchester United)

One of the best central defensive partnerships in Manchester United's history first came together when United paid a then-British record for a defender – £2.3m for Pallister – in 1989. They won the FA Cup in 1990, the UEFA Cup Winners' Cup in 1991 and the League Cup in 1992, but it is for their performance as part of the title-winning side of the 1992/3 season that Bruce and Pallister will stick long in United fans' memories. They conceded just 31 goals in 42 League games. Bruce and Pallister were also part of the double-winning side of 1993/4.

4. Darren Huckerby and Dion Dublin (Coventry City)

Darren Huckerby was signed for Coventry in 1996 for £1m by then Coventry boss Gordon Strachan. Huckerby and Dublin struck up a dynamic partnership after Huckerby's arrival, with tall solid Dublin complimenting the small and speedy Huckerby. They produced a 24-goal partnership in the 1996/7 season, which kept Coventry in the Premier League. Their 38-goal partnership in 1997/8, which saw Dublin finish joint-top Premier League scorer, also saw Coventry in their highest ever Premier League finish (11th).

The pair were reunited at Norwich City in 2006 when Dublin signed for the Championship side. The club finished 16th and 17th in consecutive seasons before Huckerby left for the MLS and Dublin retired from football.

3. Romario and Hristo Stoichkov (Barcelona)

The mercurial pair played together in 1993/4, which turned out to be one of Barcelona's most famous seasons. They shone in a group that included Pep Guardiola, Michael Laudrup and Ronald Koeman. Brazilian scoring sensation Romario was signed by Barcelona after winning the Dutch League three times and boasting an impressive scoring record for PSV Eindhoven. He scored a remarkable 30 goals in 33 League games, with Stoichkov adding a further 16 League goals to the partnership. Stoichkov's wand of a left foot and deft technique complimented the explosive Romario perfectly, and their goals helped Johan Cruyff's side to a La Liga title. The League win will be remembered by the Catalan faithful for a 5-0 hammering of bitter rivals Real Madrid in the Nou Camp, with Stoichkov's artistry helping Romario to plunder a marvellous hat-trick.

Both Romario and Stoichkov left Barca in 1995, and while the Bulgarian returned in 1996 to make fleeting appearances alongside another Brazilian scoring sensation at the Nou Camp, Barcelona fans will more fondly remember his partnership with Romario in 1993/4.

2. Dwight Yorke and Andy Cole (Manchester United)

Trinidadian striker Dwight Yorke signed for Manchester United in the summer of 1998, arriving from Aston Villa for £12.6m. His first season at the club saw him link up with Andy Cole, with the pair displaying an almost-telepathic link at times. The duo scored 53 goals in all competitions in 1998/9 season, and helped guide United to an unprecedented treble of Premier League, FA Cup and Champions League. Their partnership was best embodied by a remarkable goal against Barcelona at the Nou Camp in the quarter-final of the Champions

League, where a series of one-touch passes resulted in one of United's most memorable goals.

The pair briefly were reunited at Blackburn and helped the Lancashire club finish 6th in the 2002/3 season, qualifying for the UEFA Cup.

1. Alan Shearer and Chris Sutton (Blackburn Rovers)

Chris Sutton became the most expensive player in English football when he signed for Blackburn from Norwich in the summer of 1994 for a fee of £5m. He joined up with Alan Shearer, who had finished the 1993/4 season with 31 goals in 40 games. The pair linked up to great effect in Blackburn's title-winning 1994/5 season, with Shearer grabbing 34 goals and Sutton scoring 15. They were nicknamed the SAS (Shearer and Sutton).

Strange superstitions

Footballers, like all elite sportsmen, are highly superstitious. In a game where things can be decided by one millimetre's difference, the mentality is that you should do all you can so that your sky god will bestow upon you success and achievement, and tear it away from your opponent. In a game where technology and science has become so important, it's something of an anomaly to have such a deep belief in luck. But they do, bless them. We're all prone to it, though. Lucky socks are not uncommon. A certain route to the ground, perhaps? It's the same thing. If superstition is the poetry of life, as Goethe suggested, be prepared for some god-awful comedy doggerel.

10. Paul Ince
Would only put his shirt on once he entered the pitch, and he had to be last out of the tunnel.

9. John Terry
He has to use the same urinal before every match and if someone is using it, he will wait for it to be free, rather than using a different one. He also has to sit in the same seat on the team bus. He always listens to the same CD en route to the stadium (Usher), and he always ties a band three times on his socks.

8. Midlands Portland Cement
Back in 2008, the Zimbabwean side Midlands Portland Cement first-team squad were sent into the crocodile-crowded Zambezi river for spiritual cleansing; 17 went in, 16 came out.

7. David James
Believed to be one of the most superstitious of footballers, James admitted to having many complex pre-match rituals, one of which includes spitting on the wall in the dressing room urinals. It's not clear whether he tips the cleaning lady heavily at Christmas.

6. Laurent Blanc
His pre-match ritual in the tournament involved kissing Fabian Barthez's bald head before kick-off in every match.

5. Bobby Moore
Bobby would only put his shorts on when the rest of his teammates had already

done so. Martin 'Laugh a minute' Peters realised what was going on and would wait for Bobby to put on his shorts before once again dropping his own. And so on. Gentler times, dear reader, gentler times.

4. Johan Cruyff
When Cruyff was at Ajax, he would slap his keeper Gert Bals in the stomach and then spit his chewing gum into the opposition's half before kick-off. Children, do not try this at home, as it is antisocial and could land you with a fine for littering.

3. Gary Lineker
He would never shoot in the warm-up for fear of 'using up his goals' and not being able to score in the match, which is the reverse of what Fernando Torres does at Chelsea.

2. Neil Warnock
During a winning run, he will stop at every traffic light on the way home, even if it's green. This is of course against the Highway Code, but Neil has a plan for that, too. If he's stopped by an overzealous traffic copper he morphs into his alter ego, Winifred the Old Lady, owing to his resemblance to a moaning old lady. He gets off every time.

1. Gennaro Gattuso
Purely in terms of originality does the pocket battleship make it to number one in the list. You can keep your urinal preferences, your spitting, your clothing rituals, your smelly pants. Give us a man who read a few pages of Russian writer Fyodor Dostoevsky's work prior to each game in the 2006 World Cup. On the loo. Fyodor Dostoyevsky's work, as you well know, explores human psychology in the troubled political, social and spiritual context of 19th-century Russian society. It seemed to do the trick: Italy won the World Cup. Perhaps England's stars should take note and pull down a dusty volume of Dickens from the shelves in the library?

Best WAGs

Post-Germany 2006, career advisers up and down the country have had to forcibly remove 'WAG' from options forms. This isn't Miss World, or indeed Miss Manchester, so we have a strict list of criteria for our top WAGs. Beauty is definitely one of those factors, but it's also about how successful they've been in their own career, how successful their partner has been in football, and whether or not they've been involved in scandal.

10. Mellissa Satta
The tattooed ex-Pompey midfielder got lucky when he left struggling Portsmouth to move to AC Milan in 2010. He met Italian model Mellissa Satta and settled well into life at the San Siro. However, the couple's bedroom activity led to Prince Boateng getting injured and thus having to sit some games out on the sidelines. We're sure his manager was delighted.

9. Irina Shayk
She's the current girlfriend of Cristiano Ronaldo. The 26-year-old Russian model has been in the *Sports Illustrated* Swimsuit edition for five consecutive years. Imagine having to go poolside next to those two.

8. Christine Bleakley
A new arrival to the WAG scene, she's engaged to Frank Lampard. Adrian Chiles approves, and that's good enough for us.

7. Stacey Giggs
We all know what happened here. Soap Opera isn't the phrase. We're in awe of her standing by her man.

6. Cheryl Cole
Poor old Cheryl Cole. She had it all – the girl band, the footballer husband and the Saturday night TV show. But then Cashley and Simon Cowell let her down, her band mates took a break and it would appear her stylist had a few days off too. However, just like Newcastle she's on a mini roll right now – they're almost Champions League standard, she's back in the charts. Top tens all round.

5. Shakira
The 'Hips Don't Lie' singer has been dating Gerard Pique for some time. Her drop of the shoulder wouldn't look amiss on the pitch at the Camp Nou and arguably, she's the best singer in the list.

4. Abbey Crouch

The Stoke City striker certainly landed on his feet when he started dating – and then married – lingerie and catwalk model Abbey Clancy. Clancy first came to our attention when she came second on TV programme *Britain's Next Top Model*. Crouchy certainly hasn't settled for second best in our eyes.

3. Coleen Rooney

Her relationship with Wayne started in their high-school days. Whilst we like the teenage love story, most of us can think of nothing worse than marrying the person we kissed in the school playground. Coleen was very young in 2006 so we're hoping she was easily led and the perma-tan, extensions and shopping bags permanently attached to her arms are a teenage phase...

2. Louise Redknapp

A worthy runner-up to Victoria Beckham, pipped to the post mainly because Spice Girls were better than Eternal. She's been with Jamie for 'literally' years and works as a presenter and model. Beautiful, clever and with her own career.

1. Victoria Beckham

No question, Posh is the ultimate, original WAG. She's the epitome of 'Wagism'. Spotted by David in the video for her Spice Girls hit 'Say You'll Be There', her black catsuit won her the man. She's since gone on to design catsuits (well frocks) of her own for her fashion range. Pop star, fashion icon and married to David Beckham. You'd think that would be enough to make you smile.

Biggest badge-kissers

Badge-kissing by players is a relatively new trend in the Premier League, a wonderful and imaginative way for players to show the fans that they care and their love for the club in equal measure. If the money is right...

10. Thierry Henry – Arsenal
He won two Premier Leagues and three FA Cups with Arsenal and lost to Barcelona in the 2006 Champions League Final in his time at Highbury. He often professed his undying love for the North London club. Then he moved to Barcelona in 2007 for £16.1 million. Henry returned to Arsenal in January 2012 for six weeks.

9. Craig Gardner – Aston Villa/ Birmingham
He signed for Villa when he was 15 and claimed he had the best days of his life at his boyhood club. He moved to arch rival Birmingham in 2010 and kissed the badge when he scored. He said that 'he was a bluenose and has been all his life'. Then Birmingham got relegated, and he signed for Sunderland in June 2011.

8. Samir Nasri – Arsenal
He kissed the Arsenal badge a few times. Then he left Arsenal to join City in the summer of 2011 for a fee around £19 million. Moreover, he added injury to insult when he told the fans that he was leaving to win trophies and that they lacked passion.

7. Charlie Adam – Blackpool
Charlie Adam kissed the badge of the Blackpool shirt at White Hart Lane in the 2010/11 season. At the end of that season, he joined Liverpool for a fee of around £9 million.

6. Cesc Fàbregas – Arsenal
The former Arsenal skipper used to kiss the Arsenal badge every time he scored. He moved to Barcelona in August 2011 for a fee of £35 million.

5. Ian Wright – Arsenal
He admitted that kissing the Arsenal badge in front of Palace fans was a big mistake. He then claimed he loved Palace. Later on, he kissed the Arsenal badge again on the final day of 1992/93 season, when he scored the goal to relegate... Palace.

4. Frank Lampard – Chelsea

Lampard frequently kisses the Chelsea badge, but has so far not moved anywhere. Watch this space...

3. Alan Smith – Leeds United

He's a boyhood Leeds United fan and kissed the badge countless times. When they were relegated at the end of the 2003/4 season, Smith was the last to leave the pitch and shared a few tearful moments with the fans. Eighteen days after Leeds were relegated, Smith signed for Manchester United, Leeds' bitterest rivals.

2. Fernando Torres – Liverpool

Torres often claimed he loved Liverpool. In fact, he loved the club so much he often kissed the badge after scoring. He then moved to Chelsea for £50 million in January 2011.

1. Wayne Rooney – Everton

Be careful what you say in public. Rooney once claimed 'once a Blue, always a Blue'. He then left his club Everton in 2004 and signed for Manchester United in a deal worth £27 million.

One-club legends

In the world of football, there are huge names who have dedicated most or all of their lives to one club. Players who refused to let go, even after their retirement. These great men need celebrating. So let us raise our glasses to the loyal legends of football.

10. Alessandro Del Piero
Del Piero stayed with Juventus when they got relegated to Serie B in 2006 to help the Italian giants regain promotion back to the top flight. While key players left the club, he decided to stay, despite interest from a host of big European clubs. He's been with Juve since 1993 and made over 500 appearances.

9. Ryan Giggs
We couldn't separate the two United legends Giggs and Neville, both stars of the United Youth team of 1992 and now embroiled in United history. In his 22 seasons at United, Giggs has won 12 Premier League titles, four FA Cups and two Champions League trophies and he's still going. He claims it's down to yoga, but we think there's something in the water at Carrington. Giggs, Neville, Scholes, Fergie himself...

8. Gary Neville
Gary Neville's 602 appearances for Manchester United place him firmly as an all-time Old Trafford great. He joined them as a trainee aged just 14 and captained the under-18 side to the FA Youth Cup in his first season as an apprentice. Maybe one of the more hated figures by other teams but certainly one you would love to have on your side. And he's endeared himself to us even more by remaining as impartial as he can when commentating on United in his new role as a pundit.

7. Billy Wright
Wright played 541 games for his beloved Wolves side. He served during the Second World War, and also served his country well in football, becoming the first player in the world to earn 100 caps and captaining them 90 times. He even made Wolves one of the most attractive sides in Europe in the 1940s and 1950s. We repeat, one of the most attractive footballing sides in Europe. Legend.

6. Trevor Brooking
Sir Trev ran games for West Ham in the same way he has conducted himself as a

one-man PR for the club since. A measured, effective and loyal gentleman, and a true legend at the club, he spent his whole career at Upton Park playing 635 games and then having a stint as caretaker manager and as a director. He still goes to most of the home games.

5. Pat Rice
He made 528 appearances for Arsenal, was a double winner and then captained them to an FA Cup victory. As if he hadn't given the Gunners enough, he then dedicated 44 years to the club as a coach. Player, captain, coach and all-round nice guy.

4. Franco Baresi
Nicknamed 'the little one', Baresi is hailed as one of the greatest players ever to grace the game. Voted AC Milan Player of the Century, he retired in 1997 having served 20 years at the club. The number 6 shirt was retired in his honour.

3. Tony Adams
The traditional defender led Arsenal to unrivalled success during his 19-year spell: four League titles, three FA Cups, two League Cups and a UEFA Cup Winners Cup. He picked up 717 games for the Gunners and went on to captain England. Arsenal still miss his presence.

2. Matthew Le Tissier
Having played 540 games for Southampton, Le Tissier remains one of the finest English players ever produced. With only a handful of England caps to his name, he was axed by Glen Hoddle before the 1998 World Cup. Oh, how we could have done with his penalty-taking prowess.

1. Nat Lofthouse
As well as scoring nearly 300 goals for Bolton, Lofthouse went on to manage the side, becoming chief scout and then the club's president. A true one-club man.

Biggest fall from grace

The urge to snigger as the mighty fall from grace is incredibly powerful. One minute they are attracting the wild cheers of the crowd, the next their powers have faded, sometimes thanks to lengthy spells spent in the company of models and champagne bottles. Here are ten players whom the gods proved were human after all.

10. Adriano

The powerful ex-Inter Milan and Brazil striker was destined for great things whilst playing in Milan, but his work ethic was questioned when he was caught out in nightclubs, which resulted in him getting dropped by Brazil. This started a terrible decline. In 2010, Adriano won the 'Bidone d'Oro' award – awarded to the worst player in the Serie A – for the third time. At just 30 years old, he was released by Corinthians.

9. Ronaldinho

Once up there with the best players in the world, Ronaldinho has declined spectacularly since departing Barcelona. Moving to AC Milan, his goal-scoring record was nowhere near as impressive as when at Barcelona. This meant a move back to Brazil, like Adriano. How the mighty have fallen, at only 32 years of age.

8. Christian Vieri

Recently retired Christian Vieri has really fallen off the radar since his free-scoring Inter Milan days. Back in the day, Vieri used to score for fun. But then he left Inter Milan for rivals AC Milan. He wasn't a regular starter for Milan and was soon dropped from the Italian national team. In a bid to re-find his striker's prowess, he moved to Monaco, Atalanta, Fiorentina, and then back to Atalanta. He didn't find it.

7. Chris Sutton

After huge early success at both Norwich, then more notably at Blackburn, where he won the Premiership title, Chris Sutton's stake was at a premium. In 1999, he made a £10 million move to Chelsea, but in 28 games he only scored one League goal. He redeemed himself with a move to Celtic but should have quit while he was ahead as spells at Birmingham, and then Villa (brave move) were not successful. Maybe Le Tissier was onto something.

6. Darius Vassell

After successfully graduating from the Aston Villa academy, and playing first team football at Aston Villa for four years, Sven Göran Ericsson called Vassell to the England squad on 22 occasions, where he scored six goals. He also played in World Cup 2002 and Euro 2004. After leaving Villa, Vassell had an unsuccessful time at Manchester City, then moved to Turkey, where he was greeted like a legend, but couldn't repay the fans with goals. This prompted a move back to England with Leicester City in the Championship. Where he couldn't even get a game for them.

5. Angelos Charisteas

Whilst playing for Werder Bremen, Angelos Charisteas was on great form for Greece in the European Championships of 2004. He helped Greece to a shock victory in the competition, and life could not have been rosier. But success bites, and Charisteas has moved around ever since the tournament, but never been successful nor settled anywhere. He moved back to Greece to play for Panetolikos FC.

4. Vicente

Vicente Rodriquez made 243 appearances for Valencia, winning La Liga twice. He also won 38 caps for Spain. In his prime, he was linked with a €40 million move to Real Madrid, and was widely regarded as one of the best wingers in the world. In his late 20s, however, Vicente suffered badly from injuries which led to his release from Valencia, and he made a somewhat shock move to Gus Poyet's Brighton and Hove Albion. Lovely place, Brighton, but not quite Madrid.

3. Adrian Mutu

The Romanian striker was destined for great things when he moved to Chelsea for around £15.8 million. After being there for just over a year, however, Mutu failed a drugs test for cocaine, was sacked by Chelsea and received a seven-month ban from football. Since the end of a successful spell at Fiorentina, Mutu has plied his trade for Cesena, who were relegated to Serie B in 2012.

2. Diego Milito

In his first season at Inter Milan, Milito helped them to treble-winning glory, scoring the winning goals in the Champions League Final, Coppa Italia, and on the final day of the Serie A season to win the League title. After this incredible 2009/10 season, Milito failed to emulate this and struggled to get a start.

1. Michael Owen

The ex-England and Liverpool wonder kid's career went downhill after moving to Real Madrid. An injury-plagued few seasons saw him play only 36 League games before moving back to England to join Newcastle. Again, injuries hindered his progress and he played only 71 games in four unsuccessful seasons. After being released by Newcastle United, he had a shock move to Manchester United, but played just 31 times in three seasons before being released.

Football Jokers

Every office has one. And by 'office', we also mean football club. They are always men, though, aren't they? When was the last time a woman put cling film across a lavatory bowl? Actually, come to think of it, Jo (who does the buttons and the switches on **606**) loves a practical joke. The evening when she sent the new boy out for some waterproof teabags will live long in our memories. So here they are, our jokers in the pack when the pack only contains jokers. Funny, if the joke's not on you.

15. Bristol Rovers
Rovers used April Fool's Day to unveil their new 'shocking pink' kit on their website. Surprisingly, the strip caused such a positive stir that the club really did introduce it as their third kit, with some of the proceeds going to charity.

14. Jimmy Bullard
Back in 2009, when Bullard equalised for Hull to earn a 1-1 draw at Manchester City, the midfielder sat his fellow players down in a circle and wagged his finger at them. It was imitating what Hull manager at the time Phil Brown had done the season before in the same fixture when they were 4-0 down at half time.

13. David Luiz
Back in the days when both played for Benfica, David Luiz engineered an incident in which teammate Angel Di Maria reversed into a girl and was caught out by the police. The prank ended with David Luiz coming out and laughing at his friend, who was in handcuffs by then.

12. Mark Bircham
Bircham once scared the whole QPR squad by bringing a snake into work.

11. Nicky Butt
A classic prank that went royally wrong. Nicky Butt was sneaking up behind the Manchester United keeper with a kettle, aiming to touch his bare bum. But when Schmeichel quickly turned around, it was the other side that received the scalding. Jaap Stam revealed that this story was his funniest memory of the club:

> 'Nicky had to run for his life as Peter chased him all around the Cliff a few times, leaving us in tears from laughing. Unforgettable!'

10. Robbie Savage

Back from the days when our Robbie played with David Bentley at Blackburn, he pretended to be Steve McClaren and gave Bentley his own little call-up. Putting on Steve's voice, he told Bentley that he really wanted him in the England team. (Bentley was expecting his first call-up and the whole team knew it.) Bentley doesn't usually answer private numbers but, knowing that Steve McClaren's call would be from a private number, he answered this one. When the real Steve McClaren later rang on a private number, he refused to answer.

This story did have a happy ending: David Bentley got his England call-up. In 2007, he was a substitute in England's 3-0 win over Israel at Wembley.

9. Wimbledon

Back in the 1990s, Wimbledon were the biggest pranksters around, hence their nickname – the Crazy Gang. One of the classic stories is when John Hartson signed for Wimbledon in 1999. He arrived for his first day of training in a nice clean Armani suit. When he was returning from the training pitch, getting ready for his first press conference, he noticed a fire and panicked. All the other lads laughed. It was his suit that was on fire, along with everything he'd come with. So he had to wear an old training kit to the press conference.

8. Paulo Di Canio

When the Italian was at Celtic, he roomed with the team captain Peter Grant. Paulo knew that Grant had a phobia of fish, so when he went to bed he sneaked downstairs and got a large salmon head, put it in a plastic bag and into his bed. It ended in Di Canio having to lock himself in the bathroom as Grant chased him around the room like a madman.

7. Robbie Savage (the victim)

When Robbie Savage arrived for his first day's training following a loan move to Brighton and Hove Albion, assistant manager Bob Booker had dressed up in a car-park attendant's fluorescent jacket, complete with goofy teeth and Robbie Savage-esque long blond hair. Booker said, 'I think you're great.' Unaware he was the subject of a prank, Savage politely obliged and even posed for photos with the 'fan' as the team and manager looked on.

6. Gianluca Vialli

The ex-Chelsea player manager was quite the joker. When he played together with Graham Souness at Sampdoria, he got his own back after Souness pushed him in a lake by putting itching powder in his pants and cutting his trouser legs off. His joking may have grabbed him some headlines, but it didn't help his international career. Vialli missed out going to the 1994 World Cup in the USA after he put Parmesan cheese in Italy manager Arrigo Sacchi's handkerchief.

5. Mario Balotelli
Returning to his car after Manchester City's two-week summer tour, he found that his teammates had put a holdall full of kippers in there before they'd left.

4. Joey Barton
When moving to QPR in 2011, Joey Barton didn't waste any time in making practical jokes. He obviously didn't agree with his teammate Jay Bothroyd's Ugg boots, which he cut in half. Back at the beginning of the 2011 season, Barton tweeted a picture of a highchair with Shaun Wright Phillips on it asking if anyone had seen the 5'5" midfielder: 'Anyone seen @swp29 he's not in his seat at dinner. #searchpartyforweeman.' We're fairly sure his teammates are too scared to do anything but laugh.

3. Rio Ferdinand
Rio Ferdinand knew that David Beckham hated lateness. So he hired a taxi driver to give him a tour of Manchester before Beckham jumped out in Moss Side in sheer frustration.

2. More Rio Ferdinand
Rio was getting so good at these wind-ups that they gave him his own TV mini-series for it – *Rio's World Cup Wind-ups*, just before the 2008 World Cup. He managed to prank nearly every player from that World Cup. One of our favourites is one in which John Terry helped out Rio Ferdinand. Under the cover of a lunch invitation, an over-keen waiter – guided by Rio – kept on asking for Shaun Wright Phillips' autograph for increasingly unbelievable brothers, cousins, etc. The owner created an awkward scene in the restaurant, and got escorted out for harassing the England player.

1. Paul Gascoigne
We could have a whole list just of Paul Gascoigne's pranks. This is a man who went to the pub in his England kit, including boots, just hours after playing for England. He has blagged 'goes' on a workman's pneumatic drill and an open-top red London bus. When Ginola arrived at Everton for his first day in 2002 he arrived to the sight of Paul Gascoigne in a wig saying, 'Because I'm worth it'. Gascoigne also stuck the whistling bit of a whistling kettle up Newcastle captain Glenn Roeder's exhaust pipe, causing the car to be heard up to a mile away.

Cleverest players

Without wishing to revert to stereotype, footballers have not particularly shone in the brains of Britain department, often issuing utterances that would not be out of place in a primary school playground As ever, though, there are the great exceptions. All together now – 'You're smart and you know you are...'

10. Sócrates
The Brazilian 1982 World Cup captain is up there with the all-time greats, despite never winning an FA Cup. He wasn't just talented at football, he had a brain too. He was named after a Greek philosopher. He was also nicknamed 'the Doctor' and held a doctorate in philosophy. The Brazilian was also involved in politics before dying at 57 in December 2011.

9. Steve Coppell
Whilst at Tranmere Rovers, Steve Coppell started an Economics degree at Liverpool University. He successfully completed his degree before signing for Manchester United. He played more than 300 games for United and won 42 England caps. He has managed a number of clubs including the appropriately named Reading.

8. Graeme Le Saux
Known as one of the most intelligent footballers of the 1990s. Le Saux started an Environmental Studies degree, before having to cancel it because of that annoying thing called first team football at Chelsea.

7. Shaka Hislop
Kids usually want to be either an astronaut or a famous sportsman. Well, Shaka Hislop has been both. The former Trinidad and Tobago number 1 worked for NASA. He also studied in Washington and graduated with a degree in Mechanical Engineering. After his career, Hislop took up the assistant coaching role at Quinnipiac University in the USA.

6. David James
He might not have a university degree, but his charitable work and love for art makes him smarter than your average footballer. He set up the David James Foundation, helping young people in Malawi and he also pens a column for *The Observer*.

5. Gundi Bergsson

The Icelandic international, Bergsson left Bolton in 2003. He then studied and became a full-time lawyer. He also hosts a TV show in Iceland called *4-4-2*.

4. Iain Dowie

Believe it or not, before playing professional football Iain Dowie completed a Masters degree in Aeronautic Engineering at the University of Hertfordshire. He also started working for British Aerospace. So you could say he was over the moon.

3. Nedum Onuoha

At school, the boy did well grabbing 8 As at GCSE and 3 As at A Level. When Stuart Pearce was Manchester City manager, he was asked by a player, 'You seen Nedum anywhere, boss?' Pearce replied, 'No, but he's probably splitting the atom or something around the back there!'

2. Frank Lampard

Lampard is reported to have a higher IQ than Carol Voderman (over 150) and to be in the top 0.1 per cent of most intelligent people in the country. When a club doctor went to Chelsea to conduct some IQ tests, he didn't reveal Frank Lampard's score but said it was one of the highest sets of marks he'd ever seen. Lampard was educated at Brentwood School in Essex, obtaining 12 GCSEs – including an A in Latin.

1. Clarke Carlisle

Clarke won the Britain's Brainiest Footballer title in 2002. Which is not surprising. The lad graduated from Staffordshire University with a degree in Professional Sports Writing and Broadcasting and then went on to make an appearance on *Countdown* in February 2010, where he beat the reigning champion Adam Guest by 89 points to 55. He also appeared on *Question Time* when the programme visited Burnley. He is currently the PFA Chairman.

Iconic midfielders

The midfielder is the most important link in your team. He is the light, silky, skilled individual whose brilliance and vision continually brightens up the game, or he is the engine, a snarling all-tackling machine, whose passion and determination pushes the team ever forward to victory. Whatever your choice of player here are ten of ours.

10. David Beckham

Playing for Manchester United on 265 occasions and Real Madrid 116 times, as well England 115 times (and captaining them for many of these caps) shows the scale of David Beckham's success. Since leaving Real Madrid he has been playing in America for LA Galaxy as he tries to up the profile of football in the States. Away from football, Beckham does an exceptional amount of charity work, is married to a pop star – Victoria Adams – and was integral to London's bid to host the Olympics in 2012.

9. Clarence Seedorf

A similar player to Edgar Davids, just without the goggles. Having previously played for Real Madrid and Ajax, he now plays for AC Milan, and has done so since 2002. Seedorf has won the Champions League with three different clubs – Ajax in 1995, Real Madrid in 1998 and Milan in 2003 and 2007. Clarence also has 87 caps for the Netherlands.

8. Steven Gerrard

One-man club Steven Gerrard is a hero in Liverpool and, for many, one of the best midfielders in the world in recent years. His quality on the ball, work ethic, eye for a goal and all-round play, as well as his outstanding captain-like ability have led him to become an iconic midfielder.

7. Claude Makélélé

You can't get any more iconic than Claude Makélélé. The ex-Real Madrid and Chelsea defensive midfielder has his own position – 'the Makélélé role' – which is said to be just in front, guarding the defensive line. Not known for his goal-scoring touch, Makélélé received his plaudits for doing the simple things exceptionally well. Plus, no one else in the world has ever had a position named after them.

6. Ryan Giggs

He is the biggest footballer to have come out of Wales. Although stories about his personal life have recently been made public, on the pitch he has still been voted the greatest Premiership footballer since it began in 1992. He has scored in every Premiership season and still puts in exceptional performances in every game he plays.

5. Luis Figo

The Portuguese legend was arguably one of the best players ever – playing over 100 times for Real Madrid, Barcelona and Inter Milan as well as 127 times for Portugal proves this. His time at Real Madrid was during the ever-successful 'Galactico' era, in which every player was up there with the best in the world at the time.

4. Roy Keane

The controversial ex-Manchester United midfielder and captain was the club's leader through their recent glory years. He's an iconic midfielder because of his aggressive style of play, and an extremely competitive attitude which led to him excelling as captain. His performance against Juventus in the Champions League semi-final of 1999 remains a landmark.

3. Patrick Vieira

The French midfielder, most notable for his nine-year tenure at Arsenal, won three League titles, and four FA cups with the Gooners and was a major part of their unbeaten season as he was the club captain. His work ethic, style of play and presence put him in our top three.

2. Paul Scholes

The diminutive ginger wonder has been around the first team set up at Old Trafford for the better part of 20 years. It isn't just the Manchester United fans that appreciate the Oldham-born's talents, though – check out Zinedine Zidane's thoughts: 'My toughest opponent? Scholes of Manchester. He is the complete midfielder.' And just for good measure, Edgar Davids said, 'I'm not the best. Paul Scholes is.' High Praise.

1. Zinedine Zidane

Can you get any more iconic that Zinedine Zidane? The best player of our lifetime, and arguably one of the best players ever, the former Juventus and Real Madrid midfielder had it all – vision, skill and goals. Plenty of goals. His humble demeanour also made him an idol for many young players. Although his career ended badly, head-butting Marco Materazzi in the chest in the 2006 World Cup final, you can't take away what a fantastic midfielder he was.

Dressing room incidents

Let's get ready to rumble as we present those fiery moments when players attack players, players attack coaches or players just act in the daftest possible way and end up in a whole heap of trouble. Or in some cases, just in a heap.

10. Jacob Mellis
Mellis was sacked by Chelsea after he admitted setting off a smoke grenade and sparking a full-scale evacuation of the club's training ground in Cobham.

9. Tony Pulis and James Beattie
The pair came to blows in the dressing room in 2009 after Stoke's 2-0 defeat to Arsenal. Beattie objected to Pulis's order that the players should report for training on a day that had been agreed for their Christmas dinner / party. Note to self: Never get in the way of a man and his office party.

8. Andy Carroll and Steven Taylor
The pair had a fight at Newcastle's training ground over one of Carroll's ex-girlfriends in 2010. Both needed surgery after the incident. Taylor had a broken jaw, and Carroll needed surgery on his hand.

7. Mick McCarthy and Roy Keane
Roy Keane was sent home from the Republic of Ireland's 2002 World Cup squad after a falling-out with manager Mick McCarthy. Keane told the world it was due to the unprofessional approach of the management team.

6. John Terry and Wayne Bridge
The pair were close friends until it was alleged that Terry had been secretly seeing Bridge's ex-girlfriend, Vanessa Perroncel, and made her pregnant. Terry said he had been consoling the lingerie model after her split from Bridge, and the inevitable had happened. Bridge refuses to shake Terry's hand when facing his old teammate.

5. Raymond Domenech and French players
At the 2010 World Cup, Domenech fell out so badly with a number of French players that the whole squad threatened to boycott the tournament. During a 2-0 defeat to Mexico, Nicolas Anelka and Domenech argued so badly at half time that the striker was sent home. The next day, Domenech had to intervene in a physical row between Patrice Evra and trainer Robert Suverne. After the

incident, the team announced they would be boycotting the tournament and returning home. They didn't but instead lost 2-1 to South Africa and went home in disgrace.

4. Mario Balotelli and Marco Materazzi

While teammates at Inter Milan, the pair came to blows after the Champions League semi-final first-leg victory against Barcelona in 2010. Balotelli threw off his Inter shirt and gave the fans the middle finger after being substituted. It was later reported that Balotelli and Materazzi had a heated row in the tunnel.

3. John Hartson and Eyal Berkovic

The pair were involved in a training ground bust-up while playing for West Ham in 1998. John Hartson kicked Berkovic in the head after a tackle. Hartson was severely reprimanded, and Berkovic later said, 'If my head was a ball, it would have been in the corner of the net,' which, given Hartson's scoring record, surprised a lot of West Ham fans.

2. Ashley Cole's rifle

Ashley Cole fired an air rifle at Tom Cowan, a Loughborough Sports Science student, in the dressing room of the club's Cobham training ground in 2011. Cowan suffered a flesh wound and the Chelsea player was fined £250,000, which is just two weeks' wages. Jokes about Ashley's weapon were never uttered in the 606 offices.

1. Beckham's boot

After Manchester United's FA Cup defeat at home to Arsenal in 2003, Sir Alex kicked a boot which hit David Beckham in the United dressing room. The incident left Beckham needing stitches above his left eye. Sir Alex later joked that if he had meant to hit his star player in such a manner, he would still be playing football. United lost the match 2-0.

Largest players

When you think of the modern-day footballer, you think they are super fit, athletic and quick. This isn't always true, however, and it is not a necessity in football. If you give some players the ball, they can do amazing things with it. Indeed, most of the players on our list were very good, and naturally gifted. There's also a couple of players who used to be world superstars, but have enjoyed a few too many burgers recently.

10. Neil Shipperly
After gaining a few extra pounds, a few people rather unkindly dubbed the former Crystal Palace centre-forward Neil Chipperly. True, he does look a little rounder these days than he did in his youth, but after a total of 447 appearances for nine different clubs, we think he's maybe earned his rights to have that extra portion of chips or ten.

9. John Hartson
We at **606** towers think that the 6'1" (and slightly stocky) Hartson could have just as easily plied his trade in Rugby Union on the second row as he did as a striker.

8. Adriano
When the Brazilian was signed to Corinthians, the club actually staged an intervention in a bid to help the striker shed the pounds. They ordered him to stay in the team's hotel, following a strict, doctor-supervised diet and exercising three times a day. Unfortunately, it wasn't enough and he was let go at the end of the 2011/12 season.

7. Andy Reid
This midfielder credits a love of a well-known bakery chain brand (ahem) for his excellent work rate and surprising speed. This is music to our ears; perhaps the thought of a dozen sausage rolls the next time we're slogging away in the gym will motivate us to work harder?

6. Mark Viduka
Celtic fans have a nickname for this striker from down under – FLB. What could this stand for, we wonder? Fantastic Lovely Ball-skills? Football Loving Boy? Erm no, not quite. It's Fat Lazy B******. A bit harsh really – he scored 30 goals in 37 League appearances, which isn't that bad at all. Maybe the Hoops

faithful feel that he could have done even better if he'd had fewer deep-fried chocolate bars.

5. Ronaldo

Multiple honours then, multiple chins now... Our younger readers might be surprised to learn that there was a time when Ronaldo was a fearsome presence up front for both club and country. He also won the prestigious Ballon d'Or twice and the FIFA Player of the Year an astonishing three times, putting him alongside the great Zidane and Messi.

4. Neville Southall

Big Nev made nearly 600 appearances for Everton in goal and proved that an extra layer of padding when you're a keeper is a good thing. He helped the Toffees win 2 League championships, 2 FA Cups and a European Cup Winners Cup. Logic surely dictates then that the more of the goal you fill, the less room there is for your opponents to put the ball past you...

3. Dean Windass

OK, we feel a bit mean putting this 42-year-old veteran on the list – maybe he can attribute his impressive 19-season career to an extra sneaky pie here and there? He's lasted longer than most pros these days – a fact he accredits to his fitness-loving wife – so he's obviously doing something right!

2. Neil Ruddock

With a nickname like 'Razor', if you didn't know who former Liverpool, Southampton and West Ham hard man Neil Ruddock was then you might imagine him to be sharp, slim and, er, shiny. Definitely not Mr Ruddock! But when you realise this nickname came from a heavyweight boxer by the name of Donovan Ruddock (known as Razor 'cos of his deft punches) it makes a little bit more sense...

1. Diego Maradona

Towards the end of his career, the sprightly Argentine began to become slightly more rotund, something that was particularly noticeable during the '94 World Cup in the USA. We can't help but feel that God had a hand in things here as an act of revenge for '86...

One-club wonders

If we were David Attenborough, we would be offering a mellifluous and atmospheric voiceover along these lines:

'And we see now an extremely rare sight... The "One-Club Wonder" is very seldom spotted now. A change in the footballing habitat has meant that these loyal servants, spending all of their most useful years serving just one master, big or small, are almost extinct, driven to the edge of oblivion by employment law and extreme wealth.'

We should pause to savour football's most loyal players.

10. John McDermott: Grimsby Town, 1987–2007 (647)

Right-back John McDermott is one of only 17 players in the history of English football to have played more than 600 Football League matches for a single club.

9. Paolo Maldini: Milan, 1984–2009 (647)

Five European Cups, seven Scudetti, three intercontinental titles, five European Super Cups and a Coppa Italia were still not enough for Milan's fans, who booed him off on his last appearance for the club in 2009.

8. John Askey: Macclesfield, 1984–2003 (698)

Macc Lads legend John Askey scored with his first touch on both his debut against Morecambe in 1987 and also his side's second goal in his last game – a 3-2 win over Rochdale.

7. Stelios Manolas: AEK Athens, 1979–1998 (700)

Despite offers from Porto and Monaco, Stelios Manolas, one of Greece's finest footballers, stayed put at AEK, captaining them for 19 years.

6. Colin Cowperthwaite: Barrow, 1977–1992 (704)

Scoring 282 goals in 704 appearances, Colin Cowperthwaite was unsurprisingly voted Barrow's all-time greatest player.

5. Ricardo Bochini: Independiente, 1972–1991 (740)

El Bocha was a childhood idol of Diego Maradona. Winning eight international titles and four Argentine championships, he was one of the best playmakers in the world in the 1980s.

4. Jimmy Dickinson: Portsmouth, 1946–1965 (764)

All hail the player they called Mr Portsmouth himself. This true gent was never booked nor sent off in his 19 years for Portsmouth. Amazing for a defender!

3. John Trollope: Swindon Town, 1960–1980 (770)

Left-back John Trollope almost didn't beat Jimmy Dickinson's all-time appearance record, but a terrible start to the 1980/1 season meant he was recalled to the side for another few games.

2. Lars Høgh: Odense Boldklub, 1977–2000 (817)

The only keeper in the top ten, Lars Høgh (pronounced Lars Høgh) won three Danish championships and three Danish Cups with OB, and was voted best Danish goalkeeper five times. Wønderful.

1. Max Morlock: FC Nuremberg, 1940–1964 (944)

German legend 'Maxi' Morlock was one of the most popular players in the 1950s and 1960s. He led Nuremberg to League titles in 1948 and 1961, and in 1962 to the German Cup. He was a member of the West German team that won their first World Cup in 1954. In 2006, Nuremberg fans started a campaign to have their stadium renamed in his honour but were overpowered by a sponsor with a large chequebook.

Footballers' cars

The day they abolished the maximum wage and allowed footballers to negotiate their own wage deals, they inadvertently saved the car manufacturing business. For footballers, cars are the ultimate status symbol so it is no surprise that over the years we have seen some real top gear action.

10. El Hadji Diouf – Gold Cadillac
Nothing says bling like a gold Cadillac. The striker was seen driving around Manchester in the gold car. Surely, El Hadji Diouf is not trying to attract attention to himself?

9. Wayne Rooney – White Range Rover
We feel sorry for whoever Wayne Rooney gets to clean his car. He changed his Range Rover from silver to white with one of those lovely chocolate sweet-style wraps.

8. Djibril Cissé – Plymouth Prowler
Djibril Cissé does everything to stand out: bright boots, bright hair, scoring goals, getting sent off. He's always doing at least two of them! Why should his car be any different? The Plymouth Prowler is more Batmobile than automobile.

7. William Gallas – Chrome Mercedes
William Gallas's chrome Mercedes looks more like a speedboat than a car. Maybe he thought he was actually buying a speedboat to get up and down the Thames and play for all those London teams. William's a big car collector with his garage having an estimated combined worth of £500,000.

6. Mario Balotelli – Bentley
Mario Balotelli crashed his £140,000 Bentley in Manchester city centre. That's just one of a list of things he's got into trouble for. Maybe in his next car he'll have his own firework display?

5. Jermaine Pennant – Aston Martin
Usually just being a footballer attracts women, however Jermaine Pennant wanted more appeal. So he decided to make his car one big mirror. His Aston Martin, worth around £130,000, had a chrome wrapping and had women doing their lippy when Jermaine hit a red light. Flash.

4. Robbie Savage – White Lamborghini

When your team are sitting at the bottom of the table, you would think the players would be more suited to a Ford Focus than a Lamborghini. However, if anyone was going to try and pull this off, it would be Robbie Savage. Yes, he turned up to training at Derby in a white Lambo. He hasn't dared turn up to **606** in it yet, but we're sure the day will come.

3. Stephen Ireland – Romantic Bentley

Stephen Ireland might give off the image of bit of a hard man in the middle of the park, but he proved he's just a softie with his customisations on his Bentley GTC Convertible, reported to be worth around £260,000. He had red leather seats put in with stitching of a romantic message over a heart. His alloys even had his girlfriend's initials on them. Those wheels reportedly cost £5,000.

2. Stephen Ireland – Pink Range Rover

Now, this is a joke, isn't it? First the Bentley (see above) and now a Range Rover, with pink alloys and pink seats! We can't imagine the stick he got when turning up to training in this!

1. Portsmouth's Reliant Robin

In 2008, the Portsmouth squad all chipped in and bought a Reliant Robin. I wonder how many weeks they had to save between them to afford that? Whoever was Donkey of the Week would drive it to training.

Golden oldies

Some players see no reason why the passage of time should interfere in any way with their careers. Impressively, they simply ignore Father Time and carry on playing, year after year. **606** salutes those whom age simply cannot wither.

10. Paolo Maldini

Il Capitano had dedication, dedication, dedication, playing until he was 41 and spending all 25 seasons of his career at AC Milan. He won the Champions League five times, seven Serie A titles, a Coppa Italia, five Super Coppa Italias, five European Super Cups and two Intercontinental Cups.

9. Teddy Sheringham

Party boy, footballer and gentleman for nine clubs in a 24-year career, Sheringham is the oldest outfield player to have played in the Premier League, and he did so just 95 days short of his 41st birthday. Sheringham eventually retired at 42 after a spell at Colchester Utd. Whilst there, he was the oldest player in all four divisions of the Football League.

8. Roger Milla

Cameroon's goal celebration pioneer announced himself to the world with his corner flag dancing antics in the 1990 World Cup as a 38-year-old. He scored four goals before Cameroon were finally knocked out 3-2 in a close encounter with England in the quarter-finals. Milla is the oldest player to play at a World Cup finals. In 1994, at the age of 42, he played in a group match against Russia, and on top of that he scored, thus making him the tournament's oldest scorer.

7. Romario

The prolific Brazilian frontman and well-travelled genius of the field, Romario's career took him across five of the seven continents. The only continents he's not played on are Africa and Antarctica. A man that claims to have scored over 1,000 goals briefly came out of retirement as a 43-year-old substitute in a Brazilian 2nd Division match. He now spends his days as a politician, mainly being embarrassed by the World Cup 2014 preparations in Brazil.

6. John 'Budgie' Burridge

Created an incredible career playing for 29 different clubs, 15 of them in the Football League, which is still a record today. He finished his career as player-manager of Blyth Spartans and is still the oldest player to have played in the

Premier League, for Manchester City, at 43 years and 162 days.

5. Marco Ballotta
He's the oldest player to play in the Champions League, aged 43 years and 252 days, beating the previous record held by Alessandro Costacurta. Ballotta is still the oldest player to play in Serie A at 44 years and 38 days for Lazio.

4. Peter Shilton
The goalkeeping record-breaker, MBE, short-lived twinkle toes and after-dinner speaker retired aged 47 after a short spell with Leyton Orient that took him through the barrier of 1,000 competitive matches. He still holds records for most caps earned for England with 125 and the most appearances at the World Cup finals with 17.

3. Neil McBain
Way back in 1947, and 16 years after initially hanging up his boots, the Scottish wing-back had to turn his hand to goalkeeping after an injury crisis struck New Brighton. New who? Yes they are no more, but at 51 he is the oldest player to have played in the Football League.

2. John Ryan
Just for the sheer cheek of it, this oldie gets in, even though he didn't touch the ball during his brief jaunt onto the football field. The cosmetic surgery entrepreneur and chairman of Doncaster Rovers dared to dream himself onto the pitch in the last minute of a Conference match against Hereford United in 2003 at the age of 52. This got him into the Guinness Book of Records as the oldest player. Audacious!

1. Sir Stanley Matthews
Known as the wizard of dribble, Matthews is the oldest player to have played in the top flight of English football at the age of 50, and he is the oldest player to pull on an England shirt. He even played on for local sides until the age of 70. In a career that saw him spend a total of 19 years at Stoke and 14 years at Blackpool, Matthews became an FA Cup winner in 1953 in what was dubbed the Matthews Final. Blackpool were 3-1 down to Bolton but, thanks to his contributions, Bolton came back to win 4-3. After retiring, Matthews coached around the world, most notably an all-black team in South Africa during that country's harsh apartheid era. The team was known as 'Stan's Men'. Breaking all the rules in all the best ways, he is our number one top golden oldie.

Hardnuts

From the completely crazy to the passionate and committed, there are many tough-tackling, hardnut football players. Some may feel aggrieved at not making it into our top ten, but just don't give them our number, will you!

10. Zinedine Zidane
The former Real Madrid and Juventus midfielder is considered to be up there with the best head-butters.

9. Joe Jordan
He squared up with Gennaro Gattuso in the San Siro in a Champions League match and Gattuso head-butted him. Jordan didn't even flinch. Hard as nails.

8. Julian Dicks
He's definitely an underrated hardnut, who played for Birmingham, West Ham and Liverpool. He's snuck into the list. Better keep him happy.

7. Paul Ince
Had many great battles in the centre of midfield for Liverpool and Manchester United. He's not one to be messed with. He's the Guv'nor.

6. Duncan Ferguson
There's a reason why he got loads of red cards.

5. Neil Ruddock
He played for Southampton, Liverpool, West Ham United and Swindon Town and was a stalwart in defence. His nickname is 'Razor' for a reason.

4. Terry Butcher
Probably most remembered for the head injury he sustained playing in a World Cup qualifier against Sweden. He had such a bad cut to his head that the blood soaked through the bandages and turned his white England shirt red. Talk about taking a hit for the team.

3. Stuart Pearce
Everyone knows about 'Psycho'. Described by many as 'the scariest opponent' they have ever faced.

2. Vinnie Jones

A very close second. Famed for his hand-to-ball movement, if he says jump, you say 'How high?'

1. Roy Keane

It's all in the eyes. And Keano's eyes do something to us. Fill us with fear. Even as a pundit.

Iconic number 9s

They have one mission and one mission alone – to put that ball in the back of the net. They may play like a donkey for 89 minutes, but if they get the winning goal in the last minute of the game they are forgiven every bad pass and wild tackle. No wonder people envy the striker. Here are ten amazing practitioners of the art.

10. Samuel Eto'o

Eto'o is the most decorated African player of all time. The African Player of the year in 2003, 2004, 2005 and 2010 has had a distinguished career at club and international level. Cameroon's captain began his senior career at Real Madrid in 1997, but was loaned out to several teams in Spain to gain experience. One of these teams was Mallorca, and he was sold permanently to the Balearic club in 2000. He holds the record for most La Liga goals in the club's history (54) and his goal-scoring exploits attracted the interest of the Catalan giants Barcelona. Barca paid just over £18m for the striker and he won La Liga in his first two seasons with the club. He scored over 100 goals in five seasons and won the Champions League twice. He won the treble (League, Cup and Champions League) in his final season with the team. Eto'o signed for Inter Milan in 2009 as part of the deal that took Zlatan Ibrahimovic to Barcelona and was an instant success at the San Siro. He became the first player to win two consecutive European 'trebles' after winning the League, Champions League and Coppa Italia in his first season at Inter. He sensationally moved to super-rich Anzhi Makhachkala in 2011, who reportedly made him the highest-paid player in the world on a rumoured salary of over £300,000 per week. His international career has also been remarkable, making his full debut at the tender age of 15. He won Olympic gold in 2000, the African Cup of Nations in 2000 and 2002, and is Cameroon's all-time top goal-scorer with 53 goals.

9. Dion Dublin

When Dublin started playing for Cambridge United they were in the Fourth Division. His goals helped Cambridge achieve successive promotions up to Division One. During their FA Cup run in 1991, Manchester United manager Sir Alex Ferguson noticed the striker and took him to Old Trafford for a fee of £1 million. He went on to play for Coventry City, Aston Villa, Celtic, Norwich and England and is one of few players to reach the 100 club – scoring 111 goals in the top flight. Known as one of football's gentlemen he was capped four times by England.

8. Filippo Inzaghi

Fans will be familiar with Pippo for his passionate celebrations and for perennially being offside. It is his goal-scorer's instinct that has made Inzaghi one of the top scorers in Italian club football history. He broke onto the scene at Atalanta, where he was top scorer in Serie A with 24 goals in the 1996/7 season, scoring against every side in the League and finishing the year as Serie A Young Footballer of the Year. He then moved on to Juventus and created a formidable partnership with Alessandro Del Piero and Zinedine Zidane, winning Serie A in his first season at the Old Lady. The most successful period of Inzaghi's career has undoubtedly been with Milan. His time at the San Siro has seen him win Serie A, the Champions League and the European Super Cup twice and the Coppa Italia and Club World Cup. He is also the second-highest scorer in European club competitions with 70 goals, and reached the pinnacle of his international career by winning the World Cup with Italy in 2006.

7. Adam Stansfield

Adam Stansfield lost his battle with bowel cancer in August 2010, which resulted in Exeter retiring his number 9 shirt for nine seasons. The club also helped to set up two separate charities in Stansfield's memory. Stansfield wore the number 9 shirt on every single one of his 158 appearances for Exeter. Across his career for Yeovil, Hereford and Exeter, Adam made 260 appearances and scored 92 goals.

6. Ally McCoist

Alistair Murdoch McCoist MBE is a club legend at Rangers. In a 15-year playing spell at Ibrox, he scored 355 goals, making him their all-time top scorer. He has cemented his place in Ibrox legend by taking over the managerial reins following the departure of Walter Smith in the most difficult period in the club's history. He won 10 SPL titles in his time at Rangers, winning the League Cup nine times and the Scottish Cup once. He was also the European Golden Boot winner in 1992 and 1993. He captained his country and was their number 9, scoring 19 international goals to make him Scotland's fifth-highest scorer. McCoist finished his career at Kilmarnock, finally hanging up his boots in 2001.

5. Sir Bobby Charlton

While Bobby Charlton was not a traditional centre-forward, he wore the number 9 throughout an incredibly distinguished career with Manchester United and England. Having survived the Munich air disaster in 1958, Charlton received his first call-up to the national team in that year, scoring a thumping volley on his debut against Scotland. His club career saw him win the League three times, the FA Cup once and he captained his side to the 1968 European

Cup in Lisbon, scoring twice in the final. He was England's number 9 during their triumphant 1966 World Cup campaign, in which he finished with the FIFA Golden Ball, for best player at the tournament. His goal-scoring exploits for club and country have gone unrivalled to this day. His record of 249 goals for United still makes him top scorer for the club and his 49 international goals has not been bettered by any Englishman.

4. Dixie Dean

Dean is considered by many to be the origin of the 'traditional English number 9', an Everton club legend who played in the 1920s and 1930s. He grabbed a quite incredible 349 goals in 399 appearances for Everton, and once scored a record 60 League goals in a season. At the peak of his career, Dean earned £8 per match. The highest possible praise for Dean came in 1980, from a legend of arch-rivals Liverpool. Bill Shankly said about Dean: 'Without doubt, he is the greatest centre-forward the world will ever see. He belongs in the company of the supremely great, like Beethoven, Rembrandt and Shakespeare.'

3. Robbie Fowler

The Kop dubbed him 'God', and there can surely be no higher compliment for a striker who scored almost 200 goals in two spells at Liverpool. He never quite transformed his prolific club form into international form, grabbing seven goals in his 26 England appearances. He was part of the Liverpool side that won the UEFA Cup, FA Cup, League Cup and European Super Cup in 2001 and was famously one of the Spice Boys at Liverpool, wearing those white suits to the 1996 FA Cup final.

2. Ronaldo

Dubbed 'The Phenomenon' by the Italian press, and R9 by his sponsors, he gave defenders nightmares at the peak of his powers and was named FIFA World Player of the Year three times. He burst onto the European scene as a teenager at PSV Eidnhoven, scoring 54 goals in 57 appearances before moving to Barcelona for just one season, where he grabbed 47 in 49. After moving to Inter Milan in 1997, he had trouble with various injuries and was famously rumoured to have had a fit before the 1998 World Cup final. In spite of losing the final in France '98, he holds the record for goals scored at World Cup finals, with 15 in total. He has also won the World Cup twice, in 1994 and 2002. He crossed the divide in two of the world's great rivalries, winning La Liga and scoring for fun as part of Real Madrid's Galactico project and also turning out for AC Milan. Ronaldo finished his career at home in Brazil with Corinthians.

1. Alan Shearer

The record goal-scorer in Premier League history (with 260 goals) needs no introduction. He scored a remarkable 112 League goals in 138 appearances for Blackburn Rovers and fired them to the Premier League title in 1994/5. He won the Premier League Golden Boot in three consecutive seasons: 1994/5 (34 goals), 1995/6 (31 goals) and 1996/7 (25 goals). He signed for hometown club Newcastle for a then world record £15m in 1996, and he went on to beat Jackie Milburn's goal-scoring record for the Toon, bagging 206 goals in 404 appearances. Shearer led the line for England for eight years, and scored 30 goals in 63 caps before retiring (some think prematurely) from international football before he had turned 30.

Least popular moves

The fans hate it when players move from one team to a rival or, as they perceive it 'disrespect the club' in any way. And so it should be. There are plenty of reasons that players come out with for wanting to leave a club – wanting to play Champions League football, or give themselves a better chance of playing internationally, to name a couple. Some are telling the truth, some are making excuses; fans see straight through this. We're not asking for much, just some respect and honesty upon leaving. So we've whittled down ten of the least popular moves that we can think of. Agree...?

10. Gareth Barry
Gareth Barry spent 12 years at Aston Villa and became their captain. There was a long transfer saga between Barry and Liverpool, with them having several bids rejected. Barry publicly criticised his manager and said he wanted to leave for Champions League football. This didn't go down too well with Villa fans and, when he finally made a move away from Villa park to Manchester City, he became a very unpopular figure at his former club.

9. Frank Lampard
West Ham United fans have still not forgiven Frank Lampard for leaving the Hammers. Frank's dad, Frank Lampard Sr., became assistant manager under Harry Redknapp at West Ham, but when his dad was sacked, Lampard Jr. loyally said he would never play for the club again. Chelsea came calling and Lampard moved from his boyhood club to Chelsea. West Ham fans to this day give him a lot of stick for this.

8. Gael Clichy
No football fan wants to see a player move just because of the money, and Clichy basically admitted he did this. When Emmanuel Adebayor went to Arsenal, Clichy stated that any player that goes to City is just going for the money. He went on to say you have to choose between a big club or a rich club. Two years later the full back executed a full about turn and ended up at City. He reportedly said he had moved because he was sick of losing.

7. Samir Nasri
Nasri upset many of the Arsenal faithful when he made the move from the Emirates to Manchester City, a team he referred to as 'the club of the future'. He refused to sign a contract extension at Arsenal, holding out for a move that

doubled his salary. Samir didn't even address the fans; he just said his move wasn't anything to do with money but the chance to win trophies. Not sure the Arsenal fans believed his reason for going.

6. Emmanuel Adebayor
When Arsenal signed Emmanuel Adebayor in 2006, he was one of the most exciting players in the Premier League. But his poor attitude led to Wenger selling him to Manchester City. What puts him where he is on the list was when he scored against Arsenal. He ran the complete length of the pitch and celebrated in front of the Arsenal fans. To add insult to injury, Adebayor later moved to Tottenham on loan.

5. William Gallas
Any player to play for three London clubs has got to be pretty flighty, but when those three clubs are Chelsea, Arsenal and Tottenham, we have a serious offender on our hands. Gallas went to Arsenal from Chelsea as part of a deal, with Ashley Cole going the other way. Gallas went on to be Arsenal's captain. He was later stripped of the armband by Wenger after he claimed there were morale issues in the Arsenal camp. Then, when Arsenal refused to live up his wage demands, rivals Spurs came knocking and Gallas moved there in 2010.

4. Ashley Cole
Ashley Cole grew up an Arsenal fan and came through the Arsenal youth system. He won League titles and was part of the 'Invincibles' that went the whole season unbeaten. In 2005, Cole was fined by the Premier League because of attending meetings with Chelsea representatives. Cole was reported as not happy when he only got offered £55,000 a week in a new contract by Arsenal as Chelsea were offering £90,000 a week. Cole made the big money move in 2006 and is known as Cashley Cole to many fans.

3. Sol Campbell
Any player that makes the move across North London from Arsenal to Tottenham (or vice versa) will be branded as disloyal by the fans. So when Sol Campbell left Tottenham after nine years to become Arsenal's highest-paid player, Spurs weren't too happy.

2. Carlos Tevez
If anyone makes the move from one side of Manchester to the other, he's not going to be popular, especially when it's a character like Carlos Tevez. After helping West Ham stay up in 2007, Tevez made the move to Manchester United and enjoyed success. But when he got offered a new contract, he fancied a

move over to the blue half of the city. Since moving to Man City, he has handed in two transfer requests.

1. Wayne Rooney

Wayne Rooney grew up in Liverpool and was a life-long Everton fan. He was part of their youth set-up from the age of 9 and scored at the age of 16 on his debut. Everyone was after the wonder-boy Wayne Rooney, but he revealed a shirt that read 'Once a Blue, always a Blue'. Not exactly true: at the age of 18 he signed for Manchester United. But what makes him our number one most disloyal player? Well it's got to be that kissing of the United badge in front of the Everton fans at Goodison Park. The game was a feisty one and, when Rooney got booked for a foul on Mikel Arteta, the fans gave him some stick. He responded by kissing the red devil badge. Ferguson responded by bringing Rooney off.

Top 10 Mario Balotelli moments

Modern football rarely brings fans such characters. Within a game more alien to fans then ever we have overpriced, media-savvy players unable to find a connection with cheering fans. Then there is Mario Balotelli. A man who disregards any media training, living life to grace the football pitch whilst entertaining fans both on and off it.

10. Mario the Dart-Thrower
Balotelli was fined a week's wages having been caught throwing darts at youth players from a training ground window. Manager Roberto Mancini was not at the training ground when the incident happened – when the cat is away...

9. Press Pass for Mario
Mario surprised everyone at Inter Milan's training ground when he rocked up at the press conference unveiling the club's new manager, Andrea Stramaccioni. He had a few days off from City so popped over to Milan, as you do, to congratulate his former coach on getting the job. He bowled up at the top table, kissed and shook the hand of Stramaccioni and then sped off in his Ferrari.

8. Mario the Honest Man
Mario's performance in the FA Cup final against Stoke was one to remember mainly for his post-match TV comment. Asked if it was his best game that season, he replied, 'My whole season was sh*t. Can I say that?' Er, we think not.

7. Mario the Firework Displayer
How does one prepare the night before a Manchester derby? With a fireworks display, of course. The fire brigade had to go to Mario's mansion in the early hours of the morning as he attempted to let off fireworks from his bathroom. Perfectly normal behaviour.*

6. Mario the Firework Displayer, Pt 2
The morning after the bathroom pyrotechnic show the night before, Mario duly delivered by scoring a brilliant goal against United. The message on his undershirt – 'Why Always Me?' – has since become iconic and was printed courtesy of City kit man 'Chappy'. City went on to win the game 6-1. We hope Chappy has patented the slogan.

---

* Please don't try this at home.

5. Mario the Cool Cucumber
During a 5-1 rout over Norwich in December 2011, Balotelli fired a shot at keeper John Ruddy which rebounded up into the air. Standing in front of an open goal, all Mario needed to do was head it into the net. Why would he do that? A shrug of the shoulder towards the ball and it was in the net. Eastlands understandably went crazy.

4. Mario the Personal Shopper
After consultations with the new cleaner, Mrs Balotelli sent her lad Mario off to buy a list of supplies, including an iron, a mop and a hoover. Hours later, Mario returned with a giant trampoline and two Vespas, forgetting all the cleaning products.

3. Mario the Magician
Having been in awe of a magician at the Trafford Centre, Mario invited him home to learn some tricks. And learn them he did – the cameras caught Mario, sitting in an executive box with his kid brother for a game against Fulham, placing a small towel over a cup and waving his hands around like a pro. The only thing missing was Debbie McGee.

2. Mario the AC Milan Player
When playing for a club like Inter Milan, you certainly don't want to be caught wearing AC Milan colours. That's unless you're Mario, of course. Appearing on an Italian comedy show, Mario was presented with the famous red and black shirt with his name on the back. Any sane Inter player would quietly put it in his bag to dispose of later. Not Mario – he was soon seen with it on his back.

1. Mario the Charitable
Of all our Mario top ten, we sincerely hope number one is true. After winning £25,000 at a casino, Mario stopped on his way home to give £1,000 of it to a homeless person sat outside. We always knew he had a heart of gold.

Meteoric rises

One minute they are nobodies, people you could sit next to on a train and not blink once. The next they are all over the papers and TV, thrilling the fans with their mercurial skills and dynamic play. From zero to hero in a second, here are **606**'s top ten meteoric rises to the very top.

10. Joe Hart

Whilst he was playing for Shrewsbury, Manchester City spotted a serious amount of potential in Joe Hart and signed him in 2006. After a few loan spells, most notably at Birmingham in the Premiership, Joe Hart is now considered to be one of the best goalkeepers in the world, and England's number one.

9. John Ruddy

Signed by Everton from Cambridge in 2005, Ruddy never got his breakthrough with the Toffees, only making one appearance and undertaking many loan spells. Ruddy craved stability and in 2010 Norwich signed him. The following season, Norwich got promoted to the Premiership. Even more remarkably, Ruddy was picked by Roy Hodgson for England's Euro 2012 squad. He had to pull out due to a broken finger, but his selection confirmed his swift rise through the ranks of English football.

8. Dion Dublin

When Dublin started playing for Cambridge United, they were in the Fourth Division. His goals helped them achieve successive promotions up to Division One. Dublin caught Sir Alex Ferguson's eye during Cambridge's impressive FA Cup run in 1991, and he moved to Old Trafford for £1m at the end of the 1990/1 season. He went on to play for Coventry City, Aston Villa, Celtic, Norwich and England and is one of few players to reach the 100 club – scoring 111 goals in the top flight.

7. Chris Smalling

Playing for Maidstone United in 2007 in the Isthmian League, Fulham spotted Smalling and signed him to Craven Cottage. Having made his Fulham debut in May 2009, he was signed by Manchester United in January 2010, for about £8 million. He has since made 35 first-team appearances and, if it hadn't been for a late injury in the season, Smalling would almost certainly have been part of Roy Hodgson's Euro 2012 plans.

6. Andre Villas-Boas

In 2008, Andre Villas-Boas was not on anybody's radar, but he got his breakthrough in 2009. AVB began managing Academica, helping them to escape relegation. This prompted a move to FC Porto, where he won the League and the Europa League in his first season. This success led to Chelsea approaching him as he was meant to be the 'new Mourinho'. It did not work out for AVB at Chelsea, but he has been given a second chance to prove himself in the Premier League as the manager of Tottenham Hotspur.

5. Alex Oxlade-Chamberlain

'The Ox' made his debut in 2010 for Southampton and in July 2011 signed for Arsenal for around £12 million. He was a revelation for Arsenal in the 2011/12 season, exciting fans with his pace and direct style of football and scoring two goals. This led to him getting a call-up to the full England squad for the Euro 2012 tournament.

4. Dale Jennings

In 2010, Dale Jennings made his Tranmere Rovers debut. One season and 26 games later, the 19-year-old signed for European heavyweights Bayern Munich for £1.8m! He has made 20 appearances so far for their second side.

3. Theo Walcott

The winger and former BBC Young Sports Personality of the Year, having played 21 times for Southampton in the 2005/6 season, was signed to Arsenal in 2006. Walcott was then a shock call-up to the 2006 World Cup, although he didn't play a game. He has, however, played 149 games for Arsenal and 28 times for England since, and has cemented his place in the England squad.

2. Carl Jenkinson

In 12 months, Carl Jenkinson went from playing non-League to first-team football in the Premier League and Champions League. Jenkinson was playing for Charlton, but had loan spells at non-League Eastbourne Borough and Welling. He made his debut for Charlton in December 2010 and by June that season he had signed to Arsenal (for £1m). A leg break to Bacary Sagna meant that Carl got some football in the Premier League and Champions League. In just his second start, however, he was sent off against Manchester United as Arsenal lost 8-2.

1. Ian Wright

Ian Wright came into football late compared to players today. He signed his first professional contract at the age of 22, at Crystal Palace. Before that, Ian was playing for non-League Greenwich Borough. He went on to become one of the greatest goal-scorers the English Leagues have seen, winning titles and FA Cups at Arsenal and going six seasons in a row as Arsenal's top goal-scorer. Ian Wright scored 185 goals for Arsenal, a record. Well it was until a man called Thierry Henry turned up.

Most disruptive footballers

When they play for your side, you have nothing but praise for their wholehearted commitment to the cause. You defend them to the hilt. Yet if they play for the opposition, there is no other figure in football you love to hate than the disruptive player. Here are our ten. You got a problem with that, son?

10. Bruce Grobbelaar

The Sun published articles claiming Bruce Grobbelaar was involved in match fixing. One of the games that it was alleged he took money for was Liverpool's 3-0 loss against Newcastle in 1993. He later received £85,000 in libel damages. But the court cases and talk about Grobbelaar must have disrupted the team.

9. Roy Keane

During the 2002 World Cup, Roy Keane caused so much disruption in his team that he was sent home. Initially, Keane pulled out of the team after a reported training room bust-up with goalkeeping coach and former Celtic player Pat Bonner. Manager Mick McCarthy managed to convince Roy to stay. Keane then spoke to the *Irish Times*, criticising the nation's World Cup preparations, and McCarthy tried holding clear-the-air talks – which resulted in Keane going home. McCarthy said, 'I cannot and will not tolerate being spoken to with that level of abuse being thrown at me so I sent him home.'

8. Pierre van Hooijdonk

When Pierre van Hooijdonk was playing for Nottingham Forest in 1998, he handed in a transfer request, saying he was not happy with the lack of signings coming into the club. His request was refused, so he went on strike and trained at NEC Breda (Dutch team). He left the club at the end of the season for Vitesse. Nottingham Forest were relegated.

7. Mido

When Egyptian coach Hassan Shehata decided to substitute the striker Mido in the 80th minute of the semi-final at the 2006 African Cup of Nations, while the game was at 1-1, the ex-Spurs man was not at all happy, and had to be ushered away from the coach. Yet when the player who came on for him, Zaki, scored a header with his first touch to take Egypt to the final, Mido ran down the pitch celebrating. Egypt went on to win the final against Ivory Coast in a penalty shoot-out.

6. William Gallas

Any player who has played at Arsenal, Chelsea and Spurs in his career and worn the armband for two of them (Arsenal and Spurs) is likely to cause some problems. When he made the move from Chelsea to Arsenal in the summer of 2006, Chelsea claimed that the French defender had refused to play in the FA Cup semi-final against Liverpool in the 2005/6 season (a semi-final that Liverpool won and then went on to beat West Ham on penalties in the final). Chelsea also claimed that Gallas said he would score an own goal if they started him in the first game of the season.

At Arsenal, he caused more controversy in the game against Birmingham in the 2007/8 season. His team mate Eduardo had suffered a sickening leg break and then Birmingham scored a controversial injury-time equaliser from the penalty spot. Gallas, who was then captain, kicked the advertising board and then sat on the halfway line as the final whistle went, refusing to leave the field of play. He had to be dragged off by the Arsenal coaching staff. He was stripped of his captaincy and dropped from the squad after questioning teammates' bravery and accusing another player of disrupting morale.

Then, in the summer of 2010, William Gallas moved to Arsenal's North London rivals Tottenham, making him an instant hate figure amongst the Arsenal fans. And just to top it all off, he became Tottenham captain.

5. Cristiano Ronaldo

Cristiano Ronaldo is one of the world's best players, but he has still managed to cause some disruption in dressing rooms. In the 2006 World Cup, England crashed out of the quarter-final to Portugal, and Wayne Rooney was sent off. There was much controversy around the sending-off. Although Rooney had stamped on Portugal defender Ricardo Carvalho, the referee hadn't seen the incident. Ronaldo ran over to the ref, resulting in Rooney pushing him away. This was when the red card was shown. As Rooney departed, Ronaldo looked over and winked at the Portugal bench. Alan Shearer, who was part of the BBC commentary team, said after the game, 'I think there is every chance that Wayne Rooney could go back to the Manchester United training ground and stick one on Ronaldo.'

4. Jens Lehman

Lehman caused real problems among the Arsenal team when he threw his toys out of the pram in 2008 after losing his place in the Arsenal team to Manuel Almunia. Lehman told the world that Almunia hated him and sarcastically added it was 'amazing to know someone hates you at the club you play for.' When Lehman left Arsenal in 2008, after his final game against Everton, he said that Wenger would have been sacked if he was the Germany manager. Lehman was brought back to Arsenal in the 2011/12 season and played his 200th game for Arsenal against Blackpool at the age of 41.

3. Julian Dicks

When Harry Redknapp took over at West Ham in 1994 his first signing was left-back Julian Dicks, a move Harry seriously came to regret. Redknapp later said that Dicks was the most disruptive professional he had ever worked with. He even managed to disrupt the West Ham squad that got relegated in 2011. Dicks labelled them all as lazy.

2. Stefan Effenberg

German international Stefan Effenberg famously gave the finger to his own fans at the 1994 World Cup finals in USA. The Germans were struggling against South Korea, and the fans started getting on his back. Germany won the game 3-2. He was substituted and sent straight home from the World Cup finals. Berti Vogts, Germany's coach at the finals, said, 'It was the last straw. I will not allow a player to make an obscene gesture like that to the crowd. As far as I am concerned, Effenberg is over as an international player. He has done too much in recent years. There were also internal problems during the European Championships [in 1992 in Sweden].' It was also reported that, as a youngster at Borussia Monchengladbach, he had 'borrowed' the manager's jeep to escape from training and then crashed it.

1. Joey Barton

Joey Barton is without a doubt one of the most disruptive footballers in the Premier League. When he was playing for Newcastle back in 2008, he was sentenced to six months in jail for assault and affray. He served 74 days and walked back into his £71,000-a-week contract at Newcastle. Earlier in his career, at Manchester City, he was banned for six games after a training ground fight with teammate Ousmane Dabo. The attack left Dabo with several cuts and bruises and a suspected detached retina. Still at City, an accident was reported in which Barton apparently burnt reserve player Jamie Tandy's eyelid with a cigar at the Manchester City 2004 Christmas party.

It seems Man City brings out the worst in him. During the final game of the 2012 season, Barton, by now a QPR player, attacked Carlos Tevez, kicked Sergio Ageuro, attempted to head-butt Vincent Kompany and tried to assault Mario Balotelli. He was banned for a record 12 games by the Premier League.

Player quotes

Out of the mouths of babes... the surreal, the stupid and the inspired, perhaps they should just stick to playing. Nah, why take away the fun? Here are ten quotes to justify every stereotype about the footballer.

10. 'Everything in our favour was against us.'
  – Former Tottenham midfielder Danny Blanchflower masters the art of contradiction

9. 'I definitely want Brooklyn to be christened, but I don't know into what religion yet.'
  – David Beckham

8. 'I'm more afraid of my mum than Sven Göran Eriksson or David Moyes.'
  – Wayne Rooney in playful mood at a press conference before an England friendly with Slovakia. Rooney played for Everton at the time.

7. 'I faxed a transfer request to the club at the beginning of the week, but let me state that I don't want to leave Leicester.'
  – Stan Collymore tries to appease the Leicester fans

6. 'I have a good record there. Played one, won one, and hopefully it will be the same after Saturday.'
  – Steven Gerrard

5. 'I think that France, Germany, Spain, Holland and England will join Brazil in the semi-finals.'
  – Dubbed the greatest player of all time, you'd think Pelé would understand the concept of a tournament...

4. 'I've had 14 bookings this season, 8 of which were my fault, but 7 of which were disputable.'
  – Former Tottenham, Newcastle, Middlesbrough and Everton midfielder Paul Gascoigne can't do maths

3. 'I would not be bothered if we lost every game as long as we won the League.'

– Mark Viduka. He played for Leeds, Celtic, Newcastle and Middlesbrough.

2. 'I've never wanted to leave. I'm here for the rest of my life and hopefully after that as well.'
– Alan Shearer explains his love of Newcastle

1. 'I couldn't settle in Italy. It was like living in a foreign country.'
– Liverpool legend Ian Rush joined Juventus for £3.2 million from Liverpool. He had one season at Juve in 1987/8.

Players who never lived up to their potential

The curse of advance publicity has rendered many a promising talent a no-go from the start. Such has been the expectation heaped upon their shoulders, very few of them have ever lived up to the hype. Here are ten who have had to juggle great expectations, as well as a football, and failed.

10. Florent Sinama Pongolle

Great things were expected of the former Liverpool youngster – until the club decided he had no potential and he was moved on to Spain. Again, he failed to live up to the hype and ended up at Sporting CP. He is currently on loan at Saint-Etienne, scoring a measly three goals in 2011/12.

9. David Bellion

Like Sinama Pongolle, the former Manchester United youngster was expected to deliver great things. However, he never really kicked on, which led to him moving back to France, to Nice and then Bordeaux, where he is struggling to cement himself in the first team.

8. Anthony Le Tallec

Again, another Frenchman starting up in England, again, with Liverpool, again with supposedly loads of potential. However, after not scoring in 17 attempts for Liverpool, he was shipped out on loan on many occasions. Liverpool then deemed him not good enough for their squad, so Le Mans signed him, where he has struggled for goals. He was last seen playing for French club Auxerre.

7. Freddy Adu

Whilst playing for DC United at 14 years of age, Freddy Adu was expected to be moved on to bigger and better things, with all the big teams taking a look at this wonderkid. However, staying in the USA and moving to Real Salt Lake instead of Inter Milan or Juventus proved to be a bad career move. Freddy finally got a big move to the Portuguese giants Benfica in 2007, but after many unsuccessful loan spells he returned to the USA and is now playing for Philadelphia Union.

6. Fred

Frederico Chaves Guedes (nicknamed Fred) was scoring for fun in his early 20s for Lyon and was constantly linked with top European clubs. However, after choosing to stay at Lyon, Fred declined as a player and is now back in Brazil playing for Fluminense, where he is scoring for fun again. But then it is the Brazilian League, where they don't have defenders.

5. Michael Bridges

The former Leeds striker caught attention in his first season at Leeds when he scored 19 goals. Ever since, he has been on a decline and unsettled everywhere he goes. After travelling around the lower Leagues, he is now playing for Newcastle Jets out in Australia.

4. David Nugent

When at Preston North End, David Nugent received many plaudits, and even played for England once, despite playing in the Championship. Although he turned out in the Premiership for Portsmouth and Burnley, he never really kicked on as was expected, and is now playing for Leicester in the Championship.

3. Jody Morris

Jody Morris was an exciting young player for Chelsea, coming through the youth ranks with the likes of John Terry. He made 124 appearances for Chelsea and even wore the captain's armband briefly in the absence of Dennis Wise on 12 April 2000 when they played Coventry. But as players like Didier Deschamps, Roberto Di Matteo and Emanuel Petit came in, Jody found it hard to keep up. In 2003, he went to Leeds and then moved on to play for Millwall and Rotherham. In 2007 he went to Scottish side St Johnstone.

2. Francis Jeffers

Making his debut for Everton at 16 years old, at Old Trafford, shows that Jeffers must have some real talent. After doing well for Everton, Arsenal signed him for £8 million in 2001. Jeffers was described as a 'fox-in-the-box' type of player. Sadly, he failed to live up to this billing and went into terminal decline. Now, after spells in the lower Leagues of England and in Scotland, he's recently been released by Newcastle Jets in Australia, and he's only 31.

1. Jérémie Aliadière

The French ex-Arsenal striker holds the record in the FA Youth Cup for the number of goals scored. You'd think he'd kick on from this impressive record. Well he didn't – he scored just one goal in 29 appearances for Arsenal. The

Gooners sold him to Middlesbrough, where he scored 11 in 78. Now playing for Lorient, back in France, and only scoring two goals for the club, he is still struggling to live up to such early potential.

Players most likely to get a red

Predicting when the red mist will descend on a certain player and result in him being ordered from the field of play is a custom that all fans now practise during a game, usually taking bets on the minute the player will lose his rag and the type of foul he will then execute.

10. Neymar
The Brazilian starlet is being chased by a host of top clubs, but they ought to keep an eye on his disciplinary record. He's only in his third professional season, but he's already picked up three red cards and 46 yellows.

9. Nicolás Burdisso
This Roma defender has been known to get in a scrap or two. In 2011/12, he notched up three red cards, and over his career he's picked up 46 yellow cards.

8. Djibril Cissé
Before the 2011/12 season, Djibril Cissé was better known for his blond-bombshell hairstyle or his title as the Earl of the Manor of Frodsham than for being a red-card risk. That all changed after his mid-season switch to Queens Park Rangers from Lazio. After scoring on his debut, he was sent off in his second game against Wolverhampton Wanderers. Amazingly, he kept up this unusual pattern until the end of the season – either scoring or getting sent off in every game he played. His record for QPR in the 2011/12 season was eight games played, six goals, two reds, seven games missed through suspension.

7. Kevin Muscat
The former Wolves centre-back has an atrocious disciplinary record. In his 19-year career, he picked up 12 red cards and 95 yellows. He now plays for Sunshine George Cross in the Australian Regional League.

6. Paul Cooper
Not exactly a household name, our Mr Cooper. In fact, he's an amateur player for Hawick United in Scotland. He has also got a bit of a temper. In a game against Pencaitland in 2010, Cooper was sent off for misconduct, and then shown a further five red cards for abusing an official. He received a two-year ban.

5. Wayne Rooney

As a result of his temper, Rooney missed the first two group matches of England's campaign at Euro 2012. Wayne was sent off against Montenegro after kicking a player. He usually loses it when someone robs the ball off him as he is bearing down on goal. You can see him bubbling up like a cauldron on the pitch. Although he has tamed slightly.

4. Richard Dunne

The Aston Villa defender has been red-carded eight times in his 15-year career, so far. He is currently tied with Duncan Ferguson and Patrick Vieira for the most red cards in Premier League history. Come on, one more will do it Richard!

3. Lee Cattermole

The tough-tackling, combative central midfielder has turned himself into something of a liability. In his first match as Sunderland captain in the 2010/11 season, he drew a red card. He also got sent off later in the season for a tackle on Lee Bowyer which drew boos from the Sunderland fans.

2. Gennaro Gattuso

His outburst against Joe Jordan after the Champions League match between Tottenham and AC Milan in 2011 summed up what a loose cannon the Italian midfielder is. OK, he's tenacious, but you can wind him up very easily.

1. Mario Balotelli

He joined Manchester City from Inter Milan in August 2010. He's been given four red cards in two seasons while at City and is a prime target for opponents wishing to get him sent off. He is often subbed – much to his disgust – to avoid yet another red card.

Other sports are available...

They always say that in life you should have something to fall back on if things go amiss. Well, here are some footballers who, if they got their P45s tomorrow, could move very easily into another sport. Talented buggers.

10. Brad Friedel
The granddaddy of Premier League football had a choice of sports to take up professionally back in his native USA. Friedel excelled in ice hockey, tennis, baseball and American football. While an All-State basketball player in Ohio, he was invited to try out as a walk-on for UCLA's basketball team.

9. Zlatan Ibrahimovic
The maverick Swedish international is not just proficient in football. 'Ibra' has also continued to practise taekwondo in Italy, receiving an honorary black belt from the Italian national team. This may explain some of his ill-tempered antics.

8. Roy Keane
In his playing days at Old Trafford, Roy Keane earned a reputation as a no-nonsense midfielder – just ask Alan Shearer or Patrick Vieira. Keane expressed a passion for boxing as well as football and took up the gloves from the age of 10. The Irishman boasts an impressive record, winning all 40 of his bouts.

7. Lomana LuaLua
The DR Congo striker scored some spectacular goals during his time with Newcastle United, but it's his goal celebration that we all remember so well. LuaLua was a talented junior gymnast, and his celebration was series of backflips followed by a backward somersault. Perfect 10.

6. Wayne Rooney
Boxing – honestly, not a joke. He boxed as a form of training until he was 15 and his club, Everton, advised him to give it up. He sparred but never competed, though his gym-owning uncle rated him as being good. Thankfully, Wayne doesn't hit people these days.

5. Alan Hansen
He was and indeed still is a golfer. At the age of 16 he had a handicap of 2. He was even a reserve for Scottish Boys in a fixture against English Boys back in

the 1970s. Turning out for the English that day was the soon-to-be Scottish Sandy Lyle. Hansen was also in the Scottish volleyball squad.

4. Chris Smalling

The promising defender made the remarkable rise from Maidstone United to Manchester United, but football isn't the only sport he excels at. Smalling was a martial arts champion as a child: 'I was a national judo champion when I was younger. I started when I was about 6 or 7 and quit just before I joined Fulham. I've got medals somewhere.'

3. Leon McKenzie

The recently retired striker comes from a champion boxing family. His father Clinton was once the British light welterweight title-holder and uncle Duke, a former three-weight world champion. That probably explains why he always loved a tussle with opposing defenders when through on goal.

2. Rio Ferdinand

Rio Ferdinand is regarded as one of the classiest defenders of his generation but as a child he also took part in gymnastic classes and even ballet! Way before winning the first of 81 international caps for the Three Lions, Ferdinand represented the London Borough of Southwark in gymnastics at the London Youth Games and even won a scholarship to attend the Central School of Ballet in London.

1. Phil Neville

Before playing for Manchester United and Everton, Neville was a useful opening bat and captained the England under-15 cricket team. He was also the youngest player ever to play for Lancashire's second XI until his record was broken by some bloke called Flintoff.

Strangest injuries

Nothing riles us more than players writhing around in agony on a pitch only to jump up right as rain within moments of a spray from the magic can. Yes, we're looking at you, colleague Robbie Savage. How the unfortunate gentlemen listed below must wish there had been a spray on hand to magic away the following inflictions, comical, excruciating, and innocuous. We're not sure whether to laugh or just shout 'ouch'.

10. David Batty – Toddler's tricycle
Never one to shy away from a tackle during his Leeds, Blackburn and Newcastle days the midfielder stuck to his principles and refused to duck out of the way when his daughter headed towards him on her tricycle. Batty was recovering from an ankle ligament injury at the time which may have slowed his movement but as his daughter wasn't far out of nappies we're not sure her speed was Lewis Hamilton-esque. The injury damaged his Achilles tendons and kept him out of the side for several weeks on top of his original injury.

9. Leroy Lita – His own bed
You wake up, you stretch out to get some life into your limbs, but for fine athletes like Leroy Lita this burst of activity resulted in a pulled leg muscle. His team, Reading, had already been relegated but we wouldn't have liked to put in the call to the gaffer to explain why we couldn't come training that day.

8. Svein Grøndalen – Moose
No, dear reader, if you were expecting a hilarious anecdote about Norwegian Svein Grøndalen waking up next to a rather plain woman, you are looking in the wrong place. Have TalkSport got a book of lists? Maybe try that. No, we mean an actual moose. Grøndalen was in training for a friendly against neighbours and fierce rivals Finland when he unknowingly awoke a sleeping moose (stop it) that was none too happy about being roused from its slumber. The moose charged (really, stop it), forcing our hero to roll down a hill to safety. He survived the attack, but had to have a leg injury stitched up, meaning he missed the match.

7. Darren Barnard/Liam Lawrence – Dog
In joint seventh, Welsh international Liam Lawrence and former Chelsea midfielder Darren Barnard. Darren slipped on some doggy wee-wee and was out of action for five months with an ankle ligament injury. Liam Lawrence stretched the whole 'man's best friend' thing when he tripped over Fido on the stairs.

5. Alan Wright – Ferrari

At 5'4", Alan Wright wasn't the tallest of players and was often mistaken for the club mascot. Being the height of your average Year 4 pupil meant that he overstretched whilst reaching for the accelerator pedal of his Ferrari and strained his knee.

4. Kirk Broadfoot – Eggs

He really did end up with egg on his face. He got a little too close when inspecting poached eggs in the microwave. One exploded and scalded the poor Rangers defender's face. Do them in a pan, you numpty. Dash of white wine vinegar. They're not even poached in a microwave.

3. Dave Beasant – Salad cream

'He's reached high for the jar of salad cream... It's falling... Oh! He's missed it, it's plummeting to the floor... He's trying to catch it on the top of his foot... It's... Ouch! It's severed the tendon in his toe.'

2. Ever Vanega – Car

'Oi! Vanega! Handbrake!' How the Valencia midfielder must have wished for a well-meaning fan to scream things at him when he was refuelling before a vital clash against Barcelona. Result? Fractured foot, out for six months.

1. David James – TV remote

Calamity James added to his own legend by doing his back in whilst reaching for the TV remote. Reports that he was rewinding a particularly attractive shot of himself remain unconfirmed. Goalkeepers and remotes, like Argentinians and petrol stations, shouldn't mix – similar injuries have also befallen Carlo Cudicini and David Seaman.

Players who don't look like footballers

Face it, the footballer has a certain look – rugged, well built, full of testosterone and attitude. Yet there are some whose looks and build suggest they may well have taken completely the wrong path in life.

Here are ten of them.

10. Andy Carroll

His lanky appearance places him firmly behind the counter at your local takeaway.

9. Grant Holt

The Carlisle-born Norwich striker looks more like he'd be suited to a construction yard rather than a football pitch.

8. Shaun Derry

The QPR central midfield player looks like your average nine-to-five, Monday-to-Friday office worker, reading the paper on the 7.55 into town.

7. George Elokobi

Looking at the size of him, he shouldn't be playing football. He should be putting his massive frame to better use, by being a rugby player, or boxer. Or doorman.

6. Marouane Fellaini

The Belgium and Everton midfield looks like he should be wearing white flares and dancing to disco music, mainly because of his huge afro. The fact he's 6'4" doesn't make him look any more like a footballer.

5. David Luiz

David Luiz's hair and his 'different', gung-ho approach to playing mean that he doesn't look like he should be playing football. Instead, you could see him alongside Peter Crouch, stacking shelves in his local supermarket, but loving it at the same time.

4. David Seaman

When David Seaman had his moustache and ponytail, he looked less England's number one and more Spanish Matador *numero uno*.

3. Ricardo Carvalho

The ex-Porto, Chelsea and now Real Madrid centre-back does not look like a footballer. His face and hair make him look more like an artist.

2. Carles Puyol

Puyol's shaggy hair means he'd be more suited to being a hippy than a footballer. Peace.

1. Peter Crouch

Peter Crouch's long, lanky features do not suit a footballer, but would not look amiss alongside Magic Johnson at the LA Lakers. We're surprised Sebastian Coe didn't try to get him to moonlight for the GB Basketball team in London 2012.

Players who missed major games and tournaments

The cruel winds of chance blow upon us all, but especially this breed who came so close to playing in the final of a major trophy but were made redundant because of their behaviour in the semi. If you could only turn back the hands of time...

10. Andreas Moeller (1996 Euros final)
Despite Andreas Möller breaking England fans' hearts when he scored the winning penalty in the Euro '96 semi-final, he missed the final after picking up a yellow card earlier on in the match. Germany still went on to beat Czech Republic 2-1 after extra time.

9. Darren Fletcher (2009 Champions League final)
Darren Fletcher missed the 2009 Champions League final. In Manchester United's semi-final against Arsenal, Fletcher was sent off for a foul on Cesc Fàbregas. Replays showed the decision was a harsh one. United appealed the red card, but were unsuccessful.

8. Pavel Nedved (2003 Champions League final)
Pavel Nedved missed Juventus' Champions League final against AC Milan in 2003 after getting booked just eight minutes from time for a silly foul on Steve McManaman. The booking was enough for him to be suspended. Nedved scored in the semi-final as his Juventus team beat Real Madrid 3-0. Juventus went on to lose the final 3-2 on penalties. Pavel Nedved was the recipient of the Ballon d'Or in 2003.

7. Michael Ballack (2002 World Cup Final)
Michael Ballack's 75th-minute goal against host South Korea in the 2002 World Cup semi-final was enough to put Germany into the World Cup final. But Ballack picked up a yellow card just before he scored his match-winning goal, which meant he was suspended for the final. Brazil beat Germany in the final 2-0.

6. Laurent Blanc (1998 World Cup Final)
French defender Laurent Blanc missed the 1998 World Cup final on his own turf when he was sent off in the semi-final against Croatia. Referee Jose Maria

Garcia decided that Laurent Blanc had hit Slaven Billic when Billic hit the ground in a dramatic fashion. That was Laurent Blanc's first sending-off in his career. France were 2-1 up at this point and they held on to that lead until the end of the game. In the final, France beat Brazil 3-0.

4. Alessandro Costacurta (1994 Champions League final & 1994 World Cup final)

Missing a major final must be gutting. But can you imagine missing two in the same year? Costacurta received a red card in the Champions League semi-final against Monaco, but his AC Milan team mates went on to win the game. They also went on to win the final against Barcelona 4-0. Less than two months later, he received a yellow card in the World Cup semi-final against Bulgaria and missed Italy's final with Brazil, which they lost on penalties.

3. Dani Alves and Eric Abidal (2009 Champions League final)

In Barcelona's second-leg semi-final against Chelsea, Dani Alves picked up his third yellow card of the knockout stages and Eric Abidal saw a straight red for a tackle on Nicolas Anelka. Barcelona went through to the final on away goals after a 1 1 draw at Stamford Bridge (Iniesta scoring in the third minute of added time). Barcelona still went on to win the tournament, beating Man Utd 2-0 at the Stadio Olimpico in Rome.

2. John Terry, Ramires, Meireles, Branislav Ivanovic (2012 Champions League final)

After a historic victory against Barcelona in the Champions League semi final, Chelsea faced Bayern Munich at the Allianz stadium (Munich's ground). But when John Terry received a red card for a kick out on Alexis Sanchez, he was out of the final. Ramires (who scored one of the goals in the semi-final) was also booked along with Meireles and Branislav Ivanovic, which meant they were suspended for the final against Bayern Munich. Chelsea went on to win the Champions League on penalties.

John Terry still lifted the trophy in his full kit. The kid that blows the birthday candles out at every party.

1. Roy Keane and Paul Scholes (1999 Champions League final)

Manchester United had to win the Champions League and ultimately the treble without the heart of their team. Roy Keane and Paul Scholes were both booked in Manchester United's semi-final against Juventus, which they won. United were 2-0 down on aggregate in this game after the opening 11 minutes of the second leg in Turin, but United managed to get two goals back though

Roy Keane and Dwight Yorke, which meant they were going through on away goals. Andy Cole made sure, with a goal seven minutes from time. They had to go to and play Bayern without Roy Keane or Paul Scholes, but still won the tournament.

Played with most clubs

They are guns for hire. The mercenaries. The nomads. The midnight flitters. They tell you they love you, and they often perform, but you turn over in the morning and they're gone.

10. Teddy Sheringham
Teddy Sheringham finally ended his career at Colchester aged 42. He graced nine different teams altogether, with two spells at Tottenham. He might not have as many shirts as others, but his trophy cabinet is bigger – he won nearly everything he could in his career.

9. Nicolas Anelka
Nicolas 'Super Nic' Anelka is a goal-scorer for any team he plays for and many clubs have taken advantage of this. His trophy haul is impressive, but what's got him on this list is the scale of clubs he's been to, from Real Madrid to Bolton. Ten clubs and counting.

8. Andy Cole
Andy 'Andrew, please' Cole is one of the Premier League's all-time top goal-scorers with 187 goals. The majority of these were scored for Manchester United and Newcastle. But there were plenty more he played for – ten, to be exact.

7. Craig Bellamy
The little Welshman that gets around, Craig Bellamy has pulled on the shirt for ten clubs. He gets the ball, and one thing is on his mind: heading for the goal. This single-minded approach, and thirst for games meant he even agreed to a season-long loan to Cardiff City in the Championship, having been left out of Manchester United's Europa League squad.

6. Robbie Keane
The Irish striker might not have spread his wings as much as the other contenders; however, to play for 12 clubs is pretty impressive. Having started at Wolves he's been around – Inter Milan, Liverpool, Celtic and LA Galaxy to name but a few.

5. Christian Vieri
Despite having played for Inter Milan for six years, Christian Vieri has still

managed to play for 12 teams including arch rivals AC Milan. Other ports of call were Monaco, Atalanta, Fiorentina and Juventus. He was also the world's most expensive player at one point, with Inter Milan paying £32 million for him.

4. Jimmy Glass

The only goalkeeper to make the list is Jimmy Glass. Jimmy is most famous for scoring a last-minute winning goal to keep Carlisle United in the Football League in 1999. But he played for 13 clubs during his career, which stretched to playing for non-League Kingstonian and Lewes.

3. Ade Akinbiyi

Ade Akinbiyi is remembered for two things – resembling the Incredible Hulk when he ripped his shirt off to celebrate, and playing for numerous clubs. His 14-club journey has taken him everywhere from Stoke City to the Houston Dynamos.

2. Marcus Bent

When Marcus Bent was a hot prospect at Brentford in the mid-1990s, he attracted many clubs and ended up pulling on the colours of 16 of them – most famously for Everton, Charlton and Ipswich Town.

1. Steve Claridge

Appropriately, Steve Claridge has played for two 'Wanderers'. No other man can match his desire to play for every single club in England. He even came out of retirement to play for Gosport Borough of the Southern League Division One South and West. This itchy-footed striker played over a 1,000 professional games in a career which spread over two decades. It would be easier to name the clubs for whom he *hasn't* played, but here goes: Fareham Town, Bournemouth, Weymouth, Crystal Palace, Aldershot, Cambridge United, Luton Town, Birmingham City, Leicester City, Portsmouth, Wolverhampton Wanderers, Millwall, Brighton & Hove Albion, Brentford, Wycombe Wanderers, Gillingham, Bradford City, Walsall, Worthing, Harrow Borough and Gosport Borough.

Quirky keepers

At the highest level, goalkeeping is all about mentality. Which is lucky, as most keepers are mental. You have to be, really, to actively want to stand directly in the way of the ball. Look at the way most defenders cringe and twist when they're in the wall. Not your goalkeeper. He is 13 stone of flesh that must throw himself in the path of the advancing attack, like a slightly unhinged moving fence. Goalkeepers are born odd and go even odder. This was one of the hardest lists to write, because pretty much all goalkeepers could have made it. So here are our ten quirkiest keepers in the quirkiest of positions.

10. Jens Lehmann

Known to Gooners as 'Mad Jens', this masterful keeper's talent was matched only by his eccentricity. Over-keen to come rushing out of his area, he made the world stand up and applaud when he gave Didier Drogba something to really dive about when he shoved him over in 2006. His war of words with Oliver Kahn was hilarious, and he put it in a nutshell about losing his place to 'Faulty' Manuel Almunia: 'He does not have my class.' Whilst playing for Stuttgart, he relieved himself behind an advertising board.

9. Hugo Gatti

Our first 'El Loco', meaning 'the Madman', on the list is Hugo Gatti of Boca Juniors and Argentina. Often bored with keeping goal, Gatti would frequently join his defenders, his midfielders, his strikers, and also nip off to give the stewards a hand during the match, too, we expect. Anyone who said about Maradona: '*Es un gordito que juega muy bien al fútbol*' ('He is a fatty who plays football very well') is OK by us.

8. Harald Schumacher

Talented he may have been, but Germany's Harald Schumacher will forever only be known for one thing: an attack on Patrick Battiston of France in the 1982 semi-final against France which left the Frenchman with missing teeth and damaged vertebrae. If he'd done it in the street he could have been charged with assault.

7. Marcus Hahnemann

The former Fulham and Reading keeper keeps hens in his garden and listens to heavy metal music to psych himself up. He also loves guns and stalks deer in Berkshire in his spare time.

6. Ramon Quiroga

Another 'El Loco', he was very much a fan of the 'attack is the best form of defence' mentality, and would often be found attacking opposition players as far forward as the centre circle, such as in the 1978 World Cup when he fouled Poland's Grzegorz Lato whilst playing for Peru.

5. Fabien Barthez

Looks like the sort of player whose hair jumped away from him in fright. He loved to perform stopovers and dribbles past opposing strikers and famously tried to outwit similarly mental Paolo Di Canio by raising his hand and pretending that offside had been blown. We imagine Paolo thought Fabien's raised hand was simply a special salute. Laurent Blanc liked to kiss his shiny head before France matches.

4. David James

The side parting, the dreads, the bleached dreads, the Afro, the bleached curls, the skinhead, the 'number 3 all-over', the 'goatee-scouse' beard-thing, the headband, the ponytail, the perm... the man's had a *lot* of haircuts. He became known as Calamity James after a string of errors which he blamed on too much PlayStation. His name on the England team sheet always made fans wince.

3. René Higuita

This Columbian, our third 'El Loco', will forever be known for his magnificent scorpion kick against England in 1995, literally blocking a literal shot from literally Jamie Redknapp. He was also known for taking set pieces, and scored from both free kicks and penalties.

2. Neville Southall

The Cartman of the top division, sulky, overweight – sorry, big-boned Southall sulked against a goalpost in true Cartman style when his teammates were in the dressing room while Everton were three goals down to newly promoted Leeds. They lost the match 3-2.

1. Bruce Grobbelaar

You could write an entire book on 'Grab the Air', as he was known by schoolboy fans of teams other than Liverpool in the 1980s. Famed for his athletic ability, and a confidence that surpassed even that of Nicklas Bendtner, he became the first African to win a European Cup. During penalties in the 1984 final against Roma, he first pretended to eat the goal net, putting off Bruno Conti, who duly skied it. And then, in a piece of gamesmanship that will live on for ever, he wobbled his legs at Francesco Graziani, who also missed. Liverpool won 4-2.

Biggest fibs in football

Imagine if every word you ever said was recorded for posterity. 'Mr Smith, you stated to your wife in December of last year that your boss had saddled you with a late project on a Thursday evening. In fact, it has just been revealed by a source close to your best friend Jonesy, that you in fact were in the pub when you called Mrs Smith, and ended up in Starz Nightclub that evening. Care to comment?' So spare a thought for these unfortunate ten. What you could get away with, they couldn't.

10. UEFA's claims about stopping racism
It may be true, it just sounds like a lie when you fine Denmark's Nicklas Bendtner more money for an ambush marketing stunt involving his pants than you do for countries whose fans exhibit racism.

9. Harry Redknapp
2004: On links with Southampton whilst Portsmouth manager: 'I won't go down the road – no chance.'
2005: On links with Portsmouth while Southampton manager: 'I've no idea where this has come from. It is absolute nonsense, a stupid rumour.'
2008: On links with Spurs whilst Portsmouth manager: 'It's absolute rubbish. Portsmouth is my club – I feel immense loyalty. To leave would be a betrayal. This is my last job in football.'

8. Backing Rangers
April 2012: Singaporean businessman Bill Ng promises his £20m bid for Rangers will stand, even if the club's debts continue to rise. To be fair, he didn't walk away. For two days.

Places 4, 5, 6 and 7 – The dreaded 'vote of confidence' from the boardroom...

7. Ron Atkinson at Aston Villa
'Deadly' Doug Ellis backs 'Big' Ron Atkinson on 7 November 1994, before showing him the exit 'early doors' on 10 November. (Villa missed a trick, by the way. Surely an after-dinner tour of the ground from 'Big and Deadly' would be a winner.)

6. Emiliano Mondonico at Novara
In January 2012, Novara president Massimo De Salvo hires Mondonico, stating his faith in the new manager, before sacking him just a few weeks later.

5. Mario Lepe at Universidad Católica
18 April, 2012 in Chile: Universidad Católica president Jaime Estévez reinforces his faith in Mario Lepe before sacking him *the very next day*.

4. Marcelino Garcia at Sevilla
2010: Sevilla president José Maria del Nido offers his wholehearted support to Marcelino Garcia before sending him his P45 just a month later.

3. Roberto Mancini – September 2011
When asked if Tevez would ever play for Manchester City again, Roberto Mancini replied 'Carlo can't play with us... with me, no. He's finished.' Fast forward six months and he's back in the City squad and helping them to the Premier League title. 'Mancini' means 'forgetful pragmatist'.

2. Stephen Ireland – September 2007
Stephen 'Stupid' Ireland (copyright Sven Göran Eriksson) pretended not one but two of his grandmammies had passed away in order to be excused international duties. Both were suitably surprised to read of their own deaths and Ireland was rumbled by the press. He has gone the full Barthez, after pretending for years that he had a lovely, glossy head of hair.

1. Ali Dia – November 1996
Almost unbelievably, Graeme 'I'm Nobody's Fool' Souness became everybody's fool in 1996 when he received a call from someone claiming to be 'George Weah', recommending his 'cousin', Ali Dia. It won the cheeky chancer a month's contract at Southampton, and one start. It worked for Jamie Redknapp, though – some reckon he's had an entire career based on his dad being Harry Redknapp.

Strangest hobbies

Footballers are a strange bunch. Whilst one accepts that we all have interesting, alternative hobbies, finding out our footballing heroes have hobbies of their own is that little bit more weird. As fans, we expect them to be out on the training ground constantly practising, and having no lives. Similar to teachers, who we used to think went into the cupboard at the end of the day and didn't come out until next morning.

10. Wayne Rooney – Drumming
In between shouting at referees and scoring the odd goal, Rooney loves drumming.

9. Paul Scharner – Parachuting, bungee-jumping and water-skiing
In his spare time he likes to dabble in extreme sports.

8. Manuel Almunia – Museums
After watching *Saving Private Ryan*, Almunia now enjoys visiting Second World War sites.

7. John Terry – Fishing
When he's not catching Van Persie and other fast strikers, John Terry likes catching fish.

6. Carlos Tevez – Band member
The Man City man is a member of Argentinian band Piola Vago. Cringe.

5. Andrey Arshavin – Women's fashion designer
So that's where he gets that catwalk strut from.

4. Nolberto Solano – Trumpet-playing
Solano sees himself as a good trumpet player. He likes blowing his own trumpet.

3. Theo Walcott – Children's books
Theo enjoys reading and writing children's books. He does still look like a kid, so it's not a surprise, really.

2. Daniel Agger – Tattoo artist

Not sure which would be more painful - getting a tattoo from Daniel Agger, or watching him play for Liverpool?

1. Cristiano Ronaldo – Bingo

The Real Madrid man loves going to the community centre and joining in with the oldies. He even puts a grey wig on...

Stroppiest players

William Shakespeare once wrote that hell hath no fury like a woman scorned. They obviously didn't have professional footballers back in those days...

10. Robin van Persie
After going down to Wigan at home in April 2012, Van Persie was called a bad loser by Wigan captain Gary Caldwell, who said the striker had refused to shake his hand at the end of the game. Van Persie denied the claim later, although he may have been following orders, since his manager Arsène Wenger had stormed off down the tunnel, ignoring Wigan manager Roberto Martinez.

9. Eric Cantona
Man Utd v Crystal Palace, 25 January 1995: Having badly fouled Crystal Palace defender Richard Shaw, Eric Cantona was shown the red card. As he walked to the tunnel, a Palace fan named Matthew Simmons shouted abuse at Cantona that he believed to be racist. So he launched a flying one-man kung fu kick at the hapless Simmons. Cantona was arrested for assault and received 120 hours' community service on appeal. He was also banned for the rest of the season.

8. Roy Keane
Prior to the 2002 World Cup, Roy Keane asked Republic of Ireland manager Mick McCarthy to his house to talk about the forthcoming campaign. This move astounded many. Not even Sir Alex had ever been invited to Keane Mansions. According to Keane, a plan was hatched which included dietary requirements and training schedules. On arrival in Saipan, Keane claimed none of his suggestions had been taken on board and so in a fit of anger he announced he was quitting the tournament. Cue absolute mayhem and the Republic's campaign in tatters.

7. Wayne Rooney
Never mind the fact that he looks like a scaled up baby, he can also act like one. During the 2012 World Cup in South Africa, England drew 0-0 with Algeria. The England fans were booing, and the England striker wasn't happy about it and decided to have a stroppy rant to the nation.

6. Zinedine Zidane
That head-butt in the 2006 World Cup final against Italian defender Marco

Materazzi was the great player's final act on a pitch. Thankfully, Zidane will always be remembered for much more than reacting to extreme provocation and the fact that his career as a professional footballer was drawing to an end.

5. Neville Southall
In a 1991 game against Leeds, Everton goalkeeper Neville Southall was so appalled by his team's performance and the 3-0 deficit they had racked up, he refused to go to the dressing room at half time, preferring to stay on the pitch. His teammates took note and pulled back two goals.

4. Carlos Tevez
The Manchester City player threw one of the biggest strops in the history of the professional game after he (allegedly) refused to appear as a substitute before his club were beaten 2-0 in the Champions League away at Bayern Munich. It was all a 'misunderstanding', of course...

3. Didier Drogba
Didier Drogba was forced to make a full apology to ref Tom Henning Ovrebo after the controversial 2009 Champions League semi-final at Stamford Bridge won by Barcelona deep into stoppage time. Chelsea – and indeed most people watching – were convinced that the ref had denied the London side four clear penalties. At the final whistle, Drogba ran to confront the ref before turning to the cameras and letting loose with a stream of expletives. He later said, after watching his actions on TV, that he had overreacted a little.

2. Mario Balotelli
Where do we start with young Mario? How about at Upton Park in 2010 when he missed an easy early chance, flew into a sulk, got himself booked and was taken off by manager Mancini in the 62nd minute for his own protection. Balotelli stormed off the pitch, not even looking at his manager, as the West Ham fans sang, 'What a waste of money.'

1. Paolo Di Canio
In a League game against Bradford, the mercurial Di Canio had three penalty appeals turned down. So he did what any other player would do. He sat on the ground and demanded manager Harry Redknapp sub him. Redknapp told him what to do with his request.

Teammate bust-ups

Teamwork. It is the secret to success, we are told. And not just on the football field; who among us has not been subjected to horrendous attempts by managers to build a team ethic? As a nation, we are now horribly familiar with the white water rafting or paintballing teambuilding exercise.

Pull together and we can achieve much more. One twig on its own will snap, but a bundle of twigs bound together is strong. If you're in a hot air balloon about to crash into a building, throw the weakest one out. No, that's not right, but you get the gist.

There's no 'I' in team, but there is an 'i' in both disharmony and hilarity.

10. Steve McManaman and Bruce Grobbelaar, 1993
Shy, retiring South African stopper Bruce Grobbelaar, one of Liverpool's greatest ever keepers was not, it is fair to say, best pleased with the clearance effort of shaggy-haired mumbler Steve McManaman. He made his point like a gentleman, grabbing Mac by the throat. The whole episode then descended into a playground pushing match.

9. Ricardo Fuller and Andy Griffin, 2008
Stoke conceded. Striker Ricardo Fuller decided Andy Griffin was to blame and had a quiet word in the dressing room. That's what should have happened. Instead, just before the restart, he slapped his captain across the face and got shown a card, the colour of which matched the nasty inflammation on the cheek of Andy Griffin – bright, angry, red.

8. Emmanuel Adebayor and Nicklas Bendtner, 2008
Nicklas Bendtner: not only the world's greatest striker, but one whose poor clothing choices can start actual fights. No, it's not the pink boots; this beef started when Adebayor questioned Super Nick's repeated breaching of Arsenal's 'no trainers in the dressing room' rule.

7. Stan Collymore and Trevor Benjamin, 2000
This one has the ignominy of not even featuring in a first-team match. During a reserves game against Charlton, the much-travelled Trevor Benjamin (28 clubs) and the similarly peripatetic Collymore (ten) started an argument, which continued in the dressing room. The result? Our Stan refused to come out for the second half.

6. Craig Bellamy and John Arne Riise, 2007

'Hello, and welcome to another episode of Brits Abroad, where we take a look at how the British behave on holiday. We're at the Vale do Lobo resort, Portugal, where pint-sized Brit Craig Bellamy takes out his frustrations on his Norwegian friend John, with a golf club.'

5. John Terry and Wayne Bridge, 2010

Although this only ever manifested itself in a rather limp 'shunned handshake', it's one of the most well-known footballing bust-ups of recent years. Mr Loverman Terry has pressed the play button on the Luther Vandross with a number of what the tabloids used to call 'lovelies' over the years. Except that one of these lovelies was his teammate's ex-girlfriend, Vanessa Perroncel. John, John, John. Never on your own doorstep.

4. Joey Barton and Ousmane Dabo, 2007

We know! Joey Barton! Normally the peacemaker, Joey acted completely out of character back in 2007 when he assaulted his teammate Ousmane Dabo, who needed treatment for head injuries. If it had happened on the pitch, it would have been a red card. As it happened at Manchester City's training ground, Joey got a four-month suspended sentence.

3. Olof Mellberg and Freddie Ljungberg, 2010

The Sweden World Cup camp was plunged into chaos when Aston Villa's Olof Mellberg and Arsenal's Freddie Ljungberg had an altercation over a tackle in training. Mellberg's tackle was later than Delia Smith's husband's breakfast the morning after the 'Let's be 'avin' you' outburst, and Fred had to be stopped from doing something really quite horrid to Mellberg, like pulling his hair or giving him a nasty Chinese burn.

2. John Hartson and Eyal Berkovic, 1998

Old-fashioned ginger number 9 John Hartson gave Eyal Berkovic an old-fashioned boot to the face during training. John tried to help Eyal to his feet and was treated to a punch on the leg. In what might be termed a slight overreaction, Hartson unleashed a mighty kick from the boot that would go on to deliver 167 top-flight goals. Ouch.

1. Lee Bowyer and Kieron Dyer

One way to distract your home fans from the fact that you are 3-0 down to Aston Villa is to start beating seven shades out of one of your teammates. This was either a brilliantly planned attempt to break Villa's rhythm and concentration, or a disgraceful incident which brought shame not only to

Newcastle United but to football itself. You decide. Lovable rogue Lee Bowyer and one of football's last gentlemen, Kieron Dyer, were both sent off. It looked like Bowyer was ahead on points just before the ref stepped in.

Most bizarre behaviour

'He's big, he's lazy, we think he's f****** crazy...' Takes a lot of mental pressure to stay at the top as a footballer. The ever-present ghosts of injury and loss of form hover above you at all times. You wonder who is plotting against you in the dressing room, on the training ground. Will those girls you just spent the night with squeal to the press and humiliate your wife and children? Is your drinking getting that little bit heavy? Is it any wonder then that at some point in his career the footballer spectacularly implodes? We think not.

10. Darius Vassell
The former England striker missed several games while playing for Aston Villa in 2003 when he drilled through his toenail at home with a power drill. His attempt at DIY surgery was to relieve pressure on a swollen toe. Instead he got an infection, which required further medical attention.

9. Sergio Goycochea
The former Argentine keeper had a rather bizarre ritual for penalty shoot-outs – urinating on the pitch. This is all started in the 1990 World Cup quarter-final against Yugoslavia.

The rules of the game are that you can't abandon the field before the match finishes but when you've got to go, you've got to go – or at least that is his excuse. They won that quarter-final, and then he did it again in the semi-final against Italy in the shoot-out, and they won. So from then on, he did it before every shoot-out. It still wasn't enough for them to win the 1990 World Cup, losing in the final 1-0 to West Germany.

8. Steve Phillips
There is no doubt that the Bristol City keeper has bottle, just in a very bizarre way – he can't change his water bottle.

'When I walk into the dressing-room the first water bottle I pick up I have to keep with me for the rest of the day. It doesn't matter how dirty or battered it gets, I can't use another one or else it's bad luck. And not only that, but once it's empty our kitman Roger Harding – and only him – has to refill it from a new bottle. Roger is the only other person allowed to touch my bottle. I don't let anyone else anywhere near it.'

Steve Phillips played for Bristol City for ten years before making a controversial move to Bristol Rovers in 2006. He eventually moved to Crewe in 2011. You could say he never bottled it...

7. François Zoko

Ivorian striker François Zoko revealed some bizarre injury-healing methods during his time at Carlisle United. In September 2011, during a midweek cup defeat to Accrington Stanley, he injured his wrist. He then branded himself fit for the game at the weekend after manager Greg Abbott found the striker with his hand in a teapot. Abbott commented: 'At half time at Accrington I saw François with his thumb in a pot of tea. It nearly blew my head off when I saw what he was doing. The glare he got from me was enough for him to take it out. I'm not sure why he was doing it – maybe he was trying to keep it warm. But he ended up scalding it.'

Zoko did make an appearance in the following game against Hartlepool, but they lost 2-1, and the striker failed to score.

6. Temuri Ketsbaia

Temuri Ketsbaia's classic celebration against Bolton is one of those moments that always pops up on the Premier League highlight reels. The Georgian striker came off the bench in a 1998/9 season League game against Bolton and, after he scored, he ripped off his shirt and threw it into the crowd, tried to take off his boots and started kicking the advertising hoardings. He also shrugged off concerned-looking Philippe Albert. When commenting on the bizarre act, he said, 'I was just happy to score.'

5. Paul Gascoigne

It was reported that, one hour after playing for England, Gazza went and met his 'showbiz pals' Danny Baker and Chris Evans in a pub in Hampstead, of course wearing his full England kit and boots.

4. Maradona

We all know the classic Maradona moment of madness when he decided to use his hand to put in a goal against England then called it 'the hand of God', but there were other moments during his time as Argentina's coach for the 2010 World Cup. In preparation for the tournament, he managed to call up over 100 players in just a year and half, including a call-up for a 36-year-old Areil Ortega for a friendly against Haiti, who hadn't been previously selected for Argentina since 2003. He also bizarrely dropped two Argentine greats – Javier Zanetti and Esteban Cambiasso – for the World Cup 2010.

3. Ashley Cole

In February 2011, it was revealed that the English defender 'accidentally shot and wounded' a work experience student at Chelsea's training ground in Cobham. The Chelsea defender was reported to have been hanging around the training complex with the .22 calibre air rifle when he fired at 21-year-old Tom Cowan. The Chelsea fans responded by shouting 'Shoot' every time he got the ball and 'Ashley's gonna shoot ya!' echoed around the terraces of Stamford Bridge.

2. Eric Cantona

In 1995 at Selhurst Park, in a game between Crystal Palace and Manchester United, Eric Cantona kung fu kicked Palace fan Matthew Simmons after he verbally abused him. This resulted in him being sent off. He was also sentenced to two weeks in prison which was reduced on 31 March 1995 to 120 hours of community service. Arguably the most bizarre aspect of this story is the first press conference after the attack: the Frenchman sat there and then said, 'When the seagulls follow the trawler, it's because they think sardines will be thrown into the sea. Thank you very much.' Cantona returned to action for Manchester United on 1 October 1995 and scored a penalty in a 2-2 draw with Liverpool.

If all that wasn't enough, he decided in 2012 that he wanted to become a politician and tried to become a candidate in the race for the French Presidency. It then emerged that it was all just a publicity stunt.

1. Mario Balotelli

Here are some highlights from the man's time in England: throwing a dart at a youth-team player at the club's Carrington training academy in March 2011; gate-crashing his former club Inter Milan's press conference as they unveiled their latest manager Andrea Stramaccioni in March 2012; letting off fireworks in his house the night before the Manchester derby in October 2011, and then posing as a firework safety ambassador; going for a curry the night before City's clash with Chelsea and then being caught having a swordfight with rolling pins at 1 a.m.

ENGLAND

Best England Captain

Being the captain of your national team is the pinnacle of any footballer's career. In England, we've seen great leaders lead teams to famous victories. England's first captain was Cuthbert Ottaway in 1872, and since then over 100 more players have led England out. We've had tears, bandaged heads, penalty shoot-outs, World Cups and lots of goals. But most of all, England captains have been national ambassadors for the country all over the world and made the English proud.

10. Johnny Haynes
Anyone that Pelé says is the best passer he has ever seen deserves his place in this list. Haynes, who played his football for Fulham, was captain during the 1962 World Cup and in a big 9-3 win over Scotland.

9. Paul Ince
Despite only being captain of England seven times, he made history when he became the first black England captain. The image of him in a bloodied head bandage from the goalless draw against Italy in 1997 is an unforgettable one for any England fan.

8. Gary Lineker
Before he took his seat on the *Match of the Day* sofa, Gary Lineker scored a lot of goals and captained England. Lineker was just one short of equalling Bobby Charlton's record of 49 international goals and led England out at Euro '92.

7. Peter Shilton
Peter Shilton had to make the list! Despite only captaining the England team 15 times, he has the record for most capped English player with 125 caps. He has filled in as captain for major tournaments, including the 1986 and 1990 World Cup finals.

6. Alan Shearer
One of the most memorable number nines England has ever produced. He captained England 34 times from 63 caps and scored 30 goals.

5. Tony Adams
Tony Adams is a natural born leader and had all the qualities of a great captain. He was vocal, led by example and gave everything he possibly could every time

he wore an England shirt. He captained England at Euro '96 on his own soil and showed responsibility by giving up the armband after admitting he was an alcoholic.

4. Bryan Robson

Nicknamed 'Captain Marvel', the Manchester United midfielder led out the England team 65 times, in two World Cups. He was unlucky with injuries and he could have worn the armband even more.

3. David Beckham

Beckham captained England 58 times and wore the armband with pride, giving everything for the Three Lions. One of the most memorable moments for Beckham came when he led by example with a last-gasp free-kick against Greece to take England into the World Cup finals.

2. Billy Wright

Billy Wright captained England 90 times, something only Bobby Moore can match. He was also the first England player to surpass 100 caps. Wright set a fine example never being booked or sent off in his entire career.

1. Bobby Moore

'My captain, my leader, my right-hand man. He was the spirit and the heartbeat of the team. A cool, calculating footballer I could trust with my life. He was the supreme professional, the best I ever worked with. Without him, England would never have won the World Cup.' – Alf Ramsey.

We can't see anyone arguing with this one. Every England fan from any generation will see Bobby Moore as a legend. The inspirational leader led his England team to win the World Cup in 1966, an achievement that will never be forgotten. Our number one had to be the captain of the team who achieved the greatest moment in the country's footballing history.

He has been described as the greatest defender that they ever played against by Pelé, Franz Beckenbauer and Sir Alex Ferguson. Scottish manager Jock Stein said: 'There should be a law against him. He knows what's happening 20 minutes before everyone else.' And his statue outside Wembley Stadium reads:

'Immaculate footballer. Imperial defender. Immortal hero of 1966. First Englishman to raise the World Cup aloft. Favourite son of London's East End. Finest legend of West Ham United. National Treasure. Master of Wembley. Lord of the game. Captain extraordinary. Gentleman of all time.'

Best England performances

Since winning the World Cup in 1966, the England team has had to live up to huge expectations. In a lot of games their nerve has failed them and they have turned in performances the whole country is still trying to forget. Yet there are times when the lads turn on the style we all know they are capable of and brilliantly remind us what a force they can be in international football. Here are ten performances that set England alight.

10. England 4-2 Czechoslovakia (Friendly 1990)

These days, England friendlies are about as exciting as watching paint dry. This was a good performance and set England up nicely for Italia '90. Paul Gascoigne was England's standout player. It was one of those nights where everything he touched turned to gold.

9. England 2-0 West Germany (Friendly 1975)

West Germany hadn't lost since their World Cup triumph the year before (which England didn't even qualify for) and England were desperate for a win against their arch rivals, having not beaten them since 1966. On a wet night at Wembley, England put on a dazzling display to sweep the Germans aside.

8. Argentina 2-2 England (4-3 pens) (1998 World Cup quarter-final)

A strange one to put in the list for 'Best England Performance' particularly when they lost the match and were eliminated from the tournament. The manner of performance was everything it should be from an England side in a World Cup quarter-final. It was courageous, passionate. Looking back at this game, England really were desperately unlucky.

7. Yugoslavia 1-4 England (Euro '88 qualifier)

Yugoslavia, at the time, were a decent team, and on paper, looked like they would cause England a fair few problems. Not so. England turned on the style, racing to a 4-0 lead in the first 25 minutes. England manager at the time Bobby Robson said afterwards that 'we looked unbeatable in that opening half an hour'.

6. England 3-1 France (1982 World Cup)

England were making their first appearance at a World Cup for 12 years, and returned in emphatic style. They took France to the cleaners, with a Bryan

Robson goal after just 27 seconds. France eventually finished fourth in the tournament.

5. England 2-1 Portugal (1966 World Cup semi-final)
Portugal had the unstoppable Eusebio, who was banging in goals for fun, prior to this match. Bobby Moore dealt with him superbly well though, and England claimed a legendary victory, setting up the big final with West Germany.

4. Argentina 0-1 England (2002 World cup)
After being sent off against Argentina in 1998, David Beckham had a chance to make himself a legend, and get revenge over the Argentineans from the penalty spot. He smashed it straight down the middle, and England held on for a memorable victory.

3. England 4-1 Holland (Euro '96)
This was a truly brilliant display from England, as they ripped into the Dutch from the first minute. The best of the four goals was Shearer's second which was worked beautifully. Steve McManaman and Paul Gascoigne picked their way through the Holland defence, before teeing up Teddy Sheringham who, instead of pulling the trigger, laid it off to Shearer who rifled it into the roof of the net.

2. Germany 1-5 England (2002 World cup qualifier)
A totally brilliant performance from England. Carsten Jancker opened the scoring for the Germans, but what happened after that was quite remarkable. Michael Owen claimed a hat-trick, the Germans missed chances, and Emile Heskey scored. It was one of those nights where everything went England's way.

1. England 4-2 Germany (1966 World Cup final)
This has to be in the best England performances of all time for an obvious reason - they actually won something!

Memorable England managers

There have been some great mangers come and go over the years, but the fact remains, England has still only won one tournament in its international history. Still, some great managers have tried and failed, and in doing so left us with some great memories.

10. Don Revie
Did an amazing job with Leeds, but sadly couldn't replicate that with England, failing to qualify for the European Championships in 1976.

9. Fabio Capello
The FA's choice of Fabio Capello to manage England seemed to herald a new era in English football... Capello was a born winner, a man who had created success at every club he managed, once even guiding Roma to the Scudetto. England, however, defeated him. Despite early success, an increasingly hostile press annoyed by his bad English and some ego-driven players – who were outraged by being asked to turn their mobile phones off when they were working – created mountains he could not scale. He resigned after the FA stripped Terry of his captaincy. Said to be outraged by the move, he was probably relieved that he had just been handed a get-out-of-jail card.

8. Kevin Keegan
He had the worst win percentage of any England manager ever. So what did he do? He walked away. After Germany beat England at the last ever game at Wembley Stadium, Keegan admitted he was out of his depth and going home.

7. Graham Taylor
Taylor only managed to win 18 of his 38 games, but was the subject of one of the best football documentaries ever when he foolishly allowed a camera crew to follow him around as he attempted to get England to qualify for the 1994 World Cup. He failed badly, and the sight of Taylor on the touchline telling the linesman to thank his mate the ref for costing him his job, remains priceless.

6. Glenn Hoddle
Hoddle was much respected by the England squad for his tactical awareness. However, his employment of faith healer Eileen Drury raised eyebrows, as did his religious beliefs. When he told the press that physically challenged people had been bad in a previous lifetime, not even Moses could have saved him his

job. That situation and his religious comments secure Hoddle's place in our top ten.

5. Sven Goran Erikson
Sven makes the list, just because of his habit of saying, 'Wellllllllllll...'

4. Terry Venables
Terry Venables was named the England 'coach' by the FA rather than being given the traditional 'manager' title. Bizarrely man-management was one of his main strengths – perfect for players like Paul Gascoigne, Venables was a father figure for the wayward genius and able to realise his potential. His management of England in Euro '96 was exemplary, again taking the team to the semi-finals to lose to Germany on penalties.

3. Steve McClaren
McClaren had worked with Ferguson at United and proved his managerial worth at Middlesbrough. But the England job proved too much. His friendly approach – he famously called Steven Gerrard 'Stevie G' all the time – and lack of nous eventually led him to being called 'the Wally with the brolly'.

2. Sir Bobby Robson
Unfairly vilified by the press prior to Italia '90, Robson managed to turn things around and guide England into that classic semi-final encounter with West Germany in Naples. The 1990 penalty shootout will always stick in the memory. So close and yet so far. It was Robson who defined Gazza as 'daft as a brush', and Robbo whose passion for the game and huge dignity meant his sad passing in 2009 was mourned by football fans everywhere.

1. Sir Alf Ramsey
He did something no other England manager has come close to emulating: he won the World Cup. A legendary figure.

The Ultimate England XI

We're all managers at heart, hence the popularity of Fantasy League nationwide. And we've all, at times, claimed we could do a better job than most managers. But who would make it into your all-time top England XI. And could it beat 606's? We don't think so...

Peter Shilton (Goalkeeper)
A very close-run thing between him and Gordon Banks, but it has to be Peter Shilton, who boasts a record of an unequalled 125 England caps, as well as 66 clean sheets.

Gary Neville (Right-back)
He made 85 appearances for England and is known for wearing his heart on his sleeve for both England and Manchester United. He would have made a great England captain, but unfortunately played in a generation with Tony Adams, Alan Shearer and David Beckham.

Stuart Pearce (Left-back)
His passion, commitment and no-nonsense tackling meant 'Psycho' could play at the highest level and not look out of place. His courage after missing a penalty in the World Cup semi-final against Germany in 1990, to later return and bury a penalty against Spain in Euro '96 was testament to his character.

Bobby Moore (Centre-back)
Lifting the World Cup at Wembley is something every Englishman dreams of. But only one man can say he's done it, and that man is Bobby Moore. He got 108 caps for England, scoring two goals.

Tony Adams (Centre-back)
It was tough to pick a partner for Bobby Moore. Terry Butcher is a great contender, but Tony Adams just sneaks it. Adams made 66 appearances for England, but it was his leadership skills and mentoring of younger players that set him apart. After the Euro '96 semi-final defeat to Germany, he was urging the players to keep their heads up and show their appreciation to the England fans. A great captain and leader.

John Barnes (Left-midfield)
Left-midfield has been a problem area for England over the years, but not

while John Barnes was available for selection. The goal against Brazil in the 1984 World Cup is his most memorable for England, breezing past several defenders before burying it.

David Beckham (Right-midfield)

We have never produced a better crosser of the ball or dead ball specialist than David Beckham. The last-minute free kick against Greece at Old Trafford proved the fact that when we needed him to produce something spectacular at the most crucial moment, he delivered. Becks was so close to being the only Englishmen to ever appear in five World Cups, but unfortunately tore his Achilles tendon.

Bobby Charlton (Centre-midfield)

He is still England's highest ever goal scorer after 40 years. He was such a massive part of the 1966 winning team, and his ferocious shot stung the palms of many great goalkeepers. More often than not, though, the keeper couldn't get anywhere near his shots.

Bryan Robson (Centre-midfield)

Skippered England for 65 of his 90 caps. Unfortunately for him, and us, injuries plagued him in the 1986 and 1990 World Cups. With a fully fit Robson, maybe we could have gone all the way.

Alan Shearer (Striker)

Proven to score all types of goals – tap-ins, long-range beauties, headers and penalties, Shearer could do the lot. It was tough to leave Geoff Hurst out, but it speaks volumes about Shearer's ability to keep out a man that scored a hat-trick in a World Cup final. The most natural goal scorer this country has ever produced.

Gary Lineker (Striker)

His goal-scoring ratio is outstanding for England, with over a goal every two games. He fell one goal short of Bobby Charlton's goal-scoring record for England, with Lineker on 48. Lineker never received a single yellow card throughout his career.

Underwhelming England call-ups

To be fair, no England cap is pointless. Who among us would not want to be able to say to our grandchildren, 'I played for England'? Andy Cole, for example, would love to be able to say that. Hang on, the phone's ringing. Hello? Yes, that's us, **606**. What's that? He did? When? Oh. Sorry about that. Anyway. To play for England at any level should be an honour. Even if it is only once. Or twice. The choices below then, are not pointless, they are just a little underwhelming. So here they are: the crumbs beneath the table of international football. The bit-part players. The discarded bits of footage on the cutting room floor of 'England: The Movie'. But let us be clear – these players still have one more England cap than you. In fact, they have one more England cap than most footballers.

10. Michael Ball
No, not that one. The footballer. Michael Ball's one and only cap came in Sven's first game in charge in February 2001 – a friendly against Spain at Villa Park. England won 3-0, but neither the three goals nor the clean sheet were down to left back Ball, who was, to use the schoolboy joke, left back in England for the 2002 World Cup finals.

9. Anthony Gardner
When Anthony Gardener finally put a string of games together for Spurs, Sven decided to give him a call-up. The auspicious date came in March 2004 at the Nya Ullevi Stadion in Göteborg, Sweden in March 2004. The game finished 1-0 Sweden, the goal unfortunately being conceded minutes after Gardner came on as a substitute for Jonathan Woodgate.

He never played for England again.

8. David White
In 1992, David White was called up to the England team by Graham Taylor. The game was against Spain at Estadio El Sardinero and it finished 1-0 Spain. White missed a glorious chance early on in the game when he rounded the keeper and failed to finish in an open goal. He was replaced by Paul Merson. It took 11 more years for another Manchester City player to play for England – Shaun Wright-Phillips.

7. Theo Walcott
Yes, we know he shouldn't be on this list. But he doesn't make it on here

because of his underwhelming performances. Theo may well have been so-so for England at the 2006 World Cup. Or he may have been amazing; a scintillatingly fast unknown quantity to unlock miserly defences. He was picked by Sven without having seen him play. Mind you, no one had really seen him play – he hadn't yet made an appearance for Arsenal. To take him to a World Cup was odd enough. But to take him and *not* play him was way worse. Sven, this number seven is for you.

6. Steve Guppy

In 1999, Kevin Keegan handed Steve Guppy his one and only cap in a friendly against Belgium. Guppy was 30 when he got a call-up in the game which England won 2-1 in the friendly held at the Stadium of Light. The one and only cap was even more surprising, as Keegan signed Guppy for Newcastle in 1994 but he only played once before he sold him.

5. Michael Ricketts

Ricketts was the first Bolton player to get an England cap for 40 years when he made his debut under Sven Göran Eriksson. His only cap came against Holland in a friendly in February 2002 ahead of the World Cup that year. It was a typical friendly where in-form strikers are picked, expected to replicate their League form internationally, and then left behind for tournaments when they fail. The game finished 1-1 at the Amsterdam Arena.

4. David Nugent

On paper, David Nugent's England record has a mesmeric symmetry to it: P1 G1. But behind that Messiesque statistic lies a darker story. In a move that would invite a dead leg or similar playground punishment if you'd tried it at school, Nugent chased Jermaine Defoe's shot, which struck the keeper on the way through and was trickling over the line. Nugent triumphantly smashed the ball into the net, claiming the goal. He was not called up again.

3. Gavin McCann

In what is becoming a bit of a running feature in this list, McCann was yet another surprise Sven call-up. In February 2001, everyone's fifth-favourite Swede (after ABBA) had his first game in charge of England against Spain at Villa Park. There were many surprise inclusions in the squad, including Gavin McCann who only played 45 minutes. The only 45 he ever played in an England shirt. England won the game 3-0.

2. Francis Jeffers

And here we go again: another Sven-Göran Eriksson one-match wonder,

Francis Jeffers came on as a sub in a friendly against Australia in February 2003. To be fair to the lad, he did score one goal in his one game, which looks rather better than the statistics of his time at Arsenal where he averaged 0.17 goals per game. Jeffers came on as a sub with another debutant – Wayne Rooney. Whatever happened to him?

1. Peter Ward

There's a kind of pride to be taken in taking the shortest amount of time to do something. Being the fastest is not to be sniffed at. It's the slacker's modus operandi: get in, get it done in the minimal amount of time, get out. The job's a good 'un. And so it goes with Peter Ward, former apprentice engine fitter at Rolls-Royce, Brighton legend. He is one of the select band of footballers to be awarded the 'wonderland' song, and he played for England. What more do you want from life? Even if he did only come on in the 85th minute against Australia in May 1980, making his international career the shortest ever. Who cares? How many caps have YOU got?

Worst England performance

The zenith of England's performances as a football team came with their glorious World Cup victory in 1966 when their brilliant play and team spirit placed English football at the top of the world.

Here are ten examples when for one reason or another they didn't quite reach those heady heights.

10. Croatia 2-0 England (Euro 2008 qualifier)
England crashed to a 2-0 defeat in Zagreb, after Eduardo opened the scoring for the Croatians, goalkeeper Paul Robinson completely missed his kick for the second goal, which effectively sealed the points. Another England goalkeeper horror show, but the team were also to blame for being outclassed.

9. Poland 2-0 England (1974 World Cup qualifier)
A rare error from Bobby Moore and a red card for Alan Ball meant England slumped to a disappointing 2-0 defeat to Poland. The result was crucial in England failing to qualify for the tournament.

8. Morocco 0-0 England (1986 World Cup)
Another scoreless, woeful draw against African opposition in a World Cup group match. Sound familiar? Ray Wilkins was sent off for England in a pretty poor display. They did recover though, and if it wasn't for a 'hand of God' might have won the tournament

7. England 2-2 Macedonia (Euro 2004 qualifier)
A game which will be remembered for another David Seaman blunder as he allowed his opponents to score direct from a corner. Expected to sweep Macedonia aside, England's embarrassment was compounded in stoppage time, when Alan Smith was sent off.

6. Norway 2-0 England (1994 World Cup qualifier)
Poor prior results meant this was a huge game for Graham Taylor's side. They had to win to have any chance of qualifying for the 1994 World Cup. Naturally, England lost 2-0 and in doing so created very few chances. Taylor took a tirade of abuse from England fans and the media following the result, a barrage that only intensified when England failed to qualify for the tournament at a later stage. Unsurprisingly, Taylor then resigned.

5. England 0-1 Germany (2002 World Cup qualifier)
In the last England game at the Old Wembley, Kevin Keegan's men didn't do the stadium justice, as they slumped to a poor 1-0 defeat to Germany. Dietmar Hamman's free kick proved the difference at a rain-soaked Wembley. It turned out to be Kevin Keegan's last game in charge.

4. Germany 4-1 England (2010 World Cup)
Losing to the Germans is never nice, but this was an absolute thumping. You can look at the Frank Lampard 'goal that never was' and blame the officials, but this performance capped off a woeful World Cup from England. As it turned out, Capello never got a chance to put England's tournament football right, as he walked out nearly two years later.

3. England 2-3 Croatia (Euro 2008 qualifier)
The game that meant England failed to qualify for Euro 2008. Steve McClaren stood a lonely figure on the touchline (brolly in hand), as England turned in a shambolic display. They found themselves 2-0 down after Scott Carson fumbled Niko Kranjcar's shot into the net, followed by Ivica Olic claiming a second for the Croatians. England came back to make it 2-2, but Mladen Petric smashed a 25-yarder past Carson to seal the win for Croatia and the sack for McClaren.

2. England 0-0 Algeria (2010 World Cup)
England's worst performance for years, which resulted in **606** receiving the most calls in the programme's history. England had been handed a fairly easy group consisting of the United States, Algeria and Slovenia, but of course they had to make very hard work of it, drawing against USA 1-1 in the opening match, before producing this dour bore draw. Wayne Rooney's camera rant at the end of the match only irritated the England fans even more.

1. Northern Ireland 1-0 England (2006 World Cup qualifier)
An embarrassed England lost 1-0 to Northern Ireland at Windsor Park, thanks to David Healy's goal. The closest England came to scoring was a David Beckham free kick hitting the crossbar, but in truth it was a poor England display and Northern Ireland fully deserved the win.

Worst England players

As much as we adore the England national side, we have had some memorable disasters waiting to happen. Some players have put on the shirt without deserving it, some have more caps then they deserve. Either way their career will always be remembered for their time at England not so much for their club performances. Others may disagree, but here are our nominations for the Top 10.

10. Keith Curle
Curle spent many of his formative years in the lower Leagues. Graham Taylor selected the then Man City player securing him three caps in 1992.

9. Stuart Ripley
The Blackburn right-winger collected his first cap in 1993 and then waited four years to collect his second.

8. Geoff Thomas
Graham Taylor's selection has to be questioned with Thomas collecting nine caps from 1991 to 1992. If you were playing during Taylor's reign, you had a decent chance.

7. Seth Johnson
Johnson making it into an England kit is a mystery that Sherlock Holmes would struggle to solve. Starting only one game in 2000, the then Leeds Utd player never returned.

6. Carlton Palmer
Famous for being berated by Taylor for his inability to 'knock it', Palmer was involved in England's failed USA '94 qualifying bid.

5. Kieron Dyer
A hot prospect picking up his first cap at the age of 20. Despite the numerous injuries, he has still notched up 33 caps, failing to score at all. Is he not meant to be attack minded?

4. Scott Carson
We already have Robert 'Flappy Hands' Green and David 'Calamity' James, but Scott Carson needs no middle name. Forever enshrined in McClaren's England

legacy, making only three appearances he will forever be remembered for that moment against Croatia in 2008.

3. Emile Heskey

Fans still struggle to understand Heskey's football prowess. Apart from scoring against Germany, this rather unimpressive striker has notched up 62 caps, scoring just seven goals.

2. David Nugent

With his one cap one goal, the unbelievable finish following Defoe's strike that was already goal bound has to be a moment of embarrassment for all. It's safe to say that neither Jermain nor his England teammates were impressed. Nor were we.

1. Michael Ricketts

A meteoric demise clouds Ricketts, having once been considered the next big thing. Scoring 15 goals for Bolton in 2002, he had the call-up against Holland. He never scored again that season and never played for England again.

STYLE

Best bald footballers

Baldness has always been with us. Bald players have also always been with us. What's changed is how it's dealt with. In the past, great baldies like the Charlton brothers may have attempted to minimise the visual effects of baldness by taking a ten-inch lock of hair and pasting it across the hair-free dome of their noggin. Surely they didn't think anybody was fooled by that? These days, with hair transplants, baldies like Wayne Rooney can have hair taken from any part of their body and have it transplanted onto their heads. Now that's magic.

So here they are: the con-artists, the brazen shavers, the comb-overs, the comb-forwards, the wiggers and the weavers.

10. Stephen Ireland
It's been a tortuous and difficult journey for Stephen, but he has finally embraced his baldness and looks all the better for it. He's tried various things: the Caesar style comb-forward, a transplant, a weave, a wig, and now, the classic footballer's haircut of choice – the polished shiny top.

9. Brad Friedel
Only really makes it in because his name is an anagram of 'R! Baldie Fred'. He did have hair at one point, though. There are photographs. It was back in the 1930s.

8. Ralph Coates
Who can forget the magnificent sight of Ralph Coates sprinting down the wing at White Hart Lane, with a hair-sprayed flap of hair, hinged at one side, bouncing up and down?

7. Bob Stokoe
The *fin de siècle* comb-over belonged to Sunderland's FA Cup-winning manager.

5.= Bobby and Jack Charlton
Splendid matching attempts at disguising a square foot of bare scalp.

4. Attilio Lombardo
Fans of Crystal Palace remember the Bald Eagle so well. The hair was a comb-over without the comb-over. The length on the sides starkly contrasting with the shiny pink top, this was a haircut way past its time, and certainly far too old for a man of barely 30.

3. Jaap Stam
The best example of the intimidating skinhead look, Stam's naked head was part of United's treble-winning side in 1999.

2. Roberto Carlos
Roberto Carlos, bless his 40-inch thighs, never really had anything going for him in the looks department, and couldn't even compensate with luxurious locks. Still – he's sitting in his mansion staring at one World Cup, four La Liga and three Champions League medals, and we're sitting here hoping Chappers isn't going to shout at us for making a bad cup of tea when he gets in. Carlos wins.

1. Zinedine Zidane
So gifted that an art-house movie was made which consisted solely of footage of 'Zizou' shot during one match with 17 cameras, this iconic player's control and passing is perhaps never going to be bettered. A player of sumptuous talent, Zidane won every trophy going in the game: a World Cup, a European Championship, two Serie 'A' titles, two Champions Leagues... the list goes on and on. And yes – he did it all with no hair.

Best beards

For a long time you were more likely to see a beard on the tea lady than you were on the striker. And then, relatively recently, facial hair started to become fashionable again. Although, if you think about it, by removing the beard on a daily basis, we remind ourselves that in fact, the state of beard-dom is the natural state. But then 'Top Ten Best Not-Beards' would be quite hard. Therefore, we bring you: the Top Ten Best Footballing Beards.

10. David Beckham: 'The Neck Rug'
If anyone else had grown a beard like that, we'd have berated them. But Becks can get away with anything, even a beard which only grows on the neck, with a few stray strands on the upper lip.

9. Frank Lampard Senior: 'The Standard'
Father of Chelsea and England midfielder Frank Junior, he roamed around Upton Park with a standard beard. Not too short, not too long. Definitely a beard.

8. Djibril Cissé: 'The Blond Neptune'
Resplendent in peroxide yellow, Cissé's effort makes the list purely for its showiness. Magnificent, and named after the Roman god of water and the sea, and beard pioneer.

7. Olof Mellberg: 'Das Boot'
During his time at Aston Villa, he was fully bearded. The most ample on the list, giving famous Ljungberg kicker Mellberg the air of an extra in classic submarine-based war film *Das Boot*.

6. Ricky Villa: 'The Gaucho'
In between herding cattle on the plains of 19th-century Argentina, the Spurs legend was top of the beard league during his time at White Hart Lane.

5. Sócrates: 'El Senhor'
The ex-Corinthians and Brazil midfielder was a superb player, and you have to admire his beard, too. Luxuriant and hypnotic, a perfect match for its owner.

4. Abel Xavier: 'The Chameleon'
Sometimes it was blond. Sometimes it was dark. Sometimes it was two-tone.

It has specialised cells, chromatophores, which contain pigments in their cytoplasm, allowing the beard to blend in with its background.

3. George Best: 'The Totty Tickler'

If anyone else had attempted to pick up five Miss Worlds in three hours whilst driving down the M62 on the way to his boutique with The Beatles swigging Dom Pérignon in the back with a beard like that, he would have been laughed out of the wine bar. But on Gorgeous George, the ladies loved the tickle.

2. Alexei Lalas: 'The Chin Helmet'

British football fans had never seen a beard like that on anyone associated with football before the 1994 World Cup. It was a beard associated with unseemly things like American thrash metal. It had no place in 'soccer'. You might have seen one on fans of 'Hand-egg', of course. But not on an actual footballer. Lalas shoots in at number two for sheer all-American balls.

1. Jimmy Hill: 'The Reckon'

Normally with a chin like Jimmy's, a magnificent conical appendage over three feet long and with an extra pair of nostrils in the end, you can either hide it, or you can be proud of it. Jimmy went one step further, by covering it in a beard which accentuated the chininess of his chin. In so doing, he supplied a useful device for schoolchildren everywhere, who suspected their friends of making something up. 'The Reckon' is Jimmy's legacy to the world.

Best hairstyles

In the olden days, footballers were ordered to maintain a neat short back and sides at all times. Then came the mavericks with their desire to look and act like pop stars (George Best, RIP) and, before you knew it, every footballer in town was spending the afternoon at the local salon, dyeing and twisting their hair into a spectacular riot of colours and shapes. Bill Nicholson et al must be turning in their graves.

10. David Luiz

Many people have tried and failed with the mini-bouffant, but it looks brilliant on David 'Sideshow Bob' Luiz. The Chelsea and Brazil defender would now be unrecognisable without his curly locks. Top-drawer, David, truly a cut above the rest.

9. Steven Pienaar

Cornrows look great if you have the swagger to pull it off. Pienaar might be diminutive but he's certainly got the confidence to carry off the cornrows and braids look. Can't imagine Wayne Rooney would carry it off quite as well.

8. Barry Venison

Barry Venison had the courage to take on some of the best in terms of long-haired footballers. Hailing from a time when fashion was non-existent, Barry has the long hair and dirty face thing down to a tee. We think he deserves a place in here, if only because it's the best mullet we've seen from an English player. Ever.

7. Cristiano Ronaldo

Some people may call him greasy; we call him preened. To within an inch of his life. Hair-gel bosses would have died and gone to heaven if they could have signed this kid up. He uses so much, it's a wonder he scores as many headed goals as he does without the ball skimming off his head. Unless, of course, the hair-gel provides an extra bit of grip.

6. Cesc Fàbregas

A move to Spain has done wonders for the former Arsenal captain. His hair appears to be a reflection of a new-found, relaxed state of mind. The Barcelona midfielder has some cracking sideburns on him and a 'bedhead' look that every student in the UK would look at longingly.

5. Fernando Torres

Torres has always had a great head of hair. Since his arrival in England and Liverpool in the summer of 2007, he has shown off his blond locks. And when he's not showing off his blond locks, he wears a headband on the pitch. Which is nice.

4. Roberto Baggio

You have to admire his courage for appearing in public like this, let alone playing in a whole World Cup with it. Nicknamed *Il Divino Codino* ('the Divine Ponytail'), he lit up Italia '90 with his silky skills... and his hair.

3. Zinedine Zidane

Simple but effective. The French legend had a shaved head for most of his career, giving him the appearance of a footballing monk. Except it was us that worshipped the Frenchman. Especially for that goal in the Champions League Final in 2002, an astonishing goal on club football's biggest stage. Simply unbelievable.

2. David Beckham

Becks has had hundreds of different hairstyles, and while they have not always been brilliant, he nails it 90 per cent of the time, often starting new trends. His Mohican cut in particular started a mass exodus to the barbers by thousands of his adoring fans and left parents and teachers despairing at the many stripy kids in front of them.

1. David Ginola

He was the face of a well-known hair company thanks to his salon-style hair. It was long and it was blowing in the wind, and it summed up his elegance on the pitch. He's gone on to marry a model and set up his own vineyard. We reckon his hair is still as beautiful as ever.

Best moustaches

Here at **606**, we do love a 'tache, maybe because it reminds us of happier times, when the game was played in the true Corinthian spirit of great sportsmanship. Or maybe it is because it reminds us of that outright psychopath Yosser Hughes sitting next to Graeme Souness in Alan Bleasdale's brilliant TV drama *Boys from the Black Stuff*. We still haven't decided.

10. Charlie Paynter
Charlie Paynter was born in Swindon in 1879 and spent time working as an electrician before joining West Ham. Injuries meant that he never played for the first team and was later appointed as reserve-team trainer. He was eventually promoted to first-team manager and spent 18 years as manager from November 1932 to August 1950.

9. Tommy Smith
Tommy Smith was an ex-Liverpool defender who in February 2012 sold his prized collection of 75 League title, FA Cup, UEFA Cup and European Cup winners' medals. He made £137,000 from the auctions. He said the money meant more.

8. Giuseppe Bergomi
Giuseppe Bergomi spent his whole career at Internazionale and was the captain during the 1990 World Cup finals for Italy. He made the Euro '92 squad but didn't get another call-up until he was a surprise inclusion in the 1998 World Cup squad.

7. Willie Miller
Willie Miller was a Scottish international and a player described by Sir Alex Ferguson as 'the best penalty box defender in the world'. He holds the record for most appearances for Aberdeen, coming in at 556, whilst he also made 65 appearances for Scotland.

6. Billy Hughes
Billy Hughes's career took in spells at Sunderland, Derby County, Leicester City, Carlisle and, in 1980, San Jose as he joined the burgeoning NASL (North American Soccer League). Hughes has the unfortunate record of only winning one cap for Scotland, which came in 1975.

5. Ronald Spelbos

Ronald Spelbos was a former Dutch central defender. He made over 240 appearances for AZ Alkmaar in a career which also took in Club Brugge and Ajax, whilst making 21 appearances for the Netherlands.

4. Brian Kilcline

Brian Kilcline was certainly one of our favourites in this list – his moustache was described as 'a 'tache being a 'tache' by some. His career was as wayward as his facial hair – he had spells at no fewer than seven clubs.

3. René Higuita

René Higuita, otherwise known as 'El Loco', had some seriously unstylish hair – both facial and otherwise. Alongside his poor hairstyles, El Loco is also known for his scorpion-kick save for Columbia against England at Wembley in 1995.

2. Carlos Valderrama

Another Colombian known as 'El Pibe' that just had to be included. Who could forget the colourful midfielder – in fact, who could miss him, with his blond afro and distinct moustache. In a career that spanned 21 years and took in 11 clubs, Carlos played in Europe for Montpellier and Real Valladolid. He also made 111 appearances for Colombia.

1. Ruud Gullit

Ah, our very own Ruud – one of the finest defenders of his generation, with a club career spanning six clubs and two separate spells at Milan and Sampdoria. Gullit had numerous outlandish hairstyles, not to mention outlandish facial hair.

Best kits

A football kit represents a team, so it's vital they get the ingredients right. The colour combinations and the badge are vital in creating a shirt that the fans feel proud to wear, especially as the top is now worn by most fans to games.

Since football began, they have gone through many different phases from the simple to the over the top, from short shorts to loose-fitting shorts and from baggy tops to skintight tops. Kits often reflect fashion of the time – just look at some of the kits in the 1990s, bright colour combinations and some rather shocking patterns.

There have been so many iconic football shirts in history that we'd like an exhibition in the V&A, but a top ten list will have to do for now.

10. 2011/12 France home kit
If you look at many modern-day kits, there is nearly always an influence back to their kits from before the 1970s, and this France kit is no different. The simple blue kit with the old-school France logo mixed with a modern fit and a red finish on the sleeves is very easy on the eye.

9. 2011/12 Barcelona home kit
The red and blue stripes of Barcelona have been graced by some of the world's best ever players. But it wasn't until 2010 that they were paid to have a sponsor on their shirt – the Qatar Foundation. The deal was worth around £25m, and we think that this sponsorship made the kit a little classier and more modern – the 2011/12 home kit being our favourite.

8. 1999 Manchester United home kit
It's hard to question a kit that a team won the treble in. This classic, iconic Manchester United shirt was a simple design with a modern twist. A classy shirt for a classy group of players.

7. 2005/6 Arsenal away kit
The 2005/6 season for Arsenal was their last at Highbury, so they had a special set of shirts. Their home kit was more of a redcurrant colour, taking influence from the 1913 shirt. But we've gone for the blue away kit of the same season – navy blue with a subtle yellow finish.

6. 2002 Italy home kit
The Italians are always ahead in fashion, and this even includes their football

kit. Their 2002 shirt was the first skintight kit – a feature of most modern-day football attire. Italy were there first, with this cool kit in their traditional colour of blue.

5. 1979 Nottingham Forest home kit
The 1970s were just great for kits, weren't they? Nottingham Forest's 1979 home shirt, in which they won the European Cup, is a proper retro kit. Three white stripes down the sleeve of this red shirt made for a classic.

4. 1990 England home kit
Gazza crying, Lineker throwing his hands in the air and Waddle's hair – the 1990 World Cup shirt is undoubtedly one of England's most iconic. It's the shirt in which we came so close to reaching the World Cup final.

3. 1974 Holland home kit
You couldn't imagine a Holland shirt that wasn't orange, could you? Holland have a history of producing some great shirts, but the one for us is the 1974 kit, sold now mainly as a 'Cruyff Classic' with the famous number 14 on the back. Another classic design – bright orange with a black finish. We're also a big fan of the retro Holland lion on this shirt.

2. 1970 Brazil home kit
When we talk international football in the 1970s, there was only one team – Brazil. The yellow of Brazil is a tradition, and in the 1970 this simple yellow kit with a green finish represented class and skill. Players such as Pelé, Carlos Alberto and Rivelino are still considered by many as the best squad ever. So the kit had to make the list, didn't it?

1. 1966 England World Cup winning kit
Now we usually associate England shirts with the colour white, but the 1996 World Cup winning shirt is one big exception. This iconic red jersey has been an influence for more recent England kits. For us, this has to top the list of best kits – it's simple and cool, and England won the World Cup in it! Football kits have gone through many different phases, from plain designs to wacky ones (see 'Worst Kits'). But for us, simple is always best and this kit certainly ticks that box.

Footballer accessories

Players today like to stand out whenever possible, hence the current trend towards bright orange boots and gaily coloured hairstyles. Players are also aware that there is always something one can add to the traditional boots, socks, shorts and a top look that will ensure their individuality on the pitch – even if their talent won't.

10. Electronic tags
Following a drink-and-drive conviction, Jermaine Pennant had to play a match in 2005 for Birmingham with an electronic tag monitoring his every move.

9. Gloves
The influx of foreign players has played a huge part in the introduction of gloves in our game. Now a common sight, we feel it's almost a part of the kit. When Andrey Arshavin, born and raised in Russia, is unable to handle the English climate, what have things come to?

8. Bandanas
A few players have gone for the bandana look to get the attention of the fans, but Nigerian defender Efe Sodje wore his red bandana to attract the scouts – to good effect, having played for ten clubs and counting.

7. Superman pants
Celebrating his goal for Man City at Eastlands, Stephen Ireland drew down his shorts to reveal Superman undies. All to Martin Petrov's delight.

6. Alice bands
Now home to Tevez and Torres. We have David Beckham to thank for turning this accessory from girls' hairband into 'acceptable male accessory'.

5. Edgar Davids' goggles
With a rare eye condition, the great Edgar Davids was allowed to wear special sunglasses in the field of play to improve his vision. His ability on the field will never surpass this glaring feature.

4. Facemasks
We have been treated to some impressive facemasks on players with facial injuries but none better then when Fulham's Argentine striker Facundo Sava

pulled out a Zorro mask every time he scored. We witnessed it seven times.

3. Petr Cech's headguard

Following a Stephen Hunt challenge inside the first 20 seconds of a home match against Reading, the Chelsea goalkeeper underwent surgery, resulting in this new headguard. It makes him look like Batman. On a bad day.

2. Gum shields

There has been a sudden surge in this new protective item on the field of play. Tottenham's Sandro flies the flag high.

1. Snoods

Banned in 2010 by the football elite for potentially causing serious neck injury to players like Nasri and Balotelli, who needed the extra protection from the cold. Players do need the extra protection, don't they?

Poor taste in clothes

Until relatively recently, footballers dressed much the same as us mere mortals for one simple reason: they didn't earn that much more than us. Who can say that, if footballers before the 1980s had been as moneyed as today's stars, they wouldn't have dressed just as poorly? Dixie Dean in his Moghul Emperor Babur outfit, replete with diamonds? Stanley Matthews in harem pants made from virgin buffalo hide? Nat Lofthouse in a chainmail shirt fashioned entirely from shipbuilding rivets? Maybe not.

Unfortunately you can't escape the fact that someone with terrible taste who earns £3.5m per year will not instantly be transformed into a style icon. He will remain someone with terrible taste who spends an obscene fortune on terrible clothes. The only difference is that more people will laugh at him.

So here they are. The dumb dandies, the non-fashion parade, the dedicated followers of the fashion faux pas.

10. Emmanuel Eboué
Seek out, if you will, images of Mr Emmanuel Eboué, lately a cult hero at Arsenal, now plying his frantic trade at Galatasary, after the final whistle in the game between Arsenal v Manchester City in January 2011. City manager Roberto Mancini cannot quite believe the get-up of the man he's just shaken hands with. Upon his head, what looks like a chainmail baseball cap, several sizes too large. Eboué is also wearing what can only be described as a migraine of a shell-suit.

9. Andrey Voronin
Andrey looks like he buys his entire wardrobe by backing up a transit into one of those men's fashion shops that offer high-end fashion at rock-bottom prices but are always closing down. The King of 'with a twist' fashion, this stonewashed, bleach-twisted, acid-washed, multi-hued, transfer-printed shell-suited lump would look out of fashion in Ukraine. Which is unfortunate, as he's from Ukraine.

8. Carlos Tevez
If only the pint-sized striking striker was as inspired and skilful in his fashion sense as he is when bearing down on the opposition's centre-halves. Exhibit A: Carlos Tevez's own clothing range, seemingly designed by a drunken airbrush artist from 1993. To make matters even more baffling, it is said to have the word 'Manchester' on it. You know, Manchester: 'What's wrong with the city? The weather, everything. It has nothing.' (Carlos Tevez, 2011)

7. Robbie Savage

Ever wondered what an Afghan hound would look like after a trolley dash through the 'beige' section of the Armani store? When designer shops see him approach, they take the normal stuff off the racks, get the clobber marked 'early 1990s – jumble sale?' out and mark it up by 500 per cent. Good job he wears it all so well.

6. Cristiano Ronaldo

These are silk shorts that a Mayfair madam might think were too revealing as underwear. You know what? I'm wearing them as outerwear. Outside. In public. I'm going to team them with a pink T-shirt. Because I am Cristiano.

5. El Hadji Diouf

Our theory with Diouf is that he knows everyone apart from his mum hates him. He then seeks to embody that hatred in his clothing. His clothes are the metaphorical embodiment of everyone in the world's dislike for him. You hate me? Here are my awful clothes. Take that.

4. Dunga

Yes, Dunga. His dress sense is somewhat ropey. Carlos Caetano Bledorn Verri's taste in clothes is so bad he drives us to poetry. He never misses an opportunity to wear silver, or nylon suits you wouldn't buy from your local market trader, or the multicoloured 'shirts' of the American suburban middle-aged dad.

3. Djibril Cissé

We may have been swayed by the steam-punk bleached-blond mutton chops, but we contend that beards are in fact an item of clothing and should be addressed as such. He got married in a style which can only be described as fancy-dress. With a walking cane. And a hat. In red. He looked like the Argos Shaft but claimed to be a Lord.

2. Michael Ballack

Doing for Germany's fashion reputation what he did for so many opponents' shins during his time with Chelsea, this combative midfielder has found what he thinks is his fashion groove – the shirt that looks like your auntie's curtains. Any curtains will do, but ideally patterns fashionable in the early 1980s. He doesn't have the mullet, or the droopy moustache, but bad shirts he has.

1. The entire Liverpool team (1996 FA Cup final)

Here are the rules for cream-coloured suits: acceptable if you are in warmer climes and it is the 1920s, or you are author Tom Wolfe. The only men who might disagree with this choice are our very own Robbie Savage – who had an extension built onto his home in 2002 just to house his cream-coloured suit collection – and perhaps David James, for it is he who is responsible for this aberration. He was an Armani model at the time, and so his Anfield teammates assumed he knew what he was doing when he picked these out for them. He didn't.

Worst haircuts ever

Why do footballers do such strange things? Looking at our list, most of the players on here were not spectacular, but had outrageous hairstyles. A cynic might think that this is an attempt to compensate for their lack of ability, but we just think that they're an olive short of a pizza. Ruud Gullit, David Beckham and Robbie Savage can count themselves very lucky not to be included in our list.

10. Neymar
The Brazilian striker thinks he's the man when it comes to hairstyles. He's not quite as vain as Cristiano Ronaldo, but he certainly gives him a run for his money. His worst was the one when he looked like he had a tarantula on his head.

9. Chris Waddle
The former Newcastle, Sheffield Wednesday and Tottenham man had a nightmare hairstyle. You could be forgiven for thinking it was a wig.

8. David James
Let's be honest, he's had some real shockers in his career. The side parting has to be worst though.

7. Abel Xavier
Another ex-Liverpool player with an horrific hairstyle. The bleached-blond hair really brightened up Merseyside, as he also played for Everton.

6. Rigobert Song
Now there's a blast from the past. A quick Google search will show that his hairstyles have gone downhill drastically from his Liverpool days, and his hair was shocking then!

5. Jason Lee
The proud owner of the pineapple chant. 'He's got a pineapple on his head' was aimed at Jason Lee, when he was a Nottingham Forest player during the 1990s.

4. Marouane Fellaini
What is it with Merseyside and hairstyles? Him and his hair have been at Standard Liege and Everton, and his hair can only be described as a 'toned-down Valderrama'.

3. Taribo West

He had a good carer, playing for AC Milan, Inter and Auxerre, as well as stints in English football with Derby and Plymouth. He had a shaven head, with two large spikes on either side and, to be fair to him, he did keep the same style his whole career.

2. Ronaldo

Ronaldo seems to keep popping up in our lists, and not necessarily for good reasons. After making our list of largest players, his hairstyle during the 2002 World Cup gets a bashing here. He shaved his whole head, but kept a patch unshaven at the front. Did he fall asleep while shaving his head and forget to do the rest? Or are we just making excuses for him?

1. Carlos Valderrama

The hands-down winner. It's fair to say he's more known for his crazy hairstyle than for his playing ability, which wasn't great. He made 111 appearances for Colombia, sporting his look, which can only be described as a bush, which wouldn't look out of place on a circus clown. He deserves the number one spot, because it must have taken ages to materialise into this style. We are talking years of grooming and growing to get this spectacular result, and for that dedication we should applaud him. We may never see his like again.

Worst kits

Modern manufacturing technology has brought clothing industry great advantages. The first sewing machine was invented in the 19th century, streamlining garment manufacture. Global trade meant that textiles from all over the world could be used to make clothes. And then, you could not only make clothes from natural things like cotton, you could make them out of plastic. Up until the 1980s, football kits were simple items. Either one colour, striped, or in the case of the avant-garde, with sleeves and trunk *in completely different colours*. Unless you were a goalkeeper, who wore green, and *only green*. They did not 'wick away' sweat. They were 'technical' in the sense that you were 'technically' heaving a stone of your own body fluids around the pitch.

And then, in the 1980s, everything changed. What once would have – and should have – remained on a clothing designer's gargantuan steam-powered computer, could now be transferred onto an actual item of clothing. Which you would pay eight or nine times the cost of manufacture to wear. These psychedelic monstrosities, these visual aberrations which not only defied the laws of aesthetics but also the laws of nature, could be yours for only a week's wages or so.

We wracked our brains and recalled these long-suppressed horrors from the depths of our subconscious...

10. Cameroon 2002 kit

When all the kits came out for the 2002 World Cup, there was one that stood out a mile. For some reason, Cameroon went against tradition and decided that they didn't want sleeves on their shirts. Or perhaps their laundry service mixed up the football and basketball kits.

9. Everton goalkeeper 2011 shirt

The metaphorical battlefield of the combative Merseyside derby may have been the inspiration for this stealthy Everton goalkeeper shirt. We're not quite sure why they decided to make Tim Howard look like he was the latest recruit in the forces.

8. Mexico 1998 home kit

The only actual psychedelic kit on this list. The Aztecs were well-known users of psychoactive substances in a religious, shamanic, or spiritual context. And in the late 1990s, it seems, during brainstorms for the design of the national side's kit.

7. Dundee 1953

When we think football kits, we don't think tartan. When Dundee went on a tour in South Africa, they decided they would see how the brown checked pattern went down. It was reported that the South African media referred to them as 'the Tartan Troops from Tayside'. Still popular with the nation's grannies, who lined them with fur and now wear them to the Post Office to pick up their pensions.

6. Norwich 1993 home kit

A prime example of not doing something just because you can. Digital design was becoming commonplace in the early 1990s, and if you wanted to make it look like a flock of migrating birds with gastric illness had dive-bombed you at the training ground, then you could. But you shouldn't.

5. Manchester United 1996 away kit

The Fernando Torres of football kits. Huge amounts of money were spent on this design as it was thought that the grey would appeal to our jeans-wearing masses, thus providing the funds to buy another Djemba-Djemba or Veron. But the kit itself ended up being subbed at half time when United went three down at Southampton.

4. Arsenal 1991 kit

Any kit which is nicknamed the 'bruised banana' is not on to a good thing. The kit that Arsenal wore in the early 1990s was bright yellow with faded black zigzags across it. Just to finish off the brand, badge and sponsor are in a bright red. We're not fashion experts but we know red and yellow doesn't work.

3. England Euro '96 goalkeeper shirt

Look, children. That's David Seaman. Yes, what a funny-looking man! Now, who wants an England shirt? Everyone! Who wants an England Euro '96 official goalkeeper's shirt? Anyone? Anyone?

2. Mexico 1994 World Cup goalkeeper kit

They've given the world tequila and tacos, but they are also responsible for some of the most awful, eye-offending football kits the world has ever seen. With their second entry in our top ten, this migraine of a jersey didn't even fit properly – the sleeves flared *out* toward the cuffs.

1. Hull City 1992 home kit

Imagine an episode of *Dallas*, in which high-class trophy wife Sue Ellen Ewing, wife of oil magnate J.R. Ewing, is played not by Linda Gray but by burly old-fashioned target man Dean Windass. That is the only possible scenario in which this fake tiger-skin nylon monstrosity would be appropriate. Or maybe if Hull signed ex-Spice Girl and Eddie Murphy WAG Mel B. To add insult to injury, it bore the sponsor 'BONUS' on the front, perhaps the richest irony on this list. This kit ticks all the boxes on our bad kit checklist. Unflattering, inappropriate, overblown, and completely taste-free. Amidst a stinking rundown of turds, this is the one that won't flush. Hull City 1992–1993, *606* salutes you!

IN PLAY

Best ever matches

They arrive only once in a blue moon. They are as rare as metal money in a footballer's pocket. These matches rise above the everyday, possessing all the elements of great drama: a protagonist and an antagonist, motivated, convincing characters and a great prize at stake. Of all the lists in our book, this one's bound to cause the most controversy, so here's what to do. Write an email, detailing why we left the match between [INSERT YOUR TEAM HERE] and [INSERT THEIR OPPONENTS HERE]. Go into as much detail as you can, and be as outraged and indignant as possible. Print the email off, tear it into four equally sized pieces and spike them on a nail next to your lavatory, where your views will be put to good use.

10. Liverpool v AC Milan (2005 Champions League final)
The miracle of Istanbul. Milan were 3-0 up at half time but, after a stirring team talk from manager Rafael Benitez, Liverpool stormed back. Goalkeeper Jerzy Dudek was the hero, saving Andriy Shevchenko's penalty, and making a string of incredible saves during the match to deny Milan. Liverpool won the match on penalties to claim their fifth European Cup.

9. Benfica v Real Madrid (1962 European Cup final)
Real had dominated the European Cup for years prior to this game. The match was played at the Olympic Stadium in Amsterdam and Madrid soon took control, racing into a two-goal lead, courtesy of legendary striker, Ferenc Puskas. Benfica pegged them back but, just before half time, Puskas completed his hat-trick. In the second half, Benfica shackled Di Stefano, Puskas's main source of supply and then Eusebio hit his stride, winning a penalty and scoring two goals to give the Portuguese side the Cup.

8. Real Madrid v Frankfurt (1960 European Cup final)
Glasgow's Hampden Park was the venue for this incredible match, attracting 134,000 people through the turnstiles. Real Madrid won the match 7-3 in what is widely regarded as the best European Cup final ever. It was Real's fifth successive triumph in the tournament and their exhibitionist style opened up people's eyes to the wider European game.

7. Chelsea v Liverpool (2008 Champions League quarter-final second leg)
Liverpool *almost* produced a classic comeback. They were 3-1 down from the

first leg heading to Stamford Bridge and finally went down 7-5 on aggregate. The game remained in the balance until the eighth minute of extra time when Frank Lampard scored. Lampard had just lost his mother, Pat, and had only decided that day he was able to play. Drogba added the winner that sent Chelsea through to their first ever Champions League Final. On the final whistle, manager Avram Grant knelt on the touchline and said a prayer for the victims of Auschwitz. It was quite a night.

6. West Ham v Liverpool (2006 FA Cup final)

Admittedly, FA Cup finals aren't normally known for their swashbuckling, end-to-end excitement, but this game was a genuine classic – one of the best FA Cup finals of modern times. West Ham can count themselves extremely unlucky not to have won the cup. The Hammers were leading 3-2 in injury time, but then Steven Gerrard stepped forward and scored a piledriver from long range to force extra time. The final score was 3-3 (aet) and Liverpool won 3-1 on penalties.

5. Liverpool v Newcastle (1996 Premier League match)

Both clubs were still in contention to win the League, and were breathing down Manchester United's neck. The teams went toe to toe before Stan Collymore grabbed the winner in the second minute of extra time to send Liverpool fans into delirium. Afterwards, Liverpool manager Roy Evans said the 'entertainment was up there with the best', and no one disagreed. The match was crowned Match of the Decade in 2003 when the Premiership celebrated its tenth anniversary. Still regarded as one of the best Premier League Matches of all time.

4. Italy v West Germany (1970 World Cup semi-final)

Germany and Italy were two of world football's powerhouses at the time and the score was 1-1 heading into extra time, with a last-minute equaliser from Germany defender Schneillinger cancelling out Italy's 1-0 lead. There were five goals in extra time, with Italy coming out eventual winners. They went through to the final to play Brazil, losing 4-1. Franz Beckenbauer, 'Der Kaiser', played most of the game with a dislocated shoulder.

3. Manchester United v Bayern Munich (1999 Champions League final)

Mario Basler opened the scoring in the Nou Camp for Bayern who then went on to dominate for large parts of the match. Fatally, Bayern failed to kill United off and, with minutes to go, Alex Ferguson made two inspired substitutions, bringing on both Teddy Sheringham and Ole Gunnar Solskjaer. In stoppage time, United came from 1-0 down to win it 2-1 with goals from each of the substitutes.

2. England v West Germany (1966 World Cup final)

The greatest day in English football history. A match so significant, so important to the English psyche, that decades on, the English still can't stop going on about it. England won the match 4-2 after extra time, with a hat trick from Geoff Hurst. 94,000 people packed into Wembley to watch the match, although some 750,000 claimed to have been there.

1. Newcastle v Arsenal (2011 Premier League match)

Arsenal were cruising at half time, 4-0 up, with some of the Newcastle fans leaving in disgust at half time. They should have stayed seated. In a remarkable comeback, Newcastle scored four second-half goals to earn a draw, their final goal – a screamer from Tiote – sending shock waves throughout the land.

Best celebrations

They say scoring a goal in front of a packed stadium is the greatest feeling one could possibly ever experience. To that end, football fans have been blessed with some of the most iconic, dramatic and creative pieces of celebratory performances. Many live long in the minds and deserve recognition. Tardelli's screaming winner for Italy 1982, Jimmy Bullard's imitations of manager Phil Brown's half-time on-pitch rant and Robbie Fowler snorting the white lines did not make the cut but these did.

10. Eric Cantona
Scoring with a sublime chip against Sunderland in the 1996/7 season, Cantona celebrated with a blank expression as he glared at the fans around him. Not arrogance, just class.

9. Ryan Giggs
Scoring a remarkable winning goal against Arsenal in the 1999 FA Cup semi-final, Giggs sent Man Utd fans into chaos, at least until he took off his shirt in euphoria, revealing a love rug any ex-*Big Brother* contestant would be proud of.

8. Halldor Orri
When Icelandic team Stjarnan converted a penalty in extra time, the scene was set to perform the celebration they so vigorously practised. Requiring seven of his teammates, goal-scorer Orri imitated a fisherman reeling in a catch wonderfully performed by teammate Johann Laxdal, who was picked up by four other players and Orri, before being 'photographed' by another teammate. Practice time on the training pitch well spent, for sure.

7. Stuart Pearce
Having famously missed a penalty in the 1990 World Cup, the stage was set for Pearce to exorcise his demons. Exorcise he did, netting his spot kick against Spain in Euro '96, punching the air, screaming like a man possessed, and sending England to the semi-finals.

6. Bebeto
Many have attempted his rocking celebration, but they will never match Bebeto's original for Brazil in World Cup 1994 against Holland. Marking the birth of his third child, Bebeto was joined by Romário and Mazinho.

5. Roger Milla

The Cameroonian came out of retirement for the 1990 World Cup at the tender age of 38. Getting on the score sheet, Milla ran over to the corner flag, gyrating his hip for the famous wriggle.

4. Mario Ballotelli

Having performed his own firework display from his bathroom, causing local authorities and his nation's press to work overtime, there was much attention on the Italian striker on the day of the Manchester derby. Slotting in two goals, Ballotelli revealed the shirt that sums up his career to date and that will define the next decade of Premier League football: 'Why Always Me?'

3. Peter Crouch

The robotic dance will live long in English memories. Scoring in a pre-tournament friendly in 2006, he caused kids up and down the country to try it for themselves.

2. Jurgen Klinsmann

Having arrived at White Hart Lane with a reputation for diving, there was no better way to mark his mark his first goal on his debut then running to the home fans with a dive to remember.

1. Paul Gascoigne

Photographed on a dentist's chair during a drunken night out in the build-up to Euro '96 sent creative juices flowing in the England camp. Scoring a fine goal against Scotland, the dentist's chair was a moment that will long live with English fans.

Best Premier League seasons

It's brought untold riches to football. As recently as 1986, the television rights to England's top division were worth £6.3 million over two years. In June 2012, a deal was signed for £3 billion for 2013 to 2016. An eye-boggling sum of money. Money on that scale has meant that the Premier League has attracted the world's best talent, both players and managers. It's the most popular League in the world, with a much more attacking mentality than Italy or Spain. Not only does it make for great radio (we hope!), it also means that over its 20 seasons we've had some amazing journeys and some nail-biting climaxes. Here are our top ten.

10. 2010/11

Champions – Manchester United

Relegated – West Ham, Blackpool and Birmingham City

Manchester United were crowned champions of the 2010/11 season, which was their 19th English League title, breaking Liverpool's record. It was also the first season in which there was a 25-man squad cap.

Golden Boot – Dimitar Berbatov, Carlos Tevez (20 goals)

Goals – 1,063

PFA Player of the year – Gareth Bale

FWA Player of the year – Scott Parker

PFA team of the year – Edwin Van der Sar (Man Utd); Bacary Sagna (Arsenal); Nemanja Vidic (Man Utd); Vincent Kompany (Man City); Ashley Cole (Chelsea); Nani (Man Utd); Samir Nasri (Arsenal); Jack Wilshere (Arsenal); Gareth Bale (Tottenham); Carlos Tevez (Man City); Dimitar Berbatov (Man Utd)

9. 2002/3

Champions – Manchester United

Relegated – West Ham, West Brom, Sunderland

The 2002/3 season was the first in which the January transfer window came into effect, which brought moves such as Jonathan Woodgate's from Leeds to Newcastle for £9m and Robbie Fowler from Leeds to Man City.

One of the most memorable aspects of this season was Arsenal's meltdown. They began in March, moving eight points clear at the top of the table, but with United's game in hand they managed to peg back the Londoners and finish the League five points above them.

Golden Boot – Ruud Van Nistelrooy (25 goals)

Goals – 1,000
PFA Player of the year – Thierry Henry
FWA Player of the year – Thierry Henry
PFA Team of the year – Brad Friedel (Blackburn); Stephen Carr
(Tottenham); Sol Campbell (Arsenal); William Gallas (Chelsea); Ashley
Cole (Arsenal); Patrick Viera (Arsenal); Paul Scholes (Manchester United);
Kieron Dyer (Newcastle United); Robert Pires (Arsenal); Thierry Henry
(Arsenal); Alan Shearer (Newcastle)

8. 2003/4

Champions – Arsenal
Relegated – Wolves, Leeds United, Leicester City
A season that will live with Arsenal fans for ever, the season Arsenal went
unbeaten.

2003/4 was also the first season of Abramovich being the owner of Chelsea.
The Russian bought Chelsea in June 2003. He spent £100m that summer,
purchasing players such as Damien Duff, Claude Makelele, Herman Crespo
and Juan Sebastian Veron. Chelsea ended the season second, 11 points
behind Arsenal. Manchester United slipped down to third. It was their first
season without David Beckham, who moved to Real Madrid for £24.5 million,
and Rio Ferdinand received a lengthy ban for failing to attend a drugs test.

All three teams in the relegation zone ended up on 33 points, and two
of the teams who went down (Wolves and Leicester City) had been newly
promoted. They were joined by Leeds United, who just three seasons before
reached the Champions League semi-final.

Golden Boot – Thierry Henry (30 goals)
Goals – 1,012
FWA Footballer of the year – Thierry Henry
PFA Player of the year - Thierry Henry
PFA Team of the year – Tim Howard (Manchester United); Lauren
(Arsenal); Sol Campbell (Arsenal); John Terry (Chelsea); Ashley Cole
(Arsenal); Steven Gerrard (Liverpool); Frank Lampard (Chelsea); Patrick
Viera (Arsenal); Robert Pires (Arsenal); Thierry Henry (Arsenal); Ruud Van
Nistelrooy (Manchester United)

7. 2007/8

Champions – Manchester United
Relegated – Reading, Birmingham and Derby
This one went right down to the wire. United ended up victorious, winning
on the final day of the season, knowing that Chelsea would take the title if
they bettered United's result. At the bottom, Fulham survived at the expense

of Reading, who went down, along with Birmingham and Derby.

    Golden Boot – Cristiano Ronaldo

    Goals – 1,002

    FWA Footballer of the Year – Cristiano Ronaldo

    PFA Player of the Year – Cristiano Ronaldo

    PFA Team of the Year – David James (Portsmouth); Bacary Sagna (Arsenal); Rio Ferdinand (Manchester Utd); Nemanja Vidic (Manchester Utd); Gael Clichy (Arsenal); Cristiano Ronaldo (Manchester Utd); Steven Gerrard (Liverpool); Cesc Fabregas (Arsenal); Ashley Young (Aston Villa); Emmanuel Adebayor (Arsenal); Fernando Torres (Liverpool)

6. 2004/5

Champions – Chelsea

Relegated – Crystal Palace, Norwich City, Southampton

Abramovich's expensively assembled superstars set a new points record of 95 on the way to the title. At the bottom of the table, West Bromwich Albion survived, making them the first team to do so after being bottom at Christmas. Palace, Norwich and Southampton all dropped.

    Golden Boot – Thierry Henry

    Goals – 975

    FWA Footballer of the Year – Frank Lampard

    PFA Player of the Year – John Terry

    PFA Team of the Year – Petr Cech (Chelsea); Gary Neville (Manchester Utd); John Terry (Chelsea); Rio Ferdinand (Manchester Utd); Ashley Cole (Chelsea); Shaun Wright-Phillips (Manchester City); Steven Gerrard (Liverpool); Frank Lampard (Chelsea); Arjen Robben (Chelsea); Andrew Johnson (Fulham); Thierry Henry (Arsenal)

5. 1998/9

Champions – Manchester United

Relegated – Nottingham Forest, Blackburn Rovers, Charlton Athletic

Even by Manchester United's standards, this was quite a dramatic end to the season. United were behind to a poor Spurs side in their final match of the season. If United failed to win, the Gunners would take the title by beating Villa – but United hit back, rendering the Gunners' own victory meaningless. Forest, Blackburn and Charlton all went down.

    Golden Boot – Dwight Yorke, Michael Owen, Jimmy Floyd Hasselbaink (18 goals)

    Goals – 959

    FWA Footballer of the Year – David Ginola

    PFA Player of the Year – David Ginola

PFA Team of the Year – Nigel Martyn (Leeds Utd); Gary Neville (Manchester Utd); Sol Campbell (Tottenham Hotspur); Jaap Stam (Manchester Utd); Denis Irwin (Manchester Utd); David Beckham (Manchester Utd); Emmanuel Petit (Arsenal); Patrick Vieira (Arsenal); David Ginola (Newcastle); Dwight Yorke (Manchester Utd); Nicolas Anelka (Arsenal)

4. 1997/8
Champions – Arsenal
Relegated – Crystal Palace, Barnsley, Bolton
With a charge for the title that included winning 14 out of 16 matches since Christmas, Arsenal won their first Premier League, finally clinching the title with a spectacular 4-0 win over Everton at Highbury. They also won the FA Cup, giving them their second 'double'. At the other end, Everton stayed up only on goal difference from Bolton.

Golden Boot – Chris Sutton, Michael Owen, Dion Dublin (18 goals)
Goals – 1,019
FWA Footballer of the Year – Dennis Bergkamp
PFA Player of the Year – Dennis Bergkamp
PFA Team of the Year – Nigel Martyn (Leeds Utd); Gary Neville (Manchester Utd); Gary Pallister (Manchester Utd); Colin Hendry (Blackburn Rovers); Graeme Le Saux (Chelsea); David Beckham (Manchester Utd); Nicky Butt (Manchester Utd); David Batty (Newcastle Utd); Ryan Giggs (Manchester Utd); Michael Owen (Liverpool); Dennis Bergkamp (Arsenal)

3. 1995/6
Champions – Manchester United
Relegated – Bolton Wanderers, QPR, Manchester City
Famous for Kevin Keegan's on-camera meltdown, the 1995/6 season was the archetypal rollercoaster ride that is loved by football fans all over the world. A bruising battle between Keegan's Newcastle and Ferguson's United, which culminated in United clawing back a ten-point gap. Bolton, QPR and Manchester City went down.

Golden Boot – Alan Shearer (31 goals)
Goals – 988
FWA Footballer of the Year – Eric Cantona
PFA Player of the Year – Les Ferdinand
PFA Team of the Year – David James (Liverpool); Gary Neville (Manchester Utd); Tony Adams (Arsenal); Ugo Ehiogu (Aston Villa); Alan Wright (Aston Villa); Steve Stone (Nottingham Forest); Rob Lee (Newcastle); Ruud Gullit

(Newcastle); David Ginola (Newcastle); Les Ferdinand (Newcastle); Alan Shearer (Blackburn Rovers)

2. 1994/5

Champions – Blackburn Rovers

Relegated – Ipswich Town, Leicester City, Norwich City, Crystal Palace

Fuelled by Jack Walker's cash injection, Blackburn beat United to the title by a single point. Forest achieved their highest Premiership finish with third. And look away, Tractor Boys: Manchester United's 9-0 dance of death over Ipswich Town was the Prem's biggest ever win. Unsurprisingly, Ipswich made the drop, along with Leicester City, Norwich City and Crystal Palace.

Golden Boot – Alan Shearer (34 goals)

Goals – 1,195

FWA Footballer of the Year – Jurgen Klinsmann

PFA Player of the Year – Alan Shearer

PFA Team of the Year – Tim Flowers (Blackburn); Rob Jones (Liverpool); Gary Pallister (Manchester Utd); Colin Hendry (Blackburn Rovers); Graeme Le Saux (Blackburn Rovers); Tim Sherwood (Blackburn Rovers); Matt Le Tissier (Southampton); Paul Ince (Manchester Utd); Jurgen Klinsmann (Tottenham Hotspur); Chris Sutton (Blackburn Rovers); Alan Shearer (Blackburn Rovers)

1. 2011/12

Champions – Manchester City

Relegated – Wolves, Blackburn and Bolton

This was the 20th season of the Premier League and won the award for best season in the Premier League's 20 Season awards.

Title, Champions League places and one relegation place all rested on the last game of the season. The two Manchester clubs were level on points and when the final whistle went in Manchester United's game, they were champions. However, two late goals in stoppage time for Manchester City by Edin Dzeko and Sergio Aguero won City the League on goal difference. It was Manchester City's first title in 44 years.

All three promoted teams – Norwich, Swansea and QPR – stayed in the League, with QPR staying up on the final day, despite losing to Manchester City on the final game of the season. The Champions League places went right down to the last day with Newcastle, Tottenham and Arsenal all battling for the two spots. Newcastle lost at Everton, who just missed out. With both Arsenal and Spurs winning, Arsenal finished third and Spurs fourth. On the last day of the season, Spurs celebrated their fourth spot but became Bayern Munich fans as, a week later, Chelsea played Bayern Munich in the Champions

League final. If Chelsea won, they got Champions League football; if Bayern won, Spurs qualified for Europe's biggest competition. Chelsea won and broke the Cockerel's heart.

Golden Boot – Robin Van Persie (30 goals)

Goals – 1,066

Premier League player of the year – Vincent Kompany

Premier League manager of the season – Alan Pardew

PFA Player of the year – Robin Van Persie

PFA team of the year – Joe Hart (Man City); Kyle Walker (Tottenham); Vincent Kompany (Man City); Fabricio Coloccini (Newcastle); Leighton Baines (Everton); David Silva (Man City); Yaya Toure (Man City); Gareth Bale (Tottenham); Scott Parker (Tottenham); Robin van Persie (Arsenal); Wayne Rooney (Man Utd)

Best own goals

The own goal is the footballer's ultimate nightmare. You could have played like Pelé for 89 minutes, but then put one in your own net and you will be forever tarred with the brush of huge public humiliation and ridicule. Here then – we announce gleefully – are ten moments those named would really rather forget.

10. Chris Brass
Probably the unluckiest defender ever. Whilst at Bury, Brass attempted an overhead clearance. However, he smacked the ball against his face, breaking his own nose in the process, and saw the ball fly into the back of his own net.

9. Franck Queudrue
From 30 yards out, Franck Queudrue smacked a left-footed volley into the back of his own net, whilst playing for Lens.

8. Peter Enckelmen
Olaf Mellburg gave Peter Enckelmen a simple throw in to control, which he failed to do. The ball got a slight touch from Enckelmen's studs, as it went under his foot, which led to it being given as a goal.

7. Djimi Traore
A cross came in from a Burnley player and, not appearing to be under much pressure, Traore somehow swivelled with the ball, with a tremendous bit of skill, but putting it in his own net.

6. Wayne Hatswell
Whilst playing for Forest Green against Morecambe in the FA Cup, Hatswell made what seemed an easy clearance, under no pressure, look rash. With no one around him, a few yards from his own goal, he just leathered the ball into the top corner.

5. Lee Dixon
The Arsenal defender did an impressive chip over the keeper into the goal. Shame it was his own keeper, into his own goal.

4. Colin Hawkins
The calamity Brighton defender scored a very impressive diving header own

goal at his near post. The pace that the ball went in on off Hawkins' head was so impressive that even Brighton fans were laughing.

3. Brighton
Whilst playing Liverpool in the FA Cup, three – yes, three – of Brighton's goals in the 6-1 defeat were own goals. Liam Bridcott managed to put two past his own keeper before Lewis Dunk helped shoulder the shame and joined him with a big fat OG next to his name.

2. Jamie Pollock
Whilst playing for Manchester City, Pollock's own goal saw Man City relegated. Pollock guided the ball away from the QPR strikers before executing a header into the back of his own net.

1. Gary Neville
Who can forget this own goal? Whilst playing for England away at Croatia, Gary Neville attempted to pass the ball back to England keeper Paul Robinson, only for the ball to hit a bobble in the pitch and bounce over the keeper's foot to put England two down in a Euro 2008 qualifier. England failed to qualify for the European Championships.

Best saves

These are the real heart-in-mouth moments, when the ball seems destined to end up in your net and somehow your goalkeeper defies gravity and all manner of laws of physics to claw the ball away and save the day.

10. David Seaman, Arsenal v Sheffield United, FA Cup semi-final 2003

There was a goal-mouth scramble, and Paul Peschisolido looked like he'd nestled the ball in the back of the net at Wembley with a header from point-blank range. Somehow Seaman dived and scooped the ball back from the goal line and away from danger.

9. Bogdan Lobont, AC Milan v Ajax, Champions League quarter-final 2003

Milan's Christian Brocchi's shot took a huge deflection and was heading into the top corner. Lobont was wrong-footed, but managed to spring across the goal and keep the ball out spectacularly. It was debatable whether the ball crossed the line, but regardless it was an incredible save.

8. Bruce Grobbelaar, Liverpool v Everton, FA Cup final 1986

A mix-up in defence meant Graham Sharp's header was looping over Grobbelaar and into the net, but the Zimbabwean keeper leapt like a leopard to touch the ball over the bar.

7. David Seaman, Germany v England, World Cup qualifying match 2001

Seaman threw himself down to tip Jorg Bohme's shot around the post. England went on to win the match 5-1.

6. Toni Turek, Germany v Hungary, World Cup final 1954

Hungary's Hidegkuti fired a fierce volley which was rocketing towards the top corner, but Turek threw a hand out and it sailed over the bar.

5. Gregory Coupet, Barcelona v Lyon, October 2001

Coupet was lobbed by his own defender and was backtracking, but managed to tip the ball onto the bar, leaving Rivaldo with a free header at goal to score. Coupet got up and saved the header.

4. Peter Schmeichel, Manchester United v Rapid Vienna, Champions League 1999

The great Dane, Peter Schmeichel showed that he used to watch Gordon Banks as he pulled off a Banks-esque save. He got himself across the goal and pushed the ball wide. The crowd celebrated the save like it was a goal.

3. Jim Montgomery, Sunderland v Leeds United, FA Cup final 1973

An incredible double save, with Montgomery comfortably saving the first diving header. The follow-up from Lorimer he somehow pushed onto the bar and away from trouble. Sunderland went on to win the cup, 1-0.

2. Gordon Banks, England v Brazil, World Cup 1970

Pelé rose above everyone and beautifully placed a header in the corner, but Banks launched himself across the goal and pushed the ball up and over the bar.

1. Rene Higuita, England v Colombia, friendly 1995

One of the most famous goalkeeper moments, dubbed the 'Scorpion Kick'. Higuta obviously felt like he had had enough of this boring game. He let the ball pass over him and then quickly brought his feet up, over his head and volleyed the ball away. Quite a remarkable and acrobatic move.

Best comebacks

Breathless, unforgettable, unbelievable – these are the games still talked about today as fans try to work out how either their team managed to throw away a commanding position or how their team managed to stage a comeback worthy of Lazarus himself. Great games, incredible memories, here are **606**'s ten to make you celebrate – or cry.

10. Charlton v Huddersfield, 1957
Charlton went down to ten men early on after Derek Ufton dislocated his shoulder (Charlton had no subs) and Huddersfield scored two goals before half time. Charlton pulled one goal back, but Huddersfield used their man advantage and soon had a 5-1 lead. This didn't knock Charlton down – Johnny Summers then scored five goals, which included a six-minute hat-trick, putting Charlton 6-5 ahead. Stan Howard equalised for Huddersfield with just four minutes to go. But in the 89th minute, Johnny Summers assisted John Ryan to give Charlton a 7-6 victory at the Valley. Summers later said that he had to change his boots at half time because his started breaking – imagine if his boots had been fine for the whole 90 minutes!

9. Arsenal v Newcastle, 2011
Newcastle came back from 4-0 down to earn an amazing draw against Arsenal. Theo Walcott opened the scoring after just 44 seconds, before DJoirou scored in the third minute. Robin Van Persie then added another to make it 3-0 Arsenal within 10 minutes. Van Persie then made it four after 36 minutes, and many Newcastle fans contemplated going home right there and then. Luckily, many stayed to watch an amazing comeback by the Magpies. Arsenal's Diaby was sent off on 49 minutes and on 70 minutes Joey Barton scored a penalty. The fightback was on. Just five minutes later, Leon Best scored Newcastle's second. In the 82nd minute, Jonas Gutierrez was fouled by Francesc Fabregas to give Newcastle another penalty, that Joey Baron converted. Then in the 87th minute came the equaliser from Cheik Tiote, a screaming 20-yard shot that sent the Newcastle faithful into seventh heaven and Arsène and his boys into despair.

8. Everton v Southampton, 2003
Two goals from Tomasz Radzinski gave Everton a 2-1 win over Southampton. James Beattie gave Southampton the lead, his 17th of that season. But when a young Wayne Rooney came on and crossed the ball for Radzinski to score

on the 85th minute, the fightback was on. Radzinski scored the winner in the second minute of stoppage time.

7. Arsenal v Spurs, 2008

Arsenal were just minutes away from establishing major bragging rights over their North London rivals Spurs. The Gooners were 4-2 up right up until the 89th minute, when Jermaine Jenas scored. Incredibly, a minute later Aaron Lennon scored in injury time to grab a 4-4 draw. The first person to celebrate with him was an ecstatic Spurs fan who ran onto the pitch.

6. France v England, Euro 2004 (Portugal)

Zinedine Zidane scored a free-kick and a penalty in injury time to give France a win and break England fans hearts inside the Estadio Da Luz and at home. Frank Lampard gave England the lead and when Wayne Rooney won a penalty, England fans anticipated a 2-0 lead. Sadly, David Beckham saw his spot-kick saved by Fabien Barthez. Zidane's penalty came in injury time after David James took out Thierry Henry. Another reason this game is remembered is because Zidane was sick seconds before striking the winning penalty. That goal left a lot of other people sick as well.

5. Mansfield v Bristol City, 2002

Bristol were 4-2 down in the 87th minute of this game before the remarkable comeback at the Field Mill. Brian Tinnion scored from the penalty spot on 87 minutes. Five minutes into injury time, Leroy Lita put a goal in to make it level at 4-4. Then pretty much from the kick-off, Christian Roberts scored from around 20 yards to cap an amazing night.

4. Tranmere v Southampton, 2001

Tranmere set up a FA Cup quarter-final with Merseyside rivals Liverpool in 2001 with a remarkable comeback against Southampton (managed by Glenn Hoddle). Tranmere, managed by John Aldridge, were trailing 3-0 at half time to Southampton, but Paul Rideout was the hero when he scored a second-half hat-trick. The comeback started on 58 minutes when Paul Rideout scored the first of Tranmere's goals, he then scored again on 71 minutes and 80. With just seven minutes of the game remaining, Stuart Barlow scored the winner to mark an amazing comeback. A pitch invasion followed the game, although later on Tranmere might have wondered why they bothered. Liverpool pushed them aside 4-2 in the quarter-final.

3. Manchester United v Bayern Munich, 1999

Manchester United had already won the title and FA Cup, and were looking to grab the Champions League for a memorable treble. Their main concern was that they were missing their two vital centre midfield players, Roy Keane and Paul Scholes, through suspension

The game started well for Bayern Munich when Mario Basler put Munich 1-0 up after six minutes, with a free kick. United dominated the rest of the half, but failed to score the important equaliser before the break. In the second half, the German side looked more likely to score with Stefan Effenberg, Mehmet Scholl and Carsten Jancker all going close.

Ferguson knew he would have to make a change. Teddy Sheringham came on in the second half for Jesper Blomqvist and gave United a lifeline by scoring in the first minute of stoppage time. Incredibly, United attacked again, and the ball fell to Ole Gunnar Solksjaer, who had come on as a late sub for Andy Cole. Solksjaer had a reputation for being a 'super sub' and when he converted a David Beckham corner to poke the ball in the roof of the net, the United fans went wild.

2. Manchester City v QPR, 2012.

The final game of the season, and Manchester City and Manchester United were both poised at the top of the table, level on points, with City having the better goal difference. City just had to match whatever United had done.

When it got to the 90th minute, City were 2-1 down against ten men. The United game had finished, and they were at that point champions. When Edin Dzeko headed in a David Silva corner, the fightback was on as City ran back up the pitch with the ball. Then, in the 93rd minute, Sergio Augero put the ball in to Mario Balotelli, ran on, received the ball back, skipped over a Taye Taiwo tackle and then rifled the ball past Paddy Kenny in the QPR goal. The Etihad erupted and Manchester City won their first title in 44 years.

1. Liverpool v AC Milan (AET), 2005

Maldini scored in the first minute to give Milan the lead and then Herman Crespo scored two goals not long before half time to make it 3-0 Milan at half time in the Champions League final.

In the second half, a different Liverpool side came out. By the time it got to the hour mark, Liverpool were level through goals from Steven Gerrard, Vladimir Smicer and Xabi Alonso. After a goalless 30 minutes of extra time, the game went to penalties. Jerzy Dudek saved penalties from Andrea Pirlo and Andriy Shevchenko to help Liverpool to their fifth Champions League title.

Many believed the decision to bring on Dietmar Hamann at half time gave Liverpool the advantage as he was brought in to man-mark Kaka, the most influential player in the first half. Steven Gerrard also took lots of credit for his performance in the second half.

Best goals

Everyone who has played football will remember their best goal to their dying day. The difference with the players listed below is that the cameras were there to capture the moment they thrilled the world with their sublime skill. By the way, did we tell you about our best goal? We picked the ball up on the halfway line...

10. Tony Yeboah
Leeds v Wimbledon, Premier League match, 1995/6 season
An outrageous volley from just outside the box rightfully won Yeboah the goal of the season.

9. George Best
San Jose Earthquakes v Fort Lauderdale, 1981
He picked up a pass just outside the box and jinked his way past the Lauderdale defenders, almost toying with them with ease, before slotting it home

8. Papiss Cissé
Chelsea v Newcastle, May 2012
His goal at Chelsea in May 2012 was stunning. He hit from the corner of the penalty box with the outside of the right foot and it swerved over Cech and into the net.

7. Lionel Messi
Barcelona v Getafe 2007, Copa Del Rey semi-final
A copycat of the Maradona goal against England, he picked it up inside his own half and ran rings around the Getafe defence, rounded the keeper and slotted it home.

6. Zinedine Zidane
Real Madrid v Bayer Leverkusen, 2002 Champions League final
Roberto Carlos broke down the left and delivered a high ball to the edge of the box where Zidane steadied himself and smashed it on the volley with fantastic technique into the top corner.

5. Wayne Rooney
Manchester United v Manchester City, Premier League match, February 2011

Nani crossed the ball into the box and Rooney spectacularly produced an overhead kick which flew into the top corner past Joe Hart. In May 2012, it was voted Premier League Goal of the 20 Seasons.

4. Roberto Carlos
Brazil v France, the Tournoi, 1997
One of the best free kicks of all time, Carlos struck it from halfway inside the France half, with the outside of his foot, and the ball moved inside Fabian Barthez's left-hand post.

3. Ryan Giggs
Arsenal v Man United, 1999 FA Cup semi-final
In the famous treble-winning season for Manchester United, Ryan Giggs arguably scored the goal of the campaign. When you get to extra time, you expect players to get tired legs; not Ryan Giggs. He ran down the line, past player and player, and then smashed the ball into the roof of the net.

2. Dennis Bergkamp
Newcastle v Arsenal, 2002 Premier League match
One of the most memorable goals of the Premier League era saw Bergkamp receive the ball with his back to goal, he flicked it one way, turned the other around the player and then brilliantly put it in the top corner.

1. Diego Maradona
Argentina v England, World Cup semi-final, 1986
While the match was shrouded in controversy because of 'the hand of God', the match also involved one of the best goals of all time. Maradona picked the ball up inside his own half, and beat four England players, who he left trailing in his wake. He then rounded Shilton and slotted it into an empty net.

Cancelled and postponed fixtures

We've all been there. You're seated in the ground just before kick-off. The team you're about to play are, in fairness, quite a bit better than your team. Despite your professed loyalty, you know what's coming. You wish the match could be postponed for the best of reasons – my team is not good enough yet. Who amongst us hasn't wished for something bizarre to happen, for the match to be called off and the pools panel to adjudicate a win for your team? Behold, the bizarre, the unfortunate and the brazen reasons for calling off matches.

10. South Sudan v Uganda Cranes, 2012
Admittedly, South Sudan was only declared an independent state in July 2011 but that still left organising committees seven months to plan this football game. As reasons go, 'a lack of sufficient time to plan the match' is right up there with 'My dog ate my homework'.

9. Narbonne v Petit-Bard Montpellier, Narbonne, 2012
A referee refused to officiate a French women's football match, when players for one of the teams took to the pitch wearing Muslim headscarves.

8. Truro, 2012
A number of matches in Truro, Cornwall, had to be called off after a Roma family moved onto pitches.

7. Exeter v Scunthorpe, 1974
With just nine players fit, including two goalkeepers for the home side, Exeter attempted to officially postpone this fixture. When they were refused permission, they decided to unofficially postpone the match by simply refusing to travel to Scunthorpe. Whilst this ploy did work, it did cost them in fines and compensation. The points were awarded to Scunny, and this remains the only fixture in Football League history never to have been played.

6. Middlesbrough v Blackburn, 1996
In 1996, injury-struck Middlesbrough called off their Premier League fixture against Blackburn without permission from the FA. They were deducted 3 points and fined £50,000. The replay resulted in a draw, but Boro were relegated knowing that those three points that were deducted would have kept them up.

5. 1965/6 Blackburn Season

Thankfully, polio has, in this country at least, been eradicated. But Blackburn were forced to start their season later than anyone else back in 1965, postponing their opening set of fixtures due to a local outbreak. Bottom of the League before even kicking a ball, Rovers were soon relegated.

4. Moroko Swallows v Jomo Cosmos, 1998

One overused footballing cliché is 'a bolt from the blue'. Back in 1998, in South Africa even the laziest of commentators could have used this phrase safe in the knowledge that it was factually correct. Three players were knocked unconscious by lightning and two were taken to hospital. Needless to say the match was abandoned.

3. Liverpool 1987/8 season

When a Victorian sewer collapsed under Anfield's Kop End, Liverpool had to postpone their first three home Division One matches of the 1987/8 season, delaying the home debut of Liverpool legend John Barnes. We are avoiding references to Liverpool falling into the brown stuff since their 1980s heyday.

2. Sheffield Utd v Oldham, 1985

An unexploded Second World War bomb found near Bramall Lane forced the postponement of their Second Division game against Oldham in 1985. The match was played three days later.

1. Torquay v Portsmouth, 1999

The League Cup first round fixture at Plainmoor just happened to be on the same date as a total eclipse. Despite the date and time of the eclipse being known for several thousands of years, police decided at the last minute that they were not able to handle the influx of tourists as well as policing the game. Following negotiations with the representatives of the moon and the sun, plod discovered that postponing the eclipse was not an option. The game was eventually played six days later.

Most card-happy refs

The men in black probably take up more air time on **606** than any other subject matter. So when they act like pantomime characters with more moves than Marcel Marceau, we cannot help but give them our own version of critical acclaim. Their preferred prop of red and yellow cards mean they often give more interesting performances than the 22 men around them, so here's our top ten uses of the cards.

10. Ken Aston, 1970

A special mention at number ten for the ref who started the red and yellow card system we know and love today. Although a caution and send-off system was already in place, it sometimes wasn't actually clear as to who had actually been booked. So it was that ex-ref Ken Aston (he took charge of the infamous 'Battle of Santiago') was inspired by the red and amber signals whilst sat at traffic lights and decided to adapt their colour and respective meaning into our game. Clever, huh?

9. Jose Manuel Barro Escandón, Recreativo Linense v Saladillo de Algeciras, 2009

In this seemingly innocuous regional Spanish fixture, history was made when the ref dished out a record-breaking 19 red cards after a mass brawl broke out on the pitch, involving several members of the crowd. The cause of this fight? A Recreativo player getting sent off. The match was hastily abandoned and the referee marched to the dressing rooms to hand out another 18 red cards. Quite why three players escaped without punishment remains a mystery.

8. Chelsea v Sheffield United, 1992

He may now be more well known for his 'ardman image in films, but back in the day he was a bit of an 'ardman on the pitch as well. Vinnie Jones holds the record for the fastest ever yellow card while representing Chelsea against his former club. Three seconds after kick-off, a foul on Dane Whitehouse. That's some quick whistle action from the ref right there.

7. Antonio Lopez, Cameroon v Germany, 2002

This first-round World Cup game saw the most yellow cards in World Cup history (the record was equalled in 2006) dished out as discipline disappeared down the drain. The late Marc-Vivien Foé was first in the book, closely followed by German striker Jancker. The players just did not learn and, by the end of the game, the ref had brandished 16 yellow cards and two reds.

6. Valentin Ivanov, Portugal v Netherlands, 2006

A bad-tempered encounter between two of the tournament's strongest teams resulted in 16 yellow cards and broke the record for the number of send-offs, with Deco, Costinha, Van Bronckhorst and Boulahrouz all seeing red. Perhaps it was Ivanov's rather stifling refereeing tactics that prevented the game becoming a true footballing spectacle, as the encounter saw only one goal. Who knows, maybe the ref just wanted to make the most of his time in the spotlight?

5. Dougie Smith, Rangers v Hibs, 1995

It's not often that the referee finds himself on the other end of a yellow card, but that's exactly what happened to Dougie Smith during this Scottish Premier Division fixture. The ref dropped his cards which Paul Gascoigne helpfully retrieved, before cheekily waving one in the referee's direction. Without so much as a hint of a smile, Smith immediately booked Gazza for the second time that match and sent him from the field of play. Even the Hibs players protested the humourless decision.

4. Bologna v Parma, 1990

After striking an opponent in this Italian League game, Bologna's Giuseppe Lorenzo was sent off after just ten seconds. We know Italian football is all about passion, but this was maybe going one step too far.

3. Cross Farm Celtic v Taunton East Reach Wanderers, 2000

You can't help but feel sorry for the recipient of the fastest red card in history. As the whistle was blown to kick off the game, Cross Farm's Lee Todd exclaimed 'F*** me, that was loud'. Unfortunately for him, the ref was in earshot and promptly sent him off after only two seconds.

2. Gary Bailey, Hatfield v Hertford Heath, 2009

This has to take the biscuit for the most unusual red card ever issued in a game of football. Referee Gary Bailey kept hearing the sound of a whistle coming from the crowd during the local quarter-final cup tie he was officiating. After investigating, he discovered that the noise was coming from a parrot called Me-tu who, according to his owner, was 'getting some fresh air'. Unfortunately, Me-tu, like many footballers these days, just did not know when to shut his beak and started shouting at the players. This was the final straw and he was sent from the stands.

1. Graham Poll, Croatia v Australia, 2006

This ref loved cards so much, he dished out three to the same player, Croatian leftback Josip Simunic before remembering to send him off. Ironically, he now writes a newspaper column in which he often criticises current referees... Hmmm!

Funniest ball boy moments

They're often a team's youth players, given something to do to keep them out of trouble on match days – putting itching powder in the away team's socks and whoopee cushions in the dugout, that sort of thing. Their job is to retrieve stray balls and get them back into play as quickly as possible (unless you're a ball boy at Stoke, when your job is to apply a hairdryer to the ball before handing it to Rory Delap). But that gets boring. Standing around, occasionally tossing a ball back to some opposition player who you hate, doing kick-ups with your mates. So why not spice things up a bit?

10. Tottenham v Famagusta, 2007
Kostas Louboutis of Famagusta was certainly singing in a higher key following this anonymous ball boy's highly targeted ball return. The player actually considered clipping the lad around the ear before thinking better of it.

9. Santacruzense v Atletico Sorocaba, Brazil, 2006
With a minute of the game left and a free kick having gone wide, a ball boy decided to dribble the ball from behind the net slotting it home. Unsure what had happened, the referee went to the lineman, who thought the goal came from the free kick. The match ended 1-1.

8. Lierse SK v RSC Anderlecht, Belgium, 2010
Underdogs Lierse SK were hoping to preserve a home draw against the mighty Anderlecht. The ball went out of play for an Anderlecht goal kick and the ball boy behind the goal took so long to retrieve it that the keeper got the ball himself. The little lad wasn't done, though: he adopted the stance of a man spoiling for a fight outside a pub at midnight and had to be restrained by officials after the final whistle.

7. Hannover v Stuttgart, Germany, 2009
Stuttgart keeper Jens 'Mad Jens' Lehmann attempted to get the ball back from *der ball boy*, but instead the cheeky pint-sized joker chucked it back over Jen's head, incensing the easily incensed keeper, who said, 'I wonder if people want to see these scenes. By faking injuries and pulling stunts like those, Hannover wasted 10 minutes. I find it awful that ball boys are being taught to cheat.'

6. Grimsby v Spurs, 2005
In his customary position sitting on side of the pitch with his back against the

noticeboard, this ball boy needed no getting up. As an attempted cross missed the winger, our junior hero nodded it back for the throw-in.

5. Hapoel Haifa and Bnei Lod, Israel, 2009
When Bnei Lod's keeper ran out of his area to nod the ball well into touch, he hadn't bargained for the quick thinking of Israeli ball boy Ofek Mizrachi. He chucked a fresh ball to the home team, who threw it back into play immediately. With the keeper still stranded, Hapoel Haifa scored. But still lost 2-1.

4. Chievo v AC Milan, 10 April 2012
Scoring a 90th-minute belter to take AC Milan back to the top of Serie A with a 1-0 win, Sully Muntari was doubtless chuffed by his performance. The final whistle blew and Muntai peeled of his number 14 shirt offering it to a Chievo ball boy, who was so unimpressed he attempted to hand the shirt back. Arrogance is not a virtue, Sully.

3. Arsenal v Tottenham, 2012
It was cuddles all round as Theo Walcott put Arsenal's fifth past Tottenham in a 5-2 demolition. Wojciech Szczesny grabbed the nearest ball boy to hug it out.

2. Man City v Arsenal, 2007/8
'Play to the whistle' also applies to ball boys. With a poor cross coming in from Bacary Sagna looking like it was going out of play, this particular ball boy collected the ball when clearly still in play, causing all sorts of havoc for the officials.

1. Sevilla v Villarreal, 2011
In a number of La Liga matches, teams desperate to hang on to narrow leads told their ball boys to throw extra balls onto the pitch to confuse referees and use up time. Sevilla took it to a new level during a 3-2 win over Villarreal, when extra ball boys in the tunnel above Villarreal's goal threw balls onto the pitch when the away keeper was trying to take a goal kick. Best league in the world? Don't make us laugh.

Worst tackles

Occasionally, football finds it hard to live up to its billing as the most beautiful game in the world. Here are ten red-card moments to make you wince.

10. Ole Gunnar Solskjaer on Rob Lee, 1998

If there ever was a tackle that defined taking one for the team, this is it. With the score at 1-1, Rob Lee was through on goal. Solskjaer caught the Newcastle player and did everything he could in a tackle to stop him. Referee Uriah Rennie had no hesitation in sending him off. Beckham gave him a pat on the head as he walked off, and the Norwegian said, 'I had to.'

9. Paul Gascoigne on Gary Charles, 1991

In the 1991 FA Cup final, Gascoigne was so hyped up that his first tackle landed on Des Walker's chest. His second proved to be a terrible turning point in his career. Gascoigne lunged at Forest's Gary Charles. Charles somehow escaped injury, but Gascoigne badly ruptured his ligaments. The cash-strapped Spurs directors who had arranged a £10 million transfer to Lazio for Gascoigne saw nearly five million wiped off their fee straight away.

8. Commins Menapi on Riki Van Steeden, 2007

Commins Menapi is from the Soloman Islands and plays for Waitakere United. In a game against Auckland City, Menapi launched himself towards Riki Van Steeden with his studs showing. He missed the ball by a mile but viciously broke Steeden's leg. The last time these two teams played, Van Steeden was sent off so you could call this payback.

7. Graeme Souness on Gheorghe Rotariu, 1998

Making no effort whatsoever to get the ball, Souness rammed his studs straight into the unfortunate Rotariu's leg. He then had the nerve to fall and point at the back of his shin, as if to say he had been fouled.

6. Kevin Muscat on Adrian Zahra, 2011

This scything tackle from Kevin Muscat sent Adrian Zahra flying into the air and out of football for the rest of the season. An unapologetic Muscat – who had just returned from suspension – claimed he won the ball.

5. James Morrison on Cristiano Ronaldo, 2007

This tackle, which earned James Morrison a red card, came more from frustration than anything else. Incensed by what he saw as Ronaldo's time-wasting throughout the game, in the last minute of the match, Morrison piled into Ronaldo by the touchline. Wayne Rooney came over to stick up for his teammate and handbags at six yards ensued...

4. Benjamin Massing on Claudio Caniggia, 1990

In a famous World Cup game between Cameroon and Argentina, Claudio Canigga decided to take things into his own hands. One-nil down and with one minute to go, Cannigia picked up the ball in his half and headed for goal. He dodged two violent tackles but was completely upended by Massing who picked up a red card for the horror challenge. Cameroon won the game.

3. Nuno Claro on Georgian Paun, 2009

With Astra Ploiesti's Paun through on goal, CFR Cluj keeper Nuno Claro came steaming out of his goal to try and avert danger. Realising he would not reach the ball, the goalkeeper launched himself at the player, executing a brutal karate kick, which landed straight on Paun's stomach. The player fell instantly in agony and Claro tried to convince the ref that a red card was not at all merited.

2. Harald Schumacher on Patrick Battiston, 1982

German goalkeeper Schumacher's collision with the French defender Battison remains one of the most notorious fouls in World Cup history. The collision left Battison unconscious and without three teeth. Meanwhile, the ref gave Germany a goal kick. The match went to penalties and of course the Germans won, thanks to the heroics of their goalkeeper, who should have been sent off. Schumacher later topped a French poll of their least favourite German, even beating Adolf Hitler.

1. Roy Keane on Alf-Inge Haaland, 2001

One of the most infamous challenges ever made in the Premier League, especially when Roy Keane later admitted that his ferocious assault on the luckless Manchester City player was a deliberate payback for a foul by Haaland which had left Keane out for the remainder of the 1997/8 season. Keane ignored the ball and instead tackled Haaland's knee, putting him out of the game for months. Keane did not even bother to argue with the ref's red card.

Longest matches of all time

You know those games when you say to your mate at the final whistle, 'God, I wish that could have gone on for ever?' Well, here's ten that nearly did.

10. Leeds Badgers v Warwickshire Wolves – 57 hours

This 2010 charity match for the Meningitis Trust took 57 hours to complete and ended 425-354 to the Badgers. It is the longest match ever recorded and took place at Warwick University.

9. Stockport v Doncaster, Third Division North Cup match, 30 March 1946 – 3 hours 25 minutes

After extra time had not brought about a winner, the game continued for another 203 minutes. Reports later said that fans popped home for a cup of tea before returning to the match. Bad light eventually stopped play with the score at 2-2.

8. Cardiff v Bristol City, Ninian Park, 14 April 1945 – 3 hours 22 minutes

The game took place in the Football League North War Cup Second Round, and the teams played extra time until a winning goal was scored. Cardiff won 3-2 after 202 minutes had been played.

7. Santos (Brazil) v Penarol (Uruguay), Western Hemisphere Club Championship, August 1962

The game started at 9.30 p.m., and finished at 1 a.m. the following morning with the score level at 3 all.

6. Tunbridge Wells v Littlehampton Town, FA Cup Preliminary match, 2005

After extra time, both sides were locked at 2-2 so the match went to a sudden death penalty shootout. It took 40 kicks to decide a winner and finished 16-15 to Tunbridge Wells.

5. FC Civics Windhoek v KK Palace (Namibia), Namibian Cup tie, 2005

The match ended in a 2-2 draw and went to penalties. It took 48 kicks to separate the two sides. KK Palace eventually squeezed through 17-16.

4. Newell's Old Boys (Argentina) v America (Colombia), Libertadores Cup semi-final, 1992

The tournament is the most prestigious club competition in South America and Newell's Old Boys certainly got their money's worth when they eventually ran out 11-10 winners on penalties.

3. Burnley v Chelsea, FA Cup fourth round, 1956

Prior to 1991, FA rules meant that if scores were still level after extra time then the match would be replayed. Burnley and Chelsea met five times and, after three weeks and 540 minutes of football, Chelsea finally won 2-0. Around 160,000 people attended the five matches.

2. Ivory Coast v Cameroon, African Cup of Nations, quarter-final, 2006

The match ended 1-1 and the Ivory Coast eventually won 12-11 on penalties, thus recording the highest-scoring shoot-out in the Cup of Nations history.

1. Sheffield Wednesday v Arsenal, FA Cup third round, 1979

Arsenal needed four replays to get past Sheffield Wednesday but the effort was worth it as they won the cup that year, beating Man United 3-2 in the final.

Most memorable penalties

It is 21.33 yards squared. You are kicking a ball at it from a spot 12 yards away. The only thing stopping you is a man, standing on the goal line. You can kick it wherever you like. But then suddenly, the laws of physics seem to bend. The goal no longer seems 21.33 yards squared. It seems 21.33 feet squared. The goalkeeper grows a foot in height. His reach extends by a yard each side. Your legs suddenly feel drained. You are aware of the image of you standing in the penalty box is being beamed to eleventy million TV viewers all over the world. You anticipate the queue of callers to **606** later that evening, asking Alan Green what is so hard about scoring a penalty. The ref blows his whistle. Most of the time, it's a goal. Some of the time, however, it is most definitely not a goal, and your career becomes defined by your bottling. Which rings true – Chris Waddle, mercurial winger, floating past defenders, or Chris Waddle, who sent a 'pelanty' sailing over the bar at the 1990 World Cup to send the Germans through?

There have been some pivotal moments from the penalty spot over the years. From the heartbreaking to the ridiculous and the random, our list encapsulates the phenomenon of the penalty kick. Also, the list contains one of your favourite Motown singers. We did warn you it was random.

10. Gareth Southgate (Euro '96 Semi Final, England v Germany)
Just when you thought we might have a chance of actually winning a tournament, we were let down again on home soil at Wembley. Poor Gareth Southgate.

9. Antonin Panenka (Euro 1976 Final, Czechoslovakia v West Germany)
Panenka produced the most perfect of chips to win Czechoslovakia the European Championship at the expense of the Germans. That's not such a bad thing is it?

8. John Terry (Chelsea v Manchester United, 2008 Champions League final)
John Terry had a golden opportunity to win the Cup for Chelsea. In Beckham-esque style he slipped and the ball went wide of the post. As we all know, Chelsea ended up losing, football ended up winning, and the Terry slip became the image that launched a thousand amusing GIFs emailed to Chelsea fans everywhere.

7. Asamoah Gyan (Uruguay v Ghana, World Cup 2010)

Asamoah Gyan had a chance to make himself a legend, and send Ghana through to the semi-final of the World Cup, the first African side to get there. But he couldn't handle the pressure and smashed it against the crossbar.

6. David Beckham (England v Turkey, 2003 Euro qualifier)

In one of the most hostile of atmospheres, Becks stepped up and slipped on the penalty spot when striking the ball. This led to Turkish defender Alpay rubbing Beckham's nose in it. England qualified and had the last laugh, though. So there.

5 . Robert Pires/Thierry Henry (Arsenal v Manchester City, 2006)

The Arsenal duo got themselves in a right pickle. Pires ran up to take the penalty and touched the ball, for the incoming Henry to fire home. Except he wasn't incoming. He was standing by the edge of the penalty box. It left the normally placid Arsène Wenger fuming. For a change.

4. Johan Cruyff (Ajax v Helmond Sport, 1982)

Henry and Pires take note. Cruyff was taking a penalty with his side, Ajax, comfortably in the lead. From the spot, he played a one-two with Jesper Olson, and tucked it away. Easy when you know how.

3. Diana Ross (Opening Ceremony, World Cup 1994)

The Americans are always known for putting on a good show, but this was comical, to say the least. The 1994 World Cup opening ceremony involved Diana Ross dancing her way down the pitch and missing a penalty. Just to top it all off, the goal posts collapsed. It was very strange. At least the advertisers didn't get their way with the games divided into four quarters. Best stick to 'Hand-egg', eh, Americans?

2. Francesco Graziani (European Cup final 1984)

The first European Cup final to go to penalties will be remembered for Liverpool keeper Bruce Grobbelaar putting off Graziani by doing his 'spaghetti legs'.

1. Stuart Pearce (Euro '96 England v Spain)

Psycho's miss in the 1990 World Cup semi-final haunted him for six long years. The opportunity arose for him to take a spot kick in the quarter-final against Spain. Pearce buried it and celebrated like a man possessed, his expression like a Munch painting, six years of pain being exhaled like dragonfire. In that one moment, Stuart Pearce, a fiercely patriotic Englishman who flies the flag of St George at his home, embodied everything that English football represents to the world. And then we lost to Germany in the semis.

Most extreme games of football

Don't care if there is a hurricane coming, a volcano about to erupt or a snow-storm approaching, the game shall go on...

10. Juventus v Lech Poznan

Extreme weather can mean extreme results, or at least that's what Juventus were sizing up as an excuse even before their 2010/11 Champions League group match with Lech Poznan. Juventus went into the game needing a win to keep their qualification dreams alive but, after going one down early on, they were firmly out in the cold. An equalising goal from Iaquinta six minutes from time wasn't enough and Juve crashed out. The game was reportedly played in temperatures as low as -16C. Someone should have told them that once you run around a bit you don't even feel it. They don't get much colder than this, though.

9. Brighton Uni v Exeter Uni

Teams from Brighton and Exeter Universities competed in a two-legged tie on two different but extreme surfaces. Brighton, managed by Nigel Winterburn, won the first leg 5-3 on ice, with Exeter, managed by Martin Keown, winning the second leg 1-0 on a pitch dug out of a beach filled with seawater and with the goals elevated on banks of sand. All in aid of commercial endeavours, though their sponsors will not be named in this book.

8. Longest game ever?

The world's longest game of football lasted an astonishing 57 hours, with Leeds Badgers beating Warwickshire Wolves 425-354. Incredibly the two squads had 18 players each and players were only allowed a five-minute break per hour. No wonder they went through 1,000 energy drinks!

7. Bolivia v Argentina

Bolivia have turned in some extreme results over the years, none more so than when they beat Argentina 6-1 in 2009, their worst defeat in 60 years. At over 3,600 metres above sea level, La Paz is one of the highest grounds in world football. Lots of teams complained that they didn't have time to acclimatise to the altitude and became exhausted due to the decreased oxygen levels. For a short time, FIFA banned grounds being used above 2,500 metres, but later gave La Paz's Hernando Siles stadium a special exemption.

6. Leyton Orient v Droylesden

There have been some extreme comebacks in history, like the Champions League final that Liverpool won 3-2 on penalties after being 3-0 down to AC Milan in 2005. But when Leyton Orient were 2-0 down to non-League Droylesden with 13 minutes to go in an FA Cup second round replay, you couldn't have imagined that they'd go on to win the match 8-2 in extra time. There can't be many more extreme turnarounds than this one.

5. Christmas Day Truce

On Christmas Day 1914, legend has it that a remarkable game of football took place in France. During the First World War, troops from both sides of the trenches sang Christmas Carols to each other and then met up in No Man's Land for a kick-about. One of the last surviving participants Bertie Felstead, who died in 2001 aged 106 said, 'There could have been 50 on each side...'

4. Claypole v Victoriano Arenas

Crazy scenes in the fifth tier of Argentinian football when a match between local rivals Claypole and Victoriano Arenas descended into chaos. Two players had already been sent off in the first half, but in the second half, after some initial handbags at dawn, a mass brawl erupted. Referee Damian Rubino's match report recorded a total of 36 red cards being issued, all of the players were sent off and the other 14 were a combination of subs and coaching staff. Extreme card usage!

3. Bena Tshadi v Basanga

There have been several incidents of lightning striking during football matches in the past. None have been as catastrophic as a match in the Democratic Republic of Congo back in October 1998. In the eastern province of Kasai, Bena Tshadi were drawing 1-1 at home to Basanga when a lightning bolt struck. It was reported that 11 Bena Tshadi players were killed. Accounts in the local daily newspaper added that whilst 30 other people received burns, 'the athletes from Basanga curiously came out of this catastrophe unscathed.' Some even thought that witchcraft may have been at work.

2. The Shell Caribbean Cup

Extreme, mad, bizarre and not very well thought through was the Shell Caribbean Cup in 1994. Group matches weren't allowed to end in a draw, and in the last group game Barbados needed to beat Grenada by two clear goals to reach the finals. However, it was also decided group matches would go into extra time in the event of a draw. Why? Who knows but, to add another catch to proceedings, if extra time did occur then a golden goal would count as two goals. With eight minutes to go, Barbados were 2-0 up before disaster struck and Grenada pulled one back to make it 2-1. Or disaster until one of the Barbadian strikers realised that a draw would take the match into extra time and allow them a chance of a golden goal, so to the shock of his own goalkeeper he promptly fired into his own net. At this point, Grenada realised that they needed to score at either end to avoid extra time to get to the finals, leaving Barbados defending both ends until the final whistle. The cunningness of the Barbadian paid off four minutes into extra time when they scored again, this time in the right end, to win 4-2 and make the finals. Strange but true.

1. Bert Trautmann

For an outrageous and brave contribution to football, Bert Trautmann makes it onto the extreme list for his performance in the 1956 FA Cup final. With 17 minutes left, Man City led Birmingham City 3-1 when a collision with Peter Murphy knocked him out cold. No FA Cup subs were allowed until 1967, so Trautmann soldiered on and still managed to make some critical stops to maintain the lead. He was told he had a crick in his neck that would go away, but upon gaining a second opinion at Manchester Royal Infirmary an X-ray showed he had dislocated five vertebrae, one of which was cracked in two and two were jammed against each other. The fact that they were jammed together saved his life and his heroic performance helped City to an historic cup win.

Most controversial results

Fans secretly love losing controversially as it gives them the perfect excuse to ignore their team's failings and reply to the taunts of the opposition. Here are ten such moments, which took our breath away here at **606** and got the phone lines red hot.

10. Sunderland v Liverpool, 17 October 2009

This is probably the only moment in sporting history when a 'floater' has affected the outcome of a professional game of football. Luckily for Sunderland, the red beach ball won them the game 1-0 after Darren Bent's deflected shot was allowed to stand. Even more galling for the Liverpool fans, was the fact that it had been one of their own who had thrown the ball onto the pitch in the first place. You'll never walk alone, indeed.

9. Sheffield United v West Bromwich Albion, 16 March 2002

Players are an essential component to any football match. That's just a fact. However, when a fired-up Sheffield United faced WBA, this strategy of having players on the pitch went out the window. Known as 'the Battle of Bramall Lane', the match was abandoned after Sheffield United were left with only six players on the field. The game was eventually called off in the 82nd minute.

8. Manchester United v Tottenham Hotspur, 30 October 2010

When Manchester United's Nani scored a controversial second goal against Spurs, the word on most people's lips was 'weird'. No one had a clue what was going on, and it provided more talking points than a whole season can throw up. Should Mark Clattenburg have allowed the goal to be upheld? Was Gomes entitled to a free kick? Was it offside? And should toe-pegs really be allowed in top flight football?

7. Republic of Ireland v France, 18 November 2009, second leg of a FIFA 2010 World Cup qualifier

Thierry Henry is probably never allowed into Ireland ever again. The Frenchman, quite literally, single-handedly, robbed the Irish nation of a place in the 2010 World Cup final in South Africa when the ball was played into the box, which the Frenchman controlled with his arm (and then his hand) to cross the ball for Gallas to knock it in with ease. Although Henry has since apologised, the goal will still leave a bitter taste in Irish mouths.

6. England v Germany, 27 June 2010, first knock-out stage of the FIFA World Cup in South Africa, 2010

For as long as people talk about football, the subject of goal-line technology will forever be high on the agenda. Just ask Frank Lampard. With England 2-1 down to the old enemy, the Chelsea midfielder cracked a blazing shot from outside of the box, which ricocheted off the underside of the bar and clearly crossed the line. Alas, the goal wasn't given and the rest remains painful history.

5. Ghana v Uruguay, 3 July 2010

The 2010 World Cup provided another big talking point as Luis Suarez took on the role of 'rush keeper' and broke Ghanaian hearts in the last minute of the quarter-final as his clearance off the line with his hand denied the African team a place in history. Luckily, though, Luis Suarez saw the error of his ways and his subsequent season at Liverpool proved to be a low-key affair... Oh, hang on.

4. West Germany v Austria, 25 June 1982

This game was known as 'the Shame of Gijón' and included levels of embarrassment only previously seen at the Eurovision Song Contest. A win for West Germany by one or two goals would result in both sides qualifying for the next stage at the expense of Algeria. Germany scored after 11 minutes and neither team made any effort to change the score-line for the next 80 minutes, despite their fierce rivalry. As a result of this game being allowed to stand, FIFA ruled that in future tournaments, all final group matches would be played on the same day and at the same time. For shame!

3. Manchester United v Tottenham Hotspur, 4 January 2005

In games played without a referee, all kinds of arguments can blow up, especially if someone claims they scored when, in fact, they haven't. And that's fair enough; there's usually a minimal amount of people watching, no replays are available and the nearest thing to a referee is a passing old man walking a dog. However, there should be no excuse at Old Trafford when Premier League points are at stake. The game was 0-0 in the 89th minute with Spurs set to take a valuable point when Spurs midfielder Pedro Mendes spotted Roy Carroll well off his line and struck an ambitious effort from the halfway line. Carroll got back in time only to drop the ball two yards over the line, but Mark Clattenburg and the linesmen were too far away to see it. Cue screaming and endless debate.

2. Argentina v England, 22 June 1986, quarter-finals of the 1986 FIFA World Cup: 'the hand of God' by Diego Maradona

Diego Maradona was the original Mr Marmite (sorry Robbie). On one hand, watching the Argentine play football was the sporting equivalent of poetry – the way he sliced through defences and the way he controlled the ball effortlessly – and on the other hand, he was a podgy player with a penchant for a substance that wasn't Cola. 'The hand of God' is yet another episode in England's history of 'what could have been' since 1966 and will forever linger in the air around major tournaments like a fish finger sandwich in an elevator.

1. England v West Germany, 30 July 1966, final of the 1966 World Cup at Wembley Stadium

In case you didn't know, England won the World Cup in 1966 and Geoff Hurst scored one of the most controversial goals in World Cup history. The third England goal is proof that if you react really enthusiastically, and wave your hands in the air as much as possible, Russian linesmen will – more than likely – give you the benefit of the doubt. God bless you Tofik Bahramov!

Worst refereeing decisions

The referee is always the easiest person to blame on the pitch. They often feel the full force of blame from fans, players and managers. They usually get a pretty hard time from you on the phones too. We like to stick up for referees when we can, but if they knock you out of competitions or don't give a goal that should have been given, it's very hard. Especially when they never have to justify their decisions to the media afterwards.

Isn't it strange though, how the ref is always biased against *your* team?

10. Coventry v Crystal Palace, 1980
We feel a little sorry for the referee on this one. Palace striker Clive Allen struck a brilliant free kick that went in, hit the iron stanchion and came straight back out. The referee and the linesman both agreed not to give the goal, believing that it had hit the post. Looking back on replays, we can see why the referee thought this hit the post. But the linesman? Poor.

9. Tottenham v Chelsea, 2012
Chelsea were leading through Didier Drogba's spectacular strike when Juan Mata fired a shot into the box. John Terry threw himself at both Benoît Assou-Ekotto and Carlo Cudicini (and the ball) and all three lay in a crumpled heap on the goal line. The ball bounced back into play, having obviously not crossed the line. Mata wheeled away, celebrating, and referee Martin Atkinson was won over. Goal given. Spurs lost 5-1.

8. Manchester United v Spurs, 2004
In the dying moments of this match, at 0-0, Spurs had Roy Carroll racing back to his line as they brought on the attack. Pedro Mendes had an effort from 50 yards that Carroll got back for but then dropped it over the line. No goal given by referee, Mr Clattenburg of the amazing reappearing hair. We loved the way Carroll casually looked over to the linesman as he scooped it from behind the line. United were very lucky to escape with a point.

7. France v Germany, 1982
Replayed umpteen times on TV and never gets any less brutal. France's Patrick Battiston was clean through, only German goalkeeper Harald Schumacher to beat. Schumacher launched himself at Battiston, smashing his hips into his face. Battiston was stretchered off unconscious, with a broken jaw. The decision? Goal kick to Germany. Schumacher later went on to be the hero in the shoot-

out to take Germany through to the World Cup final, where they lost to Italy.

6. Croatia v Australia, 2006

Graham Poll's three-card brag comedy. We're pretty sure you don't have to be a referee to know a second yellow card means a red and a sending off. This pretty vital piece of knowledge for a referee obviously escaped Graham Poll's mind when he gave Josep Simunic of Croatia three yellow cards before sending him off.

5. Middlesbrough v Chesterfield, 1997

Chesterfield were so close to a famous victory that would have seen them go to the FA Cup final in 1997. They were leading Middlesbrough 2-1 when Jonathan Howard fired a shot that hit the underside of the bar and bounced over the line. The referee and his assistant failed to spot this and didn't give the goal. That game finished 3-3, and Middlesbrough won the replay to book a place at Wembley in the FA Cup final. Heartbreaking. Middlesbrough went on to lose the final to Chelsea.

4. England v Germany, 2010

Ouch. Through to the final 16, England met rivals Germany and found themselves 2-0 down. Matthew Upson got England back into it and then Frank Lampard's shot crossed the line. Unfortunately poor Jorge Larrionda's eyes aren't what they once were, and he waved play on. Germany went on to win 4-1 and knock England out of the World Cup.

3. Brazil v Sweden, 1978

It was the 1978 World Cup group stage. Brazil and Sweden were drawing 1-1 in stoppage time. Brazil fired in a corner and, BANG, Zico headed it home. Great stuff, a dramatic late winner. But no. The giants of international football had not reckoned for World Champion Jobsworth Mr Clive Thomas, truly the pedants' pedant, who blew the final whistle *when the ball came in from the corner*.

2. France v Ireland, 2010

In a 2010 World Cup qualifying play-off game, France were very, very lucky to go through against Ireland, and they had the referee to thank. It was 1-1, perfectly poised in extra time when Thierry Henry used his hand to keep the ball in play and put it across for William Gallas to put in the net. France went on to the World Cup and Ireland went home.

1. Argentina v England, 1986

It still hurts doesn't it? World Cup quarter-final with Argentina, Maradona jumps with Shilton to meet the ball with his hand and put it in the back of the net. Argentina went on to win the game 2-1 and then the World Cup. Maradona famously dubbed the goal 'the hand of God', when in fact it was the hand of a chunky, curly-haired rogue. That's ridiculous anyway – we all know God is an Englishman.

THE WORLD CUP

Best goals

Scoring in the most prestigious tournament in the world is an activity that few of us can tell our grandkids about. And when your goal is an absolute cracker, then you know the gods really have been smiling upon you. Here's ten to remember.

10. Saed Al-Owairan (Saudi Arabia v Belgium, 1994)
One of the greatest goals ever in a World Cup match came from Saed Al-Owairan in Saudi Arabia's first ever appearance at the World Cup finals. The 'Maradona of Arabia' got the ball inside his own half and beat four Belgium defenders before smashing it into the back of the net.

9. Archie Gemmill (Scotland v Holland, 1978)
In a match Scotland had to win by three clear goals to have any chance of progressing to the second round, Archie Gemmill produced one of the best goals in a World Cup match. He made it 3-1 to the Scots by playing a lovely one-two with Kenny Dalglish, beat the Dutch defence and produced an accomplished finish to rekindle Scottish hopes. Unfortunately it wasn't enough, and they were sent home.

8. Diego Maradona (Argentina v Greece, 1994)
Maradona makes two appearances on the list. The chubbier version could still produce the goods in 1994. He may have only played in two games during USA '94 after failing a drugs test, but the one goal he scored has stayed in our memories. He got the ball and played a lovely one-two before picking his spot perfectly in the top corner.

7. Bobby Charlton (England v Mexico, 1966)
The amount of distance Charlton travelled with the ball unchallenged was shocking from a Mexican point of view. They probably didn't expect him to produce a 30-yard cracker, which nearly broke the net. A great strike from England's all-time top goal-scorer.

6. Jairzinho (Brazil v England, 1970)
It needed something special to beat Gordon Banks that day, after making one of the best saves of all time from Pelé. Brazil tussled and won the ball off Bobby Moore, and then crossed for Pelé to take a breathtaking touch and flick to Jairzinho who lashed it home.

5. Dennis Bergkamp (Holland v Argentina, 1998)

He was known in England for doing this sort of thing every week. A superb individual goal, the fact it was against Argentina in the last minute of the World Cup quarter-final only made it slightly more special. His first touch brought the ball out of the air brilliantly before he smashed it home with the outside of his right foot.

4. Geoff Hurst (England v West Germany, 1966)

This one makes it for obvious reasons. Taking away the fact that it was the goal that sealed the World Cup for England, it was a great finish worthy of winning any match or competition.

3. Carlos Alberto (Brazil v Italy, 1970)

What a surprise, another amazing goal from Brazil. Do they do scrappy ones or tap ins? In the build-up to Carlos Alberto rifling it into the bottom corner, the ball was passed between no fewer than eight Brazil players, starting with the Brazilian full-back dummying two Italian players.

2. Michael Owen (England v Argentina, 1998)

He picked the ball up near the halfway line, and the acceleration he showed, leaving the Argentine defenders helpless, was fantastic to watch (from an England point of view). He lashed the ball into the top corner past Roa in goal.

1. Diego Maradona (Argentina v England, 1986)

While the match will be remembered for the infamous Maradona 'hand of God', we should not forget the incredible solo goal which followed from Maradona. He got the ball inside his own half and the England defenders stood off, which was just asking for trouble. Maradona duly punished them, by beating player after player and then burying it beyond Peter Shilton.

Best hosts

Some countries are perfect to hold tournaments in. They have modern stadiums, great transport facilities, and huge fan bases obsessed with football. That's enough about England. Here are nine other countries who have held World Cups that remain in the memory.

10. West Germany (1974 World Cup)

The tournament included Holland for the first time since 1938, which added great colour to the World Cup, and they also brought their blend of 'total football', with Johan Cryuff pulling the strings. The Germans won the tournament and lifted the World Cup trophy for the first time following the replacement of the Jules Rimet.

9. Germany (2006 World Cup)

Italy won the tournament, beating France in the final. Over three million fans watched the tournament in stadiums, and many fans partied on the streets and watched matches on big screens. It was a friendly tournament.

8. Spain (1982 World Cup)

It was the last World Cup to feature a fully leather ball. But it was the first to include 24 teams rather than 16. It was the 12th World Cup.

7. Mexico (1970 World Cup)

The World Cup was broadcast in colour for the first time. Brazil put on an incredible display to add to the dazzling spectacle, beating Italy 4-1 in the final, in Pelé's last appearance on the world stage. The intense heat made conditions difficult for the players, but brilliant for fans (at least if they had sunscreen!).

6. Italy (1990 World Cup)

The tournament set a record for the lowest-scoring tournament, with an average of just 2.21 goals per game. But the colour and drama made up for the lack of goals. It was the second time Italy had hosted the tournament, and they gave ten stadiums a complete transformation, as well as building two new ones for the tournament.

5. South Korea/Japan (2002 World Cup)

The first FIFA World Cup to be held in Asia was won by Brazil. South Korea were the surprise package of the tournament, getting to the semi-final before losing to Germany, and both host nations made it beyond the group stage.

4. Brazil (1950 World Cup)

Brazil so badly wanted to make it a tournament to remember, they built the world's biggest stadium, the Maracanã. However, 200,000 people were left severely disappointed inside the stadium when Brazil failed to complete the dream and win the tournament.

3. England (1966 World Cup)

The tournament contained one of the most enthralling and controversial World Cup finals of all time, although the tournament didn't get off to the greatest of starts. The Jules Rimet trophy was stolen from an exhibition, only to be found later by a dog called Pickles. The inventors of modern-day football, England, won the trophy on home soil for the only time in their history.

2. Mexico (1986 World Cup)

The tournament will be best remembered for the wizardry of Diego Maradona (and 'the hand of God'). Mexico became the first country to host the World Cup for the second time and this is widely regarded as the best ever World Cup.

1. France (1998 World Cup)

This tournament was played in the home country of Jules Rimet, the founder of the World Cup. The original trophy was named after him and so it was only fitting that France won the tournament. Moreover, this was the first time the World Cup involved 32 teams, which meant that sides such as South Africa, Japan and Jamaica added wonderfully to the whole spectacle.

Least memorable matches

The season has ended, domestic honours have been won, and all hostilities are put on hold until next season. Kind of. Now for the big one – the World Cup, the tournament where the crème de la crème of footballers gather to show off their amazing skills and treat the world to a month of the best football on the planet. That was the idea anyway.

10. 1990 Italy v England

Not so much dull as forgettable. It was England against hosts Italy in the third place play-off and did anyone really care? Both sides had come close to getting to the final, and this was hardly a consolation. It finished 2-1 to Italy, and was Peter Shilton's last game for England.

9. 1982 Poland v Soviet Union

The second stage of the 1982 World Cup involved teams being put into groups of three. This saw Poland, the Soviet Union and Belgium lumped together and, with Belgium losing out in both games, the group decider was an Eastern European clash. Poland had beaten Belgium by a wider margin than the Soviet Union and took to the field with the aim of keeping possession and going for the draw. They had the players to do it, too, and the ball spent a large amount of time by a Russian corner flag, grinding down both the Soviet Union and anyone watching.

8. 2010 France v Uruguay

It only took seven minutes for the Mexican wave to kick in as spectators showed more coordination in the stands than the players did on the pitch. There was disorder behind the French scenes, which can be summoned up with the words 'Raymond Domanech'. Players disagreed with his team selection and it showed. Meanwhile, Uruguay tried to be ambitious but generally failed. Even when Uruguay had a player sent off, chances were few and far between, and the only entertainment was watching Thierry Henry having the audacity to appeal for a dubious handball.

7. 1990 Ireland v Egypt

In a group of tedious games, this just about shades it as the dullest. Egypt were playing to avoid a defeat, and Ireland's long ball game was never going to break their defence. The Egyptians hardly bothered to go forward, and Ireland lacked any kind of creative flair. Irish fans do state that there was the odd shot on target but nobody remembers it.

6. 1966 England v Uruguay

It ended in triumph, but England's World Cup campaign started with this 0-0 bore-draw against Uruguay. Alf Ramsay's claim made before the tournament that England were going to win it looked a bit hollow after this. Adopting the 4-3-3 formation, there was a lack of penetration from midfield and Uruguay proved to be difficult to break down. A trend started whereby England's opening games in major tournaments tended to end in disappointment.

5. 1974 West Germany v Poland

Can't blame the Germans for this one. The pitch in Frankfurt was waterlogged and, despite the presence of a fire engine or two to pump the water away, the surface was unplayable. A shame as both teams could play a bit. Poland wanted the game, which was effectively a semi-final, called off. The Germans weren't having it. The ball barely travelled anywhere and it was a match of attrition rather than skill. Gerd Müller scored the only goal when West Germany were attacking the shallow end.

4. 1982 West Germany v Austria

Although events were not dull off the pitch, the 90 minutes of the game count as perhaps the most shameful in the history of the tournament. It was a final group game and Algeria were poised to be the first African country to get out of the group stage, unless West Germany recorded a one- or two-goal win. Then the Germans would qualify along with Austria. The German goal came in the tenth minute and then both teams stopped playing, having realised that they were both through. No shots, no tackles of note or energy expended. White hankies were waved in protest by the crowd and the match was universally condemned by the media in Austria and West Germany. Rules were changed as a result, with final group games now kicking off simultaneously.

3. 1990 West Germany v Argentina

The dullest World Cup final ever. The two teams had met in the 1986 final and that produced five goals. This match produced one, and we had to wait a long time for it. Even then it was a penalty. Argentina had played defensively throughout the tournament and got to the final via two penalty shoot-outs and after scoring only five goals. They were deprived of Claudio Canigga, who was suspended for the final, and an hour in they were deprived of defender Pedro Monzon, who was sent off for fouling Jürgen Klinsmann. The goal came in the 85th minute as Andreas Brehme converted a penalty after a very soft foul on Rudi Völler. The world cheered because they wouldn't have to sit through another half-hour of this.

2. 2006 Switzerland v Ukraine

This was always going to be a tricky one to sell: when was the last time somebody rushed home early because the Swiss were playing? Ukraine boasted the likes of Andriy Shevchenko, Andriy Voronin and Serhiy Rebrov, yet still totally failed to find the net – or maybe that's why they totally failed to find the net. There was also the novelty of there being only one booking in the game, which gives you an idea of what it was like. Sadly, this was a second-round match, so there was an extra 30 minutes of tedium before the penalties. Even then, the Swiss failed to score, but they left the tournament without conceding a goal.

1. 2010 England v Algeria

An incredibly dull 0-0 and one of the most inept England displays ever: inaccurate passing, no clear ideas and tactics deployed with all the fluency of Fabio Capello's English. It was so soul-destroying that the final whistle boos managed to drown out the vuvuzelas. Wayne Rooney questioned the loyalty of the fans, but he was lucky – he only had to play in the match and not watch it.

Most memorable matches

There is nothing like a classic international game to liven up your summer and whet the appetite for the coming season. Here are ten of our favourite matches that took place in the most prestigious football tournament of all.

10. 2010 quarter-final: Uruguay 1-1 Ghana
Uruguay prevented Ghana from becoming the first African nation to reach the semi-finals after winning an extraordinary match which ended with a penalty shoot-out. Luis Suarez saw red after handling on the line in the dying seconds of extra time. All Ghana talisman Asamoah Gyan had to do was convert his penalty to send the Black Stars through, but he agonisingly skimmed the crossbar with the last kick of the game.

9. 1998 final: France 3-0 Brazil
In a one-sided match that saw hosts France crowned World Champions for the first time, the conspiracy theories surrounding a subdued display from Brazilian star Ronaldo overshadowed the night. When the team sheets were handed out, Ronaldo's name was missing. Cue mad panic in the stands and press box alike... until the superstar appeared in the team line-up for the anthems. He had a disappointing game, and mystery still surrounds his initial omission.

8. 1990 group stage: Cameroon 1-0 Argentina
Cameroon caused a big upset defeating World Cup holders Argentina in the opening game of the 1990 finals in Italy. Making only their second appearance in the World Cup, hardly any thought was given to the Africans' chances of getting a result against an Argentine side with Maradona in his prime.

7. 1998 second round: Argentina 2-2 England
Twelve years after 'the hand of God', Argentina and England renewed their rivalry in France. This game welcomed Michael Owen to the world stage with his super solo goal. But let us not forget either Javier Zanetti's superbly worked goal from a set piece, nor David Beckham's contentious red card. Sol Campbell harshly had a goal ruled out in extra time and the 10 men of England eventually lost on penalties.

6. 2006 final: Italy 1-1 France
This match will always be remembered for Zinedine Zidane's infamous head butt on Marco Materazzi. Playing his last game before retiring, Zidane, one of

the greatest players of his generation, ended his career in disgrace by receiving a straight red card. The French magician had put his side ahead early on with a coolly taken chipped penalty, before Materazzi levelled. The Italians went on to win 5-3 on penalties.

5. 1990 semi-finals: West Germany 1-1 England

England's heroic defeat to Germany will forever be remembered for its dramatic penalty shoot-out and, most of all, Gazza's tears. Paul Gascoigne broke down after receiving a booking which would have kept him out of the World Cup final if England had got past their rivals.

4. 1982 quarter-finals: Italy 3-2 Brazil

This match had drama, fantastic goals, great saves and one hero: the spirited Paolo Rossi, who scored a hat-trick that led his Italian side to victory over a Brazil team which was debatably better than the 1970 World Cup winning side. Legendary BBC commentator John Motson said this was the greatest match he'd ever commented on.

3. 1986 quarter-finals: Argentina 2-1 England

The game was held four years after the Falklands War. Diego Maradona scored two of the most famous goals in football history. His first was the ill-famed 'hand of God', handing the ball into the net past keeper Peter Shilton. The second will forever be applauded by the football community, as 'El Diego' bobbed and weaved past six players.

2. 1970 final: Brazil v Italy

Arguably the best team to ever play the game, Brazil produced a spectacular football master class to beat Italy in the final. While Pelé and Jairzinho lit up the tournament, the winning goal scored by Carlos Alberto went down in World Cup history. As it was their third victory, the Samba boys earned the right to retain the Jules Rimet trophy permanently.

1. 1966 final: England 4-2 West Germany

Without question England's greatest moment in football history. The host conquered the West Germans in extra time. Striker Sir Geoff Hurst enjoyed his finest hour in a three lions shirt, scoring a hat-trick that has been relived for 46 years. Did the ball cross the line? The controversy continues to this day.

Most shocking results

At this level of football, any upset is bound to carry much more meaning as it results in an entire country being shamed. Here are ten terrible slip-ups that were committed in front of the whole wide world.

10. Spain 0-1 Switzerland (2010)

Spain went into the 2010 World Cup in South Africa as European Champions and favourites for the tournament. Switzerland were the first challengers awaiting them in their first game of Group H. A routine win was expected. But Switzerland weren't just going to roll over for the champions of Europe and on 52 minutes they scored through Gelson Fernandes. Nobody saw this coming; it was only Spain's second defeat in three years, a run that spanned over 49 matches. This was the first time Switzerland had beaten the Spanish and made the favourites' chances of getting out of their group pretty bleak. Spain did, however, go on to become World champions.

9. Germany 8-0 Saudi Arabia (2002)

Heavy defeats in World Cup matches have become something of a rarity. However, Saudi Arabia well and truly bucked that trend in the 2002 World Cup in South Korea and Japan, when they allowed the Germans to run riot all over their defence. This was the first time since 1982 that a side had conceded more than six goals in a World Cup match.

8. Hungary 10-1 El Salvador (1982)

Hungary inflicted the biggest ever World Cup defeat on poor old El Salvador. Yet Hungary were not even that special, failing to qualify for the second round even after this 10-1 win. The 1982 World Cup was held in Spain and won by Italy.

7. Yugoslavia 9-0 Zaire (1974)

Zaire were only the third African nation ever to qualify for a World Cup. The Zaire players were expecting to be well rewarded for their participation in the tournament but, before their game with Yugoslavia, they found out that they wouldn't be paid. The team protested by saying they wouldn't play against Yugoslavia, until their country's ruler, Mubuto Sese Seko, intervened with a series of dire threats that the players took very seriously. A highly demoralised Zaire team took to the pitch and then endured one of the most humiliating score lines ever in a World Cup.

6. Hungary 9-0 South Korea (1954)

Hungary again! It was a tournament to forget for the South Koreans. Not only did they get tonked 9-0 by Hungary, but they also lost 7-0 to Turkey. Hungary eventually lost to Germany in the final of the tournament, which was held in Switzerland.

5. France 0-1 Senegal (2002)

The opening game of the tournament provided the first of many shocks to materialise throughout this World Cup. France were World Champions at the time, but produced a lacklustre display, and didn't even make it through the group stages. Although they lost star player Zinedine Zidane to an injury, that was no excuse for this upset.

5. North Korea 1-0 Italy (1966)

The Italians were upset on English soil by the North Koreans in 1966 at Middlesbrough's Ayresome Park. No one believed the Koreans could score a goal, let alone win a game against a superpower like Italia, but Pak Doo Ik's goal shocked the world. On their arrival back in Italy, the players were greeted by fans throwing tomatoes at them. You could say the Italian players were a little red in the face. And this wasn't the only time Italy lost to one of the Korean sides in a World Cup...

4. South Korea 2-1 Italy (2002)

No one gave South Korea, the host nation, a chance against world football giants Italy, and when the Azzurri went one up everyone assumed the obvious. That was until South Korea equalized in the 89th minute to force extra time. Minutes later, Ahn Jung-Hwan headed the golden goal to send the Italians packing, and South Korea through to the quarter-final.

3. USA 1-0 England (1950)

Prior to the game, the USA team had chalked up seven straight defeats, coming in with a combined score of 45-2. The American team even had a schoolteacher and postman in their ranks but that did not stop them humiliating England, one of the world powers in football. The game is known as 'the Miracle on Grass'.

2. East Germany 1-0 West Germany (1974)

A game which, obviously, had deeper issues than it merely being a football match, given the political tension between these two countries. While East Germany won the battle, West Germany won the war, as they went on to win the tournament. The tournament was held in West Germany.

1. Northern Ireland 1-0 Spain (1982)

Spain were embarrassed on their own soil by lowly Northern Ireland during the 1982 World Cup when Gerry Armstrong scored the game's only goal. The fact that Northern Ireland had to play the majority of the second half with ten men, thanks to Mal Donaghy's sending off, made it doubly humiliating. Northern Ireland went on to win the group. Spain scraped through.

Worst goals

The World Cup is meant to bring together the best of the best of the footballing world. But sometimes, for whatever reason, things don't quite go to plan, and the resulting goals can look more like something from you'd see from the local pub team on a Sunday morning.

Goalkeepers: take note.

10. Lawal, Spain v Nigeria, 1998

Spain were leading as expected, 2-1. But, as so often happens in these tournaments, there was a twist in the third act as Lawal's half-hearted effort across the goalmouth was given a helping hand by the Spanish keeper. Cue Nigerian celebrations and, just five minutes later, another goal for the underdogs, who emerged the eventual victors. It just goes to show, the goals may not be pretty but if they find the back of the net – somehow, anyhow – then that's all that matters.

9. Robert Green's bundling blunder, England v USA, 2010

England were 1-0 up against the USA in their opening game of the 2010 World Cup but an amazing, er, balls-up, by the England keeper soon put paid to that. A chance shot on goal by Clint Dempsey should have been an easy save but instead, somehow, the ball was bundled into the net as Green flailed hopelessly. This lacklustre start to the tournament set the precedent for England's remaining fixtures, although who knows what would've happened had that infamous Lampard goal been allowed to stand.

8. Gary Neville's own goal, England v Croatia, 2006

A routine defensive move went horribly wrong when the England right-back passed the ball to his keeper... who went to clear it, missed and could only watch as the ball trickled slowly and excruciatingly into the back of the net. It was the second time Neville had got his name on the team sheet during an international. It's just a pity that neither of them were goals for his own side!

7. Francois Omam-Biyik, Argentina v Cameroon, 1990

The Nigerian striker aimed a downward header at Argentine goalie Nery Pumpido, from whom the ball ricocheted off, ground almost to a halt and rolled into the net. Oman-Biyik spun away like a Catherine Wheel and the score line remained unchanged for one of the shock results of the tournament.

6. Felix, Brazil v Italy, 1970

Who knows what was going through the Brazilian keeper's head when he gifted Boninsegna an open goal at the ninth World Cup final. Dashing out from his line, he tried to tackle the Italian striker but was outfoxed as Boninsegna tapped the ball to his left and then into the back of the net. Felix could only run around like the proverbial headless chicken.

5. Claudio Bravo leaves an open goal, Chile v Spain, 2010

Another goalkeeping blunder, this time courtesy of Chilean Bravo in his country's 2010 World Cup game against Spain. Spain were on the attack and, instead of standing his ground, Bravo made a run 20-odd yards outside his box and successfully tackled Ramos. However in doing so he lost the ball to David Villa who promptly had a shot and scored from 50 yards out as Bravo looked less Bravo than we've ever seen him.

4. Higuita thinks he's a striker, Colombia v Cameroon, 1990

Colombian keeper Rene Higuita obviously thought he was a jack-of-all-trades, as he would regularly stray outside his box to commit risky tackles or even dribble past the opposition's attackers. However he paid a strong price during this second-round game as his journey up-field was brought to an abrupt halt by Cameroonian Roger Milla, who tackled him and fired the ball into the open net.

3. Kahn... can't, Germany v Brazil, 2002

It was the World Cup final and he of that bouffant had led his side through a turbulent campaign. However, in the 67th minute it all went horribly wrong as Rivaldo fired a shot directly at Kahn, who blocked it... then somehow dropped the ball into the path of Ronaldo, who dutifully fired home.

2. England v West Germany, 1966

England has won the World Cup once and 46 years later are still plagued by the question 'but should we have won it?' Scientific evaluation has now concluded that the ball was 6cm from being a goal as it had not fully crossed the line.

1. Maradona's 'hand of God', England v Argentina, 1986

We all know the story. A defiant punch by the Argentine talisman put paid to England's hopes of progressing to the semis. It also ensured that goal was the talking point of the match rather than the beautiful solo effort by the same player a few minutes later. We'll hang on to that thought as meagre consolation.

Worst hosts

It is only right that every country should get a chance to stage the greatest football tournament in the world. But some countries just do it much better than others. Here are 606's yellow cards for those who should have known better.

10. South Africa 2010
It introduced the world to the very annoying instrument known as the vuvuzela. It also produced a brutal final with 14 yellow cards in it, which we all wished didn't have to go into extra time.

9. Colombia 1986
Colombia bid to stage the 1986 World Cup back in 1974 and won unopposed. Misael Pastrana Borrero, who had come to power as the result of a later discredited election during the summer of 1970, saw the idea of big building projects as the key to a new prosperity for the country. He was wrong. In 1982, Colombia withdrew their bid because of financial issues and because the country suffered an earthquake. Mexico got to stage the World Cup for a second time.

8. Argentina 1978
Massive security surrounded this tournament as anti-government guerrillas threatened to take disruptive action. Many people, including Holland's Johan Cruyff, were put off Argentina hosting, because of their military dictatorship.

7. Switzerland 1954
The police were deemed over the top on occasions and the organisation was a mess. FIFA seeded two teams in each group, with the strong sides facing the weak teams, and thus avoiding each other until the latter stages

6. France 1938
Because of the threat of war that hung heavy over Europe, teams had to travel by sea to France. The straight knockout meant that teams could travel thousands of miles and only play one match if they were beaten.

5. Italy 1934
Italian dictator Benito Mussolini saw the 1934 World Cup as a chance to spread fascist propaganda, and this cast a shadow over the second tournament. The

Italian team were ordered to give Nazi salutes before every game they played. All eight quarter-finalists were European, meaning that Brazil and Argentina travelled 8,000 miles for the dubious pleasure of playing and losing one game. The USA travelled over for one game too and got thumped 7-1 by the hosts. Defending champions Uruguay didn't bother to attend and certain refereeing decisions, particularly in the final, were aimed to help Italy, who won the tournament.

4. Brazil 1950

Several teams pulled out prior to the tournament, giving the groups an uneven look with two groups of four matched against one with three. India pulled out for financial reasons (though the story circulated that they were not allowed to play barefoot). Turkey also had financial reasons, while France pulled out because of the travelling involved in their group. Scotland didn't go due to bloody-mindedness: they finished second in the home internationals, having declared they would only go only if they won. There wasn't a final as such. It was a final group game and by luck it happened to be a decider between Brazil and Uruguay.

3. Italy 1990

A tedious competition of defensiveness, this was the World Cup with the lowest goals-to-games ratio. The games were so tedious that the back pass rule and '3 points for a win' were instigated afterwards. The only thing they got right, to alleviate the dullness, was at the official opening of the tournament and concerned the order of speeches. FIFA President Joao Havelange waited for the President of the Organizing Committee to hold his speech and vice versa. So no speeches were held. Italia '90 introduced England fans to the misery of the penalty shoot-out. It introduced to Scotland fans the joys of the penalty shoot-out.

2. West Germany 1974

Fear stalked this tournament because of the events at the Olympics in Munich two years before when 11 Israeli athletes were murdered by a Palestinian terrorist group. Certain teams (including West Germany and Holland) were looking for more money to play. The hosts came close to choosing a different squad if their players didn't agree to the terms offered. The Dutch held out for an incentive scheme, and Johan Cruyff refused to wear the team's new Adidas strip as it clashed with his Puma endorsement (his shirt only had two stripes rather than three). West Germany got to the final and somehow beat everyone's favourite team, Holland.

1. Qatar 2022

Temperatures reaching 50 degrees. Homosexuality illegal. Alcohol restrictions. Not looking good is it?

MANAGERS

Best managers

A glance back will show that the history many clubs boast about comes from managers who are sadly no longer with us. There are many successful managers and, in some cases, managers who have proved themselves to be the best of all time, especially at club level. There have certainly been some gems, and our game has been honoured to have them lead our teams.

10. José Mourinho (Porto/Chelsea/Inter Milan/Real Madrid)

What has the self-proclaimed 'Special One' brought to all the above clubs? A League title ? Yep, that's right, the man from Portugal is the only manager to achieve title success with four different clubs in different Leagues and four different countries.

9. Arsène Wenger (Arsenal)

You can say what you like about Arsène Wenger, but the Frenchman still has to be up there with some of the best managers ever to have taken control of a Premier League club. Despite the lack of trophies in the past **ahem** seasons, Arsène has achieved the domestic double twice, and went unbeaten during the 2003/4 season with his team of – wait for it – 'New Invincibles'.

8. Don Revie (Leeds/England)

Like his Leeds team between 1961 and 1974, Don Revie was a hard, no-nonsense leader, much to Brian Clough's annoyance. He won the English Manager of the Year award three times, winning the League twice with Leeds and narrowly missing out on the European Cup Winners' Cup in 1973.

7. Jock Stein (Dunfermline/Hibernian/Celtic/Leeds/ Scotland)

Not only has this man got one of the most Scottish names in the history of football (see 'Most Scottish manager'). Not only was he the first ever British manager to win the European Cup, but he also won nine League titles in a row with Celtic, sending him into 'superstar' managerial status.

6. Sir Matt Busby (Manchester United)

A great Manchester United manager – Sir Matt Busby's managerial record and longevity at Old Trafford can only be surpassed by the man at number one on our list. Five League Titles, two FA Cups and a European Cup speak for themselves, and the fact that this was all achieved despite one of the biggest tragedies in football – the Munich air disaster – the more credit to his character.

5. Sir Alf Ramsey (England)

On our list, only one man can claim that he's led England to World Cup glory, at Wembley... with a little help from a Russian linesman. That man is Sir Alf Ramsey. He was also considered, at the time, to be a bit of a renegade. When he took over the job, he demanded that he had complete control over the squad selection. Before that, a board of committees picked the team – can you imagine that these days? Actually...

4. Bob Paisley (Liverpool)

To say that Bob Paisley carried on Bill Shankly's legacy at Liverpool would be a factually correct statement. Fair enough, if you said that particular sentence in the pub, most of your mates probably wouldn't stick around for that long, but at least you would be safe in the knowledge that it was true. If they did stick around, however, you could continue and reel off his success at Liverpool: three European Cups, six top-division League titles and three League Cups.

3. Bill Shankly (Liverpool)

When Bill Shankly arrived at Anfield in 1959 he took a long, deep breath, rolled his sleeves up and got to work on one of the greatest transformations of a club in the history of British football. He took the Reds from the Second Division, where they had been languishing for five years, into the First Division and on to Europe, where they reigned supreme for the latter half of the 20th century.

2. Brian Clough (Derby/Nottingham Forest)

To give him his proper name, Mr Clough did not tolerate insubordination. So much as look at him with an air of arrogance and this daisy cutter would bring you down to earth faster than a pigeon carrying a vacuum cleaner. Although it didn't happen for him at Leeds, his success at domestic level was astounding: leading Derby to First Division success and dragging Nottingham Forest into Europe, and coming home with silverware, cannot be overestimated, and the fact the great man never led England out is a football tragedy.

1. Sir Alex Ferguson (Manchester)

This man oozes confidence. There's a swagger in the way he chews his chewing gum, the way he claps his hands like a primary school teacher and the way he kicks a boot that tells us that this is a man on top of his game. Hailing from Aberdeen in Scotland, this is a Sir who has single-handedly (along with some world-class players and millions to spend in the transfer market) made Manchester United the most successful team in Premier League history. When you talk about the best, Sir Alex's name is usually number one on most people's lists.

Best-dressed managers

Football managers often face tough decisions. What shall I wear today? Suit and tie to emphasise my authority? Or a casual look to suggest my likeability and warmth to the fans? It is a mind-boggling decision on the level of whether to go 3-3-4 or 4-4-2. Sartorially, the stakes have been raised in recent years, as we've seen managers from overseas come to England and different nationalities mix together.

So who tops the trend table?

10. Paul Tisdale

The Exeter manager can certainly mix it with the big boys when it comes to clothes. Not only has he taken Exeter from the Conference to the League but his love of cravats and 'Del Boy-esque' hats means he is more than worthy of his place on our list.

9. Paulo Sousa

Hailing from a Mediterranean culture that insists on smart appearances, the ex-QPR, Leicester and Swansea boss always looked effortlessly suave. Here at 606 we are scratching our heads wondering if a Welsh club has ever seen a better-dressed manager.

8. Paolo Di Canio

Di Canio is new to management. He's hit the ground running, though: appointed Swindon boss in May 2011, he has brought them promotion in his first season. He has done so with a tremendous pair of sideburns and a crazy desire to wear his Swindon scarf wrapped tightly around in his neck in blistering hot conditions.

7. Joachim Löw

Possessor of the best Beatle haircut in International Football, Joachim's modish ways have seen him successfully experiment with scarves and suits on a very impressive level. He has been snapped looking dandy in tracksuits, suggesting a highly impressive versatility, one that has seen his contract with Germany extended until 2014.

6. Andre Villas-Boas

AVB – as he came to be known – went to Chelsea off the back of winning the double with Porto in Portugal. He then made a series of baffling decisions and alienated about three-quarters of his team, and subsequently got the sack in March 2012. Now across London town at Spurs, we fear he might start missing his Kings Road shopping fix. Seven Sisters Road doesn't offer quite the same boutique variety.

5. Leonardo
If he wasn't a footballer and manager, he could have easily been a model for men's suits. We aren't jealous at all! The former Inter and AC Milan boss graced both San Siro sides with his trim, expensive-looking suits. He's the current Director of Football at Paris St Germain, and was influential in the appointment of another well-dressed manager, Carlo Ancellotti. What are the odds on them having evenings together flicking through catalogues?

4. Pep Guardiola
Now that he is taking a year off to go backpacking, it would be easy for Pep Guardiola to get complacent. After all, he had the best job in football, working with the best players in the world and winning games left, right and centre. Question is, will he leave his suit at home or will he be sporting it on mountain tops and jungles all over the world, accompanied by a white shirt and skinny tie?

3. Roberto Di Matteo
The former Chelsea midfielder led Chelsea to an astounding Champions League victory and he did so dressing like a character in the film *Reservoir Dogs*. His black suit, white shirt and black tie were hewn from classic Italian stock of the 1950s. He also wears knitted tops very nicely.

2. Roberto Mancini
Not for nothing did Mancini start his tenure wearing a Man City scarf wrapped around his neck. Not only did it instantly bond him with the suspicious Mancunians, but fans then flocked to the club shop to buy the Blue and White scarf and emulate him, thus swelling the club's overflowing coffers.

1. José Mourinho
Roberto Di Matteo is under huge pressure. Not only does he have to appease the Chelsea faithful and demanding owner Roman Abramovich, but he also has to follow in the footsteps of some of the best-dressed managers the Premier League has ever seen. Andre Villas-Boas, Carlo Ancelotti, Claudio Ranieri, Roberto Di Matteo and José Mourinho have all ruled at Stamford Bridge, and all have looked the part. We think Mourinho deserves the number one spot though. Not only has the ex-Chelsea, Porto and Inter Milan boss won pretty

much every major club honour, his ability to own the grey overcoat look and a two-piece suit is second to none. If it was a fashion league, Abramovich would be a happy man, as Chelsea would be constantly topping it.

Best international managers

To manage your country is one of the greatest honours, the pinnacle of your footballing career. After years of a gruelling workload as a club manager your reward is the crème de la crème of your country's footballing talent to work with, one game every three months to prep for and all the foreign scouting trips you could wish for. What's not to like? Here's our top ten of those who not only liked it but succeeded.

10. Aimé Jacquet (France)
Led France to World Cup victory in 1998 in their home country, trouncing Brazil 3-0 in the final, thanks to an inspired display from Zinedine Zidane. His multi-racial team did much to help French society at large.

9. Mario Zagallo (Brazil)
Along with Beckenbauer, Zagallo also won the World Cup as a player and a manager, although Zaghallo went one better by winning the ultimate trophy in football twice as a player, in 1958 and 1962 . He also managed perhaps the greatest team ever to take the field of play, and guided them to World Cup glory in 1970. He was known as 'the Professor' by players.

8. Vicente del Bosque (Spain)
He won the World Cup with Spain for the very first time in their history in 2010, which is staggering considering Spain is one of the world's footballing powerhouses. He also won Euro 2008, which meant they won their first major title since the 1964 European Championship. Del Bosque led Spain to their third major back-to-back tournament victory, in Euro 2012.

7. Vittorio Pozzo (Italy)
Prior to the 1938 World Cup, Pozzo received a very warm message from Italy's dictator Benito Mussolini, which stated, 'Win the tournament, or die.' Luckily for Pozzo, his side beat Hungary in the final to win their second consecutive World Cup. They had also won it in 1934.

6. Sir Alf Ramsay (England)
Sir Alf guided England to World Cup victory in 1966, an achievement which hasn't been matched since. He was knighted in 1967 and came very close to a repeat success in the 1970 World Cup. Sir Alf must be the only England manager to voluntarily take elocution lessons.

5. Luiz Felipe Scolari (Brazil and Portugal)

Scolari won the World Cup with Brazil in 2002 by winning all their matches in the tournament. Not content with that achievement, he then became the manager of the Portuguese national side, who lost to Greece in the Euro 2004 final.

4. Otto Rehhagel (Greece)

He was not a man known for his management of top European clubs nor had he been victorious in any major competitions, yet still Otto Rehhagel was able to guide Greece to an amazing victory in Euro 2004, beating Portugal and France on their way to success. What he did there was nothing short of magnificent.

3. Rinus Michels (Holland)

He may not have some of the silverware that other managers have won, but he sure left his mark on the game. Michels was the inventor of 'total football', which meant the full back was as skilful as the midfielder. Under the brand of 'total football', Holland finished runners-up in the 1974 World Cup. Rinus also won the European Championships in 1988, in his second stint as national team manager.

2. Franz Beckenbauer (Germany)

He is one of only two men to win the World Cup both as player and a manager. He captained his side to victory in 1974 and then coached the national side to victory in the 1990 World Cup. No wonder his nickname is 'Der Kaiser' (the Emperor).

1. Marcelo Lippi (Italy)

Led Italy to their first World Cup triumph in 24 years, winning the tournament in Germany in 2006 when they beat France in the final – the match that saw Zinedine Zidane sent off for an extraordinary head butt on Matteo Materazzi. Lippi had two stints in charge of the national team, the first from 2004 to 2006. He stepped down after winning the World Cup but returned in 2008 to lead his team to the World Cup in 2010, where they didn't even get past the group stage.

Brian Clough quotes

Brian Clough was the Best Manager England Never Had. The success he brought to Derby County and Nottingham Forest was nothing short of astonishing. On top of that he also had one of the driest wits in the business. If you ever wondered why he never got the England job, wonder no more.

10. **'If God had wanted us to play football in the clouds, he'd have put grass up there.'**
    (Grass-covered clouds are a meteorological phenomenon only found in the vicinity of Sam Allardyce)

9. **'Rome wasn't built in a day. But I wasn't on that particular job.'**
    (Clearly building a city is an easier task than managing Leeds United.)

8. **'I only ever hit Roy the once. He got up, so I couldn't have hit him very hard.'**
    (On dealing with Roy Keane and an insight into his unique training methods. If only he'd signed Joey Barton...)

7. **'I'm sure the England selectors thought if they took me on and gave me the job, I'd want to run the show. They were shrewd, because that's exactly what I would have done.'**
    (On not getting the England manager's job.)

6. **'We talk about it for 20 minutes and then we decide I was right.'**
    (Apart from not getting the England manager's job, Cloughie also failed to become Secretary General of the UN.)

5. **'Anybody who can do anything in Leicester but make a jumper has got to be a genius.'**
    (Brian Clough sings the praises of former Nottingham Forest player Martin O'Neill, who went on to manage Leicester.)

4. **'Telling the entire world and his dog how good a manager I was. I knew I was the best but I should have said nowt**

and kept the pressure off 'cos they'd have worked it out for themselves.'

(Clough's arrogance was astounding, but it's difficult to disagree.)

3. 'On occasions I have been big headed. I think most people are when they get in the limelight. I call myself Big Head just to remind myself not to be.'

(How the nickname was born – he evidently forgot about the reminder.)

2. 'I wouldn't say I was the best manager in the business. But I was in the top one.'

(Sadly his death deprives us of the live debate with José Mourinho.)

1. 'When I go, God's going to have to give up his favourite chair.'

Best manager interviews

It is perhaps the worst part of the job. You have just been taken to the cleaners by the opposition and a minute later a camera is thrust in your face and some little upstart with a microphone wants you to explain why your team is so useless. The adrenalin is pumping, the red mist descends, and out come words which are often best forgotten. Some of them are just silly. But they're all entertaining.

10. Jock Wallace

Non-ironically named manager 'Jock' Wallace – it's believed he was radically reclaiming the defamatory term – of phoenix-like Scots giants/now defunct indebted behemoth (delete as appropriate, we went to press in July) was in a hurry to get to the dressing room. Rangers had just won – won – the 1984 Scottish League Cup Final, beating Celtic – *Celtic*, mind – 3-2. Jock explained to the rookie reporter his impatience in the most forthright way possible. 'GERRONWITHITMAN,' he screamed, issuing a thankfully fake Glasgow Kiss to the callow youth. Who still has the shakes.

9. Sir Alex Ferguson

Either a rare loss of control, or a moment when his whole future flashed in front of his eyes, as he did precisely what he said he was going to, by pulling ahead of Liverpool's haul of 18 League titles in 2011. It was 2002, and impertinent and ex-Liverpool centre half Alan Hansen questioned his future. Never one to waste an opportunity to send a message to his rivals, it was succinct: 'My greatest challenge is not what's happening at the moment, my greatest challenge was knocking Liverpool right off their f****** perch. And you can print that.' They did, and he did.

8. Don Revie

Pure poetry from Don Revie, Leeds manager between 1961 and 1974. On tricky, nippy winger Eddie Gray, he encapsulated the player's mercurial nature with this beautiful one-liner: 'When he plays on snow, he doesn't leave any footprints.'

7. Ronnie Moore

At *606*, we try as far as possible to weed out the hoax callers. We have people, week-in, week-out, claiming that Chelsea is a big club, and other ridiculous statements. And we think we do a pretty good job. But they *do* get through.

Like the one who, in 2002, pretended that he'd heard that Ipswich were interested in Rotherham's dynamic and exciting manager Ronnie Moore. He'd taken them to the equivalent of the Championship on nuppence and against all odds, had kept them there. Possibly, it was said, this was as far as he, or anyone, could take them. So when the 'news' about the 'Ipswich' 'job' was relayed to him, he enthusiastically stated on live radio how excited he was to potentially be moving. He left the club in 2005, somewhat less of a messiah than he had been until that day in 2002.

6. Eduard Malofeyev

Perhaps in 30 years' time, the outbursts of obscure, strange Hearts manager Eduard Malofeyev will make some kind of sense. When asked by a BBC reporter through a translator what his thoughts were on the 2-0 defeat his team had suffered, he began a discourse on democracy, somewhat ironically. He then asked the reporter what *he* thought the problem was, 'because I don't know'. He left Hearts as the worst manager in their history, with no wins in eight matches.

5. Ian Holloway

Ah, Holloway. Which interview from the poet of Devon do we pick? A man so sought-after by media outlets he had a fully equipped 3,000-square-foot television and radio studio built in his house, in case a producer needed a pithy, self-deprecating soundbite from the man who sounds like a pirate who's been kicked in the guts one too many times. But how's this, on a horrible win over Chesterfield?

'To put it in gentleman's terms, if you've been out for a night and you're looking for a young lady and you pull one, some weeks they're good looking and some weeks they're not the best. Our performance today would have been not the best-looking bird but at least we got her in the taxi. She wasn't the best-looking lady we ended up taking home, but she was very pleasant and very nice, so thanks very much, let's have a coffee.'

4. José Mourinho

A master of the press conference, Mourinho makes it clear the game begins for him at the press conference. When asked for the line-up before Chelsea's Champions League quarter-final, said, 'Ours or theirs?' He then proceeded to correctly name Barcelona's starting 11. Not that it helped as Chelsea still lost 2-1.

3. Steve McClaren

Yesh, that one. Only a few years ago Steve McClaren would have got away with shpeaking in a hokey Dutch accent. But unfortunately, within minutshe of hish ridiculoush utterancesh on Netherlandsh television, the interview had been posted to the Chelsea Scouting Network, otherwise known as YouTube, and the resht is hishtory.

2. Walter Smith

A chick is a vulnerable, gentle little creature. Shorthand for cuteness. Look at the lovely little chick! An appropriate nickname then for 'Chick' Young, Scottish football reporter who was sent to the big bad fox's house to interview the fox, aka one of the oldest hands in all soccer, Walter Smith. Watch out, little chick! Don't ask the big bad fox why two expensively acquired Rangers players aren't good enough to play in Europe! He'll tear you apart with his long sharp teeth. Walter toyed with his prey, pointing out how ridiculous it was to suggest that two players who had played many times in Europe for other clubs weren't good enough to play in Europe. His sense of incredulity, and the ease with which he dismantled Chick Young was a joy to watch. 'If they had a bad game,' said Walter, gesturing toward the pitch, 'you're having an horrendous one tonight.'

1. Kevin Keegan

Falling foul of the mind games of number nine, above, Sir Alex Ferguson, Kevin Keegan lost it in spectacular fashion during the hard-fought 1995/6 season. Mighty Mouse uttered the deathless phrase, 'He went down in my estimation when he said that ... I will love it if we beat them. Love it.' United eventually went on to win the League.

Worst managers

Some take to management very quickly and get off to a flying start. However, the danger nowadays is, if you don't hit the ground running, the pressure mounts and fans and owners begin to question your abilities. Football is very much a results business, and owners want instant success, as a return on their investments, which, as we know, are huge. The list below are just a few of the poorest managers in living memory. A few sets of fans may still wince when they see the names.

10. Steve McClaren
Did very well at Middlesbrough, but his stint in the England hot seat was one to forget. They failed to qualify for Euro 2008 after an abysmal display against Croatia. Sadly, that's what he'll be remembered for.

9. Paul Hart
He's been at a few clubs, including Portsmouth, Crystal Palace, QPR, Swindon and Nottingham Forest. He seems to get good jobs, without ever really achieving anything in the game.

8. Iain Dowie
He relegated Crystal Palace, was sacked from Charlton and at Hull he had a forgettable tenure.

7. Tony Adams
The Arsenal legend secured 10 points from a possible 48 for Pompey and left them flirting with relegation when he was fired. He then joined Azerbaijan club Gabala FC, but left after seven months.

6. Glenn Roeder
Norwich have had some real stinkers. Roeder's record is not exactly inspiring. He took West Ham down and was then fired, and didn't exactly set the world alight at Norwich.

5. Howard Wilkinson
He was sacked from Sunderland shortly before the end of the 2002/3 season, and Sunderland were duly relegated with the (at the time) worst points total ever in the Premier League, notching up just 19 throughout the whole season. His time there was nothing short of a catastrophe.

4. Bryan Gunn

Norwich were relegated from the Championship under his stewardship, and he then led Norwich to their worst ever defeat, losing the opening game of the season 7-1 to Colchester, whose manager Paul Lambert then replaced Gunn a few days later.

3. John Barnes

His time with Celtic was atrocious and he even led them to an embarrassing defeat at the hands of Inverness Caledonian Thistle. He was then fired from Tranmere in 2009 and has since been linked to the Rwanda job. How the mighty have fallen.

2. Egil Olsen

Olsen had a torrid time as manager of Wimbledon. He was there for just under a year, and was sacked just before their relegation from the Premier League was confirmed. Since the Wimbledon debacle, Olsen has had the honour of managing traditional footballing nation Iraq.

1. Jim Fallon

The term 'back-to-back' is usually referred to when talking about success in football, but for Jim Fallon, it's the complete opposite. He secured back-to-back relegations for Dumbarton in his time at the club. He also lays claim to one of the worst records in football management. His League record at the end of his reign at Dumbarton reads: Played 46, Won 2, Drawn 5, Lost 39. Coupled with the fact he only won one home game in this time, this meant that the home fans got a little restless, to say the least. Needless to say he was fired, but why not sooner?!

Grumpiest managers

They say money can't buy you happiness, and they are right. A multi-million-pound salary for managing some of the most talented athletes in the world is not enough to assuage the cantankerousness of this sulky bunch below. Even a 4-0 win over a deadly rival only raises the ghost of a smile. Cheer up, you crotchety lot! We'd give our right arm to be where you are.

10. Kenny Dalglish
Dalglish did occasionally smile in 1995 when he won the League with Blackburn. His face didn't know what was going on. Since his less than successful return to Liverpool in 2011, the cumulative effect of paying £35m for Andy Carroll, the Luis Suarez misunderstanding and finishing in mid-table have turned 'the King' into one of the Premier League's most peevish managers.

9. Arsène Wenger
Watch out, plastic water bottles of the Premier League. The famously crabby Frenchman, despite winning three titles and four FA Cups, remains un étranger to the smile.

8. Neil Warnock
Long ago slipped into self-parody. One of our favourite pastimes in the **606** office is to turn the sound down when Neil is being interviewed and provide a comedy 'old lady' voice. The old lady must only come out on match days, though, because when he presented **606** with Robbie Savage he was a bundle of joy and there was even discussion about hairdos. Blue rinse, anyone?

7. Dave Jones
Fans of Stockport, Southampton, Wolves, Cardiff and Sheffield Wednesday will all tell you the best way to make yoghurt. Bring a pint of milk to the game and point it at Dave Jones. Blank at best, peevish at worst.

6. José Mourinho
The surly one always has his poker face on. There are rumours that he has teeth, but no one has seen them since 1992.

5. Mark Hughes
Another one for the 'old lady' treatment. Have you seen the price of stamps these days? And what about the queue in the Post Office? Pipe down, Mavis,

and have another humbug. Sparky by name, not by nature, at Wales, Blackburn, Manchester City, Fulham, and QPR.

4. Avram Grant

Looking on the edge of death at all times, Avram the miserable spreads unhappiness wherever he goes. Look up 'hangdog' in the dictionary and there's a picture of Avram Grant there, pointing at himself.

3. Steve Evans

He recently moved from Crawley to become the new Rotherham boss. What causes his perpetual grouchiness is not clear. Could it originate in looking in the mirror and seeing highlights to give Robbie's a run for their money? No – that would be a look of horror, not one of truculence. The prosecution for tax evasion? Maybe.

2. Martin Jol

If you've ever wondered which dog breed Martin Jol most resembles, it is a bulldog. A grumpy, highly strung bulldog. At Roda JC, RKC Waalwijk, Tottenham Hotspur, Hamburger SV, Ajax and now Fulham, Jol has left a trail of smashed mirrors and broken camera lenses.

1. Harry Redknapp

A surprise choice, but we have reason for it. In 2003, after Portsmouth lost 3-0 to Southampton, Harry cancelled Christmas for the players. He also banned his Spurs players from having a Christmas party in 2011, calling it 'a magnet for trouble', fundamentally misunderstanding the notion of the Christmas party. As Spurs' 2011/12 season unravelled, everyone's favourite wheeler-dealer looked less and less gruntled as the season progressed. Harry Redknapp, the Grinch of Tottenham, you win.

Managerial celebrations

Given the pressure they operate under and the day-to-day stress of managing a professional outfit, is it any wonder that when a famous victory is secured, managers suddenly lose all their inhibitions and indulge in the most silly of celebrations? Their job, after all, is now safe for at least a week. Here are ten outbursts of joy that will remain with us for ever.

10. Bob Stokoe
Remembered for steaming down the touchline to his goalkeeper Jim Montgomery, wearing a trilby hat, a raincoat and red tracksuit bottoms after beating Don Revie's Leeds Utd in the FA Cup final of 1973.

9. David Pleat
Securing promotion for Luton Town at Maine Road in May 1983 inspired David Pleat to run onto the pitch while mimicking a poor hurdler. Nearly as bad was the beige suite and cream shoes he decided to wear for the occasion.

8. Barry Fry
Barry Fry was well known for his crazy movements up and down the touchline when manager at Birmingham. When the Blues played Huddersfield to try and get promotion in 1985, it was Fry who was at the centre of the celebrations on the pitch while the stadium announcer could be heard ordering fans to return to their seats!

7. José Mourinho
The Special One was born when his Porto side knocked Manchester Utd out of the Champions League at Old Trafford with a late equaliser in 2004. Tearing down the touchline, with his arms raised, José put Adebayor's pitch-length celebratory run to shame.

6. Arsène Wenger
Wenger rarely reacts when watching his team, although football remains his number one passion. There's no clearer example of this than the jig he conducted on the touchline when the Gunners beat Villarreal in the Champions League back in 2009.

5. Bobby Robson
With a penalty shoot-out looming against Belgium in the 1990 World Cup,

David Platt's volley secured a semi-final place, causing manager Bobby Robson to emulate a one-man conga by the dug-out.

4. Graeme Souness

After Dean Saunders sealed a Cup final win for Galatasary against rival club Fenerbahce in 1996, manager Souness grabbed a huge Galatasary flag and embedded it on the Fenerbahce pitch, sparking a minor riot. He still remains – shall we say – unpopular with the Fenerbahce supporters.

3. Diego Maradona

Desperately needing a result against Peru to qualify for the Word Cup 2012, it was Martin Pelermo's winner that sent manager Maradona into a fit of jubilation, as he went running down the touchline in treacherous weather, sliding on his belly as if he had scored.

2. John Sillett

Having beaten red-hot favourites Tottenham in the 1987 FA Cup final, Coventry City manager John Sillett danced across the Wembley turf, mimicking Nobby Stiles's famous jig and pretending to drink from the trophy itself.

1. Alex Ferguson and Brian Kidd

Steve Bruce's late equaliser against Sheffield Wednesday secured Manchester United the title in 1993, leading them to a decade of glory. Sir Alex leapt from the dug-out with his hands aloft but it was assistant Brian Kidd who trumped him with an impressive series of star jumps before falling down onto the Old Trafford turf.

Funniest managerial quotes

Known for their stock-in-trade answers to any form of criticism – 'I didn't see it,' 'We battered them second half, just couldn't beat them,' 'The ref is a >&*%$## idiot,' – and desire to use the press simply for their own selfish means, the manager is never thought of as a particularly witty individual, à la Oscar Wilde. However, there have been some wonderful exceptions.

10. 'I'm out at the moment, but should you be the chairman of Barcelona, AC Milan or Real Madrid, I'll get straight back to you. The rest can wait.'
– Joe Kinnear on his answerphone message

9. 'I've told the players we need to win so that I can have the cash to buy some new ones.'
– Chris Turner, Peterborough manager before a League Cup match

8. 'They say Rome wasn't built in a day, but I wasn't on that particular job.'
– Brian Clough, being modest

7. 'If we can play like that every week, we'll get some level of consistency.'
– Sir Alex Ferguson, pointing out the obvious

6. 'We didn't underestimate them, but they were a lot better than we thought.'
– Bobby Robson after England squeezed through against Cameroon in the World Cup

5. 'If I had an argument with a player we would sit down for 20 minutes, talk about it and then decide I was right.'
– Brian Clough, never being wrong

4. 'If you're a burglar, it's no good poncing about outside somebody's house, looking good with your swag bag ready. Just get in there, burgle them and come out. I don't advocate that obviously, it's just an analogy.'
– Ian Holloway, speaking after his Blackpool side lost 4-1 to Crystal Palace

3. **'Please don't call me arrogant, but I'm European champion and I think I'm a special one.'**
   – José Mourinho, speaking to the fans after being appointed Chelsea manager in 2004

2. **'I wouldn't say I'm the best manager but I'm in the top one.'**
   – Brian Clough, saying just how he rates himself

1. **'Some people think football is a matter of life and death – but I assure you, it's much more serious than that.'**
   – Bill Shankley, stating just how important football is

Longest-serving managers

They say a week is a long time in politics. It's an eternity in football. The sport's ability to relieve you of your job in about 0.11 seconds (especially if you are in charge of Chelsea) remains unparalleled in modern day sport. We at **606** are therefore huge admirers of those able to practise the great art of longevity, so here is our top ten of those who have managed a club in the top four divisions for so long even the 90-year-old groundsman got sick of them.

10. Robert Jack (Plymouth) – appointed August 1910, 28 seasons

Yet another Scotsman paving the way for the likes of Matt Busby, Bill Shankly and Sir Alex, Robert Jack began his playing career in Scotland and ended it – as you do – at Southend. He was player-manager then manager at Southend for four seasons before returning to his old club Plymouth Argyle. During his 28 seasons in charge, Jack took them to the top of the Southern League in 1913 and seven years later took them into the Football League. In their first season in the Third Division, they finished 11th but then went on to take runners-up spots for the next six seasons. Jack finally clinched the title and promotion in 1930. All in all, he took charge of an astonishing 1,093 matches for the 'Pilgrims'.

9. Charlie Webb (Brighton and Hove Albion) – appointed August 1919, 28 seasons

In 1909, Charles Webb committed one of football's greatest ever sins. As an army soldier, he played against professional footballers. I know, shocking. This sin meant he was banned for 12 months from military football. So Webb retaliated and bought himself out of the army to join Brighton and Hove Albion so starting an amazing relationship with the club and particularly its fans. Webb was the first Brighton player to be capped at international level, the player mainly responsible for bringing the club its only major title to date when they topped the Southern League in 1910, and the provider of the club's winner in the following season's Charity Shield game against Aston Villa. Webb also set the club record for the most goals scored in the League, hitting the net 64 times in one season. An injury put paid to his playing career in 1914, and he became manager in 1919. He remained in charge of the team for more than 1,200 games between 1919 and 1947. He was so dedicated to the club he often sold tickets to games from his house. At the club's centenary celebrations in 2001, he was rightfully named a Brighton legend.

8. Arthur Dickinson (Sheffield Wednesday) – appointed August 1891, 29 seasons

If bitter rivals Sheffield United could boast John Nicholson, then Wednesday had Arthur Dickinson. With Dickinson at the helm, the Owls won the FA Cup in 1896 and 1907, the Division Two Championship in 1900, and the Division One Championship in both 1903 and 1904. Unfortunately for Dickinson, the advent of the First World War affected the club badly, and when the League resumed in1919, his team struggled. As a mark of his dedication to the club, Arthur decided to step down as manager/secretary to allow a new man in. It is an example I am sure many of us wish that others would follow...

7. Syd King (West Ham) – appointed April 1902, 30 seasons

Syd King remains one of the most colourful characters in the annals of West Ham's history. King joined the club in 1889, a year before they changed their name from the Thames Ironworks to West Ham. King played with distinction and in 1904 hung up his boots and assumed the managerial role. He managed the club for three decades. His most famous game was 1923's so-called White Horse Cup Final against Bolton Wanderers when 300,000 people crammed into the new Wembley Stadium and delayed the game for 45 minutes. In chaotic scenes, West Ham lost 2-0. The club's consolation was that they were promoted that season to Division One. King kept the Hammers in Division One for the next eight years.

6. Sam Allen (Swindon Town) – appointed July 1902, 31 seasons

Fact of football: directors are the bane of a manager's life. Not in Sam Allen's case, they weren't. He was the director who became the manager. Allen joined Swindon Town's club committee in 1895 and became a director two years later. In 1902, he was given the manager's job and, with him at the helm, Swindon won the Southern League title twice, finished as runners-up three times, and reached the semi-finals of the FA Cup twice – as well as winning the Dubonnet Cup. Unfortunately, the First World War interrupted Allen's tenure and, when football resumed in 1919, he was forced to create a new team. A year later, Swindon became a founder member of the old Division Three (South) and, over the next eight seasons, Allen steered them to seven top-six positions. Sadly, football's familiar demon – Financial Restraints – forced the club to sell their star players and the club went into decline. Allen smelt the coffee and resigned as manager. He then took up the role of club secretary which he held for 13 years. In 1941, he rightfully received the club's longest service award.

5. John Nicholson (Sheffield United) – appointed May 1899, 33 seasons

Nicholson was one of the most highly respected managers in the land, an expert on rules and the man who presided over one of the club's great eras, bringing home four FA Cups and establishing a major presence in Division One. Such was his reputation that in 1926 Manchester City tried to secure his services. Nothing new under the sun, then. In 1932, Nicholson crossed the road on his way to join up with his team who were due to play Aston Villa away. He was hit by a lorry and died instantly. He was a hero to United fans and over 6,000 of them came to pay their respects.

4. Frank Watt (Newcastle) – appointed 1895, 35 seasons

In his 35 seasons as Newcastle manager, Frank Watt set the template for the modern-day manager. No wonder he was referred to by all as the Guvnor. A former referee from Edinburgh, on arrival at the club Watt declared in a Mourinho-esque way, 'We are going to be the best team in the country.' His first move was to stop the club's directors picking the team. Having achieved that, Watt returned to Scotland and scoured his native land for players. His sharp eye brought in Hughie Gallacher, Colin Veitch and Stan Seymour, players who remain Newcastle legends to this day. His reward was to win the First Division four times and to appear in the FA Cup final five times, winning it three times.

3. Jack Addenbrooke (Wolves) – appointed August 1885, 37 seasons

When Jack Addenbrooke passed away in 1922, Wolverhampton Wanderers lost a true hero. Addenbrooke was a local teacher who, in 1883, ditched education and joined his beloved club as a player. Unfortunately, he never made the first team but he must have had something as, two years later, he was appointed manager. He steered Wolves to two FA Cup victories in 1893 and 1908, and three runner-up appearances. In 1922, he took leave due to illness and died a couple of months later. Many are of the opinion that Addenbrooke literally dedicated his life to his club.

2. George Ramsay (Aston Villa) – appointed August 1884, 42 seasons

In 1876, a 21-year-old Scotsman named George Ramsay stumbled across a bunch of cricketers playing football and threw himself into the game. In doing so, he not only initiated what is known as Aston Villa's 'Golden Era', but he actually changed the game itself. Ramsay's close control and skilful dribbling astonished those playing. This was the era of kick and run, and Ramsay's silky skills had never before been witnessed. After the game, he was besieged by requests to join the year-old club. He was appointed captain and took charge of training in which he ushered the passing game into English football. He resigned as a player and took over the manager's role, a position he held for 42 seasons. In that time, Villa won the Division One Championship six times and the FA Cup six times. Ramsey was also one of the founders of Perry Barr, a ground which allowed Aston Villa to start charging admission.

Ramsey's association with the club lasted 59 years and set the template for future Scottish managers to succeed in English football.

1. Fred Everiss (West Bromwich Albion) – appointed August 1902, 46 seasons

In 1902, Fred Everiss set the best example by leaping over the playing professional bit and becoming manager of West Brom at just 20 years of age. It took Fred nine years before he won anything as a manager, finally securing the Division Two Championship in 1911. He then put his feet up again for another nine years before winning the Division One Championship and the Charity Shield in 1920. His third major success came in 1931 when he led the Baggies to a memorable FA Cup victory. He did not pick the team; the directors of the club undertook that task until his resignation, and that may well account for his long stay. However, he's a hero in our eyes as he didn't just fade away when he stepped down in 1948. No way. He became a director, possibly so that he could finally pick the team! Fred held the position until his dying day. By then, he had worked every job at the club and must be the only man to have written the programme notes before he became manager.

Manager v manager bust-ups

Every week, managers try to tactically outwit each other. They send out scouts to examine the opposition, they look at how their oppo sets his team up and try to think of all kinds of ways to stop their adversary. When that fails, other methods come into play. Like verbal abuse, fisticuffs, etc. Far be it from **606** to be too judgemental but note how many times the words 'Ferguson' and 'Wenger' crop up on this list.

10. Arsène Wenger v Kenny Dalglish

Arsène Wenger and Kenny Dalglish were involved in a colourful exchange at the end of the 2010/11 season. A thrilling finale to the match between Arsenal and Liverpool at the Emirates that saw two injury-time penalties awarded and converted was enough to raise the temperature on the touchline. Wenger was furious that the visitors had been awarded a penalty in the 13th minute of stoppage time, leading to the altercation with Dalglish as referee Andre Marriner finally blew his whistle for full time. TV footage seemed to show Dalglish swearing at Wenger, but the pair later shook hands, and after the game the Liverpool manager dismissed the row.

9. Sir Alex Ferguson and José Mourinho

While the pair are now great friends, their relationship has not always been cosy. Ferguson refused to shake hands with Mourinho after the Champions League last 16 defeat to Porto in 2004. He was angry at what he saw as systematic diving by the Porto players throughout the game.

8. Martin Jol and Arsène Wenger

Arsenal v Tottenham, April 2006: Jol told his Spurs players to carry on playing while two Arsenal players were down injured, and Robbie Keane ended up scoring from the incident. Wenger was furious and squared up to Jol on the touchline.

7. David Moyes and Roberto Mancini

Manchester City v Everton, March 2010: Both managers were sent off in injury time following a scuffle on the touchline. Mancini was annoyed that Moyes caught the ball, and saw it as time-wasting, so he attempted to wrestle the ball off of Moyes. Everton won 2-0.

6. Arsène Wenger and Kenny Dalglish

Arsenal v Liverpool, April 2011: Arsenal conceded a penalty in the 98th minute of the match, and Wenger felt his side were hard done by. Dalglish told him to 'p**s off' as the Arsenal manager set about protesting wildly at the decision.

5. Sir Alex Ferguson and Roberto Mancini

Manchester City v Manchester United, April 2012: Mancini and Ferguson were involved in a scuffle on the touchline, with Mancini taunting the Scot. City won the match 1-0.

4. Alan Pardew and Arsène Wenger

West Ham v Arsenal, 2006: Pardew and Wenger squared up on the touchline after the Arsenal manager took umbrage at Pardew's goal celebrations. At the end of the game, Wenger refused to shake hands and was fined £10,000 by the FA for his conduct.

3. Billy Davies and Nigel Clough

Nottingham Forest v Derby, February 2010: A huge clash of players and coaching staff tarnished the match in stoppage time. During the mêlée, Davies said that Clough assaulted him from behind. Davies refused to shake his hand at the final whistle, and Clough later declined to comment. Derby won the match 1-0.

2. Arsène Wenger and Sir Alex Ferguson

These two have been involved in so many mind games and touchline altercations that in the end hate seems to have turned to love. They now share a deep respect for one another. The rivalry reached its zenith after United's match with Arsenal at Old Trafford in 2004, which United won 2-0. An unidentified party threw a pizza at Sir Alex, stoking a war of words between the pair. Arsène claiming he had not seen the incident...

1. Kevin Keegan and Sir Alex Ferguson

Keegan's Newcastle were going for the Premier League title against Manchester United when Keegan was asked to respond to a comment made by Ferguson suggesting that teams try harder against United than Newcastle. Cue the most famous managerial tirade in Prem History. 'I will love it if we beat them. Love it,' Keegan ranted. United won the title that year.

Best player-managers

It goes against nature to try and meld opposing forces together, or something like that. Anyway. You just don't do it. Like keeping a cat and dog in the same room. That's why the word 'player' and the word 'manager' should only be separated by the words 'was apparently given a good half-time talking to about his poor work rate in the first half'. They should not be separated by a hyphen. Apart from in a very few circumstances. These cross-breeds have relished the extra control they have as manager by being right there, in the thick of the action. A front-line general. And if anyone finds some footage of a player rolling his eyes and throwing his shirt to the turf in anger upon learning of his substitution, by himself, being followed by a strict telling-off as he leaves the pitch, by himself, do let us know on the usual text number. Well done to you, the band of ten mavericks who have embraced your circumstance and gone the full half-rice, half-chips.

10. Paul Incc (Macclesfield Town)
If not quite the Big-Time Charlie in the player-manager role, he kept Macclesfield Town up in 2007, appearing as a substitute (a decision applauded by the player, who thought the manager was very tactically astute) in that final game of the season. He managed franchise club MK Dons with some success before crashing and burning at Blackburn.

9. Attilio Lombardo (Crystal Palace)
Yes, the bald one. A year after signing from Juventus, he took on chalkboard as well as on-pitch duties for Crystal Palace. It was a partial success in that Palace were relegated. Can currently be found on the bench next to Samir Nasri and behind Mancini at Manchester City.

8. Romario (Vasco Da Gama)
Romario is a victim of what is known as the Law of Diminishing Returns, meaning the more you do of something, the less impressive it becomes. Like scoring 1,000 career goals.

Once a feared penalty box genius, he's now known as the slightly tragic striker who made his way round the world's 2nd, 3rd, 4th, 5th, 6th and over-60s divisions chasing that meaningless 1,000 figure. Many of them came from his time at Vasco de Gama: as a player, 324 goals, including 70 in one season, and then 15 as player-manager.

7. Paul Gascoigne (Kettering Town)

This is where 'best' starts to lose its lustre. England's clown prince, 'Gazza' Gascoigne, a man whose footballing talents were matched only by his self-destructive streak. He took the reins at Kettering Town for a magnificent 39 days.

6. Peter Reid (Manchester City)

Simian lookalike Peter 'Planet of the Reds' Reid stepped up to the managerial role when Howard Kendall left Maine Road to go a bigger club – Everton. He didn't do too badly: in 1990/1, his City side finished one place above United in fifth, and repeated that League position the next year.

5. Graeme Souness (Rangers)

One of the most successful player-managers of all time, and certainly the angriest. With a moustache that would look a touch over the top at a *Magnum P.I.* convention, proud Scot Souness led from the front, appearing 50 times and bringing home three Scottish League Cups and three Scottish Championships.

4. Gordon Strachan (Coventry)

The dinky, pocket-sized, flame-haired, short-tempered Scot led everyone's 'favourite club', Leeds, to a League title in 1992. In 1995, he got sent to Coventry. And by that we don't mean he was shunned and ignored by his peers, we mean he suffered a much worse fate – he got sent to Coventry Football Club. Initially as a mere player, he was elevated to player-manager when Big Ron Atkinson stumbled upstairs to become Director of Football. He did a good job, guiding the Sky Blues away from relegation.

3. Gianluca Vialli (Chelsea)

In the days before Abramovich's fortunes transformed Chelsea from a roguish, tough side who turned up at Wembley every year to get beaten by Arsenal into a remorseless behemoth powered by unlimited petro-chemical money, the Blues thought that the way forward was player-managers. Perhaps to save on wage bills. When Ruud Gullit departed in 1998, Vialli was one of Chelsea's star players, a fact confirmed by Chelsea's new manager, Gianluca Vialli, who regularly picked himself. He went on to win the Cup Winner's Cup.

2. Kenny Dalglish (Liverpool)

You may well be scornful of Kenny's foray into management at Anfield, but rewind 27 years and you'd be in awe of the 4'7" Scot. After taking over the reins at Liverpool, having passed their famous 'boot room' test (the penalty for failure is instant death by firing squad), he took them to three League titles, two

FA Cups and one League Cup, all whilst still dancing around the turf himself. We don't mean he was a pitch invader, we mean he was perhaps the greatest second striker in English football. He has since developed a Stewart Downing-size blind spot.

1. Glenn Hoddle (Chelsea)

Frowning Glenn was one of the most elegant and talented players of his generation. The National Football Museum Hall of Fame describes him as having 'sublime balance and close control, unrivalled passing and vision and extraordinary shooting ability, both from open play and set pieces'. Despite all that, he often has the look of a man who can't quite work out what time the next train to Chigwell leaves. He pulled off the player-manager double act twice, first with Swindon, who got promoted to the top tier, and then with Chelsea, who he got to the FA Cup final in his first season.

Best managerial quotes

In post-match interviews, we rarely get anything illuminating or incisive from a manager. They've quite often been pressed and ironed out by the media officers and will play it safe spouting platitudes about 'effort' and 'disappointment'.

But occasionally – and you'll notice that for most modern managers *mots justes* may as well be a promising centre-half from Ligue 1 – we are presented with a brilliant expression of sentiment, or a pearl of wisdom of such poetic beauty that it takes the breath away. If only for every Alan Pardew or Steve McClaren there was a Bill Shankly or a Brian Clough.

10. **'When he plays on snow, he doesn't leave any footprints.'**
    – Don Revie on winger Eddie Gray

9. **'There are no right or wrong or fair results. There's just the final score.'**
    – Otto Rehhagel

8. **'If you are first you are first. If you are second, you are nothing.'**
    – Bill Shankly, in the days before second place got you automatic qualification to the Champions' League.

7. **'It is better to fail aiming high than to succeed aiming low. And we of Spurs have set our sights very high, so high in fact that even failure will have in it an echo of glory.'**
    – Bill Nicholson

6. **'The ball is round, a game lasts 90 minutes, everything else is pure theory.'**
    – Sepp Herberger

5. **'Nach dem Spiel ist vor dem Spiel.' ('Before this game there was another one. After this game there will be another one.')**
    – Another Zen-like observation from Sepp Herberger

4. **'Professional football is something like war. Whoever behaves too properly, is lost.'**
    – Rinus Michels

3. **'Football is simple. But the hardest thing is to play football in a simple way.'**

  – The ridiculously gifted Johan Cruyff, who made most things look simple

2. **'Some people believe football is a matter of life and death. I'm very disappointed with that attitude. I can assure you it is much, much more important than that.'**

  – Bill Shankly

1. **'Football is nothing without fans.'**

  – Jock Stein pays homage to you – something today's players would do well to emulate

Most innovative managers

Managerial qualities are wide ranging and hard to apply. What works for one player may crush another. Some obsess over tactics, others opt for man-management. Here are ten great managers whose characters and vision have made great contributions to the game we love.

10. Alex Ferguson

Ferguson's man-management is second to none. When young United player Robbie Brady tried to order his food at the training ground, someone pushed in. Cristiano Ronaldo, who had just received the 2008 Ballon D'Or, jumped the queue.

As Brady left, Ferguson pulled him up. 'Why did you let him in there?'

'Well, you know... It's Ronaldo, boss.'

'You're here to try take his place, son. Don't let me see you do that again.' Simple and effective.

9. Marcelo Bielsa

Bielsa is an Argentine association football coach and manager of Athletic Bilbao. He is seen as one of the main proponents of the game's recent renaissance of total football along with former Barcelona coach Pep Guardiola. Known for his enormous collection of videotapes, which he studies carefully for hours on end, he's a man obsessed with and entirely devoted to the game.

8. Telê Santana

Santana is widely credited for the reinvention of the *jogo bonito* (Portuguese for 'beautiful game') by the vast majority of the Brazilian press. His full-attack mentality of play was best displayed with the 1982 Brazilian national squad, which fell 3-2 to Italy in the second round of the Cup. He was once considered by the media the 'last romantic of the Brazilian football', and had always been a strong campaigner for fair play and against violence in the game.

7. Guus Hiddink

One word: organisation. He coaches the Dutch brand of 'total football'.

6. Helenio Herrera

Herrera's nickname, *il Mago* ('the wizard'), was given to him by Italian sports journalists. The story behind the nickname is that Herrera would predict match scores to them before the match and, more often than not, be correct. At Inter

Milan he almost invented the now-famous Italian defensive style of play, with one player just in front of the goalkeeper. It's because of Herrera's tactical genius that managers get most of the credit for a team's win (as well as most of the stick).

5. Bill Nicholson

Spur's greatest ever manager led his team to the first Double in the 20th century and then won the Cup Winners Cup, the first British team to win a European cup. He was renowned for his inability to give out praise. When he once slapped winger Cliff Jones on the back and said well done after a game, the winger jumped back in amazement at his manager's unexpected generosity. Nicholson retorted, 'Remember son, a pat on the back is just two feet away from a kick up the arse!'

4. Sam Allardyce

Famous for wearing a Britney Spears-esque microphone to communicate with his support staff during games, 'Big Sam' initially got his pioneering ideas from his time playing in the USA in the North American Soccer League for the Tampa Bay Rowdies. The football team shared facilities with the Tampa Bay Buccaneers. Allardyce applied many practices of American football into the world of British football. When he managed Bolton, the Reebok roster featured psychologists, nutritionists, dieticians, chiropractors, a head of science and medicine, a Swedish expert of exercise and physiology, statistical analysts, and even a doctor of Chinese medicine. He also pioneered the use of computerised data to get the most out of his players.

3. Roy Hodgson – he who ties legs together

He is obsessed with two banks of four, to the extent to which he sometimes instructed his players to be tied together in banks of four when going to the cinema. It's like the 1940s Pro-Zone. Although he did once say he didn't believe in innovation. That's truly innovative.

2. Arsène Wenger

Arsène Wenger is credited with changing the junk food and drink culture at Arsenal and based part of his football philosophy on diet. He once said, 'Food is like kerosene. If you put the wrong one in your car, it's not as quick as it should be.' And he proved his theory by winning the Premier League three times.

1. Bill Shankly

'Greatest manager of all time' (Liverpool fan in 2012).

He installed the inspirational 'This is Anfield' sign in the tunnel and gave the club a sense of pride which was missing before he arrived. With the help of Bob Paisley, tactics became central to Liverpool's sense of thinking and the infamous 'boot room' was the result. Shankly deplored long-distance running on roads and insisted that, apart from warm-up exercises or any special exercises needed to overcome injuries, the players trained on grass using a ball. Everything was done systematically with players rotating through exercise routines in groups with the purpose of achieving set targets. Five-a-side games, as at all Shankly's earlier clubs, were the heart of the system and he insisted on these being as competitive as League matches. Shankly summarised the entire strategy as 'attention to detail; we never left anything to chance.'

Most Scottish managers

What do we mean by 'Most Scottish managers'? Well, they don't necessarily have to be Scottish to make the list. Ginger? Yes. Difficult to understand? Yes. Most likely to drink whisky after a game? Yes. Our criteria may be reinforcing stereotypes, but at least it's an hilarious stereotype.

10. Arsène Wenger
The Frenchman would probably disagree with this one, but our nemeses in life are usually the ones that resemble us the most (copyright: **606** staff writer, 2012). And so it is with Arsène and Sir Alex Ferguson. They hate each other so much that Arsène has picked up much of the Manchester United's manager's characteristics. Replacing the Gallic shrugs are bottle-kicking, incomprehensible mumblings and a penchant for fried foods. (Note: we cannot prove that last one.)

9. Diego Maradona
As long as we're going down the stereotype route, Diego Maradona must be considered in the grand scheme of things. Naturally talented, this is a guy who has possessed possibly the greatest footballing mind of all time; however, his taste for alcohol and, ahem, Mars Bars (thanks, 1989 Napoli shirt) means he falls into Scottish territory. True, he calmed down slightly when he took on a managerial role, but that kind of dedication to the Scottish lifestyle cannot be overlooked.

8. Alexei Lalas
The American defender was the proud owner of one of the most impressive ginger hair/beard combinations in the history of football. After his retirement from playing football in 2003, Lalas took a job as the general manager of the San Jose Earthquakes, and has since toned 'the ginger' down a tad... most likely because of all the haggis thrown his way (or something like that!).

7. Iain Dowie
Dowie isn't the obvious choice as a Scottish representative, however, look at the pale skin, the raw aggression and the obvious love for a fish supper and it's apparent that he has 'Scottish manager' running right through him.

6. Willie Macfadyen
If someone came up to you on the street, any street in the world, and told

you their name was Willie Macfadyen, it's almost guaranteed that you would instantly think 'Scottish manager!' Well, in this instance, you'd be right. The man is from a little Scottish village called Overtown, managed Dundee United between 1945 and 1954, and is the proud owner of the most Scottish name in the history of the universe.

5. Berti Vogts

Sure, he may look German, speak German and played for Germany, but former Scotland manager Hans-Hubert 'och aye the noo' Vogts is as Scottish as they come. Let's look at the facts: he was nicknamed 'the Terrier' (or 'der Terrier') because he fought hard for every ball, he played a no-nonsense game and he even managed to single-handedly fire up an entire nation when he knocked his own team, Germany, out of the 1978 World Cup when he scored an own goal against Austria. How very 'north-of-the-border'.

4. Kenny Dalglish

How could we not include 'King' Kenny? With the thickest Scottish accent in the known universe, it's amazing that he managed to cause the controversy he did during his second spell as Liverpool manager.

3. Gordon Strachan

If we had to include Kenny Dalglish because of his incredibly thick Scottish accent, then we had to include Gordon Strachan for the fact he looks like the most Scottish man alive. Stoic, almost warrior-like in stature, with a brilliant mop of ginger hair, the man from Edinburgh would not look out of place in a *Braveheart* re-enactment, shouting, 'Freeeeeeeeeeedom!!!!!!'

2. Jock Stein

Despite the fact he is Scottish, played for Celtic in between 1951 and 1956, and managed his national side, the name 'Jock' ensures his place on this prestigious list. Not only that, statistically Jock is, to date, the best ever manager of Hibs, with a win rate of 62 per cent, and he was the first person to lead Celtic to a domestic treble and European Cup victory. Scottish rating: 110 per cent (see cliché list).

1. Sir Alex Ferguson

We had to end with an actual Scot. With his rough-and-tough working-class roots, Sir Alex is as hard as nails. Only the most Scottish of managers would consider kicking a football boot near David Beckham's (previously) flawless face.

Oldest managers

Nothing like the hand of experience to guide your team through troubled waters, eh? These guys have seen it all and yet their passion and thirst for the game never diminishes. Here are ten managers born quite a long time ago but still plying their trade today.

10. Luiz Felipe Scolari (born 9 November 1948)

The Brazilian manager has taken charge of a host of clubs. He won the World Cup in 2002 with Brazil and got to the final of Euro 2004 with Portugal. He managed many teams in the Brazilian League and won nine domestic trophies there. He was hired by Chelsea in 2008, but didn't even see the season out. He went on to manage Brazilian club Palmeiras.

9. Walter Smith (born 24 February 1948)

Walter Smith has managed Rangers (two spells) and Everton, and became Scotland manager in 2004. In the same year he also had a spell as assistant manager at Scotland under fellow Scot Alex Ferguson. In 2012, he was reported to have turned down the Wolves manager post. He resigned as Rangers manager in 2011.

8. Roy Hodgson (born 9 August 1947)

Started manager career at just 28 with Halmstads in Sweden, where he won two League titles. In 1980 he joined Bristol City as assistant manager and then manager but didn't last very long and returned to Sweden, where he won more titles. He then went to Switzerland and ended up managing their national side. In 1995, he managed Inter Milan. Two years later, he took on his first job in the Premier League with Blackburn before being sacked as they found themselves bottom just a year later. He then took on more jobs outside England, in Denmark and Switzerland before managing United Arab Emirates and Finland. Between those jobs he went to Norwegian side Viking FK.

In 2007, he went to Fulham, got them their highest ever top-flight finish to ensure qualification to Europa League football and guided them to the final, but lost to Atlético Madrid after extra time. Hodgson went to Liverpool in 2010, but only lasted a year so then went to West Brom, taking over from Robero Di Matteo. In 2012, he was named England manager. He led them to the quarter-finals of Euro 2012, where they were knocked out by Italy. It goes without saying this was on penalties.

7. Harry Redknapp (born 2 March 1947)

When Harry Redknapp began his managerial career, it did not start well: his Bournemouth side lost 9-0 to Lincoln. However, Redknapp turned Bournemouth around. When he took over they were second from bottom. Four years later he won them the old Third Division. He became assistant manager of West Ham in 1992, taking over as manager just two years later, and was at Upton Park until 2001, where his biggest achievement was a fifth-place finish in 1991. He then went to Portsmouth and got them promoted into the Premier League in the 2002/3 season. Redknapp then went down the road to Southampton, Portsmouth's big rivals, but after they were relegated he was back at Portsmouth by December 2005. He went on to win the FA Cup with Portsmouth in 2008. That year, Harry landed a job at Spurs. The North Londoners were bottom of the League with two points from eight games but, by the end of the following campaign, Spurs had qualified for the Champions League.

5. Guus Hiddink (born 8 November 1946)

As well as managing Russian side Anzhi Makhachkala, Guus has won six Dutch titles, four Dutch cups and a European Cup with PSV, and a FA Cup with Chelsea as a manager. He's also managed a host of international teams: the Netherlands, South Korea, Australia and Russia.

6. Fabio Capello (born 18 July 1946)

A successful career saw Fabio play for Roma, Juventus and Milan, and win 32 caps for Italy. Went on to manage AC Milan, Real Madrid, Roma and Juventus before taking the England job. He won nine League titles and won the European Cup in 1994 with Milan. He was appointed England manager in December 2007 and resigned in 2012.

4. Dario Gradi (born 8 July 1941)

This Italian Englishman is currently Director of Football and Director of the Academy at Crewe Alexandra. He has managed Crewe, on and off, since 1983. In those 29 years, he has managed 1,404 games.

3. Sir Alex Ferguson (born 31 December 1941)

Currently managing Manchester United, Sir Alex started his playing career at Queen's Park between 1957 and 1960. He then went to play for St Johnstone, Dunfermline, Rangers and Ayr United. As a player, he scored 167 goals in 327 appearances.

Sir Alex began management when 32, with a part-time job at East Stirlingshire. He then went to St Mirren where he started full-time coaching.

With him in charge, they won the Scottish First Division in 1976/7. He joined Aberdeen in 1978 and at the time was younger than some of the senior players. After success at Aberdeen, he was appointed by Manchester United on 6 November 1986. Ferguson has won 12 titles with Manchester United and two Champions Leagues. He won the treble in 1999/2000.

2. Craig Brown (born 1 July 1940)

As well as managing Aberdeen, Brown has also managed Motherwell, Preston North End and Clyde, where he started his career. He managed the Scottish national team for nine seasons.

1. Giovanni Trapattoni (born 7 March 1939)

The wily Italian (known as the Lion in his native land,) has won ten League titles in four countries. Appointed manager of Italy in 2000, he was manager during their 2002 World Cup Campaign. He was then appointed manager of Republic of Ireland in 2008.

Youngest managers

Judging from some of your calls to **606**, as a nation we are blessed with people of all ages who know better than the manager of their team. But in reality, we're used to seeing the·grizzled faces of managers like Arsène Wenger, Sir Alex Ferguson and Neil Warnock. We see in their faces the years of intense tactical scrutiny, the high-pressure stress of top-level management having etched creases and crevices in their visages that even a plastic surgeon couldn't remove. At the other end of the spectrum are the young Turks, the Bambi-like noobs who seem to offer the promise of revolution and tactical innovation.

10. Brian Clough
Forced into early retirement at 29, Clough went on to greater success in management. He was given his chance at Hartlepool United in 1965 at the age of 30, becoming the youngest manager in the League at a club languishing in Division Four.

9. Herbert Chapman
At the age of 29, Chapman took the job at Northampton as player-manager in 1907, taking the side to two titles. He then went on to change the game, introducing floodlights and European matches. Didn't he manage Arsenal, too?

8. Valeriy Lobanovsky
With a reputation as a player, Lobanovsky took the coaching role at Soviet side Dnipro at the age of 29 in 1968. He had more success when taking charge of Dynmo Kiev in 1973, leading them to European victories.

7. Jimmy Hogan
Taking over the Dutch national side for a single game in 1910 at the age of 28, Hogan was made to manage. His tactical blueprint paved the way for such football giants as the Austrian 'Wunderteam' of the 1930s and the Hungary side of the 1950s. 'We played football as Jimmy Hogan taught us. When our football history is told, his name should be written in gold letters,' said Gustav Sebes (Hungary coach, 1949–1957).

6. Graham Taylor
Long before his reign as England coach, Graham Taylor was the League's youngest, taking on the Lincoln job at the age of 28.

5. Steve Coppell

At the age of 28, Steve Coppell was appointed manager of Second Division side Crystal Palace. Signing the hyphenated striker Ian Wright-Wright-Wright, he guided Palace to top-flight football and an FA Cup final in 1990. Steve was a bit of an outcast at Manchester United as player – he studied for a degree in economics at the same time.

4. Vittorio Pozzo

At the age of 27, Pozzo took on the job as Italian coach leading them to World Cup glory in 1934 and 1938, and oversaw the famous unbeaten run of the Italian side from December 1934 until 1939.

3. Arrigo Sacchi

In 1972, at the age of 26, Sacchi became the coach of local team Fusignano. Having managed several Italian sides, he got a phone call from Milan owner Silvio 'the Joker' Berlusconi in 1987, inviting him to manage the Rossoneri.

2. Paul Watson – Pohnpei

No, we haven't spelled 'Pompey' incorrectly. Pohnpei, as we now know having looked it up on the Internet, is one of the four states in the Federated States of Micronesia, a group of islands some way off the coast of Papua New Guinea. At the tender age of 25, Paul Watson from Bristol embarked on one of the hardest jobs in football – getting the lowest-ranked national team to win its first ever game. For no pay. His team crushed respected Guam team 'Crushers' 7-1 in 2010. One to watch, maybe?

1. Guy Roux

Beating Michel Platini in the Most Authentic-Looking Footballing Frenchman Competition, Roux took on a player-coach role at Auxerre just shy of his 22nd birthday. Roux secured top-flight football in 1980 leading them on to the Ligue 1 title in 1995/6. He managed them for 45 years, or 67 times longer than André Villas-Boas lasted at Chelsea.

Shortest managerial reigns

If you need evidence that football management is one of the world's most stressful jobs, you only need look at 'before' and 'after' photos of Steve Kean, André Villas-Boas and Kenny Dalglish, which look like someone's had a go at them with a 'comedy ageing' app on their phone. Key to this premature decrepitude is the constant knowledge that your chairman could be sitting in his volcano lair, stroking a white cat, with his finger on a button marked 'fired'. Often, there are whispers that someone's on the way out – frequently signalled by the chairman giving his 'full support'.

10. Colin Todd (Derby) – 98 days
In any normal job, 98 days is barely enough time to get on first-name terms with the local bar staff, or discover the best sarnie vendor in the vicinity. Not to mention the best skive hole in the office. But this is not normal; it is the parallel universe of football, where 17 games is plenty of time to turn a team around.

9. Brian Clough (Leeds) – 44 Days
Well documented in the superlative book and subsequent film *The Damned United*, Brian Clough's ill-starred tenure at Leeds is famous for the mutual dislike between players and manager. Clough took over a team who had won the League the previous season, having done so (he thought) by being the dirtiest, most cynical team in the country – something he told the players, who were not best pleased. He lasted just 44 days. Funny that.

8. Les Reed (Charlton) – 41 days
Lasted 41 days after being knocked out of both cups by League One and League Two opposition and flirting with relegation.

7. Paul Gascoigne (Kettering) – 39 days
Gazza attempted to kick-start his managerial career at Kettering, but sadly his alcohol problem got in the way. He lasted 39 days.

6. Steve Coppell (Manchester City) – 33 days
Steve Coppell was at Maine Road for 33 days, which equated to six games. He left due to stress.

5. Paul Hart (QPR) – 28 days
Hart lasted just 28 days at Rangers before leaving by 'mutual consent'.

4. Micky Adams (Swansea) – 13 days

Micky Adams resigned after just 13 days in charge. He managed to squeeze three games into his 13-day reign, but that wasn't enough to convince him the job was for him, so he walked out.

3. Martin Ling (Cambridge United) – 9 days

It took Martin Ling just nine days to realise he wouldn't get along with the Cambridge hierarchy.

2. Dave Bassett (Crystal Palace) – 4 days

Bassett never signed a contract with the Eagles, but put in four days' work before deciding it wasn't for him.

1. Leroy Rosenior (Torquay United) – 10 minutes

Rosenior was giving a press conference at the unveiling of his appointment, when he got a call from the chairman to say that the club had been sold and he'd been sacked. He didn't even have time to make a cuppa!

Sir Alex Ferguson quotes

Sir Alex Ferguson is without doubt one of the greatest managers ever, if not *the* greatest. His ability to mould outstanding winning teams and then rebuild them time and time again is without par in the modern game. He is also the mastermind of the wind-up and the mind game, aggravating more Premier League managers than Chelsea could ever employ. Here are ten of his best public utterances.

10. **'If he was an inch taller, he would be the best centre-half in Britain. His father is 6'2" – I'd check the milkman.'**
    – On Gary Neville

9. **'You must be joking. Do I look as if I'm a masochist ready to cut myself? How does relegation sound instead?'**
    – On whether Liverpool would win the title in 2007

8. **'When an Italian tells me it's pasta on the plate, I check under the sauce to make sure. They are the inventors of the smokescreen.'**
    – On Italians

7. **'My greatest challenge is not what's happening at the moment, my greatest challenge was knocking Liverpool right off their ******* perch. And you can print that.'**
    – On Alan Hansen questioning his future in 2002

6. **'That lad must have been born offside.'**
    – On Filippo Inzaghi

5. **'It was a freakish incident. If I tried it 100 or a million times it couldn't happen again. If I could, I would have carried on playing!'**
    – Explaining how he kicked a boot in the United dressing room that hit David Beckham in the face

4. **'He was certainly full of it, calling me "Boss" and "Big Man" when we had our post-match drink after the first leg. But it would help if his greetings were accompanied by a**

decent glass of wine. What he gave me was paint-stripper.'
– On José Mourinho

3. 'They say he's an intelligent man, right? Speaks five languages. I've got a 15-year-old boy from the Ivory Coast who speaks five languages!'
– On Arsenal manager Arsène Wenger, 1996

2. 'It's getting tickly now – squeaky-bum time, I call it.'
– On the 2002/3 end-of-season title race between Arsenal and United

1. 'I can't believe it. I can't believe it. Football. Bloody hell.'
– On winning the Champions League final against Bayern Munich on 26 May 1999

Worst-dressed managers

One way managers reigned in maverick players was to insist they wear the club uniform at all times. But what of the managers themselves? How well do they feature in the fashion stakes? Are they as suave as Mancini or as ramshackle as Barry Fry? Here are the ten managers Gok Wan would love to get his hands on.

10. Cesare Prandelli

Naturally, our 'Best-dressed managers' list contains many Italians. There are always exceptions to the rule. Step forward Italian manager Cesare Prandelli. At Fiorentina, he adhered to the club colours a little too enthusiastically by wearing all purple at some games. His move into a darker smarter suit for international duties was, we assume, part of his contract.

9. Ron Atkinson

With his dodgy trench coats and tinted glasses, Big Ron did love resembling an extra from *Only Fools and Horses*, a look he stuck to throughout his years managing Manchester United (1981–1986), Sheffield Wednesday (1997–1998) and Nottingham Forest (1999).

8. Arsène Wenger

Since arriving on these shores, Arsène Wenger has pioneered a unique 'professor' look with his grey shirt and red tie combination. However, in recent seasons, Mr Wenger has opted for a winter coat, which tends to resemble a slug or a sleeping bag. Not the epitome of style, but we have to admit it looks lovely and cosy.

7. Malcolm Allison

Clothes maketh the manager. Malcolm Allison was a flamboyant outspoken boss who dressed in big fur coats and a fedora hat, a look he usually topped off by having a big fat cigar hanging out of his mouth. Allison managed many clubs, and his striking appearance and many successes were always reflected by his equally brilliant wardrobe.

6. Diego Maradona

In the 2010 World Cup, Argentina legend and manager Maradona looked more like someone who was going to sell you a second-hand car than steer a team to the World Cup final. His oversized suits and his habit of wearing two wristwatches suggested that his tailor did not in fact possess the hand of God when it came to sartorial matters.

5. Dunga

Former Brazil captain Dunga was sacked as his country's manager in 2010 after a disappointing World Cup campaign. Many suspect, however, it was his penchant for highly dodgy shirts that did for him. Of particular interest is the lime-green number he wore to steer his team to a 0-0 draw with Colombia (2008, World Cup qualifier in Brazil). He has also been spotted sporting a salmon-colour shirt with a light tan sheepskin coat. That look works on one person and one person only. Our very own John Motson.

4. Martin O'Neill

For a self-professed fan of the highly stylish pop band the Small Faces, you would have thought that Mr O'Neill would have fashioned a look far smarter than one that relies on joggers tucked into socks and dodgy rugby-style polo shirts with big collars. However, given his penchant for jumping up and down like a man possessed every time his team gain possession, we understand a smart suit may not always be appropriate. When he returned to management after a long absence in 2011, he did so wearing his trademark look. It's nice to know that in life there are some things you can rely upon.

3. Brian Clough

Was Cloughie colour-blind? There is no other reason why anyone would think that a bright green jumper with a red polo shirt would work. But he did and fair play to him – his green sweatshirt did assume iconic status. Worst jumper, best jumper – whichever you think, it was THE jumper.

2. Tony Pulis

Every game, rain or shine, Tony Pulis wears a tracksuit. Acceptable. And a baseball cap. Less so. Unfortunately, this combination appears to reflect the entire contents of his wardrobe as, even at the 2010 FA Cup final against Manchester City, Pulis still prowled the touchline in this get-up. We all love a Cup final suit, but Pulis ignored tradition and the tracksuit/ baseball cap combo won once more. It even managed to ignite the ire of the far better-dressed Stoke fans, which is a sentence you don't often get to write.

1. Owen Coyle

We sometimes get confused whether Owen Coyle is managing the team or trying to play, given his predilection for always appearing on the touchline in shorts, football socks and training top. He looked exactly the same during his spell at Burnley where substituted players would come off the pitch and hug him instead of the man replacing them. How he manages to stay warm during cold Tuesday night games in Bolton is a mystery of our times.

OWNERS

Most-loved owners

Believe it or not, there have been some chairmen who have defied all the odds and won the deep and full approval of the fans, combining their huge financial power with an obvious love for the club they own. We salute the following men for acting like fans who have just won the Lottery.

10. Sheikh Mansour (Manchester City)

Most loved because of one thing – his money. City fans have been cherry-picking some of the world's best players since Mansour took over in 2008. He tops the football rich list, with an estimated wealth of £20 billion, and now the popularity list after his financial backing helped City to their first League title in 44 years in 2012.

9. Sam Hammam (Cardiff)

The former Wimbledon owner became a cult hero amongst Cardiff fans, when he joined in with the 'head-patting' celebration. He was seen doing the celebration in the FA Cup match against Leeds in 2002. He became Cardiff owner in 2000, after selling his interests in Wimbledon.

8. Steve Gibson (Middlesbrough)

In 1995, he became club chairman, and owns around 90 per cent of the shares. In his time at the club, Boro have moved into the 35,000-seat Riverside Stadium, won the League Cup, and been runners-up twice. They were also runners-up in the UEFA Cup in 2006 and the FA Cup in 1997. Such is Gibson's popularity, he was given the freedom of Middlesbrough after the club won the Carling Cup in 2004.

7. Elton John (Watford)

He became chairman of Watford in 1976, until he eventually sold the club in 1987. In 1997, he bought the club for a second time, but due to time commitments he stepped down 2002. Elton John is still lifelong president of the club. He has since performed concerts at Vicarage Road, in order to fund transfers and help the club out of financial problems.

6. Peter Coates (Stoke)

He was a boyhood fan of the Potters, and took over the club for the second time in 2006. When he took over, he said he wanted to do something for the area and community, not just the football team.

5. John Madejski (Reading)

No one can doubt the job John Madejski has done at Reading since becoming chairman in 1990. The club's ground, built in 1998, was largely funded by him, and is named the Madejski Stadium. The club won Division Two in 2002 and then won promotion to the Premier League in 2006 and 2012.

4. Dave Whelan (Wigan)

He bought the club in 1995 and has bankrolled their path to the Premier League, where they have been since 2005. They were in Division Three when he took over. It's been suggested that he may be considering stepping down, and passing the reigns to his 21-year-old grandson.

3. Milan Mandaric (Portsmouth)

Milan Mandaric arrived at Portsmouth in 1998 and, for the first few years, the club sat comfortably in Division One. In 2003, Pompey won promotion to the Premier League, which was largely instigated by the appointment of Harry Redknapp as manager. Unheard of for football fans, the Fratton Park faithful were often heard singing 'There's only one Milan' to the Serbian.

2. Jack Walker (Blackburn Rovers)

Walker took full control of Blackburn in 1991, and led the club to the best times in its history. He signed Chris Sutton and Alan Shearer and installed Kenny Dalglish as manager. They won the Premier League in 1995, an incredible achievement for a club the size of Blackburn. He was loved so much that Ewood Park has a Jack Walker Stand in memory of the legendary owner.

1. Jack Hayward (Wolves)

Hayward bought his boyhood club in 1990. He developed Molineux and also wiped off the club's debts. He saw the team promoted to the Premier League in 2003 after a win against Sheffield United in the play-off final at Cardiff. The club's training ground is called the Sir Jack Hayward Training Ground, and Sir Jack Hayward Way is a street outside Molineux.

Owners who think they're managers

It's their party and they will interfere when they want too, that's for sure. For many, running the club's finances and ensuring all goes smoothly is not enough. They want to be managers as well, and tacticians, and have the fans sing their names. Here are ten for whom the expression 'too many cooks spoil the broth' has no meaning whatsoever.

10. Simon Jordan (Crystal Palace)

Simon Jordan was rumoured to have interfered with team matters when Peter Taylor, Ian Dowie and Steve Coppell were managers at Selhurst Park. Jordan was Palace owner from 2000 to 2010.

9. David Gold (West Ham)

He apparently paid a visit to the training ground to give Avram Grant and the players a 'motivational talk', ahead of their key Premier League match against Blackburn in May 2011.

8. Milan Mandaric (Leicester)

Manager Martin Allen was sacked after just three games for telling owner Milan Mandaric not to interfere with team selection and transfers. There was apparently tension over the signing of Jimmy Floyd Hasselbaink. Mandaric wanted him, but Allen refused to sanction the move. Cue a big bust-up.

7. Mike Ashley (Newcastle)

In 2008, after he had left the club for the second time, Kevin Keegan said he had lost control of transfer policy. He claimed that Ashley was trying to sell players like Michael Owen behind his back, and bringing in players like Xisco without his consent.

6. Niall Quinn (Sunderland)

Roy Keane claimed that Quinn interfered with team matters during his time as Sunderland manager. By the end of his time there, Keane would not talk to Quinn, preferring apparently instead to text him. Quinn is no longer chairman of Sunderland, having left in February 2012.

5. Irena Denim (Bournemouth)

The wife of Russian owner Maxin Denim stormed into the dressing room at half time of their 1-0 defeat to MK Dons in February 2012.

4. Vladimir Romanov (Hearts)

He sacked Jim Jeffries in 2011, because of what Jeffries described as 'standing up to Romanov's interference'. Romanov is known for being very trigger-happy with managers.

3. Roman Abramovich (Chelsea)

It has been reported that Roman Abramovich likes to interfere with team matters at Chelsea. The claim has been denied by former Chelsea manager Avram Grant and former chief executive Peter Kenyon. But no one believes them.

2. Rupert Lowe (Southampton)

Stuart Gray, Saints' manager for eight games in 2001, accused Lowe of signing Ecuador international Agustin Delgado against his wishes. Delgado only made two Premier League appearances, while picking up £2m in wages and costing the club £3.5 million.

1. Steve Morgan (Wolves)

Went into the dressing room and ranted at the players after Wolves 3-0 home defeat to Liverpool in January 2012. It was their 11th game without a win and they were booed off the pitch. Mick McCarthy, the then Wolves manager, was angered by the chairman's interference, and told him so.

Most memorable owners

Having a rich foreign owner seems to be the latest must-have for the ambitious football fan. These money-soaked individuals basically play Fantasy Football for real, buying players at exorbitant prices and paying them the kind of money only bankers know about. All that sounds great, but the next ten aren't all remembered for the great things they've done.

10. Gillett and Hicks

You could say these two guys were not too popular with the fans. With their club saddled by debt, the Liverpool faithful strongly reacted to Liverpool FC being run by the two Americans. When Rafa Benitez was removed as manager, mass protests were held and the American flag burnt. Gillett and Hicks were eventually bought out and accused the fans of waging Internet terrorism against them. The fans were too busy celebrating to respond.

9. Alan Sugar

For ten years, Lord Sugar was owner of his boyhood club Tottenham Hotspur. He said 'You're fired!' to six managers, wound up the fans with his brash style and apparent desire to treat football like his computer business. Sugar stepped down as Chairman in 2001.

8. Tony Fernandes

Tony Fernandes became the QPR chairman in 2011 after buying out Bernie Ecclestone. Despite not being involved for long, he's already made a name for himself in West London by spending a lot of money and for communicating with the fans, whether it's in the stands, in the pubs of Shepherd's Bush or via Twitter.

7. Sullivan and Gold

David Sullivan and David Gold are two very ambitious owners. Since being at West Ham United, they've been chosen as the preferred tenants for the Olympic Stadium and have put cheeky loan bids in for out-of-favour Premiership stars Fernando Torres and Carlos Tevez. Oh, and they also believe West Ham will be playing Champions League football by 2017. That's ambition, and we like it.

6. Malcolm Glazer

Malcolm Glazer won control of Manchester United in 2005, which didn't go down too well with fans. They're not happy with the way Glazer's run the club, especially the huge debts that United have had to assume. Many are still wearing the club's original green and yellow scarves in protest, whilst one group of fans even started another team – FC United of Manchester.

5. Venky's London Limited
When Indian poultry giant Venky's completed their takeover of Blackburn, it all seemed so promising. But a dodgy chicken advert starring some of the Blackburn players got things off to a very bad start. The club's relegation, the owners' patchy attendance at games, and their allegiance to unpopular manager Steve Kean have not gone down too well, either.

4. Mohammed Al-Fayed
Mohamed Al-Fayed took over Fulham way back in 1997 and since then has overseen a steady rise through the Leagues. One of Al-Fayed's most memorable moments came in 2011 when he got a rather scary statue of Michael Jackson put up outside Craven Cottage. That didn't go down well with fans. His reply was that they could all 'go to hell' if they didn't appreciate it.

3. Mike Ashley
They love him, they hate him – Mike Ashley took control of the Magpies in 2007. Since then, there have been demonstrations, which have led to him nearly selling the club, a relegation, a promotion, six managers and a change of the stadium's name. Despite all that, he has clawed back huge debt, and Newcastle nearly secured Champions League football in the 2011/12 season under Ashley man Alan Pardew. Love him or hate him – it's never boring.

2. Sheikh Mansour bin Zayed Al Nahyan
Sheikh Mansour has transformed Manchester City into one of Europe's most feared teams by attracting some of the world's best players. They finally landed the Premiership title with the very last kick of the 2012 season, something their quieter neighbours didn't like at all.

1. Roman Abramovich
In 2003, a Russian billionaire arrived at Stamford Bridge and made the biggest takeover of its time. So far Abramovich's project at Chelsea has cost him over £2 billion. Yet for Roman it was all worth it when Chelsea finally lifted the Champions League trophy in 2012. Roman is most famous for the number of managers he gets through. He is currently on his eighth.

Owner decisions

They own the club, they do what they like... Owners treat their clubs in all kinds of different ways, and their decisions can either inspire or infuriate the faithful. Here are ten decisions which run the gamut from brilliant to baffling.

10. Huw Jenkins (Swansea)
In 2010, Huw Jenkins sensibly appointed Brendan Rogers, who promptly guided them to promotion to the Premier League and then into comfortable Premier League survival, playing some lovely football.

9. John Madejski (Reading)
After Steve Coppell resigned, Madeksi brought in Brendan Rodgers, who did not make much of an impact. Controversially, Madejski then appointed Brian McDermott as manager in 2010, who has guided them to the Premier League.

8. Venky's (Blackburn)
Sacked the veteran Sam Allardyce whose ability to keep clubs afloat is legendary. Replaced him with Steve Kean in 2010, who wound up the fans and then led Blackburn to... relegation.

7. Steve Morgan (Wolves)
The highly experienced McCarthy was sacked in February 2012 by a chairman fearing relegation. He appointed Terry Connor, who had never managed before, and watched him lead the team to... relegation.

6. Milan Mandaric (Sheffield Wednesday)
Mandaric sacked Gary Megson in February 2012. You could see why. Wednesday were third in the table and had just beaten local rivals Sheffield United...

5. Nicola Cortese (Southampton)
The Southampton chairman sacked Alan Pardew after a 4-0 win at Bristol Rovers in 2010. Pardew moved to Newcastle where he has been working wonders.

4. Dean Hoyle (Huddersfield)
Huddersfield were fourth in League One and had gone 43 regular season games without defeat. Therefore, the only sensible option was to sack manager Lee Clark. Which Hoyle did.

3. Mohammed Al-Fayed (Fulham)

He paid for a statue of Michael Jackson to be erected outside Craven Cottage in 2011. The fans complained so Al Fayed told them they could 'go to hell' if they didn't like it. Very diplomatic.

2. Bill Kenwright (Everton)

The decision to appoint David Moyes by Everton chairman Bill Kenwright was inspired. Thanks to his shrewd management and transfer activity, Moyes has been outstanding in his tenure at the club, ensuring that relegation is no longer a serious option. They even claimed a top-four finish in 2005.

1. Mike Ashley (Newcastle)

Chris Hughton won the Magpies promotion back to the Premier League at the first attempt in 2010. So what did owner Mike Ashley do that same year? He sacked Hughton when the club were a very respectable 11th in the table. Yet there was method in the madness. New manager Alan Pardew secured the club Champions League football.

Most extravagant owners

With the advent of FIFA's financial fair play rules, the days of benefactor-funded clubs like Chelsea and Manchester City buying success may be over. But it's not just in Britain that clubs have their mouths stuffed with cash – it's everywhere. We racked our brains for the biggest investment in a football club, and we threw personal wealth and sheer wallet-busting extravagance into the equation, too.

10. George Reynolds (Darlington)
The 'colourful' ex-safe-cracker bought Darlo in 1999 and spent £20 million on a new stadium called the Reynolds Arena. He once drove around with a cool half a million in his car boot. We hope it wasn't at the expense of a car jack. That would have been dangerous and irresponsible.

9. Lakshmi Mittal (QPR)
He paid £81.5m for a 12-bedroom mansion in London's Kensington Palace Gardens. Other famous residents of that humble street have included Princess Diana. Forbes reports, 'In 2004, Mittal threw his daughter what is believed to be the most expensive wedding in history, a $60 million, week-long extravaganza for some 1,000 guests in Paris.' We're sure lovely Vanisha (who, if she turned into a superhero, wouldn't have to change her name) is all the happier for it.

8. David Gold (West Ham)
The former Birmingham City chairman's father was an East Ender who spent time in prison during Gold's early years. David Gold's only crime is against air traffic control for overuse of his helicopter, which is often seen at the West Ham training ground.

7. Alisher Usmanov (Arsenal)
Usmanov holds interests in Facebook, which made him a *bit* of profit when it was floated in 2012. He thinks nothing of spending £40m on a house, but is also a generous charity doner.

6. Randy Lerner (Aston Villa)
Lerner took over the club in August 2006 with 59.69 per cent of Villa shares. Randy's biggest extravagance might just be private flights. His company made almost 400 trips out of East Hampton Airport between 2007 and 2011.

5. Silvio Berlusconi (AC Milan)
Where to begin? He proudly displays his vulgarity to anyone who cares. And no, that's not a metaphor.

4. Sir John Robert Madejski (Reading)
He named Reading's stadium after himself and he's got a playboy attitude that's hard to beat, even associating with a certain Cilla Black in 2004. He owns so many luxury cars, he often forgets how many he's got (we expect). They include a couple of Rollers of course, a pair of Bentleys (one to wear, one to keep), a quartet of Jaguars, a solo AC Cobra and a gorgeous red Ferrari 328 which sits inside a glass box in his home gym – laughing at him as he does his crunches.

3. Sheikh Mansour (Manchester City)
With an estimated worth of £20 billion, he's pretty much the richest man in the history of football and the universe – he could buy absolutely anything or anyone he wants, and indeed any club. So why he chose Stockport's favourite team, no one really knows. Maybe he thought he was actually buying United?

2. Suleyman Abusaidovich Kerimov (FC Anzhi Makhachkala)
Suleyman has a net worth of US$7.8 billion and is the 118th richest individual in the world. Instead of doing what any normal person would do with $7.8 billion – retire – he has launched himself headlong into the painful world of football, paying Cameroon international Samuel Eto'o over €20 million after tax per year, slightly more than the average caller on 606.

1. Roman Arkadyevich Abramovich (Chelsea)
Boats and bling galore, and he's happy to admit it: he recently purchased a £300 million super-yacht with two swimming pools (one for shopping, one for long drives), a couple of helipads (one to eat, one to keep), just the one dance floor and a single submarine. We're still waiting for the invite for tea.

Most trigger-happy owners

Chairmen used to be invisible individuals who went about their business quietly and efficiently. Not any more. Today a club's chairman is as well known as the star centre-forward. Many of these individuals tend to demand the very best from their managers and woe betide anyone who should not deliver them every cup and title in the game. In one season. Playing wonderful football. With cut-price players. On low wages.

10. Stan Flashman
You could say Barnet chairman Stan Flashman was a little volatile. After all, he apparently fired and rehired Barry Fry eight times during his nine-year spell at the club.

9. Rupert Lowe
Southampton chairmen Rupert Lowe not only enjoyed duck shooting but was pretty trigger happy with his managers as well, firing Stuart Gray after 17 games and Paul Sturrock after just 13.

8. David Gold and David Sullivan
This seasoned pair of chairmen took over West Ham in 2010 and within two years had employed and sacked Avram Grant and Gianfranco Zola. One would like to think that current manager Sam Allardyce is safe after guiding the Hammers into the Premiership. One would like to think that...

7. Vladimir Romanov
After inexplicably sacking Hearts manager George Burley after the club's best ever start to the season, Romanov then sacked Graham Rix after just 19 games, claiming he should have done it earlier. After steering Hearts to an impressive 2012 Scottish Cup Victory over bitter rivals Hibs, his most recent manager Paulo Sergio was informed that the owner had left halfway through the match and would not be present for the celebrations. Sergio has now left the club. He was Romanov's ninth full-time manager since taking over the club in 2004.

6. Freddy Shepherd
Shepherd was the chairman of Newcastle for almost ten years from December 1997 to the summer of 2007. He took the unexpected step of sacking Sir Bobby Robson just four games into a new season, despite a fifth-placed finish the season before.

5. Doug Ellis

His nickname was 'Deadly' Doug and there was a good reason for the sobriquet. In his two spells of Chairman, Ellis took on and let go 13 managers.

4. Florentino Perez

The Real Madrid president is not afraid to give big names the boot even if they have just won him everything, as Vincent Del Bosque discovered in 2003 having won the club two La Ligas and two Champions League titles.

3. Roman Abramovich

The managers' serial killer, Abramovich took over Chelsea in 2003 and has since hired and fired eight managers including Luiz Felipe Scolari, Carlo Ancelotti, Avram Grant, Claudio Ranieri, José Mourinho, Guus Hiddink and Andre Villas-Boas. Current manager Roberto Di Matteo managed to keep his job, but only just. And he won the Champions League.

2. Flavio Briatore

Briatore and Ecclestone took over QPR when it was on the verge of bankruptcy in 2007. They said they needed to make changes, and boy did they. They hired and fired John Gregory, Luigi Di Canio, Iain Dowie, Gareth Ainsworth, Paolo Sousa, Jim Magilton, Steve Gallen and Marc Bircham. Mark Hughes is currently the man in charge, looking nervously over his shoulder.

1. Milan Mandaric

At Portsmouth, Mandaric got things right from the off, by appointing Harry Redknapp as manager. Unfortunately, Harry later jumped ship for bitter rivals Southampton, returning a year later. During that period Mandaric went through Alain Perrin and Velimir Zajec, as well as caretaker manager Joe Jordan. But that is nothing compared to his stint at Leicester, where he got through seven managers in just over two and a half years. No wonder national unemployment figures are so high.

Best sponsors

Sponsors are important for one reason. One green-backed, jangling, doughy reason. Filthy lucre. The main ingredient of the modern game, after disappointment, is money. Money, money, money. Lots of lovely money. From anywhere. As much as possible. In order to pay top-flight footballers' agents the money they need to spend on pointless and expensive cars, clubs need to make the moolah. They need to find the funds. They need to bring the bread. They need to show the shekels. Brands of the world: football clubs need your money. Sometimes it works, for example when Barcelona didn't have a sponsor's logo on the shirts. At all other times it is a besmirching of the purity of the game.

'Money doesn't talk, it swears,' said the wise old Preston North End winger Bob Dylan.

Cover your ears...

10. AC Milan – Pooh Jeans
Not, unfortunately, named after the game played on Milan's Ticino River, where children throw their jeans over a bridge and then rush to the other side to see who's won. Nope. These jeans are Pooh.

9. Scarborough – Black Death Vodka
At least it's honest. 'Drink In Peace' ran the tagline. Kind of cool, in a nihilistic sort of way.

8. Denmark – Dong
You have a dong on your chest. Never tires.

7. Roma – Wind
What a load of old guff. But fart be it from us to cast aspersions on Roma's sponsors. You'll never gas what they actually do? They're a mobile phone company, which trumps some of the other sponsors on this list. Roma let rip in the Coppa Italia with Wind behind them.

6. Clydebank – Wet Wet Wet
This four-year (four-year!) sponsorship deal was a one-off – it would be more likely for a football team to sponsor a pop group than the other way round, now the music industry has virtually collapsed.

5. St Johnstone – Bonar

Excuse me, fans of St Johnstone. Would you mind if we put a bonar on your chest? We can pay good money.

4. Oxford United – Wang

And on a similar note, the Yellows were often found with a Wang between the nipples between 1985 and 1989.

3. Lyon – Le69

'Allo. Je suis un footballer française. Vous voudrais un sexy time avec moi? Vous voudrai "Le69"?'

2. FC Nurnberg – Mister Lady

Imagine if you'd overheard this sponsorship deal being discussed in a German *Kaffechaus*. You'd think you'd stumbled in on something completely different. Lots of German men discussing how much *Mister Lady* should cost.

1. Deportivo Wanka – Deportivo Wanka

This Peruvian club were formed in 1996, making them Peru's version of Chelsea. Deportivo Wanka are named after the *Wankas*, the indigenous people of Huancayo in the Peruvian Andes. The Wankas helped the Spaniards during the conquest of Peru, providing supplies and men to the Spanish army. Their splendid green home kit bears across the chest the legend 'D. WANKA'.

TRANSFERS

Best Premier League signings

Love or hate the clubs they play for, there are some players whose talent places them above all other considerations. If you love football, you are going to love their style, even if you do have to keep your admiration a secret. Here are ten such wonderfully gifted players who also proved to be of great financial worth to their clubs.

10. Carlos Tevez: Corinthians to West Ham, 2006 – Undisclosed

He got the goal that kept West Ham up at old Trafford in 2007, even though it turned out he was ineligible, which meant he shouldn't have been playing. Either way, his never-say-die play and goals helped the Hammers secure precious Premier League status.

9. Jay Jay Okocha: Paris St Germain to Bolton, 2002 – Free

Brought to the club by Sam Allardyce, he dazzled the Premier League with his silky skills. Bolton fans devised the song 'So good they named him twice' in his honour.

8. Cesc Fàbregas: Barcelona to Arsenal, 2003 – Free

The man who took over from Patrick Viera returned to Barcelona in 2011 for £35million, having won the hearts of all Arsenal supporters with his driving skilful play and crucial goals. He was Arsenal's youngest ever player, aged 16 years and 177 days when he made his debut against Rotherham United in the League Cup in October 2003.

7. Nicolas Anelka: Paris St Germain to Arsenal, 1996 – £500,000

After scoring for fun in an Arsenal shirt and helping the club to a Double, Nicolas Anelka was sold for a hefty £22.3 million profit when he signed for Real Madrid.

6. Alan Shearer: Southampton to Blackburn, 1992 – £3.6 million

Shearer's record at Blackburn (not to mention Newcastle) was astonishing, the prolific centre-forward netting 112 goals for Blackburn in 138 appearances. His goals helped Rovers to win the Premier League in 1995 for the only time in their history.

5. Gianfranco Zola: Parma to Chelsea, 1996 – £4.5 million

Scored some incredible goals, and always played with a smile on his face. Such was his talent and character, Chelsea fans voted him their best player of all time in 1997.

4. Cristiano Ronaldo: Sporting Lisbon to Manchester United, 2003 – £12 million

After David Beckham's departure to Real Madrid, United needed a replacement on the right wing. Step forward, Ronaldo. His partnership with Wayne Rooney up front proved one of the most potent in the League, and not only that – he then made United a whopping £68 million profit when he left for Real Madrid in 2009 for £80 million.

3. Thierry Henry: Juventus to Arsenal, 1999 – £10.5 million

Scored some fantastic goals and was a major influence in 'the Invincibles', the unbeaten Arsenal side of 2003/4, Henry netting 30 goals in the campaign. Arguably, one of the best players to grace the Premier League.

2. Dennis Bergkamp: Inter Milan to Arsenal, 1995 – £7.5 million

Bergkamp was signed by Bruce Rioch, but it was Arsène Wenger who undoubtedly got the best out of the Dutchman, who set the League alight with his vision and skill. His dietary habits and all-round professionalism exerted a huge influence on all footballers and changed the game for ever.

1. Eric Cantona: Leeds to Man United, 1992 – £1.2 million

United hadn't won the League for 26 years until Cantona strolled into Old Trafford. While he had his controversial moments (kung fu kicking a fan), he scored some of the best Premier League goals ever and thrilled crowds everywhere with his imperious skills.

Best transfer bargains

Sometimes we knock the wheeler-dealer manager, but when we see their players blossom into something special we envy their managerial approach. Why pay a fortune when you can use the scouting system to hunt the little gems who may one day be inscribed in club history?

10. Paolo Di Canio

Having made a name for himself pushing over referee Paul Alcock, the Italian parted with Sheffield Wednesday, with West Ham taking him for £1.75m. Proving a massive hit, he did nothing but score fine goals.

9. Ole Gunnar Solskjaer

The baby-faced assassin will forever be remembered for the winning goal against Bayern Munich in 1999. He also scored 126 goals in 336 games for United, many of them coming from the bench. He only cost £1.5m!

8. Thierry Henry

Having sold Nicolas Anelka, Arsène looked for another bit of shrewd dealing in 1999. Picking up a French winger called Henry for £11m from Juventus may have pulled the purse strings at the time but the rest is history. Bargainous.

7. Nicolas Anelka

For a mere £500,000, Arsenal was Anelka's second career destination. He was offloaded two years later for a whopping £22.3m to Real Madrid, after which he began building an impressive list of clubs to his name.

6. Steve Bull

Moving from West Brom for £65,000 to local rivals Wolves in 1986, Steve Bull became a Molineux hero and a goal machine netting 306 times including 18 hat-tricks.

5. Peter Schmeichel

£550,000 was all it cost to acquire the then Brondby keeper in 1991. Schmeichel went on to be the finest goalkeeper in the English game. A tenth of the fee Serie A club AS Bari paid for Villa's David Platt that same year.

4. Alan Shearer

£3.6m secured Shearer's move from Southampton to Blackburn. Finding the net 112 times and taking Rovers to the League title, he was then sold to Newcastle for a record fee of £15m.

3. Kevin Keegan

£35,000 was all it cost Liverpool to take Keegan from Scunthorpe. Scoring 100 goals, voted European player of the year, twice, winning three First Division titles, two UEFA Cups, two FA Cups and the European Cup doesn't seem a bad return.

2. Peter Shilton

Brian Clough jumped at the chance to get Shilton into his newly promoted Nottingham Forrest side. They went on to win the League and two European Cups. All for £250,000.

1. Dixie Dean

Moving from Tranmere to neighbours Everton for a price of £3,000, Dean went on to score 383 goals in 433 games. He even netted 60 times in one season!

Most overvalued transfers

Want to make billions? Then simply find out why some players thrive at clubs and others flop terribly. Here are ten players who perhaps now wish they had not made that move.

10. Joleon Lescott: Everton to Manchester City, 2009 – £24m

The English centre-back cost Manchester City £24m in the summer of 2009. Despite looking impressive for Everton, he's still not a regular in the Manchester City XI.

9. James Milner: Aston Villa to Manchester City, 2010 – £26m

Manchester City were famous for overspending on players, but £26m might be their biggest overvaluation. James Milner has impressed when he's played, but now 26 has still not become a regular in the City starting team.

8. Zlatan Ibrahimovic: Inter Milan to Barcelona, 2009 – £54m + Samuel Eto'o

When Barcelona paid £54m for Ibrahimovic and gave them Samuel Eto'o as part of the deal, Inter Milan must have been in seventh heaven. Whilst Eto'o continued scoring for fun, Zlatan found it very tough fitting into a Barcelona team, although he did manage to score 16 goals in his first and only season. He was moved on to AC Milan on loan for a season, and then in the summer of 2011 Milan signed him for €24m.

7. Anderson Luís de Abreu Oliveira: Porto to Manchester United, 2007 – £27m

When you sign a 19-year-old for £25m, you expect something special and, let's be honest, Anderson hasn't really delivered. After breaking into the Porto team he won the League twice, Portuguese Cup and Super Cup. Since moving to United, he has picked up a lot of silverware but has failed to become a regular starter for the team.

6. Juan Veron: Lazio to Manchester United, 2001 – £28.1m

Manchester United signed Juan Veron from Lazio for a huge £28.1m in July 2001. Veron scored seven goals in 45 appearances and, although Sir Alex called him one of the best players in the world, he manifestly failed to live up to the expectations that surrounded him. He did win the League with Manchester United, but injuries blighted that campaign. He proved to be more of a success in the Champions League, scoring four goals in one campaign. After two seasons, he signed for Chelsea for £15m. Must have been the Manchester rain.

5. Robinho: Real Madrid to Manchester City, 2008 – £32.5m

Manchester City signed Robinho on transfer deadline day when they snapped him up for £32.5m from Real Madrid. He scored 16 goals in 48 appearances. But his performances left a lot to be desired and his last act for Manchester City came when he scored against Scunthorpe in January 2010 in the FA Cup. He then went to Santos on loan before making a move over to AC Milan in 2010.

4. Andrei Shevchenko: AC Milan to Chelsea, 2006 – £30m

Another player who has worn Chelsea's number 9 shirt and not lived up to his price tag. They signed the Ukrainian striker in the summer of 2009. In his time at Chelsea, he played 30 League games and only scored nine goals. His return for Milan had been 127 goals in 193 games. After his spell at Chelsea, he returned to Milan shortly and then went back to where it all started with Dynamo Kiev.

3. Jordon Henderson: Sunderland to Liverpool, 2011 – £20m

Only 20 when he made the move to Liverpool, Henderson had made 79 appearances for Sunderland, the team he supported as a boy, scoring five goals. He was viewed as one of the game's most exciting prospects but has struggled to make any kind of impact since signing to Liverpool.

2. Fernando Torres: Liverpool to Chelsea, 2011 – £50m

Torres' record for Liverpool was exemplary – 65 goals in 91 League games, many of them superlative examples of the art of goal-scoring. Just over a year later, after a £50m move to Chelsea, Fernando Torres had only seven goals to his name.

1. Andy Carroll: Newcastle to Liverpool, 2011 – £35m

Andy Carroll was the hero of Tyneside. In the 2009/10 season, Newcastle were in the Championship and Carroll scored 19 goals in all competitions. In his first full season in the Premier League with newly promoted Newcastle, he had scored 11 goals by Christmas. Which is when Liverpool came knocking. Flush with the 50 million they had picked up for Torres, Liverpool handed over suitcases of cash to secure the big man. Sadly, after just over a year at the club, Carroll only had eight goals to his name and it was rumoured that Newcastle had bid to get him back in January 2012.

For ten million.

Controversial transfers

Nothing angers fans more than when their players head off to play for a rival. Footballers experience the taunting and derision that accompanies such moves for an awfully long time. Especially when the player in question has been at the club long enough to understand its significance. Here are ten transfers that still rankle with the faithful.

10. Nicky Barmby

Making the £6m move from Everton, Nick Barmby was the first player to have switched from Everton to Liverpool since 1959. After a successful first season, in which Barmby scored the winner against his old club, injury blighted his next season and he was shipped out to Leeds

9. Lee Clark

Beginning his career at Newcastle in 1990, Clark controversially moved to local rivals Sunderland in 1997, infuriating the Newcastle faithful. He was part of the team that won promotion to the Premiership but at the 1999 FA Cup final between Newcastle and Man Utd, Clark was spotted sitting with Newcastle fans, wearing an anti-Sunderland T-shirt. He was instantly dismissed by Sunderland and moved to Fulham before re-joining Newcastle in 2004.

8. Mo Johnston

A fan favourite at Celtic Park, scoring 52 goals in three seasons, Mo Johnston moved to the French club Nantes where he spent two successful seasons. He then announced he would be returning to Celtic. 'Celtic are the only club I want to play for,' said Johnson. Which was true until Rangers under manager Graeme Souness stepped in with a much better financial offer. Johnson instantly switched allegiances, thus incensing fans of both clubs; Rangers fans burnt scarves and threatened to hand back their season tickets. Until Johnson scored the extra-time winner against Celtic and ran to the Rangers end to celebrate.

7. Wayne Rooney

When Rooney left his boyhood side Everton for Manchester United, Evertonians despaired. They soon let their anger be known, but Rooney shrugged his shoulders and proved his transfer price by scoring a hat-trick on his full debut.

6. Denis Law
Spending his best years with Sir Matt Busby at Old Trafford, Denis Law made the move to local rivals Man City on a free transfer having declined an offer from United. He then went on to score the goal that at the time he believed had relegated his beloved team. He didn't know that United were already gone. He retired before the start of the following season after not being guaranteed a first-team place.

5. Roberto Baggio
Having won the UEFA Cup with Fiorentina and endeared himself to the club's fans with his breathtaking skill and modesty, Baggio's move to Juventus was greeted with howls of pain. Fans actually invaded the club's training ground in an attempt to make the star stay. Fifty people were hurt in a street riot that broke out later.

4. Louis Figo
Worshipped at the Nou Camp in his six years there, Figo made the move to Real Madrid in 2000 much to the fury of the Barca faithful. On his return to the Nou Camp, one fan threw a pig's head at him.

3. Ashley Cole
In his biography, Ashley Cole admitted to nearly swerving off the road in anger when his agent told him he had been offered a final £55,000 a week by Arsenal. Cashley Cole - as he was dubbed - was quickly tapped up by money-rich Chelsea and made the move. Arsenal fans responded by forging bank notes replacing the Queen with Ashley's pretty face.

2. Sol Campbell
He once said he would never leave for Arsenal and throughout his final season at Spurs resisted all offers, saying he would decide when the time was right. The deal was done soon after and Campbell moved to Arsenal on a free transfer, negotiating a hefty wage packet in the process. Spurs fans have called him a Judas ever since.

1. Carlos Tevez
'Welcome to Manchester' was the famous board Manchester City had erected when they took Tevez off United's books. At the street parade to celebrate Man City's capture of the title, Tevez wore a T-shirt saying 'RIP, Sir Alex', a reference to Ferguson's quote that City would never win the title 'in his lifetime'. Tevez apologised the next day.

Craziest transfer rumours

Such is the fans' devotion to their clubs and to the game, the media are more than happy to spoon-feed them the most outrageous tosh, safe in the knowledge that, rather than pull them up vociferously, they will be back the next day looking for even more breathtaking stories. Here are ten of our favourites.

10. From Juventus to Rangers
The *Daily Record* reported that Rangers were bidding €10 million for Juventus striker David Trezeguet. This was rubbished almost instantly by the player's agent.

9. Carlton Cole and Torres the new Anfield Dream Team
The last day of the summer transfer window of 2010 saw the *Daily Mail* report that Roy Hodgson was after Carlton Cole to be the man to partner Fernando Torres. Apparently, Liverpool were only willing to pay £7 million but West Ham wanted £10 million.

8. Vieira to North London (as in Tottenham, North London)
Back in 2009, the *Telegraph* suggested Tottenham were pondering an ambitious bid for Patrick Vieira, and had Harry Redknapp saying that Vieira actually wanted to join Tottenham. As if.

7. Napoli in for Reo-Coker
April 2011 saw Sky Sports report that up-and-coming Italian giants and Champions League participants Napoli were chasing Aston Villa midfielder Nigel Reo-Coker. He ended up signing for Bolton.

6. Eto'o to Kuruvchi
In July 2008, Eto'o was plying his trade at Barcelona when rumours started flying about that he was to sign for Uzbekistan side Kuruvchi. Nope, we've never heard of them either – but they were seemingly the source of the rumour, with their chairman claiming that 'the defining moment of the transfer was not money, but the friendly mutual relations between the management of our club and Barcelona.' Barca immediately denied this, and the following season Eto'o signed for Inter.

5. Del Piero to Loftus Road
Juventus striker Alessandro Del Piero has played for the same club for 19 years, the Ryan Giggs of Serie A if you like. So where better to end his career than... Loftus Road?! In March 2012, multiple sources reported that QPR had expressed an interest in the forward. However, this rumour may not be as crazy as it appears. A free agent at the time of writing, Del Piero himself has come forward and said that he is not ready to retire just yet. Watch this space... or maybe the starting line-up for QPR in the 2012/13 season!

4. Juventus for Wickham
London's *Metro* reported that Arsenal and Tottenham were rivalled by Juventus for the signature of Connor Wickham. He ended up signing for Sunderland.

3. Bellamy to manage Cardiff
In May 2011, the *Daily Mail* and the *Guardian* reported that Craig Bellamy was favourite to replace Dave Jones as Cardiff manager, after the club endured yet another play-off failure.

2. Blackburn to buy Adebayor
The *Mirror* stated that Blackburn Rovers were approaching Manchester City striker Emmanuel Adebayor as part of a £30 million spending spree. Madness.

1. Raul to Ewood Park
July 2011 saw the *Mirror* and the *Daily Mail* suggesting that Real Madrid and Spain legend Raul would be plying his trade at Ewood Park. The Blackburn Rovers chairman is clearly ambitious, but that's just ridiculous.

Craziest ever actual transfers

Most transfers are smooth and, in some cases, inevitable. Others, though, can either be highly controversial or just plain surreal, and those are the ones we like the best. Here are ten that got the football world talking, overexcited or extremely underwhelmed.

10. Andy Booth: Sheffield Wednesday to Tottenham

Unfortunately, if you ask any Spurs fan for his list of all-time bad players, Mr Booth's name will be somewhere near the top. He scored a resounding zero goals in four games for Spurs when on loan back in 2001.

9. David Bellion: Sunderland to Manchester United

Fergie was linked with the Black Cats reserve striker through the whole of the 2002/3 season and finally got his man. Bellion started off well but by Christmas was languishing in the reserves. A year later, he was back home in France.

8. Julian Faubert: West Ham to Real Madrid

Faubert joined West Ham from Bordeaux in 2007 for £6 million and was not what you would call a roaring success. Ex-Spurs boss Juande Ramos then brought him to Real Madrid until the end of the season with an option to buy. That deal was seriously put in doubt when Faubert was pictured asleep on the subs bench.

7. Zico: Flamengo to Udinese

Zico was named the 'White Pelé' by his numerous fans. Many considered him to be the best player in the world, and AC Milan and Juventus dutifully came knocking in the early 1980s. Zico ignored them and moved to Udinese for £2.5 million in 1983. He scored 19 goals in his first season, but injuries forced him to move back to Flamengo at the end of his second season.

6. Luis Figo: Barcelona to Real Madrid

Only a brave man would make the move from Barcelona to bitter rivals, Real Madrid. Luis Figo was that brave man. In 2000, for a then world record of £37 million, he swapped his Barcelona shirt for the all-white of Madrid. On his return to the Nou Camp, Figo took a corner and was pelted with many objects from the crowd.

5. Luther Blissett: Watford to AC Milan

A million pounds in those days could have bought you pretty much anyone in world football. AC Milan decided Blissett was their man. In his first season, he scored five goals in 30 appearances. Perhaps, he wasn't their man.

4. Allan Simonsen: Barcelona to Charlton

He was a former European Player of the Year, and after three years at the Nou Camp he could have gone to another top European Club. Instead, he chose to play his trade at the Valley, where he scored nine goals in 16 games. Unfortunately, Charlton FC couldn't afford to keep him.

3. Carlos Tevez: Corinthians to West Ham

This move was shrouded in so much mystery that inevitably something had to go belly-up. And it did. Signed on transfer deadline day in August 2006, it was later revealed that Tevez was owned by a third party, thus breaking Premier League rules. West Ham were fined £5.5 million and Tevez then scored the controversial winning goal on the final day of the 2006/7 season at Old Trafford to keep West Ham up. Newly relegated Sheffield United began a lengthy court action against the Hammers. Tevez meanwhile moved to Man United. And then Manchester City. And then played a lot of golf. And then returned to Manchester City. His life is one never-ending crazy transfer.

2. Ali Dia: To Southampton

Ali Dia pretended to Graeme Souness, then Saints boss, that he had 13 caps for Senegal and was George Weah's cousin, Souness bought the story and signed the lad. He replaced Matt Le Tissier against Leeds at the Dell in November 1996, but was so poor he only lasted 50 minutes. He has not been heard of since.

1. Sócrates to Garforth Town

Surely the most unbelievable transfer ever. At the age of 50, the Brazilian footballing legend Sócrates agreed to join Garforth Town of the Northern Counties East League for one month after meeting Garforth's owner, Simon Clifford, who ran a football school in Brazil. Clifford attributed a key part of the club's subsequent promotion to Sócrates, who sadly died seven years later.

Longest transfer sagas

News of an amazing player arriving at your club breaks in the press. Every day you excitedly tune into **606** for future developments. Weeks then turn into months then turn into years and still no movement. Which is when you realise that there was probably no truth in the matter. So you turn on **606** again and news of an amazing player arriving at your clubs starts to break...

10. Samir Nasri to Manchester City

After an impressive season for Arsenal, Samir Nasri left the red of North London for the blue of Manchester in a saga that seemed to go on for ever. You could argue that Arsenal should have offered him an extension to his contract earlier, as it was due to expire in June 2012. Nasri made his move in the final days of the August 2011 transfer window for £24 million. It was a hard summer for Arsenal as this transfer saga was running at the same time as Cesc Fàbregas's. Nasri and Fàbregas were arguably their two best players from the season before.

9. Alan Shearer to Manchester United

A top contender for a transfer that never happened, Alan Shearer had long been linked with a move to Old Trafford. Sir Alex Ferguson first tried to sign Shearer in 1992 when he was at Southampton, but Shearer opted for a move to Blackburn Rovers. Four years later, Ferguson appeared closer to sealing the deal with England's top striker but in the end Shearer would let his heart rule his head, and he signed for his boyhood club Newcastle United for £15m.

8. Thierry Henry to Barcelona

The Arsenal legend cut a frustrated figure after losing out to Barcelona in the Champions League final in 2006, and the striker fuelled speculation over his future after failing to commit to the club in a post-match interview. 'King Thierry' remained at the club for a further season, but supporters feared the sight of their talisman in the shirt of a different team. Despite pleas to stay from several teammates, Henry completed his move to Barcelona in 2007.

7. Cesc Fàbregas to Barcelona

The end to one of the longest transfer sagas in football history saw the Barca kid Cesc Fàbregas return to the Nou Camp. The midfielder left Spain to join Arsenal as a 16-year-old and always dreamt of returning to play for his boyhood club, frustrated with Arsenal's long wait for silverware. Speculation grew that Fàbregas wanted out, and he was pictured in a Barcelona shirt whilst celebrating Spain's World Cup victory, but he stayed at the Emirates for the following season. In the summer of 2011, Arsenal resultantly granted Fàbregas's decision to return home, and he left the club for £35m, signing a five-year deal.

6. Sol Campbell to Arsenal
Another of the longest-running transfer sagas in football was that of Sol Campbell. For two years the Spurs skipper was linked with moves to some of Europe's elite clubs. As his contract drew to its end, the Spurs centre-half was up there as one of the world's best. In 2001, the story came to a dramatic conclusion, with the England international signing to make a controversial move across the north London divide to arch-rivals Arsenal.

5. David Beckham to Real Madrid
David Beckham's eventual move to Real Madrid in 2003 ended a transfer saga that captured the world's attention. The darling of Manchester United edged closer to the exit door after a stray boot to the face, kicked by Sir Alex Ferguson, left Beckham with two stitches above his eye. The manager later left him out of the starting line-up for two key matches, signalling he did not regard him as indispensable. The relationship between manager and player was strained and a move was the only solution. After several months of speculation, Beckham departed England for a new quest in the Spanish capital.

4. Cristiano Ronaldo to Real Madrid
The 'will he, won't he' saga spanned three years and ended in Ronaldo becoming the most expensive player in history. It began when Ronaldo became public enemy number one for his part in England's 2006 World Cup exit. The Portugal player directed the referee to send off Wayne Rooney and pulled off the cheekiest of winks, caught on camera, leaving many to wonder how he could return to the Premier League.

In between, the saga was fuelled with rumours, lies and quirky quotes from the player himself, Manchester United manager Sir Alex Ferguson and Real Madrid director Florentino Perez. After a trophy-filled stay at Old Trafford, which included picking up three Premier League titles and the Champions League, Ronaldo eventually joined Real Madrid in 2009 for a world record fee of £80m.

3. Ashley Cole to Chelsea
Over a year before his confirmed arrival at Stamford Bridge, Ashley Cole, along with two agents, José Mourinho and former Chelsea chief executive Peter

Kenyon, were caught in a secret hotel meeting. The club were subsequently fined by the FA in one of the highest-profile 'tapping-up' cases to date. Arsenal chairman Peter Hill-Wood revealed Cole demanded a triple-wage increase in order to stay at Arsenal, whilst Cole, in his controversial autobiography, said he believed Arsenal had 'fed him to the sharks' during the tapping-up case by not publicly backing him over the incident.

2. Steven Gerrard to Chelsea

Former Chelsea manager José Mourinho had long been an admirer of Steven Gerrard. For consecutive seasons, the then Premier League champions bid £32m to prise the midfielder away from Anfield. Liverpool subsequently rejected the offer but Gerrard, frustrated and going through a spell of uncertainty, admitted he was not 'happy with the progress Liverpool has made', and that 'for the first time in my career I've thought about the possibility of moving on.' It had looked set that Gerrard would swap red for blue but, as he watched television pictures of his shirt being burned outside Anfield's Shankly Gates by dismayed Liverpool supporters, Gerrard had a change of heart. And Gerrard still waits to get his hands on a Premier League medal...

1. Carlos Tevez

The Argentinean striker has never been far from transfer speculation. In fact you can always expect his name to be circulated when the transfer window opens. His move from West Ham to Manchester United ran long into the summer of 2007, and two years later Tevez was at the centre of another saga, opting to join neighbours Manchester City.

After allegedly refusing to warm up for City in a Champions League match in September 2011, Tevez was ousted from first-team action by manager Roberto Mancini. Paris St Germain, AC Milan and Corinthians were a number of clubs linked with Tevez. But still he remains at the Etihad.

Memorable January transfers

The January transfer window was introduced in 2002. Unfortunately, it is easier to name the dud transfers than the great ones. Or is it?

10. Jason Roberts
In January 2012, 606's very own Jason Roberts moved from struggling Blackburn side to Reading. When he arrived, Reading were sitting just outside the play-off positions, but after a brilliant run they ended up going up as champions.

9. Djibril Cissé
Djibril Cissé signed for QPR for a reported £4m from Lazio in January 2012. The striker had quite a start: in every game between January and May he either scored or got sent off.

8. Papiss Cissé
In January 2012, Newcastle paid £8m for the Senegalese forward from Freiburg. On his arrival, he was handed the number 9 shirt – the most important in the club. Cissé did not let them down. He scored 13 goals from January 2012 to the end of the season and bagged goal of the season against Chelsea.

7. Ashley Young
Martin O'Neill forked out almost £10m for Young in 2007, who was playing in a struggling Watford side at the time. It was Aston Villa's record transfer fee, and Young was putting in good but not sensational performances in the Premier League. Young went on to play almost 200 games for the Midlands club, scoring 38 times, and was sold to Manchester United for a fee close to £20m last summer. Villa finished in their lowest position for seven years in 2011/12 after selling Young in the summer of 2011.

6. Luis Suarez
Just hours before Liverpool signed Andy Carroll, they signed Luis Suarez for £22.8m in 2011. Suarez began scoring straight away but made all the wrong kinds of headlines when he was involved in a racism scandal with Man United's Patrice Evra, which resulted in an eight-match ban.

5. Jimmy Bullard
In the first ever January transfer window, Paul Jewell picked up 25-year-old

Jimmy Bullard for £275k from Peterborough. He was instrumental in Wigan's promotion to the Premier League and played a key role in keeping the Latics there. He became a cult hero among football fans and compilers of blooper reels for his on-the-field antics, which included running the length of the field to attempt to score when the floodlights went out in a League Cup semi-final in 2006, and leapfrogging a pile of players during a goalmouth scramble.

4. Henry's return to Arsenal

Henry came back to his beloved Arsenal in January 2012 for a short-term loan deal during the off-season of the MLS (he was playing for New York Red Bulls). Arsenal's club record scorer had scored 226 goals in 370 games and won two Premier League titles and three FA Cups. In his first game back against Leeds in the FA Cup, Arsenal were looking for a goal to finish off the Northerners when Henry pounced in typical fashion and scored the winner.

3. Nicolas Anelka

The journeyman Frenchman had his first spell in England at Arsenal, but he will arguably be best remembered for his time at London rivals Chelsea. He moved to Chelsea in January 2008 for a fee of £15 million, almost double what Bolton had paid for him just two years before. In over four years at the Blues, he formed a formidable partnership with Didier Drogba, won the FA Cup twice and the Premier League once. In 2012, he left Chelsea to see out his twilight years in China, signing for Shanghai Shenhua in April.

2. Andy Carroll

Andy Carroll was Torres' replacement at Anfield and was signed for £35m in 2011. In his first full season for Liverpool, he played 56 games and scored just 11 goals. This compared to his 11 goals in 18 games for Newcastle in 2010/11.

1. Fernando Torres

Chelsea broke the British transfer record when they paid £50m for Fernando Torres from Liverpool in 2011. He then went 24 games without a goal before scoring against Leicester in the FA Cup in 2011/12. His first full season in the League ended with 11 goals in 32 appearances.

Outrageous transfer quotes

It's OK, the rumours are all wrong. My favourite player is going nowhere. Look, he has just held a press conference and committed himself to my club. He is going nowhere, and I have nothing to worry about. At all.

10. Clarence Seedorf: Real Madrid to Inter Milan, 1999

'People can come knocking at my door, offering a lot of money, but I'm not moving. I'm happy in Madrid. I'm at the best club in the world where we are pushing for more trophies.'

Just over a month later, Seedorf signed for Inter Milan for £13.5 million.

9. Marc Overmars: Arsenal to Barcelona, 2000

'I see a lot of good things for Arsenal in the future and I want to be here. Better that clubs are interested in you than no clubs interested in you.'

Four months later, Overmars moved from Arsenal to Barca for an undisclosed fee.

8. Christian Ziege: Middlesbrough to Liverpool, 2000

'My family are happy here. The papers would have me in for a busy summer but I want the fans to know I'm not looking to move anywhere.'

Two months later, Ziege signed for Liverpool for £5.5 million.

7. Fabien Barthez: Monaco to Manchester United, 2000

'I have not received any offer from Manchester. I can tell you I will be at Monaco next season. I'm not trying to leave my club. If a proposition comes up, I will not even take it into account. I'm fine at Monaco.'

Thirteen days later, Barthez signed for United for £7.8 million.

6. Mark Viduka: Celtic to Leeds, 2000

Peter Risdale: 'Just because we have money available, we are being linked with everybody. I wouldn't be surprised to see us linked with Elvis Presley next.'

Viduka moved to Leeds just over a month later for £6m.

5. Luis Figo: Barcelona to Real Madrid, 2000

'I want to reassure fans that Luis Figo, with all the certainty in the world, will be at the Nou Camp on 24 July to start the season, and I want to remind people that whatever is said about other clubs, Luis Figo has a

contract with Barcelona.'
He moved to Real Madrid on 24 July for £37million.

4. Darren Bent

'Do I wanna go to Hull City. No. Do I wanna go to Stoke. No. Do I wanna go to Sunderland. Yes. So stop f****** around, Levy.'

In July 2009, Spurs striker Darren Bent took to Twitter to have a swipe at Tottenham chairman Daniel Levy.

3. Cesc Fàbregas: Arsenal to Barcelona, 2011

Arsène Wenger: 'We are not under any financial need, we are well managed and that gives you one luxury in that you can decide the future of your players.'

Fàbregas moved to Barca not long after.

2. Cristiano Ronaldo: Manchester United to Real Madrid, 2009

David Gill: 'He's not for sale. He's a great player and he's part of our club.'

Ronaldo signed for Real in June 2009 for a world record £80 million.

1. Samir Nasri: Arsenal to Manchester City, 2011

Nasri joined Manchester City in August 2011 for £24million. In a parting shot, he said, 'Arsenal have good fans but they are not that passionate since they moved from Highbury. The City fans remind me of Marseille.'

Worst signings

Nothing worse than your club announcing they have just signed the best player around and have every hope that they will mature into a prizewinner – only to discover they were badly mistaken.

10. Steve Marlet: Lyon to Fulham, 2001 – £11.5m

Newly promoted Fulham looked to Steve Marlet to fire the goals to ensure a solid first year in the top flight. However that looked like a costly mistake. By the 2003/4 season, he was loaned out to Olympique de Marseille for 18 months, with his sizeable contract still being paid by the English team before it was cancelled. Al-Fayed was so incensed about Marlet's failures that he took then-manager Jean Tigana to court for allegedly overpaying players and signing them 'in secret'. Unsurprisingly, the High Court ruled in favour of Tigana.

9. Per Krøldrup: Udinese to Everton, 2005 – £5m

Signed in the summer of 2005, before even playing a game for the club, the Danish defender suffered a groin injury. Krøldrup made his long-awaited debut in a 4-0 Boxing Day defeat to Aston Villa.

8. Massimo Taibi: Venezia to Manchester United, 1999 – £4.5m

Despite a few errors on his debut against Liverpool, Taibi went on to get Man of the Match. He only played another three games, which included a 5-0 defeat to Chelsea. The biggest howler of them all was when he let slip a tame long-range effort from Southampton's Matthew Le Tissier through his legs.

7. Francis Jeffers: Everton to Arsenal, 2001 – £8m

Jeffers did not quite live up to his 'fox in the box' tag, and his time at Arsenal was blighted by injuries. The club won three trophies during Jeffers' spell at the club; he, however, did not pick up any medals. His final appearance for Arsenal came in the 2003 FA Community Shield, coming on as a substitute but then getting sent off. Jeffers later plied his trade in Australia's top flight.

6. Tiago Manuel Dias Correia (Bébé): Vitória de Guimarães to Manchester United, 2010 – £7m

Only five weeks after he signed for Vitória de Guimarães, Manchester United snapped up the Portuguese forward. It was reported that Real Madrid were keen on him, so Sir Alex moved in fast. It is fair to say Bébé hasn't quite cut the mustard and has since been loaned out to Turkish outfit Besiktas.

5. Stéphane Guivarc'h: Auxerre to Newcastle, 1998 – £3.5m

Despite goal-scoring records in France and Europe to add to his World Cup medal, many consider Guivarc'h to be one of the Premier League's worst ever Strikers, in recognition of his brief and unsuccessful spell at Newcastle United.

4. Sol Campbell to Notts County, 2009 – £10m

The former England international made a surprise move to the County Ground, agreeing a five-year £40,000-a-week deal, but after only one game, asked to be released from his deal.

3. Paul Konchesky: Fulham to Liverpool, 2010 – £3m

As one of Roy Hodgson's first buys, the left-back endured a miserable spell at Liverpool. To make matters worse, his mother publicly criticised the club and their fans on her Facebook page. Konchesky was soon shifted out on loan.

2. Alfonso Alves: Heerenveen to Middlesbrough, 2008 – £12m

After watching him scoring goals for fun in Holland, Middlesbrough decided to fork out a hefty sum for the forward, who averaged over a goal a game for Heerenveen. But it never quite worked out for the Brazilian as he scored just four goals in his only full season in England. The club were relegated and Alves was sold.

1. Winston Bogarde: Barcelona to Chelsea, 2000 – free transfer

Before entering Stamford Bridge, the defender enjoyed spells at Ajax and Barcelona. He garnered worldwide attention as, although he received almost no playing time – and no Premier League appearances whatsoever in his last three seasons combined – he preferred to see out his lucrative £40,000-a-week contract. The Blues repeatedly tried to offload Bogarde because of his inflated wages. When there were no takers, Chelsea demoted him to the reserve and youth teams.

GROUNDS

Best grounds

Part of the joy of following your football team is going to places you'd never otherwise visit. Why else go to Hull, Scunthorpe or Burnley but to find a footballing stadium worthy of a RIBA Award? Similarly, we're not sure we'd rush to Gdansk Stadium in Poland or the Kharkiv in the Ukraine if it wasn't for the excuse of 90 minutes of disappointing European Championship football. However there are some beauties which, quite frankly, we'd visit even when a game isn't on. Grounds which are stadia in their own right. Architectural delights with atmospheres to match.

10. Allianz Arena (Bayern Munich/1860 Munchen)

The stadium which hosted the 2012 Champions League Final, and where Bayern Munich and 1860 München play their home matches. The ground is lit up red when Bayern Munich play, blue when 1860 München play, and white when it's used by the German national team. Who needs Blackpool illuminations?

9. Ali Sami Yen Stadium (Galatasaray)

No architectural awards here, but it makes the list because of the atmosphere created by the Galatasaray fans. They are some of the loudest and most hostile fans in world football, and the atmosphere was always electric inside the stadium. Galatasaray moved to a new stadium in 2011.

8. Arena AufSchalke (Schalke)

Similar to the Sapporo Dome, the stadium has a slide-out pitch and a retractable roof. The scoreboard and team sheets screen hang down from the roof of the stadium over the centre of the pitch. It's like something we drew in DT lessons at school. But it's real!

7. Inonu Stadium (Besiktas)

Situated along the banks of the Bosphorus and the Dolmabahce Palace, it makes the list because it has one of the best settings of a football stadium. However, the atmosphere inside, especially in the Kapalı (the home covered end), will leave you in no doubt where the phrase 'hot-blooded' originated. Passionate is all we're saying.

6. Kaohsiung National Stadium (Taiwan)

The Kaohsiung is the first stadium in the world to be powered by the sun. It was originally built for the World Games in 2009, but now the Taiwan national football team use the stadium. It's shaped like a dragon, and we would push it into the top five if they could magic some fire from its mouth as back-up for when the sun goes down.

5. Sapporo Dome (Japan)

One of the host grounds of the 2002 World Cup, the Sapporo was built so that the pitch can be transported outside where the grass can grow naturally. It can take five hours to move the pitch from outside to inside, during which time the less green-fingered among us are concerned some of the grass might die. In its favour, England did beat Argentina there and for that alone we'll give it top five status.

4. The Maracanã (Brazil)

The Maracanã played host to the 1950 World Cup final between Brazil and Uruguay, which ended 2-1 to Uruguay. The result disappointed a rumoured 174,000 Brazilian fans, although former FIFA President Joao Havelange claims there were 220,000 people in attendance. The ground is currently under reconstruction for the 2014 World Cup in Brazil, and the child in us is hoping it is renamed the Macarena.

3. Estadio Municipal de Braga (Braga)

We've tunnelled through the Channel and through the Alps for this stadium, and what a backdrop the cliff face provides Estadio Municipal de Braga. Opened in 2003, it only has two stands due to the cliff, but it has won a number of architectural prizes which is more than we can say for many an away end.

2. Nou Camp (Barcelona)

The ground where every European football fan wants to go – and not just to watch the football. Even on non match days there is a constant stream of people traipsing out of Maria Cristina metro and heading up the road to Camp Nou just to say they've been to the home of Barca. On match days, it has one of the best atmospheres anywhere in the world but it's been pipped to the post by Wembers for sticking the away fans up in the Gods. Worse than St James' Park.

1. The Old Wembley

Who didn't grow up dreaming about playing at Wembley? The Old Wembley, that is. Wembley with its Twin Towers and grey concrete Way. Wembley with its long walk from behind the goal to the front of the Royal Box. Wembley with its low terracing so you couldn't see anything but didn't care because being there was enough. Wembley, its own board game. Correct our memories if you must, but we're sure it was always sunny at the Old Wembley, even in February. And England won the World Cup there. What more could you want from a ground? It has a very special place in our hearts.

Best entry music

It's five to three. Or twenty to eight in the evening. Yes, OK, or five to eight on a Monday. Or five to four on a Sunday. Or... look, we find it hard to keep up ourselves sometimes. Anyway, it's five minutes before the match begins. Tension's building. Everyone is in their seats – unless you're at the Emirates, of course. Prayers are being said. Toes are twitching. Cruel hope is in the heart of every supporter. It's an exciting time, perhaps the most exciting time of the whole match-day experience, in the same way that the anticipation of Christmas Eve is arguably better than the bloated excesses of Christmas Day. As the teams emerge, a song that encapsulates the sense of anticipation bellows from underpowered and annoying speakers. But that doesn't matter, because it's your song. Here are some of our favourites.

10. Man City – 'Blue Moon'
Say what you like about Manchester City buying success. There's a school of thought that says after cleventy million years in the shadow of Old Trafford, their fans deserve it. Some of those fans have been singing along to 'Blue Moon', just before watching Lee Bradbury hoof several golden chances into the back of the North Stand, since it was first written in 1934. Made famous by doo wop legends The Marcels, and now the anthem of the hated, it does at least have authenticity about it: once in a blue moon does, of course, mean very rarely. Perhaps, with the level of Sheikh Mansour's investment, it should change to 'Always' by Bon Jovi.

9. Wolves – 'Hi Ho Silver Lining'
Before they run out in resplendent orange, sorry, 'old gold', this is blasted out with the words changed to 'Hi Ho Wolverhampton'. Actually, if your kit is 'old gold', why pick a song with 'silver' in the title? Surely there's a Spandau Ballet song that's much more appropriate?

8. West Ham – 'I'm Forever Blowing Bubbles'
Made famous by pretty much every major male and female singer in the 1910s and 1920s, it has been the club's anthem since the 1920s, when Charlie Paynter, former manager, introduced it to the club. Famously sung at Highbury by Arsenal fans during 'Lasagnegate', when a Spurs side were defeated by West Ham on the last day of the 2006 season, handing the final Champions League spot to Arsenal.

7. Derby County – 'Steve Bloomer's Watchin''

'Steve Bloomer's Watchin'' is the song that the Derby players have run out to at home games at Pride Park since 1997. Steve Bloomer was a Derby legend and two Derby fans, Mark Tewson and Martyn Miller, wrote the song in his honour. Our friends at BBC Radio Derby threw their support behind it, and it was adopted as the Derby anthem. Full marks from **606** for a properly home-grown song. Premier League teams take note!

8. Newcastle – 'Local Hero'

Mainly chosen because it was written and performed by headbanded Geordie country-rock maven Mark Knopfler, this soaring guitar-driven piece was the theme to a movie called *Local Hero*, which IMDB describes as 'An American oil company sends a man to Scotland to buy up an entire village where they want to build a refinery. But things don't go as expected.' Eerily prescient. Substitute 'American oil company' for 'pile-em-high sportswear company' and 'Newcastle' for 'Scotland' and 'St James' Park' for 'an entire village' and 'a cash-making machine' for 'refinery' and you're near the truth. Howay the lads!

7. Portsmouth – 'Portsmouth'

You know the one. It's the one with a squeezebox and a flute and a tambourine that sounds a bit like 'In Dulci Jubilo'. It's a sort of camp dance number by Mike Oldfield, who also did the theme tune to *The Exorcist*, which is what Portsmouth used to finally get rid of Harry 'we need to be bold in the transfer market' Redknapp.

6. Liverpool and Celtic – 'You'll Never Walk Alone'

To some, it's a joyous affirmation of the power of community. To others, it's a threat. 'You'll Never Walk Alone' was Gerry and the Pacemakers' second number one hit, but originally appeared in the Rodgers and Hammerstein musical *Carousel*, in a scene where the male lead kills himself to avoid capture during a failed robbery. No, it's not set in Liverpool.

5. Everton – 'Theme from *Z Cars*'

Liverpool's other club and their song also has links to crime. We're saying nothing. *Z Cars* was a series about mobile uniformed Merseyside police. It's jaunty. It's catchy. It's based on the folk song 'Johnny Todd'. And it's also used by Watford.

4. Chelsea – 'The Liquidator'

Say what you like about Chelsea, they've got a rousing bit of entrance music. Harry J Allstars' instrumental reggae classic is the song that Andre Villas-Boas hears in his nightmares as he wakes up, sweating.

3. Rangers – 'Follow Follow'

Another fan-created song, this stirring hymn is based on a revivalist hymn. It was created by true fans of Rangers who were against the sectarian chanting that is still heard at some games. Rangers, we salute you! Rangers are still in operation as we go to press.

2. Sunderland – 'Dance of the Knights'

Yes, we know it's the theme to *The Apprentice*, but in terms of sheer anticipation and menace, Prokofiev cannot be beaten. Magnificent.

1. AFC Wimbledon – 'Theme from *Enter the Dragon*'

Sheer genius. Lalo Schifrin's period piece sums up impending battles in a proto-funk fashion. Bruce Lee's last, and finest, film involves an underdog triumphing against all odds, much like, we hope, AFC Wimbledon.

Most dishevelled stands

Due to the number of new stadiums cropping up around the country, finding broken-down, dilapidated stands in England's top 92 clubs is – thankfully – becoming a bit harder in 2012. That said, there have been stands that are universally hated by both sets of fans, their awfulness joining together two very disparate groups of people. Such stands make you feel like you're in the visiting end of hell, but instead of searing flames its much colder and comes complete with muddy tea and a lukewarm pie.

10. Blackfriars End, Edgar Street, Hereford United

This stand was so decrepit it had to be replaced with temporary seating, and then finally closed in 2009. It did not have a cover and was full of concrete, weeds, metal fencing and peeling paint... Nowhere we'd rather be on a cold November evening.

9. North Stand, Roots Hall, Southend United

A converted terrace stand with the seats bolted into the existing concrete, this also has a large number of pillars which block the view of the pitch.

8. Boundary Park, Oldham

Oldham's BP was demolished in 2008 as part of proposed redevelopment. However, that had to be put on hold following the financial downturn and a main stand has not since been rebuilt.

7. West Stand, Withdean Stadium, former Brighton and Hove stadium

This stand offered what we will politely call a 'restricted view'. As one Brighton and Hove fan said, 'Even with the Hubble Space Telescope it would be difficult to make out what was going on at the east end goal.'

6. Milton End, Fratton Park, Portsmouth

Formerly the only stand in the Premier League without a roof, this stand had not had a lick of paint before their promotion to the Premiership. The seats are bolted directly onto the old-style terracing, offering zero leg room.

5. The Silkmen Terrace, Moss Rose, Macclesfield Town

The peeling wooden boards at the back of the stand – and the fact the fans are penned in by big steel fences – bring this stand into the top five of our most dishevelled stands.

4. Paddock/Main Stand, Brunton Park, Carlisle United

Built in 1954, this is the largest football stadium in England which isn't all seated. The corrugated iron roof doesn't cover the whole stand and the terraces leave fans open to elements.

3. Main Stand, Underhill, Barnet

Underhill is the smallest Football League ground in London but manages to somehow have seven stands! Our favourite for most dishevelled is the main stand, which doesn't even run the full length of the pitch – it merely straddles the halfway line.

2. Grandstand, St James' Park, Exeter City

This stand stretches half the length of the pitch and provides an all seated terrace with corrugated iron on the roof. There's nothing like a bit of corrugated iron to make a rain shower sound like a monsoon.

1. East Stand, Vicarage Road, Watford

This stand really lets down the rest of a smart stadium and is expected to be knocked down soon. The only remaining part of the original stadium, it was built in 1922 and then closed in 2008 for health and safety reasons. It makes Watford the only team in the top two divisions not to have four stands open to the public.

Biggest grounds

As venues for one of the world's most popular sports, massive stadiums are crucial to satisfy the fans' need to watch 22 men kick a leather ball around for 90 minutes. **606** went all around the world and got lost in the following stadiums.*

10. Stade de France, Saint-Denis, France – 81,338
The Stade de France is used by both the French national football and Rugby Union teams. The ground hosted the final of the 1998 World Cup final, when hosts France defeated Brazil 3-0. Two years later, the Stade de France hosted the UEFA Champions League, when Real Madrid defeated fellow Spaniards Valencia 3-0, with former England winger Steve McManaman getting on the score sheet.

9. Estadio Santiago Bernabéu, Madrid, Spain – 85,454
One of the most prestigious grounds in football, the Bernabéu is home to nine-time European Cup winners Real Madrid. The ground has hosted the European Cup final on four occasions: in 1957, 1969, 1980, and the UEFA Champions League final in 2010.

8. Wembley Stadium, London, England – 90,000
The 'New Wembley' was opened in 2007 replacing the famed 'Twin Towers', which had been closed in October 2000. The home of English football hosted the 2011 UEFA Champions League final between Barcelona and Manchester United and will also host the 2013 UEFA Champions League final to mark the 150th anniversary of the Football Association. The first English player to score an official goal at the ground was David Bentley with a free kick in an Under 21 fixture against Italy.

7. Soccer City, Johannesburg, South Africa – 94,000
South Africa's impressive stadium hosted the 2010 World Cup final between Spain and the Netherlands. The stadium was designed so that fans are never more than 100 metres away from the action. Nelson Mandela also chose the stadium for his first speech after his release from prison.

6. Estádio do Maracanã, Rio de Janeiro, Brazil – 96,000
Rio de Janeiro's Estadio do Maracanã is one of the most recognisable stadiums

---

* All in the name of research. We wish.

in world football and is forever associated with a whole host of Brazilian greats including Pelé, Sócrates, Rivaldo and Ronaldo. It opened in 1950 for the FIFA World Cup but Brazil lost the final to Uruguay 2-1. The Maracanã will stage the 2013 FIFA Confederations Cup and the 2014 World Cup, as well as the 2016 Olympics and Paralympic Games.

5. Camp Nou, Barcelona, Spain – 98,787

FC Barcelona's stadium is the largest in Europe in terms of capacity. The world's very best players including Lionel Messi, three-time FIFA World Player of the Year (2009-2011), grace the Nou Camp every other week. The stadium hosted the famous 1999 UEFA Champions League final where Manchester United played Bayern Munich and came back from 0-1 down to win 2-1 in injury time.

4. Melbourne Cricket Ground, Melbourne, Australia – 100,000

The MCG is best known as one of cricket's most impressive venues but also plays host to many of the Australian national football team's fixtures. Fans have been known to host barbeques there...

3. Estadio Azteca, Mexico City, Mexico – 111,064

Mexico City's iconic Azteca Stadium is most remembered for the two World Cup finals it hosted in 1970 and 1986. It was also the venue for the 1986 quarter-final between England and Argentina, when the Azteca crowd witnessed the creation of immortal football history as Maradona's 'hand of God' moment was quickly followed by one of the greatest individual goals of all time.

2. Salt Lake Stadium, Bidhannagar, Kolkata, India – 120,000

Salt Lake Stadium is the home of the Indian national team. As well as being host to the Bhangra Boys, the Stadium is also used and shared by four of India's leading football clubs.

1. Rungrado May Day Stadium, Pyongyang, North Korea – 150,000

The May Day Stadium is regarded as the largest stadium in the world by capacity and is home to the North Korean national football team.

Terrace dance crazes

Fans don't just express themselves with songs and chants. Quite often, they invent routines that would not be out of place on *Strictly Come Dancing*. Here are ten of our favourites.

10. The Wenger
The Wenger, most commonly used by Birmingham fans, is a dance move that involves stretching your hands directly in front of you and then flapping them up and down. It's often done to the song 'Let's All Do The Wenger'.

9. The Greque
This dance is pretty similar to the Poznan (see below) but is done facing the pitch by several Greek teams in the style of a Greek wedding. Galatasaray were seen performing the dance (presumably given another name in Turkey) ahead of the 2000 UEFA Cup final against Arsenal. And it isn't just for goal celebrations.

8. The Hokey Cokey
A universal dance move that can be done anywhere and a football ground is no different, the left hand in and left hand out has been at grounds all over the country.

7. Let's all have a disco – generic dance move
Often dancing in a ground is not choreographed at all, believe it or not. It can be just be generic hand pumps and jumping. This is a generic dance move, but it's usually done to the tune of 'Let's All Have A Disco'.

6. The Huddle
Celtic's first team huddle on the pitch was in 1996 and the fans adopted a themed dance as a result. It predates the Poznan and looks very similar in that it involves fans with their arms around each other, not looking at the game.

5. The Bouncy
A Rangers dance, which involves bouncing up and down and shouting 'Bouncy' or 'Let's All Do The Bouncy'. It may lack originality but it's popular among other clubs throughout the world. It's been banned on trains in Glasgow because of the threat of derailment.

4. The Conga

The classic dance move can be seen in football grounds across the country. It's a great dance move for the terraces as it can be used to celebrate or in an ironic way to cheer up fans of teams that are losing. The conga's often done in fancy dress.

3. The Ayatollah

The Ayatollah is dance moved devised by the Cardiff City fans, and it is reminiscent of Michel Jackson's 'Thriller' dance, with some weird hand movements. They even released a song called 'Do The Ayatollah' for their FA Cup final against Cardiff in 1998.

2. The Poznan

Not since the days of the Charleston has a dance craze been named after a city. In 2010, Manchester City found themselves in the same group as Polish outfit, Lech Poznan. City won their home game 3-1, but things would never be the same again. Poznan fans sang and showed off their dance moves during the match, which involved turning their backs on the pitch and bouncing up and down. City fans have had several decades of wanting to turn their back on the pitch and so it was a perfect celebration. It made its City debut against West Brom in early November that year and has been used to celebrate ever since. To confuse the issue a bit, the dance is accompanied by a conga tune.

1. The Mexican Wave

Oddly enough the origins of this seem to lie in US baseball rather than Mexico. It was certainly witnessed at the Los Angeles Olympics in 1984 but really became embedded in popular culture when the World Cup was staged south of the border two years later. It was originally seen as sign of communal joy but if you see it at a football match it's a sure sign that what's on the pitch is spectacularly dull and it gives fans a good excuse to have a stretch. Apparently a wave needs a critical mass of around 30 people to get started and will travel clockwise in the Northern hemisphere and anti-clockwise in the Southern.

Best away journeys

Is there anything worse than travelling miles and miles to support your team only for your heroes to slump to yet another defeat? Well, at least some away games do offer a kind of compensation to help you over the misery, and here are ten of them.

10. Fulham

A trip to Fulham can be one of the best away journeys out there, especially if you're making your own way to the ground, located right on the edge of the River Thames. On a pleasant day it can be idyllic as you leave the Thames Path, head through Bishops Park and into the Putney End of the ground to be met with an away end with one of the best views in the country.

9. Brighton

Who would have thought it would have taken Brighton so long to get their own ground after leaving the Goldstone in 1997? But with the Amex Community Stadium, Brighton finally have their own home and a home to be proud of. Located on the outskirts of Brighton at Falmer, this stadium sits on the edge of the wonderful Sussex landscape and is a dramatic addition to the local skyline.

8. York City

A trip to York is always a pleasant one. The historic capital of the north is easily accessible from all of the country, and the journey into the city along the A19 is an ideal way to get to an away game. If coming via train follow the City walls and cross the river towards York Minster until you reach Bootham and the delightfully old-school Bootham (Kit Kat) Crescent.

7. Torquay United

Torquay's Plainmoor ground is located just outside of Torquay on the English Riviera. As with Newcastle and Blackpool, Torquay is one of those destinations where a weekend away is a must, and where better to spend a weekend than this delightful Devonshire resort. The journey along the A380 passes through historic towns in the South West and, despite now showing its age, Plainmoor is an attractive ground for the lower Leagues.

6. Blackpool

Blackpool has to be on the list. It's still one of the favourite holiday destinations in the country – somehow. The crumbling Victorian resort has an appeal to football fans from all parts as they head up the M6 to the crumbling beauty on the Irish Sea.

5. Bath City
We like our historic spa towns at **606**, and none come more historic than Bath. In the 18th century, it developed into an elegant town with neoclassical Palladian buildings, which blend harmoniously with the Roman baths, and is now a UNESCO World Heritage site.

4. Bristol City
Bristol is one of the most exciting cities in the UK, and a trip to either of the two Bristol clubs is well worth the journey, particularly a trip to Ashton Gate. A number of fan guides recommend taking in the city centre and its cultural waterfront. Bristol is easily accessible from all parts of the country particularly if travelling by train to Bristol Temple Meads station, not to mention easy access provided by the M5 and famous Swing Bridge.

3. Newcastle United
What isn't to like about a city that has the highest number of Gregg's bakeries in the western world? The journey up to Newcastle is one of the longest but also one of the best. Heading through the city centre towards the stadium by coach or by foot, St James' Park – the Sports Direct Arena – rises above the city like a cathedral on a hill.

2. Barcelona
Camp Nou is located close to the Sants district of Barcelona, a city situated between the sea and the mountains, and is one of the most historical, cosmopolitan and avant-garde cities in Spain.

1. Hearts & Hibs
Edinburgh is worthy of any weekend break, never mind watching a game of football! A trip to Scottish Premier League Hearts of Midlothian or Hibernian sees you watching football in one of Britain's favourite cities. Either of these fine Edinburgh clubs offer a great location to watch a game, be that at Tynecastle or Easter Road.

Floodlight failures

They're 134 years old. They're the unsung heroes of night-time football. In fact, they're only ever mentioned when they go wrong. Most of the time, they don't – 999 times out of 1,000, in fact. But when they do go wrong, everything goes wrong.

10. Derby County v Wimbledon, August 1997

Leaving absolutely nothing to chance for your first match at a spanking new stadium is crucial. Especially if you're playing football in the dark. You will need floodlights. Eleven minutes into the second half against Wimbledon at the new Pride Park stadium, out they went, and didn't come back on. The match was abandoned.

9. Dundee v Ayr, March 2012

Pure and simple. No working floodlights, no ball kicked and the game abandoned half an hour before kick-off.

8. Lots of games in Poland

In an otherwise unremarkable game between Zagłebie Lubin and Arka Gdynia in Poland, the floodlights went out in both the home leg and the away leg. Gdynia claim the moral victory; they made the repairs in two minutes, whereas in Lubin the delay was over an hour. By coincidence – or was it – the only other top-flight match in Poland on that day – the Great Derby of Silesia between Ruch and Górnik Zabrze – was also beset by floodlight problems. In 2007, Poland were playing Kazakhstan at Legia in a Euro qualifier. You guessed it. Floodlight failure. In the same year in a parallel event to the Derby County debacle, Zagłebie Sosnowiec were at home to Lech Poznan in their newly refurbished stadium, play was delayed because of... a 30-minute floodlight failure. Maybe think twice before booking that Polish electrician.

7. Wimbledon v Arsenal, December 1997

An electrician, doubtless sucking air in over his teeth and muttering about labour costs, finally put the crowd at Selhurst Park out of its misery at the third attempt to restore power. Wimbledon owner Sam Hammam commented at the time, 'This shouldn't be happening. Once was bad enough, the second wasn't pretty, and this is getting near a disaster. Unless we stop it there will be shame on the game. We are all embarrassed by it.'

6. Motherwell v Hibernian,December 2011

Someone should call Jamie Redknapp – there was a footballing scenario in 2011 where the words 'literally on fire' could be used accurately. The fire in question was in the generator room at Fir Park during Hibs' new manager Pat Fenlon's first game and which in turn caused the floodlights to fail.

5. Cheltenham v Southend, November 2010

Not a great night for League One football. This game lasted just 66 minutes before the floodlights failed, and the other two fixtures lasted a combined total of nine minutes due to waterlogged pitches at both Hartlepool and Rochdale.

4. Spurs v Luton Town, November 1991

If it hadn't been for a 15-minute floodlight outage when they were a goal down, Spurs were heading for an embarrassing home defeat in this fixture back in 1991. However after 15 minutes of rest, goals from Gary Lineker and Scott Houghton rescued Spurs' blushes.

3. Aldershot v Southend United, December 2011

There is nothing better than confusing messages being heard over a tannoy when the floodlights go out. A classic example of the left hand not knowing what the right hand is doing came on Boxing Day 2011, when players and supporters were told three times the match would be restarted following flickering floodlights in the first half. They were then told four times that the match was going to be called off. It was.

2. Marseille v AC Milan, March 1991

It's not just in the English Leagues or in Scotland where it happens. Le Floodlight failure classique stopped a 1991 European Cup match between a Marseille side featuring Chris Waddle and a classic AC Milan side featuring Baresi, Costacurta, Maldini, Rijkaard, Ancelotti and Gullit. Although not that classic, as they were a goal behind and refused to take the pitch again after the floodlights were fixed. Marseille were awarded a 3-0 victory.

1. Charlton v Liverpool, 1999: The one that never happened

In Asia, if a match is abandoned after half time, the score stands, unlike in Britain, where it's void. That was the motivation behind a Malaysian betting syndicate who'd managed to bribe a Charlton Athletic security supervisor into giving the Malaysians access to the generator room, where they hoped to install remote control devices to cut the power after half time. Police were tipped off and happily the game went ahead without disruption. Charlton won 1-0.

Best commentary positions

For football commentators, the office is the football stadium. Located in prime locations around the grounds, the press box is where great commentary moments are born. Less comfortable than you think, leg room is at a premium, and lord help you if you need the toilet during play. No gossiping round the water cooler here, it's all about the coffee machine at half time. And far be it for us to let refreshments on offer sway our judgement... Here are our favourite 'offices'.

10. Villa Park
For years, the perfect commentary position bang on the halfway line – until they decided in their wisdom to move it away from the halfway line. Fortunately, the standard of the food has remained top notch and it's one of those grounds you always make sure you have a good few hours of 'prep' time in – to get ready for the game, obviously.

9. Millennium Stadium
A stadium with state-of-the-art facilities and a great view from the box to boot, this was a ground that rated highly amongst our commentators. No mention of the grub, though...

8. Emirates Stadium
Arsenal manage two entries in our list, so they obviously have their priorities right when planning their grounds. This is not the last time you will read about the food in this list... really, it's a wonder that commentators can lift the microphone to their mouth in between bites! Please note that at the Emirates it's all about the ice cream.

7. Feethams
Feethams was Darlington FC's much-loved home for 120 years and when the club moved in 2003 many of the fans were devastated. If their experience was anything like our commentator's, though, we can fully understand their upset. 'In the old TV gantry, we used to lower down a rope and the pie shop underneath would send up pie and peas for half time!'

6. St James' Park
Jackie 'Wor' Milburn was a legendary Newcastle centre forward and their second-highest goal-scorer of all time. The Magpies decided to name their

then newly built West Stand in honour of this adored player, and it is here that the press and commentators are housed to oversee the action on the pitch. Our man with the mic loves the view from the window of this particular media box.

5. Chelsea

The quality of the catering seemed to be a major factor in how our commentators rated their experiences in the media box – baffling really, until you consider the fact that, while the quality of the football may be unreliable, at least the food comes up with the goods. So maybe next time you hear 'what a beauty that was', the pundit is referring to the culinary delights of the pie he was nibbling on at Stamford Bridge.

4. Anfield Centenary Stand box

Being suspended from the roof of a stadium certainly isn't an ideal position for those who have a fear of heights, but the Centenary Stand box was a big favourite amongst our team. No flags or banners obscuring your view, no worries about a particularly vocal fan interrupting your commentary... in fact, the only company you'd be likely to have would be a couple of lonely pigeons.

3. White Hart Lane (mid-tier halfway line)

'Front row of the mid-tier halfway line! Not the gantry!' This commentator was very keen to emphasise the point, which just goes to show that even in football commentary, the right position is everything. There is also the gantry commentary position which you will be familiar with from the aerial view shots seen on *Match of the Day*. Perfect for seeing all the action.

2. Highbury

For Arsenal fixtures 'back in the day', the 5 live team would have to don a collar and tie when commentating at Highbury as they would be camped out in the Director's Box. Would you like a canapé to go with your post-match analysis, sir?

1. Man City

Our man in the know didn't seem too bothered about whether he could see the action on the pitch (you know, so he could do his job effectively) but was more concerned about having a clear view of the 'delicious' carvery generously provided by the club for media staff! A comfortable working environment makes a big difference to the working day.

Best groundsmen

Part scientist, part magician, these tanned heroes are literally responsible – and we actually mean literally, not in the Jamie Redknapp 'metaphorical' sense – for ensuring that our gilded millionaires have a level playing field. Times have moved on from the days when a man called Alf would walk across the pitch on a Friday with a fork, aerating the soil, and tossing some builders' sand into the wet bits. These days it's all plant physiology and advanced turf machinery qualifications. So **606** salute the people who ensure our beautiful, modern, free-flowing game runs as best it can.

10. Vincent Vlaminck
Vincent is Anderlecht's Head Groundsman and deserves to be in the list because of what he has had to deal with. Anderlecht's ground – the Constant Vanden Stock Stadium – is a problem, because its sides and corners are hidden from light and wind, which means the grass begins to die in the winter, like Tottenham's title challenges. This has seen Vlaminck take up a system that uses synthetic fibres to ensure that the pitch stays healthy.

9. Rico Salomons and Remy de Milde
Between them, our noble strike duo take care of Feyenoord's pitch. The De Kuip stadium is almost 70 years old, but the pitch has been re-laid just five times in that period, though it's hosted more European Finals than any other. Controversially, the club have recently moved back to natural grass, after a spell with synthetic fibres.

8. Paul Burgess
Paul is one of British groundsmanship's biggest exports, currently plying his trade in La Liga as Real Madrid's Head Groundsman. The young Paul joined the club that loves signing them young – Arsenal – in 1996 as an 18-year-old and was made Head Groundsman just four years later. He was nominated for Premier League Groundsman of the Year in every year he was at the club, winning it three times.

7. Paul Ashcroft
From one Paul to another: Ashcroft took over from Burgess as Arsenal's Head Groundsman in 2009. Since their move to the Emirates, Arsenal have been at the forefront of discovering new ways of maintaining and developing pitches. Paul won Premier League Groundsman of the Year in 2009 and 2012 for his

work on the Emirates' beautiful 'bowling green' surface.

6. Sander Xavier

If there's one holy temple to pure football that requires a pristine carpet-like surface, it's Barcelona's Camp Nou. The dizzy heights achieved by Pep Guardiola's all-conquering side could only have been achieved by a purity of purpose – pass, pass, pass – matched by their Groundsman – grass, grass, grass. Barca's large pitch is also used for countless concerts and other public events over the years, but the pitch still looks perfect.

5. Darren Baldwin

Tottenham's Groundsman has won a title more recently than Spurs. Darren is always a fixture in nominations, and won Premier League Groundsman of the Year in 2007. He has a tough job, as White Hart Lane is covered in a lot of shade – and not just the type that's been casting a shadow over Tottenham from the other end of the Seven Sisters Road.

4. Terry Forsyth

There is an Anfield byelaw that states that 50 per cent of people working for Liverpool must be called 'Terry'. Liverpool's Principal Groundsman joined the club aged 17 as an apprentice and is in charge of keeping Anfield carpet-like, as well as Melwood and the Youth Academy.

3. Dan Duffy

Dan is Head Groundsman at Swansea, who in 2011/12 won plaudits for their positive, passing game – showing that you don't need to park the bus as a promoted side to retain top-flight status. Paul won the IOG Professional Football Groundsman of the Year award in 2009 for his great work at the Liberty Stadium and also won Football League Groundsman of the year at the end of the 2008/9 season.

2. Jonathan Calderwood

Aston Villa's Groundsman was in the running to win the Premier League Groundsman of the Year award for the second consecutive year in 2011. Take That concerts held at Villa Park that summer meant that Calderwood and his team had just four weeks to prepare the pitch for the new season, rather than the usual 12 weeks.

1. Alan Ferguson

Alan was the Ipswich Groundsman for 12 years, winning Groundsman of the Year seven times in that period, making him the Pep Guardiola of groundsmanship. He's also a wise man, turning down the offer to become Head Groundsman at the hapless New Wembley. He did leave eventually, though: in July 2011, Ferguson became Head Groundsman at St George's Park, the FA's National Football centre in Burton.

Best music when a team scores

For many, the only sweet music you want to hear is the percussive hiss of ball hitting nylon string, followed by the deafening roar of your fellow supporters. But some teams do attempt to gild the lily by playing some actual music at those moments. We at **606** are ambivalent about such practices and prefer the sweet music of applause, but each to their own. Here's our favourite celebratory tunes.

10. Scotland – '500 Miles'
Did you know The Proclaimers are Scottish? It's true. You learn something new every day. They were originally called The McProclaimers and used to perform wearing kilts made of defeated English 13th-century soldiers' hair. (Not really.) Every time the Scots score a goal at Hampden, the crowd breaks into a rendition of '500 Miles'. It's a special sound not often heard.

9. Bolton – 'I Feel Good'
During the Allardyce era, it was heard pumping out at the Reebok after yet another soulless punt into the channels had paid off.

8. Norwich City – 'Samba De Janeiro'
Was there ever a city less like Rio de Janeiro? Apart from Stoke, of course. The sub-tropical paradise of Norwich, where locals stretch out in the searing sun, next to a flooded gravel pit, to watch tanned athletes perform trillions of kick-ups before repairing to a beach bar for a Caipirinha. For a few seconds at least, this flat corner of East Anglia is transformed into the Maracanã.

7. Middlesbrough – 'Reach Up (Papa's Got A Brand New Pigbag)'
There's not a name in the world that cannot be improved by the replacement of the letter 'S' with a 'Z'. The Perfecto Allstarz felt that Pigbag's deathless funk classic could be improved by some rudimentary house beatz, and Middlezbrough felt that was what was needed to ice the cake of a Boro goal.

6. Ipswich 'Chelsea Dagger'
Nice and easy to sing along to, with its durp, durpy durp, durpy durp, durpy durpy durp chorus, it sounds exactly like a pub full of Ipswich fans before a game.

5. Blackpool – 'Glad All Over'

'Itch All Over' might be more appropriate after a night in one of Blackpool's less salubrious flophouse B and Bs.

4. Watford – 'Chase The Sun'

Italian dance group Planet Funk's anthem is well-known to Darts fans, but Watford also use the song when they score at Vicarage Road. Which means that this is a song that... wait for it... GETS THE HORNETS BUZZING.

3. Leicester – 'Fire'

Serge Pizzorno and Tom Meighan from Kasabian are lifelong Leicester fans. They are like the Edward Lear of mainstream indie rock, spouting poetical verses about effigy burning and spilling guts on wheels. Which they then want to taste. Why would you wanna taste guts? Guts, we should add, that have been on a wheel? What's wrong with a match-day burger, like everyone else?

2. Borussia Monchengladbach – 'Maria'

The only song on the list that sounds terrible on record and amazing when shouted from the terraces. A product of camp German techno band Scooter, 'Maria' goes doop doop doop doodoodoodoo doop. Over and over again. Magnificent.

1. Fleetwood Town – 'Theme from *Captain Pugwash*'

The Cod Army are currently in the Conference, but have secured promotion to League Two for next season, where 'The Trumpet Hornpipe', as it is actually known, will ring out around Highbury Stadium whenever they score. Highbury Stadium is, of course, almost *in* the sea, hence the maritime connection.

Best names for grounds

In the money-soaked world of football, everything is up for sale, including your ground's name. Who would have thought it? I mean, in our day, you didn't have all this...

10. The Foote Field
Does what it says on the tin. The venue of home games for Edmonton FC who play in the North American Soccer League.

9. The Old Spotted Dog Ground
Home of Clapton FC, who play in the Essex Senior League. Attempts to rename it the 'Lesser spotted fan ground' have come to nought.

8. Dick's Sporting Goods Park
Get that into a chant, if you can. It's the home of the Colorado Rapids, and you'll never guess who sponsors the stadium.

7. Wankdorf Stadium
As if the name wasn't enough, it was the home ground of 'Young Boys', Berne. Sadly, the ground was demolished in 2001 and replaced by the far more boring Stade de Suisse.

6. Gay Meadow
Easily the most bucolic and least threatening name in English football. It conjures up images of picnics and wasp stings and times gone by. It's time has gone by: it was floored in 2007. The New Meadow now exists and the name isn't a reflection of the playing surface.

5. The Keepmoat Stadium
Home grounds are often referred to as a fortress. Doncaster's is named after parts of one.

4. The King Power Stadium
Formally the Walkers Stadium and occasionally known as the crisp bowl, Leicester City's ground is now named after a Thai travel company, though you'd never guess that from the name. We're guessing here that there's a potato-based snack takeover going on by a resurgent KP – don't let the name fool you.

3. The KC Stadium

Sadly not sponsored by the main man of the Sunshine Band – Sunshine and Hull don't usually go together.

2. The Weston Homes Community Stadium

Colchester's new gaff and built on the site of the former Cuckoo Farm. Sadly, the stadium clock wasn't altered accordingly.

1. The Sports Direct Arena

Known to the locals as St James' Park, Newcastle. The name change is appropriate as football is more about commerce these days than saintly behaviour. And at least it's a sports sponsorship unlike some we could mention.

Old-fashioned grounds

The trend may be for spacecraft-style mega-arenas with hot and cold running wi-fi and organic nut burgers brought to your seat by lifelike robots, but this country boasts dozens of proper stadiums. By 'proper' we mean four stands. At most. We mean stadiums with one ladies' toilet. And cold water, if there's running water at all. We mean stadiums that *actually move* when a goal is scored. You can keep your Lego bowls. What we want is four metal sheds overlooking the field, where the wind blows colder inside the ground than it does outside. The footballing equivalent of Route One – here are the **606** team's favourite old-fashioned grounds.

10. Exeter City – St James' Park
Formed in 1904, Exeter City have always played at St James' Park. Prior to this, the land was used for fattening pigs. Despite playing a very solid 4-4-2, the pigs regularly met an unfortunate end. Some may say the porkers were of more use than the players in the 2003–2008 Exeter sides, when they dropped into the Conference.

9. Burnley – Turf Moor
This ground couldn't be more northern if it was shaped like a whippet and had its own pigeon loft. It's even got 'moor' in its name. When it rains at Turf Moor, notice how it passes your face horizontally. You need a hat and gloves here in August.

8. Luton Town – Kenilworth Road
Did we say a maximum of four stands? We meant a maximum of five. To get in to the Oak Road End you enter the ground through what looks like your friendly local neighbourhood garage but is in fact a gate in the middle of a row of terraced houses.

7. Accrington Stanley – Crown Ground
'Who are they?' is one question it is obligatory to ask when the name 'Accrington Stanley' is mentioned. Younger readers should ask their mums and dads. Other questions should be: Is it possible to have two main stands where one would normally sit, with a gap in the middle? Can you compensate for the slope in your pitch by having fewer rows of seats at one end? Is it acceptable to have your terracing *behind* your seating? The answer to the last three is 'yes'. The answer to the first one? Exactly.

6. Cowdenbeath – Central Park

Central Park normally conjures up images of sophisticated New Yorkers enjoying pastrami sandwiches in the sun. Central Park stadium in Cowdenbeath does not, it would be fair to say. With a stock car racing track around the edge of the pitch, and floodlights handily restricting the view, Central Park is a proper ground. One of the stands is even called the Old Stand.

5. Macclesfield Town – Moss Rose

Famed for its old-fashioned yet oddly futuristic main stand – which supports its roof despite having no supporting pillars running across the front of it. The Silkmen's Ultras congregate in the Star Lane End, where, like at Accrington's Crown Ground, the terracing is behind the seating.

4. Portsmouth – Fratton Park

At the time of writing, Pompey were still in the Championship, having been fined ten points for entering administration. Their financial woes cannot be attributed to wild spending on their stadium. Like a suburban bank manager, over gin and tonics and the golf club, Portsmouth is strangely proud of having a 'mock Tudor façade'. One of the stands only had a roof added for the 2007/8 season, but the atmosphere here is always top-notch.

3. Dagenham & Redbridge – London Borough of Barking and Dagenham Stadium

Any stadium which has a stand known as 'the Sieve' due to its leaky roof has to make the list. And being situated next to the Sterling Works factory, known for its manufacture of armaments, gives it a hardworking northern edge we wouldn't necessarily associate with Essex's finest.

2. Brentford – Griffin Park

If you're given lemons, make lemonade. If you're under the Heathrow flight path, sell advertising space on the roof of one of your stands, to catch the eye of passengers landing at the airport, which is only a few miles away. The view from the seat of your 747 is probably better than that from the rear of the Braemar Road Stand, which looks more like a long flat cave than a terrace. The Brook Road Stand is known as the Wendy House.

1. Fulham – Craven Cottage

Fulham have had ten grounds overall, second only to QPR in the footballing nomad stakes, but they settled at Craven Cottage 1896. The original 'cottage' stood where the centre circle now is; the present-day 'cottage' is a pavilion designed by Archibald Leitch in 1905, along with the astonishing redbrick façade of the Johnny Haynes Stand. Outside that is a statue of legendary inside forward Johnny Haynes. Other club legend Michael 'Moonwalking' Jackson, is commemorated by a statue in the ground which is only visible if you're seated in the Riverside Stand.

Best services

The only highlight (listening to **606** aside) of a 300-mile return trip to see your team lose on FA Cup third round day is pulling into the services for a visit to the lavatories and some refreshments. Not to mention eyeballing the other rival supporters' coaches when the coach companies have failed to coordinate 'visiting hours'. They rescue us from boredom, hunger and the fan who had one too many dribbling on your shoulder. The respite may be temporary, but the 'Services 1m' sign should never be underestimated.

10. Hilton Park, M6, between J10a and J11

It may be home to the same bland, generic, soulless brands but it is also one of the best places to people-watch in the country. Don't be surprised if rival fans start chanting towards each other over overpriced organic coffee. 'You don't know what you're doing!'

9. Clacket Lane services, M25, between J5 and J6

They feature Roman remains that were found when the site was constructed, with one display called 'The History of Titsey'. MUST BE A JOKE IN THERE SOMEWHERE!!!!

8. M4 Cardiff West

The first services when you cross the Severn Bridge, Cardiff West services are a relief to anyone with a fear of high winds or heights. They also featured in a Christmas Special of *Gavin and Stacey*, which means, as football fans, we're effectively visiting a film set. Our very own Universal Studios when en route to Cardiff Arms Park or the Liberty Stadium.

7. Lancaster services, M6, between J32 and J33

Overheard in **606** Towers: 'It looks a bit like Wembley, so that's what I tell the kids.' If you like Wembley's twin towers, you'll like Lancaster service station. The Pennine Tower stands tall in the centre of the service station and is visible from miles around. If you squint, you could almost be on Wembley Way. Almost.

6. Tiverton services, M5, J27

There's free parking for up to two hours at Tiverton. This means if you're on a marathon journey to watch your team play Exeter City, you can rest easy, and cheaply, while you take a break for a post-match powernap on the way home.

5. Knutsford service station, M6

If you're northbound on your way to Manchester or Liverpool, then this is the service station for you. It was one of the first in the country and even has a restaurant on a bridge! The stand-up comedy show *Rhod Gilbert and the Award-Winning Mince Pie* is based on his experience here and at service stations in general.

4. Winchester services, M3

This is where Jeff Stelling, presenter of *Soccer Saturday*, does his research on the week's football.

3. Central Gar Main St, Kyle, Ross-Shire

Placed just on the mainland side of the Isle of Skye, this petrol station is one of the most essential filling-up spots for any fan planning to drive to a game, just because of the sheer distance to any football ground.

2. Cumbria's Tebay service station, M6, between J38 and J39

It has won the British Academy of Gastronomes Grand Prix of Gastronomy award for its home-made and locally sourced fare. As one 606-er says, 'A wonderful stop-off en-route to any North East away games, featuring a farm store with local ales and ciders along with gourmet pies and scotch eggs.' Sold.

1. Watford Gap services

Watford Gap were the first services in Great Britain. When it celebrated its 50th anniversary in 2009, a petition was created to have 'Watford Gap' added to the Oxford English Dictionary for its relevance to the north-south divide.

Southerners claim that there is no culture or sophistication north of Watford Gap, and northerners claim that the line forms the boundary of humour, humility and humanity. On any away trip, crossing this line makes you truly feel like you're in enemy territory. You and your tribe are soon to do battle.

Worst away trips

Here on **606**, we love a call from a coachload of fans with a six-hour journey ahead after losing to Carlisle. We feel we are doing our bit for public service by entertaining you for a third of the journey at least. But Carlisle away would be like popping down the road for some of the clubs below.

10. Montreal Impact – Houston Dynamo

The burgeoning Major League Soccer movement in the USA can throw up a number of hellish away trips for US soccer fans, none more so than the trip between Montreal and Houston. Recently admitted to the Eastern Conference, Montreal Impact faced an away trip to Houston Dynamo in July 2012, coming in at a whopping 1,875.91 miles, taking an estimated one day and seven hours. Dedication isn't the word.

9. Vancouver Whitecaps FC – LA Galaxy

Another exhausting away day in the MLS comes from the Western Conference, where the newly admitted Vancouver Whitecaps faced LA Galaxy, this time a mere 1,124.06 miles to travel.

8. Real Sociedad – Malaga CF

In La Liga, sides can often travel long distances across Spain's vast regions. Take, for example, Real Sociedad from the northern city of San Sebastian in Spain's Basque region and their trip to Andalusia to play Malaga CF, with a distance of over 600 miles for the clubs to travel. When you consider a trip like this, it becomes clearer why opposition fans don't travel much across Spain.

7. Godoy Cruz – Olimpo

Despite the large concentration of Primera Division clubs across Buenos Aires, there are a number of clubs in Argentina's top division spread across the vast swathes of Argentina's land mass. Take for example Godoy Cruz in the Mendoza Province of Argentina; their home ground the Estadio Malvinas Argentinas is a total of 664 miles from their farthest rivals, Club Olimpo, based in the city of Bahia Blanca in the province of Buenos Aires.

6. Ceara – Internacional

As with their Argentinian cousins, Brazilian football fans are some of the most dedicated in South America, especially when you consider match-ups like this. From Fortaleza in north-east Brazil, Ceara fans have to make one of the longest journeys in world football as they travel to the far south-east of Brazil to face Sports Club Internacional of Porto Alegre, a journey totalling over 2,500 miles making this one of the most arduous away trips in world football.

5. Zenit St Petersburg – Tom Tomsk
With the strength and power of Russian football increasing with each season, the number of foreign players arriving to ply their trade increases with each transfer window. For players like Chris Samba and Samuel Eto'o, playing for Anzhi Makhachkala, long-distance journeys for games are the norm. But how about this match-up, as Russian giants Zenit St Petersburg faced an away trip from hell as they travelled to the most easterly club in Russian football, Tom Tomsk. Tomsk is located on the Tom River and is one of the oldest cities in Siberia. Any Zenit fans travelling to Tom Tomsk would face a distance of over 1,948 miles if travelling by air. Any daring travellers undertaking the journey via road would be facing a distance of just under 2,800 miles. Here at 606, we suggest the Russian FA doesn't ever arrange this game for an evening kick-off.

4. Udinese – Catania
Fancy seeing a Serie A game? How about this match-up between the most northerly side in Serie A and the most southerly side, Catania? Udinese, based in Udine close to the Slovenian border, face an away trip of over 880 miles when they travel to Sicily to face Catania at the Stadio Angeloa Massimino. It may be one of the longest but also one of the most rewarding as it sits on the east cost of Sicily facing the Ionian Sea.

3. Valenciennes – Ajaccio
Who would have thought the promotion of Corsican side Ajaccio in 2011 would cause issues for perennial Ligue 1 mid-table dwellers Valenciennes? But with the promotion of the Corsicans, Valenciennes now face an away trip of over 825 miles to reach the Stade Francois Coty in Ajaccio, with a journey from one of the most northerly points in France to Corsica, an island that is closer to Italy than it is to the French mainland. This is not an away trip for the fainthearted.

2. CD Tenerife – Racing Santander
For Spanish football fans of a certain age, CD Tenerife were a regular fixture in Spain's top division as they spent nine years in La Liga through the 1990s. They eventually returned to the top League in 2009/10 where they faced Racing Santander and a trip to the Estadio El Sardinero in Santander. A trip coming in at a mere 1,437 miles.

1. Plymouth Argyle – Anywhere

Despite now residing in League Two, after subsequent relegations and financial crisis crippling the club, Plymouth were playing in the Championship in 2009 and, after the relegation of Middlesbrough and Newcastle United from the Premier League, Plymouth faced the two furthest away days in English football. The trip to Newcastle saw Plymouth clock up 820 miles whilst the subsequent trip to Middlesbrough was small in comparison with only 750 miles for Plymouth to travel. Over an average season, Plymouth travel in excess of 10,000 miles, making the Pilgrims' fans some of the most dedicated in the UK.

Best stands

As grounds are rebuilt, the notion of the four-sided stadium, with its separate stands will surely be consigned to history – at least in the top leagues of the world. New stadiums are now elegant, curvaceous ovals and circles, all smooth, undulating lines designed for ultimate supporter enjoyment. There will be no place for the 'stand', although these new grounds do, at least in name, still retain an element of that historical notion – the Clock End and North Bank at Arsenal's super-modern Emirates Stadium, for example. Below, we give you our favourites.

10. North Bank, Emirates Stadium

As much spaceship as football stadium, Arsenal's ground is the envy of fans everywhere, particularly a bit further up the Seven Sisters Road, where Spurs are busily clearing the ground for their own modern stadium. Whilst 'the Library' at Highbury had its detractors, it was always a much noisier stadium than its nickname suggests. And those Arsenal fans who do sing have congregated in the north west corner of the ground. A perfect blend of the modern football experience and old-fashioned unbridled love for the team.

9. Easter Road's Famous Five stand (The Leith San Siro/The Holy Ground)

Any stand with the guts to have 'famous' in its name had to be included. With an impressive cantilevered roof and a capacity of 4,000, this is the only stand in the country to have a staring competition with the pitch, and win. The pitch was widened to match the stand, not the other way round.

8. Gwladys Street Stand, Goodison Park

If you're going to be named after one of your gran's friends, or maybe your actual gran, you had better be something special. And a proper club like Everton deserves a proper stand. This is where Everton's ultras, the Very Blue Noses, sit. Or rather, stand. If Everton win the toss, the captain always chooses to play toward the Gwladys Street End in the second half, in the hope that the ball will be sucked into the net by sheer toffee power. The fans also politely applaud the away keeper. Capacity is over 10,000.

7. Trinity Road Stand, Villa Park

A gorgeous piece of footballing history to rival Arsenal's famed 'marble halls', the Trinity Road stand, completed in 1922, is surely one of the finest in the world. Stained-glass windows? Check. Italian mosaics? Check. Sweeping staircase? Check. Annual battle with the relegation zone? Check. Well, you can't have it all. Referred to as 'the St Pancras of football'. For those of you outside London, St Pancras is London's most beautiful railway station.

6. Sheffield Wednesday, Hillsborough Stadium – South Stand

Ubiquitous stadium architect Archibald Leitch built this in 1915, and it underwent a major refurbishment for the 1996 European Championships. They added an upper tier, a new roof, 30 executive boxes, two conference suites, a bar, a restaurant, office space, a travelling menagerie, a gold Jacuzzi and a permanent exhibition of the works of Pablo Picasso. We may have made some of those up. Capacity of over 11,000.

5. Newcastle United, Sports Direct Arena – Gallowgate End

In 2005, the Barcodes opened a new bar in the Gallowgate End, called 'Shearer's Bar' after the local sheep-shearing tradesmen who used to frequent the area before the stadium was built. Or something. The bar contains some original steps from the previous incarnation of the Gallowgate End, which were uncovered during the excavation work.

4. The Olympiastadion – Hertha BSC

The western portion (on the Marathon Arch) is open to reveal a Bell Tower to the spectators. In 1947, British engineers improved the bell tower by demolishing it. To be fair, it was the Russians who did the most damage, setting the tower on fire to destroy films that the Third Reich had kept there. It was rebuilt in 1962, however. What other stand in the world offers spectacular views of Berlin, Spandau, the Havel Valley, Potsdam, Nauen and Hennigsdorf? Eh? You don't get that in Stoke.

3. Barcelona, Camp Nou – the Main Stand

This makes the list for pure romance factor. An important footballing and political symbol, it's the biggest stadium in the Europe, which is kind of impressive, if size is your thing. If you're at the back, though, it's like watching a flea circus.

2. Leeds United, Elland Road – East Stand

Clocking in at a *mahoosive* 15,100 capacity, this replacement for the old Lowfields Stand is as old as the Premier League itself – work started during the inaugural 1992/3 season, when Leeds were – brace yourself – in the Champions League!

1. Liverpool, Anfield – The Kop

The first reference to a football stand as a 'kop' was made in 1904 about Arsenal's Woolwich ground. Since then, 27 other stands around the world have been named after a steep hill near Ladysmith in South Africa. Spion Kop was the scene of a bloody Boer War battle, and today, the noise emanating from this phenomenal and sacred part of the ground can sound like the war cry of 13,000 kopites.

Best things smuggled into grounds

At the end of the 2011/12 season, a chicken was smuggled into Ewood Park as part of a protest at owners Venky's; the chicken soon had its own Twitter account. When Darren Fletcher brought up the subject of best things smuggled into grounds, our phone lines rang off the hook and we heard more than a few beauties! Here are some of our favourites...

10. Two bricks and a plank of wood
Paul, a West Brom fan, called into to **606** to tell us a story: 60 years ago, in the days of Ray Barlow, it was early spring, sunny, and his dad was wearing a big mac while everyone else were wearing shorts and short sleeves. He walked to the back of the stand, pulled out two house bricks from his long coat, and a plank of wood from his back and put that on the bricks, then Paul on his shoulders. Best view he ever had.

9. Car door
During a friendly between New Zealand and Chile in Auckland before the 2002 World Cup, a fan ran onto the pitch carrying a car door. At the end of the match, the announcer not only asked the fans to stay off the pitch but ended the announcement by saying, 'Do not to bring car parts onto the pitch.'

8. Half of a cat
During a match in January 1982 between Charlton Athletic and Luton Town, a Charlton fan threw half of a dead cat across the Luton fans and onto the pitch. We don't know why and we don't approve but, as bizarre objects go, this is up there. We're now off to call the RSPCA.

7. Wheelbarrow
When America played Sao Caetano in the quarter-final of the Copa Libertadores, things got a bit fraught at the end of the game. American striker Cuauhtémoc Blanco had been sent off but ran out of the dressing room to get involved. The fans took this as their cue to join in the mayhem and from somewhere a wheelbarrow was thrown onto the pitch. How do you smuggle that in your handbag?

6. Coffin
17-year old Christopher Jacome was murdered in the Colombian city of Cucuta on Saturday and, only hours after his death, his friends stole his body

from the funeral home and brought his coffin along as they went to see their local side Cucuta Deportivo in action. It doesn't get much crazier than that!

5. Rubber snake

Vinnie got in touch with us to tell us how he bought a six-foot rubber snake in Hamleys then walked into Wembley with it: 'I told the steward it was a scarf and he gave me a nod and in I went. Happy days!' Lucky mascot or just weird?

4. Pantomime costume

Stoke City v Man City, 1988. The fancy dress game: two men in a panto horse costume trying to get in on one ticket. One of our favourite MCFC moments of the last 40 years. Until tomorrow, I hope.

3. Celery

Chelsea fans throwing celery onto the pitch is a tradition that began in the 1980s at Stamford Bridge. It was apparently started by Gillingham supporters due to celery growing on the pitch at the Priestfield Stadium but we are still none the wiser as to how the practice found its way to West London.

2. A scooter

In a Serie A match between Inter Milan and Atalanta in 2001, Inter snuck a scooter into the stadium. Apparently, the scooter was stolen from the Atalanta fans. The fans somehow took the scooter into the upper stand of the San Siro and after failing to set it alight threw it over the edge of the stand. Fortunately no one was hurt as the stand below was empty.

1. Beach ball at Stadium of Light

In October 2009, someone in the crowd threw a beach ball onto the pitch. That beach ball then scored a goal... kind of. Darren Bent's shot ricocheted off the offending object, sending Pepe Reina the wrong way, resulting in the only goal of the game.

606's favourite remote grounds

We all know that lonely feeling. It's 4.45, and you're two goals down. The visiting opposition are toying with you. The away fans are olé-ing. You have a premonition of one of your fellow supporters angrily calling **606** in just over an hour bemoaning the referee, the work rate, the overpaid striker's inability to convert eleventy million chances, the inexplicable substitution. You are imagining work on Monday morning and the grief you are going to get. That feeling is loneliness.

Imagine having that feeling, but being 1,760 miles from the nearest landmass. That feeling is loneliness as masterminded by Lionel Messi. Here are our most isolated stadiums, the outposts of football, the distant temples of the beautiful game.

10. England: Carlisle United, Brunton Park

It's 58 miles to their nearest rivals' ground, the Sports Direct Arena, home of Newcastle United. Brunton Park is nearer Queen of the South's Palmerston Park in Scotland than any in England. But it's not all bad. At least you can buy a round of drinks after that long trudge back after an away defeat – such behaviour was banned by the pubs of Carlisle, all of which were owned by the government until 1973.

9. Iceland: IBV Vestmannaeyjar, Hasteinsvollur Stadium

If mum has indeed gone to this part of Iceland, she'll have quite a journey ahead of her. To give them their full name, Íþróttabandalag Vestmannaeyja are in fact triple Icelandic champions and play their games in the bijou but spectacular 1,500-capacity Hasteinsvollur Stadium, on an island off an island, many miles off the coast of Lýðveldið Ísland.

8. Scotland: Ness FC Isle of Lewis, Fivepenny Stadium

Archie Pelago was not, as you might think, a tricky Tottenham winger from the 1970s, but a way of shoehorning a slightly strained pun into this paragraph. It's also a corruption of the word 'archipelago', meaning a string of islands such as the Outer Hebrides. Ness FC's ground is on Fivepenny Machair, who is said to be quite cross about this as it's quite heavy. Not really. Fivepenny Machair is the name of an island. Sorry, Ness FC.

7. Faroe Islands: Eiois Stadium, Boltfelag

No, not the Pharaoh Islands. That's where the football is so bad the supporters start screaming for their mummies. Sorry about that. No, the Faroe Islands, halfway between Scotland and Iceland. Rugged, scenic, incredibly remote. Get there if you can – unless you're a pilot whale.

6. Faroe Islands: Við Margáir in Streymnes

Just edging it in the 'stadiums that could appear in *Lord of the Rings'* stakes, this teeny weeny ground, home to EB/Streymur who play in the Vodafonedeildin, the top division in Faroese football.

5. Switzerland: Ottmar Hitzfeld Gspon Arena

Say what you like about the Swiss, they can make a toy cuckoo jump out of a wooden box at regular intervals, they can cook you up some smashing chocolate and they can build football pitches 1.2 miles up a mountain. If you thought a five-hour train journey was arduous enough, to get here you either have to take a ski lift, hike, or jump in your helicopter and fly.

4. Russia: Luch-Energiya, Vladivostock, Dynamo Stadium

Russians: you only have yourselves to blame for your vast, sprawling communist empire. Vladivostok used to be part of what is now China. It is 4,000 miles away from Moscow, meaning a ten-hour flight. CSKA Moscow's goalkeeper Igor Akinfeev even suggested that they should play in the Japanese League.

3. St Helena Island: Francis Plain

This stadium is the best one on the island. It's also the worst. And the biggest and the smallest, and the most colourful, and the best and worst at playing the piano, because, you may have guessed, it's the only stadium. As a former British colony, it's compulsory to have a football stadium of some kind, even if the site is located in the middle of the Southern Atlantic Ocean and currently lacking an airport.

2. Bolivia: Nevado Sajama

This one sneaks in, in the '**606** special treatment' way – it's not an official pitch but it was home to the highest game of football ever played at 6,542m (21,424 feet or four miles).

1. Tristan da Cunha, South Atlantic Ocean

Tristan da Cunha is a group of volcanic islands in the South Atlantic. It is considered to be the remotest inhabited part of the world, situated 1,760 miles from the nearest land in South Africa. With a population of less than 300, the locals have managed to put together a local football team, Tristan da Cunha FC, and usually play games amongst themselves or against the crews of visiting ships. One recent game saw a local XI take on an International Salvage XI, played on one of the island's cattle fields. The locals triumphed 10-5.

Worst stadium names

How embarrassing. You fall head over heels and decide that it is only fair that your new beau should meet the other love of your life. You will take her to watch your team in action. 'Where are we going?' she asks excitedly and that's when you choke on your coffee and say, 'Um, you are not going to believe this but it's called the...'

10. Mitsubishi Forklift Stadium (capacity 3,000)
Dutch side Almere City FC play at this stadium, which is named after a forklift truck. We can't think of anything more random to name the home of a football team after so for that reason alone it makes our top ten.

9. Pizza-Hut Park – Frisco, USA (capacity 21,193)
The home of MLS side FC Dallas. The Stadium has been nicknamed 'the Oven' by its fans.

8. Hunky Dorys Park – Drogheda, Republic of Ireland (capacity 2,000)
After winning the Irish League in 2007, Drogheda United decided to change their stadium name. Hunky Dorys are crisps and snacks available in Ireland and, in a beautiful coming together of sport and junk food, the Drogheda Stadium became Hunky Dorys Park.

7. Kit Kat Crescent – York (capacity 7,827)
The Kit Kat Crescent is home of York City. It was renamed in 2005 as part of a £100,000 rescue package by Nestle, whose confectionery HQ is in York. The deal ran out in 2010 and it went back to its name of 'Bootham Crescent'.

6. The Madejski stadium (capacity 24,161)
The Madejski stadium opened in August 1998 and is named after – who else – multi-millionaire owner Chairman John Madejski. That said, the stadium is highly regarded and has been named 'Europe's Best Mid-Sized Arena' by American TV Sports Channel ESPN.

5. Sports Direct Arena (capacity 52,387)
It was a highly controversial move when Newcastle owner Mike Ashley renamed Newcastle's St James' Park the Sports Direct Arena. Sports Direct is a popular sports store that is owned by Mike Ashley. The renaming of the stadium didn't

go down well with Olympics chief Lord Coe, who revealed the news that it was to be called St James Park again for the Olympics, under strict rules over the use of commercial names. Lord Coe also added, 'It is St James' Park for the Olympics and, if I am being honest, as a football fan, it will be always be St James' Park for as long as I am watching football.'

4. Playmobil Stadion (capacity 15,500)

The Playmobil Stadion is home of Bundesliga 2 side SpVgg Greuther Furth. The stadium opened in 1910, but when two new stands were built in 1997 it was called Playmobil Stadion. It has since changed again to the much more prosaic name, the Trolli Arena. Fans think the owners are indeed off their trolleys.

3. The Bargain Booze Stadium (capacity 4,500)

Home of Witton Albion, who play their football at the Northern Premier League Division One. Witton Albion's stadium was called the Bargain Booze stadium, named after the discount alcohol brand. Thankfully, the hangover cleared and the stadium is now called the Help for Heroes stadium.

2. Cashpoint Arena (capacity 8,500)

The Cashpoint Arena is home of Austrian team Cashpoint SC Rheindorf Altach. Opened in 1990, the team's partnership with the sports betting brand Cashpoint has meant they've changed the name of their stadium and the club.

1. Arnold Schwarzenegger Stadium (capacity 15,400)

Between 1997 and 2005, this stadium – where Sturm Graz play – was named after one of Austria's finest exports. Schwarzenegger asked the name to be changed in 2005 after he became governor of California. Now known as the UPC Arena.

Longest time in a ground

We're traditionalists on **606**, and while we love the shiny new but generic out of town stadiums, they do all look and feel the same – give or take a bit of red or blue signage. So here we celebrate clubs who have stuck with their grounds and not sold out.

10. Sheffield Wednesday: Hillsborough, 113 years
Sheffield Wednesday moved to Hillsborough in 1899. They won their first game 5-1 against Chesterfield and went on to win their first 19 matches there. When they first moved to the ground it was still named Owlerton Stadium after the suburb of Sheffield. But in 1914 this area was taken into the parliamentary constituency of Hillsborough, hence the renaming of the ground.

Hillsborough is one of the most iconic stadiums in the world because of the Hillsborough disaster – an FA Cup semi-final between Liverpool and Nottingham Forest, which was held on 15 April 1989. The tragedy resulted in the deaths of 96 Liverpool fans.

9. Nottingham Forest: The City Ground, 115 years
Nottingham Forest moved to the City Ground on 3 September 1898. It was only a few hundred yards away from their old ground – the Old Town Ground. Nottingham was granted its Charter as City in 1897, and this is the reason for it being called the City Ground. It has had plenty of redevelopments, including the building of the Trent end, a 7,500-seater stand that was built in time for Euro '96. It took the ground's capacity to 30,602.

In 1998, to mark 100 years at the City Ground, Forest entertained local rivals Derby in a Premier League game that finished 2-2. At half time, there was a parade of some of the biggest players to play for the club, including an 83-year-old Len Beaumont (believed to be oldest living ex-player at the time).

8. Stoke City: Victoria Ground, 119 years
Before moving to the Britannia Stadium in 1997, Stoke had played at the Victoria Ground for 119 years. When the club played their first game at Victoria Ground it was still known as Athletic Club Ground. It later got its name from the Victoria Hotel, which was built nearby. Stoke City played their first game at the Victoria Ground in 1878 against Talke Rangers in the Inaugural Staffordshire Senior Cup Final. Stoke won 1-0. The last game at the ground was on 4 May 1997, a Division One game against West Bromwich Albion. Stoke won 2-1.

7. Everton: Goodison Park, 120 years

Goodison Park was opened on 24 August 1892 by Lord Kinnaird and Frederick Wall of the Football Association. However, the day it opened the crowd saw a short athletics meeting, some music and a fireworks display. Everton actually played their first game there on 2 September 1892 and beat Bolton 4-2. Goodison Park hosted the 1894 FA Cup final when Notts County beat Bolton, with a crowd of 37,000.

Everton were the richest club in the country in the late 1800s and attracted crowds of around 30,000. It was one of the grounds chosen to be used during the 1966 World Cup finals, and only Wembley held more games.

6. Celtic: Celtic Park, 120 years

Celtic started playing at Celtic Park in 1892. The stadium is in the area of Parkhead, which is often what it's known as. The highest ever attendance of 92,000 came in an old firm derby (against Rangers). The capacity of the stadium now is around 60,000. A grandstand was built at Celtic Park in 1898, which burnt down in 1927 but was rebuilt. From the late 1950s until 1971, the stadium was greatly improved with new stands and roofs. This made Celtic Park's capacity around 80,000. Three stands at Celtic Park were rebuilt and the main stand refurbished in the 1990s.

5. Sheffield United: Bramall Lane, 123 years

Bramall Lane has been used as a sports ground since 1855. Sheffield United have played there since 1889; before that, Sheffield Wednesday also played there. Bramall Lane was also the home of the first ever-floodlit football match in the world on 14 October 1878 between two teams selected by the Sheffield Football Association. The teams were split into the reds and the blues.

4. Rangers: Ibrox, 125 years

Ibrox stadium was originally opened in 1887 with a capacity of just 15,000. Less than 12 years later, they moved up the road to the current Ibrox. The stadium was made mostly of wooden stands. In 1902, one of the stands collapsed and killed 26 people. In 1919, after the First World War, they rebuilt the stadium for 80,000 people. But during a game against Celtic in 1971 there was another disaster, which killed 66 people.

In the 1899 season, at the original Ibrox, Rangers won the League without dropping a point. The club moved to the new Ibrox in December 1899 in a League match against Hearts.

3. Burnley: Turf Moor, 129 years

Burnley have played at Turf Moor since 1883, just nine months after the club formed. Half of the ground was redeveloped in the mid 1990s, with two new modern stands. Burnley first decided that they needed to extend the ground in 1884 after a local derby with Padiham drew 12,000 attendance, which was three times bigger than the FA Cup final that year. It was also reported that Turf Moor was the first ground to be visited by a member of the Royal Family. Queen Victoria's son, Prince Albert, was reported to have attended a game there in October 1886.

2. Preston North End: Deepdale, 131 years

Deepdale used to be a farm but hosted its first League match on 8 September 1881. It was against local rivals Burnley and it finished 5-2 to Preston. Deepdale was previously used for other sports including rugby and cricket.

There have been plenty of re-developments at Deepdale over the years to cater for the demand, and the most recent development was completed in 2008. The old Pavilion Stand (which had stood for 30 years) was demolished in 2007. This to many fans was the last piece of the 'old' Deepdale. The new 'Invincibles Pavillion' opened for the first time on 16 August 2008, when Preston entertained Crystal Palace in the first League game of that season. Preston won on that day 2-0.

1. Chesterfield: Saltergate, 139 years

Chesterfield played at Saltergate from 1871 to May 2010. The last game was against Bournemouth and Chesterfield won 2-1. They are the fourth longest-running team in the football League. Two of the original seats from Saltergate are being taken to a new permanent home at the Football League's headquarters in Preston to celebrate the history of the ground. Chesterfield now play their football at the b2net Stadium, a 10,500 all-seater stadium that cost £13m.

Memorable half-time entertainment

The half-time interval is of course the perfect time to find a transistor radio, tune in to Radio 5 live and discover the scores around the country. You'll also need a visit to the little boys' or girls' room and, if you've saved enough, possibly a pint and a pie. But if you choose to remain in your seats... well, you're in for a 'treat'. Over the years, fans have been subjected to sub-American cheerleading displays, toe-curling penalty competitions, interminable announcements about birthdays and the thrill of searching for a unique number printed in your programme for the chance to win a half-price weekend away for one in Bridlington, to be taken any time between January and February.

10. Southampton v Norwich City, 1978
When an RAF dog-handling display commenced at the Dell, the announcer clearly explained that the handler with the briefcase and a fake gun, and four inches of padding, was about to be attacked by the trained dog. A police sergeant, with his back to the pitch up until this point, heard the blank shots being fired and decided an actual armed robbery had just taken place in front of 15,000 people, and that he had his eye on a bravery medal. Our hero sprinted onto the pitch, in hot pursuit of a man in a padded suit with an empty briefcase, calling for back-up. It slowly dawned on him that his well-intended one-man crime-fighting initiative wasn't quite what he thought and had to make his way rather sheepishly back to the touchline. His authority somewhat eroded, it was decided that he should leave the pitch – but to do so meant he had to walk the walk of shame, as the exit was on the opposite corner of the ground.

9. West Ham, September 2010
Football's favourite comedy duo, David Sullivan and David Gold assured fans they were going to 'bring the fun back' to West Ham. One way of doing this would be to invest in exciting new talent, serving up the swashbuckling, attacking football West Ham has been known for. Or, at half time, you could have two seated teenagers turning over football cards in the Match Attax World Championship. With analysis from the stadium announcer. The good times were back! Bobby Moore would have been proud.

8. On Your Shed, Son – Birmingham City
What could be more entertaining than bringing an actual shed, without a roof, onto the pitch at half time? That's right, bringing out a roofless shed and getting

punters to chip a ball into the shed, to win... a shed. Or at least, a voucher toward the cost of a shed.

7. Phil Brown, Hull FC, Boxing Day 2008

Resplendent with a very normal-looking tan for someone who lives in Hull in the middle of winter, Phil Brown held his half-time talk on the pitch after going 4-0 down to Manchester City. There are ways to manage a team of highly talented millionaires, and this is not one of them. They went on to lose 5-1.

6. The Sky Strikers, Highbury, 28 September 1992

Amidst Sky's desperate attempts to engender some kind of interest, or at least reduce the animosity toward Monday night games, we remember the ill-starred 'Sky Strikers', a badly misjudged attempt to introduce some of the razzamatazz of American football or, as it is rightly known, 'Hand-egg'. It didn't work. And on 28 September, it *really* didn't work. One way to wind up the Highbury crowd is to send out cheerleaders dressed in what looks like the Tottenham kit.

5. The Red Barrows, Colchester United, 2011

No, dear reader, not a misprint. The Red Barrows are the 'Awesome, aerobatic, barrowbatic display team' from Essex. More accurately, they are some people wheeling wheelbarrows around. In formation. To be fair to them, if there was a list of the best half-time entertainment, they'd be on that. Marvellous and mad at the same time.

4. The Shamen performing 'Ebeneezer Goode', Arsenal, 1992

In the nascent years of the Premier League, Sky didn't think it was enough to have the football. We had to have pop stars miming to songs. Manchester City fans were memorably 'treated' to Undercover's cover version of 'Baker Street', whilst Arsenal's fans 'enjoyed' The Shamen's single-entendre classic. Legend has it that the Clock End amended the lyrics to something along the lines of 'He's a cad, he's a cad, the referee's a cad.'

3. The Swanky Pants Dog Troupe, Burnley, 1999

Everyone loves a dog troupe. What thrills! What skills! The marrying of man and his best friend, engaged in exhilarating hoop jumps, hind-leg walking, disco-dancing antics to delight and surprise. What's not to like? Well, what's not to like is if the dog troupe in question are very good at the 'taking the dog for a walk' skillset. In fact, they are very good at the 'taking the dog for a walk' skillset *with dogs in fancy dress*. That was it. The owners walked the dogs around the pitch.

2. Vitesse Arnhem v PSV, 2005

Two worlds collided at the Gelredome in Arnhem back in 2005 as the comedy losers from the Dutch version of *Pop Idol* serenaded the crowd with a version of Tina Turner's deathless classic 'Simply The Best'. The indescribable caterwauling is available on YouTube, should you wish to untraceably assassinate a life-long enemy. Use with caution during wartime though, as this footage is outlawed under the Geneva Convention.

1. Delia Smith, Norwich City, 2005

There could be no other winner. Our heroine took to the pitch to rally Norwich City's faithful, who had seen Manchester City erode a two-goal lead to go into the break at 2-2. What Delia probably thought was a rousing speech in the vein of Shakespeare's Henry V ('Once more unto the breach, dear friends, once more; Or close the wall up with our English dead') was actually more like your very embarrassing auntie grabbing the microphone halfway through a wedding disco. This excruciating discourse will never, ever, be beaten.

Notable ground-shares

There are a number of reasons why clubs ground-share. Maybe it's wartime, and your stadium has been requisitioned as an Air Raids Precaution office and was bombed (which is why Arsenal played home games at White Hart Lane during the Second World War). Maybe your ground is being redeveloped by an Egyptian shopkeeper (Fulham shared with QPR in 2003). Or maybe – and this is the most likely reason – you just want to halve your costs.

10. Sampdoria & Genoa: Stadio Luigi Ferraris

It's easier to think of Italian clubs which don't share grounds. Genoa and Sampdoria share the Stadio Luigi Ferraris, which holds over 36,000 people.

9. Bury & FC United: Gigg Lane

Not one of the most high-profile on the list, but FC United, formed in 2005 by some Manchester United fans who were dissatisfied with the Glazer takeover, now play their Northern Premier League home games at Bury's Gigg Lane.

8. Charlton & Crystal Palace: Selhurst Park

In 1984, Charlton were struggling financially and were forced to move out of the Valley following safety concerns. They eventually moved back in 1992.

7. Brighton & Gillingham: Priestfield

After leaving the Goldstone Ground, Brighton spent two years sharing with Gillingham at the Priestfield, a handy 70 miles away. They then moved on to the not-so-state-of-the-art Withdean Stadium, an athletics ground, before arriving at the AMEX stadium in Falmer in 2011.

6. Juventus & Torino: Stadio Olimpico di Torino

Juve shared the, ahem, Stadio Benito Mussolini with local rivals Torino from 1933 to 1990 and from 2006 to 2011. The ground was restructured for the 2006 Winter Olympics in Italy.

5. Fulham & QPR: Loftus Road

Fulham got into bed with QPR in 2002, while Craven Cottage was being redeveloped.

4. Bayern Munich & 1860 München: Allianz Arena

The two Munich clubs, Bayern Munich and TSV 1860 München share the

Allianz Arena. They moved into the ground in 2005. The stadium is lit up in red when Bayern Munich play and in blue when 1860 Munich play.

3. Crystal Palace & Wimbledon: Selhurst Park
Crystal Palace seem to be the League's most accommodating club. Originally meant to be only a temporary agreement, the share ended up lasting over 12 years, only ending when Wimbledon were controversially dissolved in 2004.

2. Roma & Lazio: Stadio Olimpico
Roma and Lazio have an intense rivalry, but chants referring to how terrible the opposition's ground is have been rendered obsolete. The *Derby della Capitale* takes place on shared ground in the 72,000-capacity stadium. The fact that Roma are the better-supported team may be down to its origins; it was created out of three separate clubs by the fascist regime in 1927, who were keen for a united Rome side to challenge teams from the north.

1. Inter Milan & AC Milan: San Siro
Milan have been in the San Siro since 1926. City rivals Inter were accepted as joint tenants in 1947. Inter were formed in 1908 after a split with AC Milan, and the two sides have remained best of enemies ever since. They have an enormous stadium in which to play out the biannual *Derby della Madonnina* (named for the prominent statue of the Madonna atop the City's cathedral). The San Siro, also known as the Stadio Giuseppe Meazza, is the largest in Italian football, with a total capacity of 80,018.

Best free seats in the country

Along with 'pretty girl in tight-fitting top', 'face-painted child singing enthusiastically' and 'old person in team colours', 'people watching the game for free' are the TV director's best friend, especially when there's not much going on on the pitch – maybe Stoke are passing it along their back four for 20 minutes or so. Here are our favourite gratis vantage points, where you don't have to spend anything to enjoy the match.

10. Hednesford Town – Keys Park
Once upon a time it was possible to see Hednesford Town's Northern Premier League games by standing on slag heaps outside the ground.

9. Charlton Athletic – The Valley
The name says it all. It's in an actual valley. If you live in one of the surrounding tower blocks, there's no need for a season ticket, just some binoculars.

8. Stenhousemuir/East Stirlingshire FC – Ochilview Park
If you live on Jamieson Avenue and are a fan of either Stenhousemuir or East Stirlingshire FC (they ground-share), then you are laughing. Your rear windows enjoy spectacular views of Scottish second and third division football on any given Saturday.

7. Leyton Orient – Matchroom Stadium, Brisbane Road
All four corners of the ground contain blocks of flats with balconies overlooking the pitch. Mmmm, imagine those balmy summer evenings spent on your balcony, a cold beer in your hand, watching League One's finest entertain you. Alternatively you could draw the curtains and watch *Corrie*.

6. Stoke City – Britannia Stadium
Owing to Stoke's 'traditional' style of play, you can often see a 'direct' Dean Whitehead pass fly 80 feet into the air from your vantage point on the hard shoulder of the A50.

5. Northampton Town – Sixfields Stadium
Thrifty Cobblers fans mass on a hill over the road from the ground, just behind the north stand, where they can see approximately 65 per cent of the pitch. Still, 65 per cent of the match for 100 per cent of nothing is not too bad.

4. Sheffield United – Bramall Lane
The Copthorne Hotel at Bramall Lane not only boasts a photocopy service, you can also watch the Blades from some of the rooms.

3. Southampton – The Dell
If you were building a block of flats that looked over the Dell, what would you call them? You'd call them Overdell Court. Those on the top floors are the envy of Saints fans – they enjoyed uninterrupted views of the match.

2. West Ham – Upton Park
Tempting as it is to draw the curtains on any side Sam Allardyce manages, hardcore Hammers fans would be delighted with their Room with a View in several blocks of flats overlooking the Boleyn Ground.

1. Norwich City – Carrow Road
The Holiday Inn Norwich City, which is incidentally ranked 5th of 56 hotels in Norwich, has a number of rooms which overlook the pitch at Carrow Road. One of which was taken advantage of by an away fan who had been ejected from the ground for persistent standing. A fellow Saints fan invited him up to his pitch-view room, but he was banned from the hotel after breaching regulations which bar 'more than two adults' in rooms overlooking the pitch on match days.

Smallest stadiums

Have you noticed that whenever a new stadium is built, there's a real focus on how big the capacity is? Well, we think it's time the smaller grounds in the Football League got some attention. Remember, it's not how big it is – it's how effectively it's used!

10. Aldershot Town – 7,100
Name of ground: The Recreation Ground/the Rec (officially the EBB Stadium)
Moved here: 1927
606 fact worth knowing: Aldershot Town were formed from the ashes of the liquidated Aldershot FC in 1992 and were able to continue playing their fixtures at the Rec.

9. Burton Albion – 6,912
Name of ground: Pirelli Stadium
Moved here: 2005
606 fact worth knowing: The stadium was opened by Sir Alex Ferguson and Brian Clough's widow, Barbara.

8. Stevenage – 6,722
Name of ground: Broadhill Way (officially the Lamax Stadium)
Moved here: 1980
606 fact worth knowing: The former Stevenage Borough won the Conference in 1996 but were not promoted as the stadium did not have sufficient crowd capacity for the Football League.

7. Morecambe – 6,476
Name of ground: Globe Arena
Moved here: 2010
606 fact worth knowing: The Shrimpers played at their old ground Christie Park for 89 years.

6. Dagenham & Redbridge – 6,077
Name of ground: Victoria Road
Moved here: 1955 (Dagenham) and 1990 (Redbridge Forest)
606 fact worth knowing: The ground has hosted numerous international fixtures including England Ladies v Sweden and England, San Marino and Cyprus youth teams in a UEFA tournament.

5. Barnet – 5,500

Name of ground: Underhill
Moved here: 1907
606 fact worth knowing: The pitch at Underhill is famous for its slope, which is over 8 feet end-to-end; an angle of 1:41 – the maximum allowed in the Football League rule book.

4. AFC Wimbledon – 5,194

Name of ground: Kingsmeadow (aka the Cherry Reds Stadium)
Moved here: 2002
606 fact worth knowing: The club have ground-shared with Kingstonian FC since their inception, from whom they purchased the lease to Kingsmeadow in 2003.

3. Accrington Stanley – 5,070

Name of ground: The Crown Ground
Moved here: 1968
606 fact worth knowing: Although the ground was acquired in 1968, it wasn't until 1970 that any competitive football was actually played there!

2. Torquay United – 5,027

Name of ground: Plainmoor
Moved here: 1921, after merging with local rivals Babbacombe
606 fact worth knowing: The roof of a stand was blown off by a gale in 1930, and one-third of the grandstand was destroyed in an early morning fire in 1985.

1. Crawley Town – 4,738

Name of ground: Broadfield
Moved here: 1997
606 fact worth knowing: Just two years after moving into their new home, Crawley Town went into administration, and then again in 2006 after being dogged by financial problems.

Worst away ends

Your team is your life. Every month you spend hundreds of pounds you really don't have travelling around the country to support them. A lot of the time it is worth it. But then sometimes you end up in places like...

10. Withdean Stadium, Brighton
Before moving to the splendour of the 'American Express Community Stadium', Brighton called the Withdean Stadium home. The Withdean wasn't in fact a designated football ground but an athletics stadium that in its past history had also doubled up as a zoo. The home stands at the Withdean were poor, but that was nothing compared to the away stand – an away stand without a roof doesn't exactly bode well, even more so when that stand is located behind a running track and at the side of a sandpit. As one contributor commented, 'The pitch is in a different time zone.'

9. Priestfield Stadium, Gillingham
Despite renovating the Priestfield completely since taking over as chairman in 1995, Paul Scally seemed to neglect the away fans, who are located in the Brian Moore Stand. This is is a temporary stand, which is fine if the rain holds off... If not, don't worry – Gillingham will happily hand out rain macs to those who prefer to watch their football slightly dry.

8. Ninian Park, Cardiff
Coming in at number 8 on the *Observer's* 'simply worst' list in 2009 was Ninian Park, the former intimidating home of Cardiff City. Away fans at the Ninian were allocated a section of the stand close to the corner flag with, for added atmosphere, a pillar obstructing most of their view.

7. Liverpool, Anfield
We advise you to avoid picking up restricted view tickets at Anfield. The view is not so much restricted as blocked by a steel pillar. With ticket prices on the rise, away supporters can be charged up to £48 for a cramped seat in the Anfield Road end.

6. Doncaster, Belle Vue
Doncaster may well have moved to a nice shiny stadium but their former home of Belle Vue offered visiting supporters the chance to experience life in a top-security prison, an open-air terrace end and ten-foot-wide mesh fencing

helping to make away fans feel welcome in South Yorkshire.

5. Blackpool, Bloomfield Road

The newly refurbished Bloomfield Road is a world away in terms of experience for away fans from that before refurbishment. Away fans were allocated a mixture of the old Spion Kop and a section of terracing delightfully described as 'the Paddock'. Part of the Spion Kop had been closed off due to safety reasons; what remained of it was a crumbling tribute to old-school football grounds. It was a stand totally open to all of the elements that the Irish Sea could throw at it, often resulting in away fans facing wind from one section of the ground and rain from the other. Meanwhile, the aforementioned Paddock saw supporters missing much of the game as they were below the pitch level by quite a substantial amount.

4. Barrow, Holker Street

It would be unfair to concentrate solely on Football League clubs in this list, so we give you Barrow's very own Holker Street. Pure football dedication is needed for an away trip to Barrow. As Holker Street is close to the coast, away fans are often treated to all four seasons in one 90-minute game. Bring parkas, cagoules, scarfs and sun cream for the terraces.

3. Newton AFC, Latham Street

Welsh Premier League side Newton AFC have a nice compact home ground which more than meets the requirements of the Welsh Premier League and even UEFA. Sadly, it doesn't offer much for away fans, who are allocated temporary seating at the South/Llanidloes Road end. This temporary seating is made up of a number of benches behind the goal and again – you've guessed it – an open-air environment.

2. Southport FC, Haig Avenue

Perhaps a controversial choice but the location of this terrace and the fact that once again it is open to the elements sees it make our list. Southport have been at Haig Avenue for over a century now, and time is beginning to tell. Once again, if you make a trip to an away game at this north-west seaside favourite, wrap up warm.

1. Portsmouth FC, Fratton Park

Financial ruin put paid to any improvements or changes to Fratton Park bar the roof placed over the Milton End. For many years the Milton End was an open-air terrace until Portsmouth finally added the roof. The terrace has also been converted to seating, which has caused numerous issues as seats are placed on old terrace steps meaning anyone who does actually sit down in the Milton End has a cramped experience. Standing pillars from the new roof can also impede the view of away fans, though the roof has helped to add to the atmosphere.

Craziest football stadiums

From the ridiculous to the sublime, there are many football stadiums around the world that are beautiful, picturesque or sometimes just downright crazy. Here are some of the crazy stadiums we've requested to do **606** OBs (Outside Broadcasts) from. Deaf. Ears.

10. Estadio Municipal de Braga
Used during Euro 2004 in Portugal, Braga's ground known as A Pedreira (the Quarry) has its 30,154 seats spread between only two sides of the pitch. At one end is a view overlooking Portugal's most northern city and at the other a quarry wall with a big screen suspended from it. Costing £54.7million, more than a million cubic metres of granite were blasted out to build it.

9. Strahov Stadium
In Prague is the world's largest stadium: it seats around 240,000 people and has nine football pitches. Although no longer in use for sports events, Sparta Prague use it as a training complex. It was also used for the 2010 World Ultimate Club Championships, which merges aspects of rugby and frisbee.

8. Janguito Malucelli
It became famous for being the first eco ground in Brazil. It can hold 6,000 people, is constructed with recycled wood, has grass-covered seats and has a hill as its main stand. There'll be more to come in Brazil with seats made of sugar cane planned for the 2014 World Cup.

7. Gospin Dolac
Home to NK Imotski in Croatia. Built in 1989, it has a capacity of 4,000 and is next to a 500-metre drop to the Blue Lake. The greatest player to come from the area – Zvonimir Boban – went on to play for Dinamo Zagreb and AC Milan, and also captained the Croatian national team that finished third in the 1998 World Cup.

6. The Allianz Arena
Home ground to Bayern Munich and 1860 München, it's the first stadium in the world to change colour and does so according to whichever team is playing there. Red for Bayern, blue for 1860 and white for the German national team. Amongst some of the stadium's features: 69,901 capacity, the roof has 2,874 air cushions, it's self-cleaning and, should snow fall, 12 sensors can measure the

pressure of the snow and trigger a pressure increase in the cushions to balance out the load. Ultra safe!

5. Igraliste Batarija

A tiny stadium in Croatia with a 1,000 capacity, it is home to HNK Trogir. It is unique because the ground is located between two 15th-century fortresses: the Kamerlengo Castle and the tower of St Marco. Perhaps more fans watch from the castle roofs next to the pitch?

4. Estadio Municipal de Aveiro

The second stadium on the list built for use during Euro 2004 in Portugal with a 30,127 capacity and now home to Beira Mar. Somewhat of a Willy Wonka entry, not because it's made of chocolate but because it's a bit quirky, like its architect. Combining many lively colours and a collection of differently shaped elements to its overall structure, it resembles a big toy for children.

3. Sapporo Dome

Hosting three first-round matches in the 2002 World Cup, the Sapporo Dome in northern Japan is one of a kind. It is home to both football and baseball teams. The wonderfully named Hokkaido Nippon-Ham Fighters baseball team play on an artificial pitch, but when it's time for the J-League's Consadole Sapporo to play, in slides the grass pitch for football matters. It takes around five hours for the transformation to be complete. From the outside it looks like a big space invader.

2. The Marina Bay Stadium

Singapore's 30,000-seater stadium hosted its first football match between Tuan Gemuk Athletic and VNNTU FC, a Sunday League amateur match. However, the match status to ground capacity ratio isn't the extreme part. The pitch is on the world's largest floating stage on the Marina Reservoir and can bear a weight of up to 1,070 tonnes. That's nearly 13,000 Robbie Savages!

1. Wembley Stadium (the new one)

Deep breath... The 90,000-seater stadium cost almost £800m, and opened nearly a year late. During construction, it had 3,500 workers on site at its peak, and at one point 3,000 workers had to evacuate due to safety concerns. The steel arch supporting the roof spans 317 metres (the world's longest), which requires beacons for low-flying aircraft. It has more toilets than any other venue in the world – 2,618, give or take a urinal.

Worst pitch ever

Kenny Dalglish is, as we write this, working on a theory that all the football pitches in England are conspiring against Liverpool. Well, Kenny, we are here to help. Pick and choose from our list of shame below and, in your next interview, claim that 'everyone else seems to do fine here. I'm not saying it's a conspiracy, but that slope was not here last week when Everton played. For us and only us, the pitch here was as bad as...' and then insert a reference to any of these ploughed fields of shame.

10. The 'New' Wembley pitch

'A disgrace' (Harry Redknapp), 'one of the worst' (James Milner), 'a joke' (Andy Townsend). Not describing our dearly beloved FA itself, but their showpiece, the new Wembley Stadium. Rather like building a car but forgetting to put in the engine, they somehow managed to build a stadium where the pitch had to be relaid 11 times in three years. Finally realising in 2010 that simply relaying the turf wasn't working, 3,000 tonnes of soil was removed, the drainage system improved, and a new pitch was laid containing artificial fibres. So far it has held up.

9. Barnet FC – Underhill – The 'Ski slope'

Being a Barnet fan is an uphill struggle. Being a Barnet player is an uphill climb. The Highways Agency once suggested that a red gradient warning triangle be placed by the touchline. (They didn't really.)

8. QPR's artificial plastic pitch

The sci-fi sounding Omniturf pitch was laid at Loftus Road in time for the start of the 1981 season. It makes this list as it was not bad for everyone, it was just bad for visiting teams. In the first season of plastic grass, QPR reached the FA Cup final as a Second Division club and then won the Second Division Championship the following season. The abnormally high bounce provided many comedy moments with keepers coming off their line. Only removed seven years later because of a change in regulations and replaced with grass.

7. Oldham artificial plastic pitch

There's a pattern emerging here. In 1986, the Latics installed a plastic pitch in order to generate more non-footballing income for the club. Cue a massive upturn in Oldham's fortunes. In 1990, the club reached the League Cup final and the semi-final of the FA Cup.

6. County Ground at Northampton

If you want to make your pitch really bad, one way is to allow people to park cars on it during the summer. The Cobblers said goodbye to their grassy car park in 1994.

5. Yeovil Town's old ground – Huish

Between 1928 and 1990, It was famous for an 8-foot side-to-side slope, which meant that if Peter Crouch stood on one side, and you layed down flat on the other, you'd only be able to see him from the nipples up. Scene of perhaps the most shocking FA Cup giant killing of all time, when Yeovil of the Southern League beat First Division Sunderland in 1948/9. Reports that Sunderland's players were found crumpled in a heap on one side of the pitch are unfounded.

4. Chelsea FC – Stamford Bridge 'beachgate'

A pre-Abramovich Chelsea attempted to inject a little Copacabana beach glamour into their workaday footballing style by laying several thousand tonnes of 'Brazilian Beach Grass' (sand) on Stamford Bridge. In 2003, Charlton attempted to get a 4-1 defeat rescinded because of it, and in 2006 Barcelona accused Chelsea of trying to sandily sabotage their tiki-taka. It worked – Chelsea won 1-0.

3. AC Milan – San Siro

One of the world's temples of football, the home of both Inter and AC Milan, rivals Wembley in one important respect: it has at its centre a ploughed field you'd stare at with trepidation if you were asked to play on it on a Sunday morning. A rough, sorry excuse for an international playing surface.

2. Avanhard Stadium

In the first match of the 2011 Ukrainian Premier League season, FC Zorya Luhansk squared up against Volyn I utsk on a pitch that, it is fair to say, had not fared well over the Ukrainian winter. In fact, it looked like it had been prepared by the *It's a Knockout* production team. Partly frozen, partly waterlogged, some grass, some not-grass, some sand, some of what looked like tar coming through all added up to a comedy nightmare of a match. The only thing missing was some giant rubber waiters to come galloping across the halfway line, trying not to spill their tray of drinks.

1. Derby County, Baseball ground 1970s

A terrible pitch with a wonderful pedigree. Derby's long-lost Baseball Ground had the reputation for having the worst pitch in the top flight since the 1930s, which in a weird way is something to be proud of. Softer than marshmallow, cutting up more easily than a pat of butter put to the hot knife, more uneven than the surface of the moon, the Baseball Ground is probably more suitable for football now it's covered in houses.

FANS

Nicest fans

A lot of the time, football fans suffer a bad press, a hangover from hooligan-driven days of yore. We at **606** see things differently and proudly present the case for the defence of the football fan.

10. Portsmouth fans
Pompey fans witnessed their team get ripped apart 5-1 by the Gunners at Fratton Park in March 2004. Thierry Henry got a standing ovation from the Pompey fans and in return gave them a salute in a Portsmouth shirt. Henry said, 'I will never forget that because you know a lot of people are really appreciating what you are doing.'

9. Real Madrid
Everyone knows of the bitter rivalry between Barcelona and Real Madrid (El Classico) but sometimes, outrageous skill will out. The Real fans applauded Ronaldinho's performance for Barca at the Bernabeu in the 2005/6 season. Barca ran out 3-0 winners with Ronaldinho getting two of the goals and producing a dazzling display which saw the Real fans on their feet.

8. Manchester United fans
Old Trafford 2003, Champions League quarter-final, second leg: Manchester 4-3 Real Madrid (Real won 6-5 on agg). After Ronaldo scored a hat-trick against them, he was substituted and received a standing ovation from Old Trafford. He was arguably the greatest player in the world at the time.

7. Aston Villa fans
Villa fans created the 'Petrov Pie' in aid of their captain Stilyan Petrov who was diagnosed with Leukaemia. The pie was on sale against Sunderland in April 2012 and a percentage of the proceeds went to the Cure Leukaemia Charity.

6. Fulham fans
One of only a few grounds in the country with no segregation in its away stand, the Putney End. They also boast the lowest number of arrests at Premier League matches in the 2010/11 season, with just 12.

5. Liverpool fans clapping off Swansea
Swansea's players were clapped off at Anfield following the 0-0 draw in November 2011. Swansea manager Brendan Rodgers said, 'Respect to the

Anfield supporters, because I don't think there are many teams that walk off here and get a round of applause.'

4. Kilmarnock fans
When Celtic played Kilmarnock at Rugby Park in April, a Celtic win would have ensured the SPL League title went to the Glasgow club. In a show of great understanding, the Kilmarnock fans gave up their seats, donating three sides of the ground to the opposition. Celtic repaid the favour by winning 6-0.

3. Liverpool fans for Rhys Jones
After the murder of 11-year-old Everton fan Rhys Jones in 2007 in the Croxteth area of Liverpool, Liverpool fans paid a moving tribute to Rhys and his family before the Champions League qualifier against Toulouse. The Everton *Z Cars* theme was played at Anfield in memory of Rhys.

2. Spurs fans with Muamba
Fabrice Muamba suffered a cardiac arrest in the FA Cup quarter-final match at White Hart Lane in March 2012. Spurs fans repeatedly chanted Muamba's name while he received treatment on the pitch, and one fan, Dr Andrew Deaner, a cardiologist, ran onto the field to assist in the treatment.

1. Ipswich fans with Billy Sharp
Following the death of Sharp's two-day-old son Luey, Ipswich fans applauded his goal at Portman Road in November 2011.

Best mascots

To make this list you must either be a highly appropriate mascot for your team, perhaps even to the detriment of your mascotness (no room here for your 'Pottermus', Stoke fans). You must exhibit a certain amount of chutzpah, you must have a certain degree of cool, retro or otherwise, you may be strange, or – and there's no way of dressing this up – the mascot must have done something funny or brave, or stupid. Like chase a streaker.

10. Angus the Bull, Aberdeen
Angus the Bull: you are delicious. You are one of the nicest things that there are to eat. You only exist as a food source for humans. You taste nice rare with a hollandaise sauce, or roast with a bit of gravy. You come from Aberdeen. Your breed is the 'Angus'. You are appropriate and toothsome. And we are hungry.

9. Bertie Bee, Burnley
Bertie makes it on here for two reasons. One, bees are dying out and this poses a threat to the ecosystem. Two, Bertie tackled a streaker. Go and find the video.

8. World Cup Willie, England World Cup finals, 1966
Mainly because we're hanging on to 1966 by our fingertips, but also because World Cup Willie, quite a crappy-looking threadbare lion, seemed to have come from a gentler time. This was an era when Bobby Moore, having just captained England to World Cup glory, returned to his house in Essex and had a barbecue with some friends.

7. Pique, Mexico World Cup finals 1986
In a move we hope is reminiscent of Alf Garnett or Al Murray's Pub Landlord, Mexico decided to point out the ridiculousness of stereotypes by using stereotypes. A sombrero-wearing Jalapeno pepper with a droopy moustache? *Gracias!*

6. Xoloitzcuintli, Club Tijuana
This fearsome beast looks like the devil's own attack dog, standing upright, like it's just walked off a Hieronymus Bosch painting. The only genuinely intimidating mascot on this list, the Xoloitzcuintli is actually a breed of Mexican hairless dog.

5. Deepdale Duck, Preston North End
He's been sent off. He had to be dragged from the pitch by his wings. Everton

tried to ban him from Goodison, for fear he would start a riot. Our favourite duck after Howard.

4. Cyril the Swan, Swansea

Who would win in a fight between a nine-foot swan and a lion? The nine-foot swan. Millwall's Zampa the Lion came off second best and feeling more than a little 'roar' after Cyril ripped off the lion's head and drop-kicked it into the crowd. Worth the £1,000 fine? Probably.

3. Chaddy the Owl, Oldham

Do we need random drug testing... for match officials? This might suggest that we do. Oldham were playing Peterborough in the 2000/2001 season and the linesman kept wrongly flagging Carlo Corazzin offside. Apparently line-o kept mistaking a seven-foot owl for the Canadian forward.

2. H'Angus the Monkey, Hartlepool

One way of throwing an insult back at someone is to reclaim it, and that's what Hartlepool have done with H'Angus. In case you don't know, the good folk of Hartlepool once hanged a monkey, thinking it was a French spy. They have been known as 'the monkey hangers' ever since.

1. Super Homem (Superman), Esporte Clube Bahia, Brazil

One way of demonstrating your footballing prowess to your opponents is to compare yourselves to Superman. Or maybe to show your familiarity with the work of 19th-century German philosopher, poet and classical philologist Friedrich Nietzsche. Whatever the reason, it's the coolest of the lot.

Best international fans

Fans are what football is all about. In international tournaments we see fans come from all over the world to provide colour and noise to support their country. But which nations' fans are the best?

10. Ireland

The Irish spread good spirits and the colour green wherever they go, and it's no different in football. Despite not being the most successful nation around, fans do anything to get to the games. One ticketless fan even disguised himself as an Estonian player to get a seat in the dugout!

9. Mexico

The Mexicans have their own way to cheer on their side, taking it too far on occasion, which doesn't always go down too well. But they are likely to be louder than any opposition in any stadium.

8. Spain

The Spanish have a lot to cheer about at the moment, being current reigning European and World Champions. The fans have been patient with a team that has notoriously choked on the big stage.

7. Italy

Italian football is known for its crazy, passionate fans. At home, they despise anyone not hailing from their region. At tournaments they bind together, getting well and truly in the spirit of any competition.

6. Germany

The ever-reliable Germans – they're a team that always gets to the latter stages of major tournaments and their fans are always right next to them! They also give huge support to their female team, who won the Women's World Cup in 2003 and 2007.

5. South Africa

When South Africa hosted the World Cup in 2010, it was the first to be held in Africa and they made it special. One of the most memorable noises from the World Cup was the vuvuzela. By the end of the tournament every fan in South Africa was blowing one.

4. England

England are one of the best-supported teams in the world. Their ticket allocation was apparently one of the quickest to sell out for the 2014 World Cup in Brazil. While you cannot deny the fans' passion, they are often guilty of getting carried away with the team's form. Well, some say carried away, we call it belief.

3. Argentina

Similar to their South American neighbours Brazil, Argentina bring the party to every stadium. Everyone in Argentina is a football fan – and with players like Lionel Messi, we're not surprised.

2. Brazil

The Brazilians have had a lot to shout about in recent history and boy do they shout, and drum and dance. Another colourful bunch, the Brazilians bring the party to every game. They're bright, colourful and very loud, creating quite the atmosphere at any stadium.

1. Netherlands

What do you associate with Dutch football? Classy, skilful and technical play? Maybe, but what about the colour orange? Seeing the Dutch support is quite remarkable – brightening up any game. And they're not a quiet bunch either!

Best pitch invasions

It is the hallowed turf, the sacred ground, the grass only the gods of football may tread upon – until thousands of fans get it into their heads that they too should get a piece of the action...

10. Swangard Stadium 2010

What do you mean you've never heard of it? It's home to the Vancouver Whitecaps and one of the more unusual pitch invasions. During a match against AC St Louis, a 2-year-old child took to the pitch and used his skill and agility to take on Vancouver's goalkeeper Jay Nolly. Nolly saved the child and put him out for a corner. 'You'll Never Beat Jay Nolly' sang the crowd.

9. West Leigh Park 2011

The scene here was Havant and Waterlooville's ground and a match with Dorchester Town. A man ran onto to the pitch wearing a mankini and proceeded to run around unchallenged. With the stewards seemingly unbothered, Dorchester Town's player-manager Ashley Vickers stepped in and wrestled the man to the ground. When Vickers stood up again he saw the referee waving a red card at him, and he left the pitch seconds after the would-be streaker.

8. Anfield 2012

You can tell how dreary a game is when the headlines the next day are all about a cat taking to the field. Liverpool played out a tedious 0-0 with Spurs, but all the action came in the 12th minute when the tabby, later named Kenny, took to the pitch and was surprised to discover he wasn't the only one there with two left feet. He bore down on Brad Friedel's goal in a manner that Dirk Kuyt could only dream of, before being taken away by one of the stewards. He's currently on loan at Yeovil Town.

7. Old Trafford 2009

A bad-tempered derby match which saw Man City's Craig Bellamy hit by a coin. He scored twice in the game including an equaliser late on, only to see Michael Owen snatch a very late winner. A fan took to the pitch to celebrate and was expertly rugby tackled by the stewards. Bellamy decided to help them out, appearing to slap the invader. Headlines involving 'The Sh*t hitting the fan' were tempting for some newspapers...

6. Gander Lane 1989

Sutton United's ground is an unlikely venue for a pitch invasion, particularly in January when the players were struggling on its surface. Coventry City were the visitors for this third-round FA Cup tie and the memories of their 1987 victory were still strong. Matthew Hanlon scored the winner for the part-timers and at full-time the home fans celebrated in the time-honoured fashion by jumping onto the pitch and then sinking into the mud and needing to be rescued.

5. The City Ground 1989

Nottingham Forest beat QPR 5-2 and some of the Forest fans got a bit carried away and took to the pitch. They reckoned without their manager, though. Brian Clough also took to the field and, disgusted at their behaviour, decided to hit a few of his own fans. He then had to face a pitch-side ban. Two of the fans apologised to him on television, and Clough asked them to kiss him. Standard Cloughie behaviour.

4. Etihad 2012

All Manchester City had to do was win at home – something they had managed to do on all but one of their previous games of the season – and the League title would be theirs for the first time in 44 years. They were 2-1 down to QPR as the 90 minutes were up. Then, entering the time added on for how long it took Joey Barton to get sent off, City scored and then scored again. Can you blame the crowd for taking to the pitch under such circumstances? Despair to elation in seconds.

3. Wembley 1977

Scotland beat England 2-1 at Wembley and won the Home Internationals (remember them?). Within seconds of the final whistle, the pitch was covered totally by Caledonian exuberance. Flags were flying, tartan was being waved and goalposts were getting broken. It looked chaotic and it probably was. For a time it was rare to meet a Scottish fan who didn't claim to have a bit of Wembley turf in his garden.

2. Maine Road 1983

A unique pitch invasion in that we know one of the people involved. Cast your mind back to the final day of the 1982/3 season and a time when football was very different. Manchester City needed a draw against Luton to stay in the top division. Luton needed a win. It was deadlock until the 85th minute, when Yugoslav Raddy Antic scored for the Hatters. Some Luton fans made it onto the pitch after the final whistle, but who was that amongst them galloping around in a beige suit with his hands in the air? It was manager David Pleat creating an iconic moment and displaying a uniform that has become every bit as famous as Brian Clough's green jumper.

1. Wembley 1966

Possibly the most iconic pitch invasion of all time. With all eyes on Geoff Hurst bearing down on West German goalkeeper Hans Tilkowski, BBC commentator Kenneth Wolstenholme notes something out of the corner of his eye and interrupts his commentary: 'And here comes Hurst! He's got... Some people are on the pitch! They think it's all over! It is now, it's four!' And if you can't feel the hairs on the back of your neck standing up, you're either Scottish or Andy Johnson.

Top ten 606 callers

606 is the UK's biggest football phone-in for a reason. You make it insightful, engrossing and, at times, utterly hilarious – and for that we thank you dearly. Here are the calls we still talk about.

10. Andy Anson on England's failed World Cup bid
Just 48 hours after England unceremoniously lost in its effort to host the 2018 World Cup finals, England's bid Chief Exec Andy Anson picked up the phone to talk the nation through our disappointment. After an unprecedented grilling by 5 live's 606 hosts Darren Fletcher and Robbie Savage, Mr Anson then faced questions from angered callers and frustrated football fans.

9. Paul on racism in England
The issue of racism is something that has been heavily debated on 606 in the past few seasons. Paul's call into the show about John Terry retaining the England captaincy was probably one of the most heated debates on the subject to date. Paul was a Chelsea fan who had tickets to an upcoming England game, but in light of an incident involving the England captain, refused to take his family to Wembley. The 'innocent until proven guilty' stance was not an option for Paul who took Jason Roberts to task.

8. Joey Barton defends himself on 606
Ricky, a Newcastle fan, was on the show saying that he hoped that Joey Barton would stay at Newcastle even though he'd been sent off after a mêlée the day before against Arsenal. Cue Mark Chapman to ask the man himself if he was staying at the Northeast club. 'Am I staying at Newcastle? I'm in Newcastle, it's hard for me to get out...' But get out he did.

7. Frank on 'Six Times Six'
606 has a regular feature called 'Six Times Six', where callers have six seconds to make their point. See what we did there? Frank was caller six and after Robbie had muttered the words, 'Caller six, name, team, point, go!' Frank failed to answer (despite producer Jo shouting down the line, 'Come on Frank!' so loudly it bled through). Dead air is always a pleasure on 606.

After the feature finished, we got Frank back on to make his point. He set off: 'Serious incidents, red cards. Debatable incidents, yellow cards... a football match is made up of 22 players. I don't like seeing games when there's a man short, especially when it happens in the first ten minutes. I'll let you get on with it. Ta-ra.' Cue howls of laughter. We decide when the call ends, not you, callers!

6. Bob the Man City fan

Bob, a Manchester City fan, was on top of the world when he called **606**. On top of Everest, in fact. As he pressed home his point to Darren Fletcher and Robbie Savage that Roberto Mancini should stay at Manchester City for the long haul, Bob encompassed what **606** is all about – eccentricity, passion and joy – in one spectacular call. Bob: 'Darren, let me educate you... this guy is good, believe me... he plays the Italian way and you've got to live with it.' **606** host Darren Fletcher could only agree: 'I've never argued with someone so much that I've agreed with.'

5. Graeme on Gary Speed's death

It was a day that hit us all hard. News of Gary Speed's death had filtered through and Darren Fletcher and (personal friend to Gary) Robbie Savage were to host the show that evening. Graeme was first on a special show dedicated to Gary, and he typified the super-emotional show that evening. Graeme had worked with him on his charity golf-day while the former Wales manager was playing at Newcastle, and paid tribute to Gary's top-class personality and his manner towards everyone he came across. His parting sentence summed it up for us all: 'He was an absolute gent.'

4. Dan the Spurs fan

A consistent hot topic on **606** is fans booing their own players. Dan was infuriated by Robbie Savage's suggestion that fans should support their team no matter what. In Dan's opinion, if the players are not filling their job criteria, then the fans – who pay a substantial amount of money to watch them – hold the right to boo them. Robbie Savage, who was booed a lot as a player, knows the feeling all too well. However, this was one argument Robbie was destined not to win. Mark Chapman suggested that players only get booed when they don't try their hardest on the pitch. Robbie responded, 'When do players not try?! Tell me?!' To which Mark replied, 'I'm fairly sure I read in a book recently, that this footballer [Robbie Savage] went onto a pitch and didn't try because he was angling for a transfer...' 1-0 Chappers.

3. Malcolm says, 'Get rid of Capello, the dictator'

England had just drawn 0-0 with Algeria in their World Cup qualifying group in South Africa with an underwhelming display and England fans were furious. None more so than Malcolm, who called up Alan Green to tell him so: 'Why was Rooney on the pitch? Why was Lampard on the pitch? Why was Gerrard on the pitch? [Fabio Capello] is tactically unaware, he hasn't got a clue, get rid of him immediately. Put Beckham in charge until we get knocked out, because he's got more passion on the bench than the players have on the pitch.'

The show still holds the record for the most calls received by **606** on one evening. Who says we don't care about international football any more?

2. Pizza gate – Robert

Trainers, pizza – we always sweat the big stuff on the show. Middlesbrough fan Robert was furious when he saw his team's coach festooned with takeaway pizza boxes after losing 3-1 away to QPR. Robbie insisted that it was a perfectly reasonable post-match meal: 'Pizzas are good for you ... I just had a pizza, chicken curry and chips.' Robert argued, 'Why can't you have good carbs? Maybe some meat, maybe some potatoes. I'd have some salad or something.'

Robbie's reply: 'WOWOWOWOWOWOWOW, you'd eat a salad? What is this, Slim-fast?!'

What a ding-dong.

1. Seven pairs of trainers – David

We like to discuss the big issues in football each week on **606**, and the seven pairs of trainers call is no exception. As Mark Chapman said at the time, 'In all my years listening to **606** as a kid, with Danny Baker then everybody who's done it since, that's one of the funniest points I think I've ever heard.' The reason for David's call was simple. He suggested that Robbie Savage had bought seven pairs of trainers in a shop and made a boy carry all the boxes to the car while he carried nothing. His point – made up or not – was that footballers in the modern game aren't in touch with the fans, nor living in the real world. Robbie was having none of it: 'David! David! I tell you what now, that's a lie... don't say I've bought seven pairs of trainers in a shop and made a little boy carry them out... you're a liar! ... People like you really wind me up!'

Famous fans

There's nothing more satisfying than seeing a celebrity jumping for joy with as much passion as your average punter. Nor seeing one trudging home having just lost the FA Cup final. Even with superstar status and millions in the bank, they're just like us, right? Football can hurt Mr Superstar, just as much as it hurts us. Spotting a celeb in the crowd also inspires the lyrical geniuses among you: when Oasis's Gallagher brothers were spotted at Spurs, chants of 'sh*t Chas 'n' Dave, you're just a shi*t Chas 'n' Dave' rang round White Hart Lane. Here's our favourite football shirt-wearing celebs.

10. Steve Lamacq – Colchester
BBC Radio 6 Music DJ Steve Lamacq has been a season ticket-holder at Colchester United on and off since 1982. He currently has one for the new ground situated right next to the M11. It's picturesque. He's sponsored games twice – and United have lost both times. On the first occasion, the Us were losing 4-0 by halftime. He says he will sponsor another game, if only to get a hat-trick.

9. Stephen Fry – Norwich
Stephen Fry grew up in Norfolk and has supported the Canaries since he was a young boy. He has described supporting Norwich as one of the great pleasures of life. Despite his playing days being largely over, he has offered up his services to Paul Lambert and apparently has a good right foot. He joined the board of Norwich City Football Club in August 2010.

8. The Chuckle Brothers – Rotherham United
Much loved for their catchphrase 'To me, to you', Paul and Barry are true Rotherham United fans and in January 2007 Chairman Denis Coleman announced that the brothers had both been made Honorary Presidents of the football club. The brothers are apparently good mates with former Rotherham manager Ronnie Moore.

7. Hugh Grant – Fulham
Before finding fame on the big screen, Hugh Grant worked as an assistant groundsman at Craven Cottage. Grant can often be seen at the Cottage, and he even joined the hordes of Fulham fans who travelled to Hamburg in 2010 for the Europa League final – only to see Fulham lose 2-1 to Atlético Madrid. And apparently in 1993, when money was tight at the Cottage, Hugh Grant put

£60,000 towards the signing of Roberto Herrera. It's always useful to have rich friends.

6. Mick Hucknall – Manchester United

Maybe the naming of Simply Red was something to do with Hucknall's red locks, or maybe it's simply because Hucknall is a massive Manchester United fan. Hucknall has supported Manchester United since he was 8 years old, and cites one man as the source of his allegiance: George Best. In 2011, Hucknall sang at Edwin van der Sar's testimonial.

5. Frank Skinner – West Brom

Frank Skinner, real name Christopher Collins, was born in Oldbury and went to his first Baggies game when he was 10 years old. Not only has the comic supported his club from the stands, he has also helped his country by co-writing 'Three Lions' in 1996, which became England's anthem in the Euros that year. According to Skinner, his all-time favourite Baggies player is Tony Bomber Brown.

4. Ray Winstone – West Ham

There are a few famous faces that can regularly be seen at the stands in Upton Park, Keira Knightley and Russell Brand to name just two. But one of the club's most famous fans, who even modelled the Umbro home kit in 2009/10, is lifelong fan and Hollywood actor Ray Winstone.

3. The Gallagher Brothers – Manchester City

Rock 'n' rollers Liam and Noel Gallagher are two of Man City's most famous fans. Noel went to his first game back in 1971 with his dad and saw Man City lose 5-1 to Newcastle United at Maine Road. The brothers are true blues and are regulars at most games.

2. Sean Bean – Sheffield United

Sean Bean is one hell of a famous fan. In 1990 when Sheffield United won their promotion, Bean got '100% Blade' tattooed on his left shoulder, and in 2002 he was appointed a director at the club. Sheffield United got relegated from the Premier League in 2006/7. Neil Warnock later resigned as manager, and Bean stepped down as director and returned to the terraces.

1. Danny Baker – Millwall

BBC Radio 5 live presenter and 606's very own genius of the airwaves, Danny Baker was born in Deptford round the corner from Millwall and is a regular at the Den. We love his unique take on life as a fan: 'When Rioch came to Millwall, we were depressed and miserable. He's done a brilliant job of turning it around. Now we are miserable and depressed.' The Candyman is the man.

Fans with instruments

If you are going to sing and dance in support of your team, it makes sense to bring in instruments of varying kinds to add to the noise and thus spur on your team. Or not, in some cases.

10. Sheffield Wednesday Band
The Wednesday Band is the same band as the England Supporters Band. 'Why are they mentioned twice, then?' we hear you cry. Well, it's because there are not a lot of different instruments you can bring to a match, and considering brass bands are like a well-known brand of toast topping made from extract of yeast, it seems only fair to let you decide if you love them or hate them. They were even banned from playing at Hillsborough until 2009.

9. Helen the Bell
Helen 'the Bell' Turner was 85 when she died. She was a regular at Maine Road for more than 30 years, and a supporter all her life. She was also a favourite with both fans and players. She was given a standing ovation on the day she rang the bell for the final time at Maine road when City moved to the Etihad in 2003. Her proudest moment came when she was invited onto the pitch to do a lap of honour with the team when City won the League Cup in 1970.

8. Bolton Drummers
The *Guardian* said this about the Reebok stadium: 'Any ground that needs a drummer is suspicious.' The drummers were installed to try and raise the atmosphere in the relatively new stadium. As to whether or not they work or make a difference, we'll leave it up to you to decide...

7. Scotland bagpipers
It wouldn't be the Tartan Army without someone belting out a tune on the bagpipes, would it? Whether it's 'Flower of Scotland' or 'Scotland the Brave', a bagpiper makes any party Scottish. And again there can be no better feeling as a football fan than being led out of a train station in Europe to go and watch your team by a bagpiper piping the Scottish national anthem.

6. Wisla Krakow – drummer and conductor
Polish side Wisla Krakow use their drummer as a conductor for a whole stand of home support. The conductor stands facing the crowd, away from the pitch, and bangs his drum while leading the fans in songs and chants to rather

dramatic effect. He should be help up as a shining example of how a drum should be used at a football game. Top Drawer.

5. Ebbsfleet United drummer

Drummers are present up and down the country as a focal point to create some atmosphere at grounds. But is there really a need for a drummer when only 70 of your fans turn up to an away game? According to a well-known video-hosting website, Ebbsfleet's drummer was banging away for the duration of one video with only eight fans around him. Ten out of ten for effort.

4. Brazil carnival atmosphere

How can you describe the party atmosphere that follows the Brazilians about? Drums, samba and scantily-clad women? There's something about those drums and the samba beat, though, that seems to make an atmosphere electric, and the Brazilians do it better than anyone else.

3. South African vuvuzelas

The long, trumpet-shaped instrument made famous in the 2010 World Cup in South Africa. The sound it makes is like a million mutated ninja bumble bees. They made watching the World Cup nigh-on impossible, unless you had the TV muted or your earplugs in.

2. Pompey Bell

John 'Portsmouth Football Club' Westwood. Yup, the man who changed his name by deed poll, the man who has 'PFC' engraved on his teeth, the man with the stovepipe hat and the curly wig, the man who insists on incessantly ringing that bell from minute 1 to minute 90. Apparently, it's to represent the 'Pompey Chimes' when, in fact, for the majority of us, it represents a headache.

1. England Supporters Band

These guys follow England everywhere. They even have their own website and are sponsored by a pie manufacturer. Who'd have thought it, football supporters being supported by pies? The England Band play in support of the England football team at home and away and have done since 1996. And they always seem to strike up 'The Great Escape' when England are cruising at 3-0.

Iconic fan outfits

It is not enough to simply show up for every game home and away. It's not enough to bore your friends silly with your non-stop talk about your club, and not enough to dedicate huge amounts of your spare wonga to their coffers. No, expressing your love to the world through clothes is equally as important. Here are ten of our favourite football Beau Brummels.

10. Blue Honeymoon
Manchester City fan Karen Bell got married in a wedding dress made from her husband's old replica shirts. Karen spent three weeks turning the kit into a dress fulfilling the custom of something old, something new, something borrowed and something blue.

Karen and Simon exchanged vows in Chester before heading to Manchester to watch their side beat Stoke 3-0. There were mixed emotions for Simon, who gained a wife clad in City colours but parted company with his collection of replica shirts.

9. John Anthony Portsmouth Football Club Westwood
Portsmouth fan John Anthony Portsmouth Football Club Westwood is a must see attraction when visiting Fratton Park. His top hat and chequered blue and white leather waistcoat, accompanied by his tapestry of tattoos and blue hair, make him one of football's most recognisable figures. John can always be seen and heard ringing his bell during games at Fratton Park.

8. Brazilian samba girls
Female Brazilian football fans have sent pulses racing on a global stage. Face paints, skimpy Brazilian crop tops and blue hot pants complete the look that most cameramen find difficult to ignore.

7. Toon fans with their tums out
In Tyneside no matter what the weather, nor even the score-line, you are likely to see at least one brave Newcastle United fan proudly displaying his belly. Not a six-pack in sight, brown ale aside.

6. The Fellaini wig
Everton midfielder Marouane Fellaini has become a cult hero at Goodison Park since arriving from Standard Liege in September 2008. Apart from his knack of scoring important goals, Fellaini's hairstyle has been a major part of

his popularity. Everton fans at Goodison can be seen sporting the 'Fellaini wig'.

5. The St George's knights
International competitions have seen a dramatic increase in England fans dressed as knights in armour with shields, swords and white and red surcoats.

4. Flags and scarves in the Kop End
Irrespective of the club you follow, the sight of Liverpool fans in the Kop donned in red, white and gold is bound to stir emotion. Liverpool fans with scarves outstretched accompanied by an array of flags is one of the most iconic sights in football.

3. Chelsea Pensioners
The Chelsea Pensioners are retired military veterans and live in the Royal Hospital Chelsea. Chelsea's first nickname was the Pensioners, and until the 1950s the club crest featured a Chelsea Pensioner.

The Pensioners can always be seen at Stamford Bridge and in 2010/11 the Chelsea kit had a red trim on the collar in a nod to their trademark red coats.

2. Sunglasses please
The brighter the shade of orange the better, as far as Dutch fans are concerned. Orange pig tails and orange inflatable objects are classic Dutch accessories.

1. The Tartan Army
In the 606 office, feeling is unanimous that Scotland fans are the best-dressed. The tartan kilt and sporran, woollen socks and Ghillie brogues accompanied by blue and white face-paint, a glengarry hat and replica shirt makes them the sharpest-dressed fans in world football.

Loudest fans

We all have something to aspire to with our football teams. Maybe it's avoiding relegation. Maybe it's signing a half-decent striker. Maybe it's the hope of a well-organised and compact 4-4-2. Maybe it's ending a game without a sarcastic clap from your fellow home fans. Maybe you'd like your team to be known for its attractive, free-flowing football. Or maybe... you want your team to have the LOUDEST FANS. In the WORLD. You want your virtual amplifier to go up to 11. You might be rubbish,* but at least you are LOUD RUBBISH.

Our methodology is more than a little flawed. The winner, though, cannot be doubted as this was a proper test undertaken by the *Guinness Book of Records* itself. A representative held up what looked like a breathalyser to measure the actual decibels in Galatasaray's niftily named Ali Sami Yen Sport Complex Türk Telekom Arena.

The rest have been whittled down to a list by the scientific method of looking on YouTube. Not really. Some of the team have actually been to some of these far-flung cauldrons of noise!

10. The Britannia Stadium – Stoke City
They may have ugly, lumpy, bumpy physical football to look at, but the Stokies are certainly loud. Relentlessly loud. Always good to have something to do when you're bored.

9. La Bombonera – Boca Juniors (Buenos Aires, Argentina)
When Boca Juniors play here, the noise is audible all the way to San Telmo. The 49,000-capacity La Bombonera is in the working-class La Boca barrio, and when ultimate rival River Plate arrives for the Superclásico, it's time for the earplugs.

8. Anfield – Liverpool
When Liverpool used to play regularly in the Champions League, the noise was incredible – but even at a normal home game, the noise is impressive.

7. Estádio do Maracanã – Flamengo (Rio de Janeiro, Brazil)
Flamengo, in a very Brazilian way, are extraordinarily loud. Particularly so when rivals Vasco da Gama visit. And it's not just the singing – the Surdo and Zabumba drums give a heart-thumping percussive thrill.

---

* We are not suggesting that all the teams on this list are rubbish.

6. Fratton Park – Portsmouth

A club so proud of their ability to raise a racket that a big internal argument went on regarding whether Pompey superfan John Westwood's famous bell and Dave Anderson's drums should continue. Some fans felt that their constant use was stopping the crowd doing what they wanted to do – belt out Pompey's traditional songs at the tops of their voices.

5. Stadio San Siro – Inter & AC Milan (Milan, Italy)

The stadium can hold 80,000 mental fans, which means that, even on an average match day, it's loud. But when it really begins to hurt is when the as Derby della Madonnina gets under way, with both sets of fans 'at home'.

4. Estadio Centenario – Penarol & Nacional (Montevideo, Uruguay)

The Centenario is the graveyard for many international sides – notably Brazil, who have only managed three wins in 20 matches here. It's another ground-share – and another raucous cauldron of cacophony. The Penarol-Nacional derby, in a country where everyone is either Penarol or Nacional, can cause the fillings to jump from your teeth.

3. Westfalenstadion – Borussia Dortmund (Dortmund, Germany)

Germany's loudest ultra-fans by some way, the crazed Dortmundistas (if that is a word) tend to out-ultra all the other ultras in Europe. Loud, proud and a lot of fun to know, they are 80,700 screaming bags of football joy. Home games, particularly European ones, are a sight to behold.

2. De Kuip Stadion – Feyenoord (Rotterdam, Holland)

Rotterdam is a true working-class city, and its inhabitants are very proud of its defiantly old-school – and defiantly LOUD – stadium. It's one of the most intimidating arenas for visiting teams and fans. The home ultras, known as 'Het Legioen' ('the Legion'), expect their players to give all for the shirt. In return, ALL the home fans roar their support.

1. Ali Sami Yen Sport Complex Türk Telekom Arena – Galatasaray (Istanbul, Turkey)

The one that cannot be argued with. On 18 March 2011, at Galatasaray's brand new stadium, Ali Sami Yen Sport Complex Türk Telekom Arena in Istanbul, with everything undertaken according to Guinness's strict World Records guidelines, Galatasaray fans recorded a reading of 131.76 decibels – loud enough to cause immediate hearing damage. Well done, the Turks!

Worst mascots

Every football club has a mascot. We're not sure why. Perhaps it spread in a kind of weird keeping-up-with-the-Joneses type way – the club ten miles down the road have invented a figurehead for the club and had an approximation of it run up in foam, so we'd better. In a way, at least that's better than some of the cynical efforts below, whose purpose is to support the football family (which of course translates as 'make a lot of money').

Anyway, after much cringing in the **606** office, here are our choices for worst mascot of all time. We were thinking though, perhaps we need one. Tommy the Telephone, maybe. Texty the Tiger. Tweety the Owl, perhaps?

10. The Jerboas, 2011 Asian Cup
For the 2011 Asian Cup in Qatar, creator Ahmed Al Maadheed decided that the thing that most represented Qatar to the world was a type of hopping desert rodent that only comes out at night and bathes in sand. Not only that, good old Ahmed decided that the mascot, singular, was not enough. No – we had to have a whole family of them. In pastel colours.

9. The Spheriks, South Korea and Japan, 2002 World Cup
They're orange! They're purple! They're blue! They're futuristic! They're rubbish!

8. Moonchester, Manchester City
All that money and the best they can come up with is this. In the world of football mascots, if you can breed a terrier with a lady, you can breed a moon with a bat. This phoned-in will-this-do monstrosity is neither fish nor fowl, and either would have been better.

7. Gunnersaurus, Arsenal
This might be acceptable if Arsenal's stadium was called 'Jurassic Park'. Arsenal, a club ahead of the game in so many ways, have even given Gunnersaurus his own official blog on the Junior Gunners section of the website.

6. Hammerhead, West Ham
Unveiling their new mascot Hammerhead in 2011, the club described him being as strong as an iron. He actually looks more like Kryten from *Red Dwarf*.

5. Pilgrim Pete, Plymouth Argyle
It's not the concept so much as the execution. The pilgrims left from Plymouth

to the New World. Fine. We get it. So why have Argyle used a leftover St Patrick's Day leprechaun outfit?

4. Lucas the Kop Kat, Leeds United

Striking laughter into the opposition is this rather unattractive unspecified big cat. Does it represent the roar from the club badge or the near extinction of both club and animal?

3. Fred the Red, Manchester United

What is it? Is it a sunburnt teddy bear? No, it's what you get when you try and make a child-friendly devil. Let's take the devil, the Actual Devil, a powerful, supernatural entity that is the personification of evil and the enemy of God and humankind, and make him appeal to children. Behold!

2. Mrs Growler, Huddersfield Town

Yes, dear reader, you read that right. The spectacularly named mascot of the Terriers looks like a terrible genetic experiment. You know *The Fly*, with Jeff Goldblum? Imagine 'The Terrier' with Bet Lynch. A humanoid dog. With mascara on. Called Mrs Growler.

1. Pottermus, Stoke City

Not another 'Gunnersaurus' type dinosaur. No, no, no. Nothing as obvious as that. Stoke City's mascot is a hippopotamus. Why's that, you ask? Come closer. It is because Stoke's nickname is 'the Potters', and within the word 'Potter' is another word. That word is 'pot'. The word 'pot' can also obviously be found in the word 'hippopotamus'! Obvious, now you know, isn't it? Other Stoke mascots that nearly made it: Sammy the Spot, a giant foam zit. Peter the Pot (he's a pot) and Oswald the Otter.

Memorable fan protests

Fans are the most important link in the ever-lengthening chain of football. Without their support and money, quite frankly the whole edifice comes crashing down. Most of the time, the fans are reasonable creatures who will sustain terrible food, drastic season ticket price hikes and poor performances with an admirable sense of humour. Yet push them too far and they will soon let you know about it.

10. Silent protest
Swedish fans felt so mistreated by their FA, in a derby between AIK and Djurgården in September 2011, they protested in silence for the first ten minutes. After that ten minutes was up, the crowd went wild. The good old silent treatment can work.

9. Man United fans
When the Glazer family took over the red side of Manchester, it saddled the clubs with debts. This didn't please United fans and they started wearing green and gold. The colours symbolised the original club that was set up by Newton Heath in 1902. The Glazers are still in control at Old Trafford and you can often see fans wearing green and gold.

8. Fan handcuffs himself to post
In a match between Everton and Manchester City at Goodison in February 2012, a fan ran onto the pitch and handcuffed himself to Joe Hart's goalpost. Apparently his reason for it was that his daughter hadn't got a job. We're not quite sure why he decided that this was the right place to protest about someone's recruitment policy.

7. Newcastle fans
Mike Ashley isn't the most popular man with the Newcastle faithful. They weren't happy at all when he sacked Chris Hughton and replaced him with Alan Pardew. They held up banners saying 'Cockney Mafia out' and sang 'There's only one Chris Hughton'. Despite the lack of support, Pardew nearly got Newcastle into the Champions League. Since then the protests haven't been as strong.

6. Blackburn fans
You could say that the whole of the 2011/12 season for Blackburn was just

one big protest against manager Steve Kean and Venky's ownership of the club. The Blackburn faithful were not happy with the way the Venky's group ran their club. The group is a big chicken brand in India, and at one protest – in May 2012 when Blackburn faced Wigan – the fans released a chicken onto the pitch.

Also throughout the season fans would shout 'Kean Out' and hold up signs with the same message. The booing at Ewood Park became a regular occurrence.

5. Genoa fans

In April 2012, fans were so disgusted by the way Genoa were playing against Siena (4-0 down after 53 minutes) that they started throwing flares onto the pitch and were climbing the barriers. The game got so out of hand that the fans ordered the players to take off their shirts as they were unworthy of wearing them. Most players agreed and took off their shirts. After a 45-minute delay, the game continued and they got one goal back but still lost 4-1. The actions resulted in the next two games being played behind closed doors.

4. Basel Fans

Lunchtime kick-offs seem to cause so much trouble. Basel fans were upset when their top-of-the-table clash with FC Luzern was moved to 12.45. This was because it clashed with the final of the indoor tennis tournament, which featured Roger Federer and Novak Djokovic. Fans were not happy because the Swiss TV networks showed the tennis, so they threw tennis balls onto the pitch.

3. Wimbledon fans

After Pete Winkelman took over Wimbledon FC, and successfully moved the club to Milton Keynes in 2003, attendances dropped dramatically as supporters set up their own club: AFC Wimbledon. The fans held trials on Wimbledon Common to find players, and between February 2003 and December 2004 went 78 consecutive League games without defeat, an all-time record in English football. The club were promoted to League football less than a decade after their formation when they beat Luton Town on penalties in the 2011 Conference Premier play-off final. This club was the first in a spate of so-called 'phoenix clubs', formed in protest at the decline of a team, and honourable mentions should go to Chester FC and FC United of Manchester.

2. Schalke Fans

We like fans with a good sense of humour and Schalke fans certainly showed that. They opened a banner saying '90 euros per ticket = 1 euro per minute? Football is not phone sex.' The banner appeared at the first leg of a Europa League quarter-final between Schalke and Athletic Bilbao in 2012, after it was announced that tickets for the return leg would cost 90 euros.

1. Liverpool fans

After the Hillsborough disaster in 1989, the *Sun* ran a front page headlined the 'The Truth', blaming Liverpool fans for the disaster. There was then an immediate boycott of the paper, and circulation in the Merseyside area went from 120,000 to 11,000 within a week. The boycott was still present at the Carling Cup final in 2012, which coincided with the launch of the *Sun on Sunday*.

Most powerful fans

If **606** were a club, we'd be Barca: unsurpassed consistent experts who are owned and run by the fans. No need for AGMs – just the weekly shows. In fact we quite like the idea of **606** presenters voted in by the fans according to promises of who or what they'll buy for you. We do fear though, that all Robbie would offer to win your vote is white trainers or a taxi! All power to the people, or in the case of the clubs below, all power to the fans.

7. Argentinian fans
The inclusion of some of Argentinian club fans on this list is nothing for them to be proud of. Gangs called *barra bravas* have taken over stadiums. Inside they start chants and light flares. Outside they make money from everything from parking to merchandise, and are so entwined with the clubs that they're reported to have taken cuts of transfers fees and even of some players' wages. The Boca Juniors group 'La Doce' (the Twelfth) are particularly notorious.

6. AC Milan
Many clubs boast a celebrity following, and politicians in particular like to align themselves to a club in an attempt to look in touch with the public. It's a little different, though, when the prime minister of your country is simultaneously the premier and owner of one of its largest football clubs. That's the situation Milan were in with Silvio Berlusconi for most of the last 20 years. Would you want to step into the PM's office to ask for a new contract or more money for players?

5. Athletic Bilbao
Athletic operate the *socio* system in the same way as Barca and Real, but they truly are a unique club. The fans and the Basque region from which they hail are so much a part of the club that they are barely distinguishable. This is because they have a long-practised policy of only allowing players from the Basque region to play for Athletic. A change from this policy would never be allowed by the fans, for whom Athletic are like a national team. Limiting themselves to a small region has not limited their playing ability – they reached the UEFA Cup final this year, beating Manchester United over two legs along the way.

4. Brentford
Fan ownership is the holy grail for many supporters, but with the money involved in the game today it's often just a pipe dream. Clubs that have been

able to do it are often 'phoenix clubs' such as AFC Wimbledon, FC United – new start-ups responding to disillusionment in the running of the original clubs. But Brentford supporters managed to raise enough money to take majority ownership of their 117-year-old club in 2006. The Bees United Supporters Trust remains in control of the club today, which is in a stable financial condition and established in League One. Some fans have even started calling themselves 'the Barcelona of League One'.

3. Galatasaray
Nothing in English football could quite prepare fans or players for visiting Galatasaray's notorious Ali Sami Yen Stadium, or as it was affectionately known, 'Hell'. Despite having a capacity of less than 25,000, the ferocity of the atmosphere created has become legendary. Dutch midfielder Edgar Davids once said whilst playing for Juventus that if they had fans like Galatasaray, no team could ever stop them. Sadly, the stadium was demolished in 2011, but their new home is the impressive 52,000-seater Türk Telekom Arena.

2. Brazilian fans
There's no point separating individual teams from Brazil in this category, because they're all guilty of it. If you think clubs in England don't give their managers enough time, count yourself lucky you don't live in Brazil. As a general rule in the Campeonato (Brazil's top flight), three consecutive losses and the fans expect a managerial change. Don't believe us? In the 2009/10 season in the English Premier League there were five managerial changes, and eight in 2010/11. In Brazil, there were 37 changes in 2010, and a comparatively reasonable 29 in 2011. There are only 20 teams in the League!

1. Barcelona/Real Madrid
The two Spanish giants are registered associations rather than companies, meaning shares cannot be bought in the club. The club's running is decided by the *socios* (members) who vote in presidential elections (Real has 60,000 *socios*; Barcelona 170,000). The result of this system is that potential presidential candidates have promised to sign certain players if they are voted in; this led to what can only be described as the nuclear arms race that was the Galácticos era. It came to a head in 2003, when both Real's Florentino Perez and Barca's Joan Laporta promised to sign David Beckham. Laporta and the Barca faithful eventually had to settle for Ronaldinho.

Quietest fans

Not all fans want to sing and shout and shake it all about, you know. Some like to savour their football in silence, their concentration only broken by the occasional burst of 'We forgot that you were here...' from the opposing fans. Here are – keep it quiet – ten vocally challenged sets of fans.

10. Peterborough
Posh have had a quick rise in recent years. Promotion in 2009 from League One to the Championship, before being relegated and then bouncing back in 2011 with a play-off final win over Huddersfield at Old Trafford. Even so, the fans have hardly raised the decibels significantly.

9. Doncaster Rovers
They've had much to cheer about in recent years: promotion from the Conference in 2003, promotion from League Two in 2004, and then promotion from League One in 2008 with a play-off victory over Leeds at Wembley. But their fans have been dubbed 'the quietest in the football League' on many forums.

8. West Brom
Second-quietest fans in the Premier League in 2011, with an average of 67 decibels. Maybe it's down to the football played under Roy Hodgson or the jokes told at half time by fellow devotee, Frank Skinner...

7. Bolton
Bolton's average decibel reading was just 69 in 2011. The atmosphere at the Reebok today is not the same as it used to be in the days where Jay Jay Okocha and Youri Djorkaeff graced the pitch. In the days of Big Sam managing at Bolton, there were many cult players whose names would be echoing around the Reebok. They haven't had much to shout about recently, having been relegated in 2012.

6. Chelsea
For a club with so much money, and success, their fans should be raising the roof off of Stamford Bridge. However, research shows that they averaged only 80 decibels in the 2011 season, which puts them ninth-best in the Premier League. And ten of those were the sound of prawn sandwiches being munched upon.

5. Blackburn

Rovers rarely fill Ewood Park. In fact, the only real noise recently has been dissent towards Venky's and Steve Kean.

4. Wigan

Wigan is predominantly a rugby town so the DW Stadium is rarely full, averaging a very average 72 decibels in 2011.

3. Watford

Even though Hornets fans have had quite a lot to shout about in recent years – FA Cup semi-final in 2003 and two stints in the Premier League in 1999 and 2006 – Vicarage Road is not exactly a cauldron of noise. They obviously need Elton John to come more often and sing to excite the fans. Then again...

2. Fulham

Once named the quietest ground in the Premier League in 2011 with an average of 65 decibels.

1. Arsenal

The old ground, Highbury, was nicknamed 'the Library'. Enough said.

Best streakers

You know those really boring games where no one on the pitch seems bothered by the result and it is cold and grey and even the referee looks bored out of his head and you just wish something would happen to liven things up? Well, here are ten games where the fans got their wish. And a whole lot more.

10. Middlesbrough v Newcastle, December 1998
Paul Gascoigne and co were confronted by a Christmas-themed female streaker during the North-East derby between Newcastle and Middlesbrough in 1998. The game ended 2-2, an inspired Nikos Dabizas grabbing a late equaliser.

9. Burnley v Preston, March 2002
During this derby at Turf Moor, it took the Burnley mascot to stop a male streaker. As he ran onto the pitch, the streaker seemed to duck and dive plenty of stewards, but not Bertie Bee, who rugby-tackled him in fine fashion. And then sprang up and celebrated. Burnley won the game 2-1.

8. Liverpool v West Ham, November 2002
When Wayne Rooney was an Everton player, obviously all Liverpool fans hated him. But one fan took this to a new level. As he paraded around the pitch totally naked, he had painted on his back 'Rooney is an...' with arrows pointing to his buttocks.

7. Charlton v Aston Villa, December 1998
During Charlton and Villa's clash at the Valley, a streaker ran on, only to be confronted by an angry Gareth Southgate. For some bizarre reason, Southgate ended up kissing him. Well, that's what it looked like, maybe he was celebrating his team's 1-0 win.

6. Liverpool v Arsenal, January 1995
During the quarter-final of the then-named Coca Cola Cup in 1995, a streaker ran out and shook hands with David Seaman, just after Ian Rush had scored the goal that put Liverpool through to the semi-final. Liverpool went on to win the Cup that year. That's naked ambition for you.

5. Porto v Celtic, May 2003
Serial streaker Mark Roberts disrupted play in this EUFA Cup final by deciding he wanted to go on a run with the ball towards goal. The keeper, Vitor Baia, debated ignoring him but did not want the embarrassment of letting a streaker score past him, so saved his weak effort on goal.

4. Dorchester v Havant and Waterlooville, March 2011
When a streaker came onto the pitch, the stewards were doing such a terrible job in waylaying him that player Ashley Vickers thought he would take matters into his own hands. But the referee didn't like the way Vickers handled the matter and gave him a straight red card.

3. York City v Grays Athletic, December 2008
Just ignore him, lad... In this game between York City and Grays Athletic, a streaker ran onto the pitch totally unchallenged by anyone. He did a lap of honour, but then didn't quite know what to do. A player approached him but, after being ignored by the stewards, the streaker lost interest and wandered off the pitch of his own accord.

2. Aston Villa v Liverpool, May 1995
This game finished 2-0 to Villa. This prompted a streaker to come on the pitch, wearing just trainers and some sunglasses. Andy Townsend seemed to enjoy it and shook his hand.

1. Leeds United v Middlesbrough, May 1997
I'm sure the majority of fans inside Elland Road didn't have their heads in their hands when this blonde streaker came running onto the pitch at Elland Road. No wonder the game finished 1-1.

Strangest fans

They spend hundreds of pounds a year watching 11 men try and kick a leather sphere into some netting with thousands of other fans. Then they phone a radio station to tell other, similarly afflicted fans what they think about the sphere-kicking. 'They', dear reader, are YOU. You oddball. But amidst that crowd of dangerous obsessives that is the football fan community of Great Britain and Northern Ireland, there lurk the *real* obsessives. And we mean that in the nicest sense of the word. Everything is relative in this world, said Wigan left-back Leon Trotsky. So we now present to you, oddballs, the oddballs' oddballs.

10. Spartak Moscow's 12th man
Spartak Moscow's Alex was stepping up to take a penalty against Russian rivals FC Saturn when a fan ran onto the pitch and scored for him. The fan then ran around Saturn's Moscow Central Park pitch in a celebration Adebayor would be proud of.

　　Unfortunately for our heroic 12th man, Spartak still lost the game 2-1.

9. Michael Jackson – Exeter City
In 2001, the singer was made an honorary director of Exeter City FC. During his appearance at St James' Park, his friend Uri Geller said, 'When I asked him what does he know about football he said, "Absolutely nothing, but I love Exeter City."'

8. AC Milan fans harness the power of 'Pacman'
The banner below the image of Pacman chasing a ghost in Barcelona colours reads 'Let's Eat Them!'

7. Fans who show their team where the goal is
After failing to score in five games, Magdeburg fans made arrows to point their side towards where they needed to score. Incredibly, it worked – but they still lost 2-1.

6. Borussia Dortmund fans and the massive flag
Before their home game against VFL Wolfsburg, Borussia Dortmund fans had a plan. We all have our own specific game preparations; some grab a pie before the game, some fans take a particular route to the ground but others – more specifically Borussia Dortmund fans – use an entire stand to intimidate the opposition.

5. Another Geordie – Pete Toogood

Pete Toogood was plucked from the Gallowgate End by Alan Pardew, who hailed him the club's 'number one fan', and even scored when he smashed a penalty past Rob Elliot during a training game. The 19-year-old, from Shieldfield in Newcastle, wears his distinctive uniform to every game and regularly waits outside the club's Benton training ground to meet his heroes. So when Pardew spotted him in the crowd, he was given a morning he will never forget.

4. Topless Geordies

They're like the 'ultras' of the northeast, the hardcore few that show off their beer bellies for the love of their club.

3. Categoria Primera A

Colombian soccer fans brought a coffin with the body of a 17-year-old boy inside to a match between Cucuta Deportivo and Envigado!

2. Pete Sampara – Liverpool FC 'Badge Man'

Liverpool badges are to Pete Sampara what spikes are to a hedgehog. On match days, you can't miss him. Just listen to his waistcoat setting off shoplifter alarms in local shops as he walks past. Pete is on his third homemade waist coat now. They're denim, which he bleaches and then dyes red, if you're interested.

1. John Anthony Portsmouth Football Club Westwood (born 1963)

Yes, him.

He has 60 Pompey tattoos. He has the club crest shaved onto his head and 'PFC' engraved on his teeth. He has a big bell, which even his fellow supporters find annoying, a large stovepipe hat, which only annoyed the little old lady who sits behind him at Fratton Park, and a big curly blue wig. He went into administration for the second time in February 2012. (We made that last one up.)

The 12th Man

Forget the substitute, the real '12th man' at some grounds are the fans who will collectively push their team to victory whilst scaring the hell out of the opposition. Here we celebrate those who have proved indispensable to their club's fortunes.

10. Besiktas
Their fans claim that it is one of the loudest grounds in Europe and goalkeeper Ben Foster agrees. He called the atmosphere the most intimidating and frightening he had experienced when Man Utd played there in 2009. Don't believe us? At one game in 2007, crowd noise reached 132 decibels, a record at the time.

9. Napoli
Back in the days when Maradona and Careca graced Napoli's San Paolo stadium, the fans created an intimidating wall of noise which helped push their team to two League titles and the UEFA Cup. Moreover, the fans stuck by their side when they were relegated to Serie B.

8. Feyenoord
At most grounds, there is a singing contingent pocketed behind a goal or in a corner. At De Kuip, the whole ground gets behind Feyenoord and they do so for the whole 90 minutes.

7. Dinamo Zagreb
The Maksimir Stadium produces a very intimidating atmosphere for away fans and players. England played at the stadium against Croatia in 2006 and were glad to get home. Even more impressive is the fact that such an atmosphere can be generated without a roof on the stadium.

6. Liverpool
A European night at Anfield is like no other and the fans have often acted as the 12th man, particularly in the 2004/5 winning campaign. That year they beat Olympiakos, Bayer Leverkusen, Juventus and Chelsea on their way to Istanbul, and one of the most memorable finals ever. Three-nil down at half time, manager Benitez told his players to go out and play for the fans. Liverpool consequently won on penalties.

5. Galatasaray

During the 1990s and early 2000s, Galatasaray often qualified for Champions League campaigns and viewers were stunned to see their fans packed out in the stadium hours before kick-off, expressing their hostility to anything that did not bear their club's colours.

4. Borussia Dortmund

The Temple of the Yellow Wall is a terrific sight of carnival and colour on Dortmund match days and is erected in the South Grandstand (the largest grandstand in the world,) by 25,000 boisterous fans.

3. Schalke

A collective that really knows how to back its team. 61,000 fans at Arena AufSchalke consistently produce a cauldron atmosphere, which seriously unnerves the opposition. Even when their side are doing poorly, they still turn out in huge numbers.

2. Portsmouth

Their fans are very loud, very loud indeed. Big teams like Manchester United, Tottenham and AC Milan have all struggled when visiting Fratton Park, which remains one of the country's most traditional grounds and therefore perfect for the fans to express themselves fully, usually by singing their trademark anthem, 'The Pompey Chimes'.

1. Boca Juniors

Their fans are nicknamed 'La Doce', which means 'the Twelfth'. Their stadium, the Bombonera, is a very intimidating ground for the opposition, as there is one very small stand, and three others which rise up vertically with the Boca fans segregated behind fencing, creating a cage effect.

Worst-dressed fans

Football fans sometimes dress quite well and, in fact, have started fashion trends from the terraces. However, those that make this list may show passion at matches, but don't necessarily check themselves in the mirror in the morning.

10. Spurs

The Champions League final wasn't just a nail-biting affair for Chelsea fans, but also Spurs fans. If Chelsea lost to Bayern Munich, Spurs would be playing Champions League football, if Chelsea win they wouldn't qualify. So the Spurs fans decided to dress in lederhosen, severely damaging their street cred. It didn't help as Chelsea won the final on penalties.

9. Bayern Munich

Frank Ribery is known as one of the best wide players in the world, but he's also known for the scar that runs down the side of his face, something that occurred during a car accident when he was just 2 years old. The Bayern fans deck themselves out in facial scars to look like the Frenchman. It's not a great look.

8. South Africa

In 2010, South Africa hosted the first World Cup in Africa. It was great to see the passion Africa had for the World Cup. But one sight that did annoy the watching millions was the plastic horn round the necks of the thousands of fans. They knew what was coming when those instruments were played – the sound of a million bees descending on the pitch. This, mixed with the clashing of bright colours, was not the best look or sound to a tournament.

7. Chelsea and Everton

Marouane Fellaini and David Luiz have brought back the afro hair style, big-time. Fellaini was the original. He moved to Everton for £12m and became a hit with the fans early on. Plenty of Everton fans started to show up at Goodison with a huge afro wig. When David Luiz came to Chelsea, he was instantly a cult hero at the Bridge, meaning afros started popping up everywhere amongst the Chelsea faithful.

6. Blackpool

Blackpool seem to be everyone's guilty conscience when it comes to football teams. But the bright orange is a little too much for us all the time. If you're sitting in the ground watching your team, you don't want to have to wear sunglasses just because of the colour of the other team's strip.

5. West Brom

The *Sun* did a survey to find the ugliest and worst-dressed fans in the country. The winners of their survey were... West Bromwich Albion. We're not really sure what West Brom have done to the *Sun*.

4. Hartlepool v Charlton

A group of Hartlepool United fans invaded London in 2012 to cheer on their team against Charlton. 171 of them painted their faces blue and wore white beards and hats in homage to their team's strip and they did it to celebrate the last game of the season. Hartlepool manager Neale Cooper said, 'The fans were fantastic. I got a message on my phone saying, "The Smurfs are invading Charlton", and that was from someone in Scotland.'

3. John Anthony, Portsmouth fan

Probably one of the most well-known fans in football, John is a sight to behold. He can be seen at every Portsmouth game with a long blue and white checked top hat, blue plaited hair and a checked waistcoat. Of course, he wears nothing underneath, rain or shine. As if that wasn't enough, he's covered from head to toe in Portsmouth tattoos.

2. St Pauli

St Pauli are often dubbed as the most left-wing team in the world. The football team of the small port city of Hamburg stand for the poor and are against the rich. They describe themselves as pirates fighting for the poor. Their flag is even a skull and crossbones. They don't hold back in how they dress, either. It looks more like Hallowe'en than a football game when you see their ground swarming with fans wearing masks and black T-shirts with their famous skull and crossbones logo. Not the best of looks.

1. Newcastle

Rain or shine, you're guaranteed to see a section of St James' Park – sorry, we mean 'Sports Direct Arena' – taken up by topless Newcastle United fans. Plenty of other fans around the country do this, but no one to the same extent as the Newcastle faithful. Most like to take off their top to show big bellies and Newcastle tattoos. Passion, we like. But for this, there is no excuse.

CHANTS

Classic chants

It's a fascinating phenomenon that grown adults will happily belt out bursts of classical music adapted with rousing, ingenious, offensive or hilarious lyrics at the football on a Saturday afternoon (or at the pub on a Friday night). No matter how bad you were in the school choir, you'll sing your heart out when safe amongst 20,000 fellow fans. High notes, low notes, who cares if you hit them? As long as you put your heart into it, right? The following ten chants are staples of any club hymn sheet.

10. 'Oh when the blanks go marching in...'
One of football's most recognisable chants started life as an American gospel hymn. Different clubs put their own spin on it, but often it will start off slow and solemn and gradually build into a frenzy. Fans can argue over who imported it first but among the dozens of clubs who regularly sing it, it's probably most associated with Tottenham Hotspur.

9. 'Que sera, sera, whatever will be, will be, we're going to Wembley, que sera, sera...'
Wembley Stadium, new or old, is the great leveller in English football. From Chelsea fans going to their fourth Cup final in six years to Darlington supporters winning an FA Trophy semi, everyone gets excited about the prospect of a trip to north-west London. Singing this (along with 'Wem-bur-leee, Wembley, we're the famous blanky blanky and we're going to Wembley...') when it happens is a rite of passage.

8. 'One blanky blanker, there's only one blanky blanker. Sing when you're winning, you only sing when you're winning...'
In the 1920s, when Cuban composer Joselito Fernandez got rejected by a girl from Guantanamo and decided to write a song about it, it's hard to imagine he knew that he'd just written the refrain that would echo around English football stadiums almost a century later. Infinitely adaptable, it's the automatic song of choice to celebrate any player with a name of four syllables.

7. 'You're not singing, you're not singing, you're not singing any more...'
It's often hard to tell at football matches whether fans get more pleasure from seeing their own team succeed or making the other team's fans miserable; this

is the ultimate expression of that central conflict. Everyone hates to be on the receiving end of it, and it's probably recognition of that fact that makes it so popular.

6. 'And it's Blanky Blanker, Blanky Blanker FC, we're by far the greatest team, the world has ever seen...'
Another of the English football fan's greatest traits is their sense of irony. Sung straight-faced and full-throated from Wycombe to Sunderland, it's testament to the fact that the football stadium is a province in which the normal rules of logic and reason just don't apply.

5. 'Glory, glory Blanky Blanker...'
This classic has been well and truly claimed by Manchester United since the early 1980s. It was recorded as their FA Cup final song in 1983, but before that it had belonged to Leeds, Spurs and originally Hibernian in Scotland. 'Glory glory to the Hibees' was recorded in the 1950s by Scottish comedian and actor Hector Nicol.

4. 'We shall not, we shall not be moved...'
This is another classic that can be traced back to an American folk song. It was even recorded by Elvis and Johnny Cash and developed as a defiant union chant in the tough economic times of the 1930s.

3. 'Blanky Blanky's red and white army...'
Managers are generally under-represented in terms of songs on the terraces, with adoration flowing more naturally to the players. But on those special occasions when the fans feel the boss is due a bit of love, this is a one-song-fits-all formula. Just insert the manager's name and the two main colours of the club, and you've got yourself a classic chant.

2. 'Come on you blanks...'
It doesn't get easier than this one, with just two notes asked of the crowd. It's also the chant that most pleasingly showcases the native accent of the team singing it – the cockney drawl of 'Caaam awn you Irons' (West Ham) and the Black Country burr in 'Cuuum on you bagguys' (West Brom) particularly stand out.

1. 'We love you blank, we do...'
The one thing all real football fans have in common is devotion. You're as likely to hear this classic sung when a team has been relegated as you are when a team wins the League. In the end, whatever happens the whole point of being a fan is that we love our blanks, we really do. There's no simpler or better way to put it.

Worst chants

Ah, the football sing-along, the time when fans bring to the terraces their witty, insightful, often side-splitting and extremely funny songs about players, owners and other fans. Or just drivel. The worst thing is they actually still make us smile, but only slightly. You just can't beat football chants, even the bad ones.

10. Chant at Reading for their captain, Adie Williams
'In our defensive foursome,
He's absolutely awesome,
From Corners he will score some,
He's Adie Williams!'

9. Nottingham Forest to the tune of 'Macarena'
'10 Danny 9 Danny 8 Danny Sonner,
7 Danny 6 Danny 5 Danny Sonner,
4 Danny 3 Danny 2 Danny Sonner,
ONE DANNY SONNER.'

8. Huddersfield Town to the tune of 'Sloop John B' about their player Lee Novak
'We've got Novak,
We've got Nova-ak,
Our carpets are filthy,
We've got Novak.'

7. Norwich City to the tune of 'Take Me Home, Country Roads'
'Take me home to Carrow Road,
To the place I belong,
Norwich City,
Pride of England,
Take me home to Carrow Road.'

6. Hartlepool to the tune of 'One Wheel On My Wagon'
'Hartlepool is my passion,
but I'm still rolling along.
Premiership don't bother me,
We'll be singing the same old sonnnnngggggg.'

5. Chelsea fans to Torres

Fernando Torres has struggled to make an impact at Stamford Bridge since his £50m move from Liverpool. However, it seems the man can do no wrong for the Chelsea faithful. No visit to Stamford Bridge was complete during 2012/13 season without hearing 'Torres, Torres, Torres' repeated over and over and over.

4. Stenhousemuir fans for their popular midfielder, Robert Love

'Love, love will tear you apart again!' to the tune of Joy Division's 'Love Will Tear Us Apart'

3. Southampton fans for José Fonte, their Portuguese centre back

'José Fonte baby, José Fonte woah oh oh!' to the tune of Human League's 'Don't You Want Me'

2. Oldham Athletic

   'Give us a T - T.
   Give us an I - I.
   Give us a T - T.
   Gives us an S - S.
   Put 'em together and waddaya got?
   Tits, Tits, Tits.
   And whaddaya wanna do with 'em?
   Oldham Oldham Oldham.'

1. Chelsea fans mocked Turkish side Galatasaray with a version of the Pet Shop Boys' 'Go West'

   'You're shish,
   And you know you are.
   You're shish.'

Best responses to chants

An ill-mannered bunch of louts most football fans, eh? No, actually. Football fans are amongst the wittiest in the land, especially when it comes to turning the verbal tables on their tormentors – as this top ten proves.

10. 'Where's your famous atmosphere?'
When there is no clever answer, just put your fingers to your lips and sing 'Shhhhh'.

9. 'Who are we? Who are we?'
The response from Villa fans during their game at White Hart Lane, having had the classic 'Who are ya?!' chant sung at them by Spurs fans.

8. '5foot4, 5foot4, we've got Arshavin, f*** Adebayor!'
Arsenal fans response to 'Adebayor, Adebayor, runs hundred metres in 10.4' in a Carling Cup game.

7. 'We're forever reaching finals,
Reaching finals in Hamburg.
We'll be on the beer while they'll be stuck here,
Watching *EastEnders* with their old dear.
We'll be on the Reeperbahn,
They'll still be in Dagenham.
We're forever reaching finals,
Reaching finals in Hamburg!'
Fulham fans respond to West Ham's 'Bubbles' chant.

6. 'We were watching *The Bill*.
What was the score in Seville?'
Rangers fans responding to 'You'll be watching *The Bill*, when we're in Seville' from Celtic, who sang this before their 2002/3 UEFA Cup final. Celtic lost 2-3 to Mourinho's Porto.

5. 'We're the right side.'
In response to: 'We're the left side' – a common exchange between two sides of a stand to see who are the loudest. You know the game is dull if you ever hear this.

4. **'You've got Di Canio, we've got your stereo.'**
Liverpool fans in response to West Ham's chant of 'We've got Di Canio'.

3. **'Rangers till July! You're Rangers till July! We know you are. You know you are. You're Rangers till July!'**
March 2012. Dundee Utd fans in response to the 'We're Rangers till we die' chants regarding financial problems at Rangers.

2. **'We hate Tuesday, hate Tuesday.'**
Millwall fans in response to Sheffield United's chant of 'We hate Wednesday'.

1. **'So are we, so are we, so are we.'**
West Ham fans respond to chants of 'going down, going down'.

Cleverest chants

There are club-specific chants. There are universal chants, where you cut 'n' paste your team's name into the gap. There are chants for players. And then there are those pieces of poetic genius that only rarely meet the ear; the chants that are a cut above the normal terrace fare. They're lyrical gems that are the footballing equivalent of the poetry classics 'How Do I Love Thee?' or 'Kubla Khan'. Seemingly constructed by a kind of lyrical hive mind, these classic chants are timeless hymns to player, team and rival.

10. 'Sunday, Monday, Habib Beye. Tuesday, Wednesday, Habib Beye. Thursday, Friday, Habib Beye. Saturday, Habib Beye, rockin' all week with you!'

To the tune of 'Happy Days', sung by fans of Newcastle United at St James' Park, and now regularly heard at Donny Rovers.

9. 'We like Eboue-boue,
We like Eboue-boue,
We like Eboue-boue,
We like E...BOUE!'

Before he was sent to Turkey on loan, Emmanuel Eboué was something of a cult hero at the Emirates. The tune is of course Reel 2 Real's 'I Like To Move It', which featured singer The Mad Stuntman, which makes it even more appropriate for a song about Eboué.

8. 'Fat Eddie Murphy, you're just a fat Eddie Murphy.'

Newcastle fans sang this to Jimmy Floyd Hasselbaink at St James' Park. Even Jimmy saw the funny side of it and broke into a smile.

7. 'We've got Morten Gamst Pedersen; Gamst Pedersen is what we need.'

Sir Bon of Jovi provides the stirring pop-rock backing; the terraces of Blackburn provide the words to the tune of Bon Jovi's 'Bad Medicine'.

6. 'Tun-cay, cay – Huth, Huth, Abdoulaye.'

Take a bow, Stoke supporters, as you sing this to the tune of 'Too Shy' by Kajagoogoo. But please spare us the Limahl wigs.

**5. 'I'm your biggest fan, I'll follow you until you love me,
   Aqui, Aqui Aquilani.'**
Great song (to Lady GaGa's 'Paparazzi'). Player, not so great. Loaned from
Liverpool to AC Milan in 2011.

**4. 'U-N-I-T-E-D.
   That spells (flipping) debt to me,
   With a knick knack paddywhack, give a dog a bone,
   Ocean Finance on the phone.'**
Manchester City revelling in the size of Manchester United's debt.

**3. 'We love Taboubi, We love Taboubi, We love Taboubi on a
   Saturday night.'**
After French midfielder Hedi Taboubi scored for Wrexham. As if you needed
telling, the music is T Rex's 'I Love To Boogie'.

2. 'Put your hands up for Dirk Kuyt – he loves this city.'
Well, someone has to. Liverpool fans to their favourite Dutchman, via 'Put Your
Hands Up 4 Detroit'.

**1. 'The Unibond, it has no nails,
   The Unibond it has no nails,
   And its anti-mould bath sealant
   Is very good, it never fails.'**
From the terrace bards of Marine FC of the Unibond Premier League. To the
tune of 'When The Saints Go Marching' in, of course. This just goes to prove that
within Britain's Leagues, enormous creativity lurks. If there was a Champions
League for songs, Marine FC, playing at Rossett Park, Crosby (capacity: 3,185
– 389 seated) would be the winners. **606** salutes you.

Most self-deprecating chants

There is nothing worse than arrogant football fans. 'He scores when he wants' is our current pet hate. So this is one of our favourite lists: the chants that make you smile, even when you feel in the depths of despair.

If you've ever started such a chant, or better still are the genius behind some of the wit below, we want to see you puffing your chest out from here.

10. Stoke City – 'We only score from throw-ins.'
After being ridiculed in the press for their somewhat 'unorthodox' tactics and high percentage of goals scored direct from Rory Delap throw-ins, Stoke fans decided it was time to accept what the press were saying and come up with the amazingly catchy 'We only score from throw-ins, we only score from throw-ins'. The fact this chant started after a 25-yard screamer from Liam Lawrence shouldn't detract from the wit.

9. Bolton Wanderers – 'Let's pretend we've scored a goal.'
Now this one is a classic because of its bizarre nature more than anything. The sight of thousands of Bolton fans celebrating 'nothing' is something special. The chant originated after the Wanderers had been on the back of a number of controversial decisions. Refusing to allow the officials to dampen their spirits, Bolton fans began chanting 'Let's pretend we've scored a goal', and jumped around to boot.

8. Grimsby Town – 'We only sing when we're fishing.'
The Mariners managed to reflect the state of Grimsby's local economy in a football chant as they came up with the wonderfully witty and factually correct (probably) 'We only sing when we're fishing'. With relegation to the Conference in 2010, it's quite understandable that the Mariners only sing when they're fishing and less so when watching their team.

7. Newcastle United – 'You stole my holiday.'
Newcastle fans had a witty response to the news of West Ham's major sponsors XL Holidays going into liquidation as they continually sang 'You stole my holiday, West Ham, you stole my holiday'. With that number of Geordies booking with XL it's amazing that they ever went out of business.

6. Darlington – 'The Football League is upside down.'
It's been a miserable few years for Darlington, lucky to still be in existence

before their relegation to the conference in 2010. Darlington fans would often turn the tables on opposing supporters with this tongue-in-cheek look at the League standings. 'The Football League is upside down / The Football League is upside down / We're going up with Carlisle / And Hartlepool are going down.' Sadly, the League wasn't upside down and Hartlepool weren't relegated, much to the Quakers' disbelief.

5. Liverpool – 'Sotirios Kyrgiakos (we can't pronounce his name).'
One of Rafa Benitez's final signings for Liverpool was the 30-year-old Sotirios Kyrgiakos. A club always willing to give a fond welcome to any new recruit, Liverpool did their best to welcome Kyrgiakos into the Anfield family; the only problem was they couldn't pronounce his name. As they sang, 'It is / A shame / We can't pronounce his name / Kyrgi-laaaa, Kyrgi-laaaa...'

4. Manchester City – 'Robinho on the bus.'
In September 2008, life for Manchester City fans changed forever as they were taken over by the Abu Dhabi United Investment Group. Before the close of the transfer window on 1 September, City made history by signing Brazil international Robinho from Real Madrid. Apparently Robinho thought he had signed for Chelsea, but he endeared himself to City fans by revealing his favourite mode of transport was the bus. Feeling he was therefore just like them, the City fans came up with the excellent 'Robinho on the bus goes round and round / Round and round / round and round / Robinho on the bus goes round and round / All day long.' Robinho left City in 2010 when he returned to his native Brazil. Reports that he was last seen on the 192 Manchester to Stockport service are still unconfirmed.

3. Wigan Athletic – 'We've won it two times.'
Another of our favourites from Wigan Athletic was sung in response to at the time European Champions Liverpool and their infamous 'Istanbul – five times'. Not to be outdone, the Latics responded with 'We've won it two times / Auto Windscreen Shield / We've won it two times', ignoring the fact that one of those times it was actually called the Freight Rover Van trophy and the Latics picked up a white van for their Wembley success. A truly inspired example of football wit.

2. Tottenham Hotspur – 'He's only got one knee.'
Ledley King has endured a tough few years by anyone's standards. England's long-term centre back's injuries have taken their toll, in particular a knee injury which requires constant treatment and prevents Ledley from training and

playing on a regular basis. Spurs fans made their feelings on the club's skipper clear as they proudly chanted, 'Ooh Ledley, Ledley / He's only got one knee / He's better than John Terry / Ooh Ledley, Ledley'.

1. Swindon Town – 'So are we.'

Swindon Town managed just five wins during the whole 1993/4 season in the Premier League and conceded 100 goals in 42 games. Not a great deal to laugh about as a fan, but we take a mini-bow to those who came up with the best retort to a chant we know. Everton fans started singing, 'Going down going down going down' to the Swindon fans. Their reply? 'So are we, so are we, so are we'. You cannot beat terrace humour.

Popular songs made into chants

Before there were the Charts, men in flat caps stood on terraces making up
pleasant one-dimensional songs to hymns such as 'Cwm Rhondda' ('You're not
singing any more') or 'The Battle Hymn of the Republic' ('Glory, glory to the
Hibees / Leeds United / Tottenham Hotspur / Man United'). Folk songs also
featured prominently, such as 'The Blaydon Races' at Newcastle. Simple times.
Then the Charts arrived. It seemed that if it was in the Charts, and you could
hum it, a fan in a pre-match pub would wrangle it into a chant. Here are some
of our favourites.

10. 'Temuri's on fire.'
Remember follicly challenged, advertising-hoarding-kicking Geordie Georgian
Temuri Ketsbaia? Well, he went on to manage Anorthosis Famagusta in Cyprus.
Who else is big in Cyprus? The Kings Of Leon, that's who.
  'Wooooooooooaaaaaah, Temuri Ketsbaia!!'

9. 'Demba Ba.'
Some surnames are made to be sung. Demba Ba could have had two entries in
our top 10. We like Newcastle United fans to the tune of 'War' by Edwin Starr:
'Ba! Huh! What did he sign for? Absolutely nothing!' But for sheer silliness we
favour West Ham fans' effort to the tune of late 1990s Chicago house pop
classic 'Get Get Down' by Paul Johnson:
  'Ba Demba-Ba Ba, Demba-Ba, Ba Ba Ba Ba,
  Demba Ba Ba Ba Ba Ba Ba Ba Ba.'

8. 'Giggs will tear you apart.'
When your city boasts the most influential post-punk bands ever, as well as
the most decorated player in Premier League history, then any song that can
marry the two deserves a spot in our top 10. Apparently Ian Curtis was a City
fan. He'd have hated this.
  'Giggs, Giggs will tear you apart again.'

7. 'Allardyce!'
West Ham fans changed Coldplay's hit 'Paradise' to the name of the manager
who guided them to success in the play-offs and put them back in the Premier
League.
  'Alla- Alla- Allardyce,
  Alla- Alla- Allardyce,

Alla- Alla- Allardyce,
Oh oh oh oh oh oh-oh-oh.'

6. 'We've come for our scarves.'

'Sloop John B' by the Beach Boys is the ubiquitous modern-day football standard. Every club has at least one version. Arsenal have the Robin Van Persie one. Liverpool have the Istanbul one. And Norwich City thought of this one for their trip to Old Trafford in 2011/12, where they went looking to reclaim the green and gold.

'We've come for our scarves,
We've come for our scarves,
We're Norwich City,
We've come for our scarves.'

5. 'Knowing me, knowing you.'

This would have been perfect if the little Estonian had played for Norwich, or Djurgårdens. But full credit to Southampton fans for knowing their Alan Partridge, and Abba.

'Knowing me, knowing you, Pahars!'

4. 'I wanna be HTFC.'

There is some debate amongst fans of FC United and Huddersfield Town as to who came up with this first. It's based on punk classic 'Anarchy In The UK' by the Sex Pistols – and all property is theft, right? And we prefer Town's lyrics.

'I am an Hudders fan,
I am a Yorkshire man,
I know what I want and I know how to get it,
I wanna destroy Bradford and Leeds,
Cos Iiiiiiiwanna beeeeeeeeeeeee HTFCCCCCC.'

3. 'That's Zamora.'

The best terrace songs are often affectionate digs at your own players. Here Fulham fans show their love to England forward Bobby Zamora.

'When the ball hits your head,
And you're sat in Row Z,
That's Zamora.'

To be fair to Bobby, we're not sure if Craven Cottage has a row Z.

2. 'Moonlight Shadow.'

Surely one of the most emotive songs can be heard regularly at the Estádio do Dragão in Porto, where the Super Dragões Ultras have adopted, curiously,

Mike Oldfield's folk-rock ditty 'Moonlight Shadow'.
'And there's no one who can shut up our love,
And that's why we sing for you Porto!
Porto! (clap clap clap). Porto! (clap clap clap).'

1. 'Blame it on Traoré.'

Liverpool won the Champions League in 2005 for the fifth time, despite having Djimi Traoré at left back. Earlier that same the season, Djimi scored a uniquely clumsy own goal in the FA Cup at Burnley. The Kop responded with this modern-day classic, to the tune of 'Blame It On the Boogie' by the Jackson 5...
'Don't blame it on the Biscan,
Don't blame it on the Hamann,
Don't blame it on the Finnan,
Blame it on Traoré.
He just can't, he just can't,
He just can't control his feet!'

Worst football songs

Normally, the only bad football song is the one being sung by your rival fans. Hypocrisy is an essential component of the football fan's psyche, and rest assured that your songs sound *just* as bad to your opponents. Football pop songs are almost always bad. It only ever works the other way round – when a top pop anthem is converted by an inspired terrace poet into a thing of beauty. We now reach the bottom of the barrel, ladies and gentleman, and we have our trusty scrapers out.

Here are our top ten least good football songs, the worst of a really bad bunch, the gnarliest of warts, the most swollen of musical pimples.

10. 'Good Old Arsenal' by Arsenal FC First Team Squad
Possibly the first FA Cup song and so has a lot to answer for. It uses a grand total of 20 different words in the entire two and a half minutes of its duration, making it less complex than a *Mr Men* book. It's also stopped Spurs fans from ever singing 'Rule Britannia' again. Got to number 16 in 1971.

9. 'Diamond Lights' by Glenn Hoddle and Chris Waddle
At least most other football songs were cobbled together to mark some kind of occasion. This appears to be a genuine attempt to start a pop career. It did get to number 12 in 1987, but no follow-up was recorded. The Everly Brothers they were not. The song has yet to be covered by either U2 or Radiohead.

8. 'We're In This Together' by Simply Red
'Three Lions' was the official football song for the England team in Euro 1996, but this insipid ditty was the official song of the competition itself. It involved Mick Hucknall walking down a players' tunnel wearing sunglasses. Easily the most unsingable thing the band ever recorded, and that's saying something. Got to number 11, but I don't think anyone noticed.

7. 'Here We Go' by Everton FC
This was based on the march 'Stars and Stripes Forever' by John Philip Sousa and recorded at the famous Abbey Road studios. Unfortunately, it featured the vocal talents of Peter Reid and Adrian Heath, amongst others, and lyrics that could have been cobbled together from graffiti in the toilets at Goodison Park. In fairness, the team had the decency to look awkward when they sang it on *Top of the Pops* in 1985. It got to number 14.

6. 'Anfield Rap' by Liverpool FC

Not to be outdone, the red half of the city got together to storm the charts and continue to unravel the musical legacy created by The Beatles. Co-written by reds' midfielder Craig Johnston, in a way which makes you understand why he chose football over music, the hip-hop tune is all about native Liverpudlians John Aldridge and Steve McMahon, laughing at their teammates' accents. Sadly they didn't sound as Scouse as Dane Jan Molby. Also features 'John Barnes' rhymed with 'bananas'.

5. 'We All Follow Man United' by Manchester United

1985 was a truly epic year for bad football songs. This one lacks so much imagination that the tune is actually nicked from Scotland's 1978 World Cup song, 'Ally's Tartan Army'. Cliché is piled upon cliché, and fans can rest assured that 'we know our aim / is winning the game'. Well, thank God for that. It made the top ten. Just.

4. 'Go For It' by Coventry City

Spurs had Chas and Dave. Coventry had Steve and Heather Taylor, who have written songs for Shakin' Stevens and Daniel O'Donnell. 'City's marching on / Lead by George and John.' Coventry's 1987 Cup song sung with all the gusto of a team who know they're never going to be in this situation ever again. It reached the dizzy heights of number 61 in the Charts and is almost impossible to find on YouTube.

3. '(How Does It Feel To Be) On Top Of The World' by England United

Featuring the odd alliance of Echo & The Bunnymen, Space, Simon Fowler from Ocean Colour Scene, and the Spice Girls, this was England's official song for the 1998 World Cup. Sadly for all concerned, it clashed with the release of 'Vindaloo' and a reissue of 'Three Lions' and disappeared into obscurity. England fans don't know how it feels to be top of the world any more than this song knows about being top of the charts.

2. 'This Time (We'll Get It Right)' by England World Cup Squad 1982

It had been 12 years since England had last played in a World Cup. Times had changed: we'd had several different governments; we'd gone decimal. Sadly, the nature of the World Cup song hadn't moved on. After the success of 'Back Home' in 1970, England got together in tracksuits to record this song as if punk had never happened. It probably has the least inspiring lyrics of any football song ever written:

'We're going to find a way,
Find a way to get away,
This time.
Getting it all together,
We'll get it right.'

They didn't get it right.

1. 'Head Over Heels' by Kevin Keegan

In 1979, it seemed Kevin Keegan could do no wrong. He was England captain, he'd helped Hamburg win the Bundesliga and had become European Player of the Year for the second year in succession. Then someone persuaded him that he could sing. Then someone else told him he could promote the song. Written by Smokey's Chris Norman and Pete Spence, who also wrote 'This Time (We'll Get It Right)', it got to number 31 in the UK but made it into the top ten in Germany where they know good music when they hear it.

PRESS

Best commentators

They have the job we would all love to do – sit and watch some of the biggest games of football and talk about them and get paid for it! Love them or hate them, commentators are very much part of the game. Here is our list of some of the best around...

10. Jacqui Oatley

'Nine minutes played, and what a crucial goal that could be!'

BBC One, Premier League, Fulham v Blackburn, 2007

As the first ever woman commentator on *Match of the Day*, Jacqui Oatley certainly knows her onions (from her Steve Sidwells). This Wolves fan has achieved her enviable position the hard way, by grafting all the way to the top... and staying there.

9. Alan Green

'Can you believe it! It was *inconceivable* that they [AC Milan] wouldn't win!'

BBC Radio 5 live, Champions League final, Liverpool v AC Milan, 2005

How could we not include one of our very own? Best known for his straight-talking style, many a referee, player, fan and mascot has been lambasted by the sharp tongue of 'Greenie', and we wouldn't want it any other way. The Northern Irishman doesn't mince his words – let's face it, not many people would have the cahoonas to say some of the stuff he says on national radio – and we like that. Alan Green, we salute you!

8. Jonathan Pearce

'He's played the game with a bag on!'

Channel 5, UEFA Cup, Aston Villa v Atlético Madrid, 1998

Not only does he have a surname synonymous with the football world, but Jonathan Pearce also has, luckily for him, one of the most distinctive voices in British sport. Cutting his teeth on programmes like *Robot Wars*, the big man's enthusiasm for football is contagious. Even when he gets given the last game of *Match of the Day*, it's hard not to be transfixed by his loud and exuberant howls during a dull scoreless draw.

7. Clive Tyldesley

'And Solskjær has won it!'

ITV, Champions League, Manchester United v Bayern Munich, 1999

When you think of football on ITV, you think of the number seven on our list. Despite not being universally recognisable in appearance, his voice is instantaneously synonymous with some of the greatest, most memorable and dramatic moments in the history of televised football.

6. Brian Moore

'Thomas, charging through the midfield, Thomas, it's up for grabs now!'
ITV, *The Big Match*, Liverpool v Arsenal, First Division title decider, 1989
This is a guy who was behind the microphone when Michael Thomas snatched the League title from underneath Liverpool's noses in the last minute of added time in 1989 and will forever be remember as one of the greats. He made *The Big Match* his own during the 1960s, 1970s and 1980s, and has a voice which reflects football in its truest colours, passionate, down-to-earth and chock-full of character.

5. Barry Davies

'Interesting... very interesting! Look at his face, just look at his face!'
BBC One, *Match of the Day*, Derby County v Manchester City, 1975
If Brian Moore is the 'gravel pit' of the football commentator's world, then Barry Davies is the silk linen (not to be confused with Barry White). With a background that goes far beyond the world of football, Barry Davies's voice has been guiding us through football's highs and lows for over five decades, and he is a bona fide commentary legend.

4. David Coleman

'He is a whole-hearted player.'
David Coleman's assessment of West Brom's Asa Hartford, who suffered from a hole in the heart
David Coleman often accidentally said things that were funny... so much so, that the magazine *Private Eye* tagged these gaffes 'Coleman Balls' after the man himself. The commentator worked at the BBC for almost 50 years and was the BBC's senior football commentator for several years from 1971, covering numerous World Cups and domestic trophies.

3. Martin Tyler

'He's round the goalkeeper... he's done it! Absolutely incredible!'
Sky TV, Sunderland v Manchester City, commentating on Sunderland's last-minute winner in the 2011/12 season
As the anchor of Sky TV's football coverage for the past 20 years, Tyler has seen more Premier League action than most. Chances are, if you've watched top-flight football in the past two decades, his voice has added to the drama.

Trusted, competent and comforting – Tyler brings all you would wish for in a commentator.

2. Kenneth Wolstenholme

'And here comes Hurst, some people are on the pitch, they think it's all over... It is now!'

There are legends of the broadcasting world, and then there are solid gold ones. Kenneth Wolstenholme's voice is assured to be forever remembered as the voice that described England's World Cup win in 1966 with such panache and class. He worked predominately in the 1950s and 1960s, covering top-flight football in a way that will probably never be heard again ('that is the pink ribbon on this luscious box of chocolates that Manchester United have given us tonight'), but the World Cup final is where his legacy shines brightest.

1. John Motson

'Oh, Ballack...' (said in a slightly familiar tone)

BBC One, *Match of the Day*, Chelsea v Aston Villa, 2008

'For those of you watching in black and white, Spurs are playing in yellow' is how he started his commentary of a 1977 League fixture for *Match of the Day* at Roker Park between Sunderland and Spurs.

There absolutely no doubt about it, 'Motty' is a national treasure and you'd be hard pressed to find anyone in the British Isles who disagrees. He typifies the UK's passion for the beautiful game, and it's been said that he contains his vast knowledge of the game in his trademark sheepskin coat.

Best press one-liners

We often mock managers and players for being clichéd, dull stereotypes. But before we turn our tape recorders on and hit record while mentally switching off, here are the characters worth listening to.

10. Gordon Strachan

When he was unveiled as Southampton manager, Gordon Strachan was asked, 'Do you feel you are the man to turn it round here?'

'No,' he replied, adding, 'If you're going to ask stupid questions, then I'll give you stupid answers.'

9. Ian Holloway

Harry Redknapp had been praising Holloway in the media, which led a journalist to ask Holloway if there was a bit of man-love between the pair.

Holloway laughed and replied, 'No.'

The journalist then asked what it was about Harry that made him successful.

Holloway replied, 'It's his curly hair.'

8. José Mourinho

The Special One was once asked in a press conference in 2007 which Premier League manager he would least like to fight. The Chelsea PR people got a little bit annoyed as they wanted to keep the questions about Chelsea. But José being as special as he is answered: 'Big Sam. He would kill me.' And he would be right.

7. Martin Jol

When the Fulham manager was asked how he felt about fans positively chanting his name when he took his team to White Hart Lane, the ex-Spurs manager replied, 'It is like you have a new girlfriend and you take her to a restaurant, and your old girlfriend is also there...'

6. Gordon Strachan

When Southampton were doing well in the League in 2003, a reporter asked Gordon Strachan what he thought about their chances in Europe.

To which he replied, 'Me and the wife are going to Spain next month.'

5. Jamie Carragher

After Liverpool's Carling Cup win in February 2012, Jamie Carragher was interviewed on the pitch by Sky's Andy Burton. Burton asked Carragher if this was the beginning of a farewell for him.

Carragher laughed and asked if he was the manager and said that he was lucky to keep his job at Sky.

4. José Mourinho

The former Chelsea boss was speaking of Sir Alex Ferguson in a press conference and said, 'When we go to Old Trafford on my birthday for the match, I will bring a nice bottle of wine. Because the wine Sir Alex gave me was bad.'

3. Branislav Ivanovic

After Chelsea's win over Barcelona at the Nou Camp in the Champions League, Geoff Shreeves asked Ivanovic if he had been booked. Ivanovic said that he had, and Shreeves broke the news that Ivanovic could not play in the final, shattering his dreams in one swoop.

2. Harry Redknapp

A journalist asked Harry if he really did not want a replay against Leeds in the FA Cup.

Harry replied, 'No, I'm really looking forward to it. I thought with a minute to go, give them a goal and go to Elland Road on a Tuesday night, as I haven't been there in a long time.'

1. Ian Holloway

When QPR manager, Holloway was asked about his side's performance.

He said 'A win's a win. It's like going out on the town and pulling a bird. Some weeks they are good-looking, some weeks they are not the best.'

Top football clichés

This section is top drawer, has real stickability, is straight from the horse's mouth, and hits the nail on the head. We've searched high and low for the crème de la crème of football clichés. But remember the important thing is that the team got three points... Do you agree?

10. 'The best form of defence is attack.'
If this is the case, why bother with a goalkeeper at all?

9. 'Good feet for a big man'
When commentators and pundits talk about big strikers like Andy Carroll and Peter Crouch, they often talk about how good they are with the ball at their feet, almost as if it's a surprise. The classic cliché of 'good feet for a big man' can be heard almost every time a big striker does something good. Especially if they pull on an England shirt.

8. 'Giving 110 per cent'
OK, statistically, the figure 110 per cent is a possibility in certain realms of mathematics, but if a player/club/manager/ball boy gives more than 100 per cent, then something special is going on.
110 per cent in the realms of possibility: Ten people go to a supermarket on Monday. Twenty-one people go on Tuesday, therefore, the amount of people who went to the supermarket has risen 110 per cent.
110 per cent NOT in the realms of possibility: A footballer plays to the maximum of his ability and magically grows another leg.

7. 'Setting out their stall'
Literally, market traders set out their stalls. How this phrase made it into the world of metaphorical football colloquialisms, we'll probably never know. But we can guess.
Warning: made-up fact alert... In 1652, Peter Snitchard managed his local village team, the Camden Crunchers. He had a bit of Italian genetics in him, so he was naturally a very defensive manager tactically. To make a living, Peter sold apples and so the only language he knew revolved around his trade... In a post-match interview with the *Plague Times*, Peter was asked how they beat their local rivals, the Kings Hot Cross Buns 7-3, and the words 'setting out their stalls' were first uttered, therefore starting a tradition of mediocre analysis.

6. 'What this game needs is a goal.'

Are you kidding? This is the most obvious sentence since William Shakespeare uttered the words 'To be, or... damn! How on earth can I finish off this stanza?' Commentators who say this particular sentence should not be commentators. What they need cannot be printed without a lengthy legal process.

5. 'On paper...'

There are no guarantees in football, so having something predicted that looks likely 'on paper' never fills any supporter with great comfort. Who writes on paper anyway, these days?

4. 'End-to-end stuff'

Come on, this isn't tennis we're talking about. Commentators love this phrase because it conjures up hectic, engrossing action in one, easy, uncomplicated phrase. What it actually means is that the game should have had more goals in it.

3. 'Take one game at a time'

Of course, this means not getting too ahead of oneself, and planning in incremental steps, but it also sits in the 'top drawer' of footballing clichés. Probably best represented by managers who don't want to be too happy about a great result in front of television cameras, this lets the audience/chairman/ fans know that he is level headed and always has a 'Plan B' up his sleeve. What it actually means is that there is no 'Plan B' and that he thinks he deserves a pay-rise. Probably.

2. 'A funny old game'

When things happen in football, this is the phrase that rules them all... Popularised by the England cohort Jimmy Greaves, you can't really argue against the logic of its meaning. At times, it is funny (both ha ha, and the other one), old and, most of all, a game. Best said by someone with a wizened voice.

1. 'A game of two halves'

Factually true (most of the time) as well as one of the few football clichés that tend to be spot-on. How many times have you watched a game that has completely turned around after half time? Liverpool coming back to win the Champions League against AC Milan, Newcastle's comeback against Arsenal after they were 3-0 down plus a stunning comeback that saw Mali score four goals in 11 minutes to prevent Angola win the opening game of the Africa Cup of Nations in 2010. These all prove, beyond doubt, that the phrase is a good'n.

Best pundits

Strong views, harsh criticism and contagious catchphrases are the best way to describe the cream of football's pundits. Interestingly, being a great player in your heyday isn't a necessity to be a good pundit. Being able to talk a good game is key. So we start on Monday, then?

10. Ron Atkinson
Big Ron was the pundit for ITV's Champions League coverage from the early 1990s to early 2000s. He can take credit for phrases like 'early doors' and 'you'd have put your mortgage on him scoring there'. He once said of a Tranmere Rovers throw-in specialist, 'This lad throws the ball further than I can go on holiday.'

9. Pat Nevin
One who you may not expect to be in the top ten, but his analysis on BBC Radio 5 live is always lively and very perceptive. He's honest, frank and can handle whatever Mr Colin Murray throws at him. Works for us.

8. Charlie Nicholas
Known as 'Champagne Charlie Nicholas', he was once popular with the ladies, believe it or not. He is a regular pundit on *Soccer Saturday* on Sky, as well as appearing on Scottish football coverage.

7. Alan Shearer
Shearer has been a regular pundit on *Match of the Day* since his retirement. His trenchant views and insistence on using the word 'done' instead of 'did' at every opportunity, has won him many admirers.

6. Jamie Redknapp
His enthusiasm and passion for the game shines through on Sky's coverage of the Premier League, and his suits and looks ain't bad either. He's a little too fond of the word 'literally' to make it into our top five, but he's up there.

5. Gary Neville
He's taken to commentary like a duck to water. A much more toned-down Neville nowadays, but he still can be controversial.

4. Mark Lawrenson
Lawro has been the BBC's main co-commentator since the departure of Trevor

Brooking. He also appears on the *Match of the Day* and *Football Focus* and is known for his world-weary opinions and slightly cynical viewpoint.

3. Andy Gray

Gray was a key part of Sky's coverage from 1992 to 2011. Some of his well-known catchphrases include 'take a bow son', 'look at the venom' and 'power and accuracy'.

2. Alan Hansen

Known for the line 'you can't win anything with kids', after Manchester United drafted in youngsters Gary Neville, David Beckham, Paul Scholes and Nicky Butt and went on to win the League, Hansen's no-nonsense approach, coupled with his passion for defending, has kept him at the top of his game for some time now.

1. Chris Kamara

He's become a YouTube hit, thanks to his mutterings with Jeff Stelling on *Soccer Saturday*. Often taken by surprise by events at games, his catchphrase is 'Unbelievable, Jeff'. And you are, Chris.

Top ten football put-downs

Laugh and the whole football world laughs with you, goes the saying. And it is true, sometimes.

10. 'If David Seaman's dad had worn a condom, we'd still be in the World Cup.'
– Comedian Nick Hancock after the defeat by Brazil in the 2002 World Cup.

9. 'Jimmy Hill is to football what King Herod was to babysitting.'
– Tommy Docherty, former football manager and player.

8. 'Porto are a bunch of girls that go down too easily.'
– Gary Neville commenting after Manchester United lost their first leg to Porto in the Champions League in 2007.

7. 'When Rioch came to Millwall, we were depressed and miserable. He's done a brilliant job of turning it around. Now we are miserable and depressed.'
– Danny Baker, Millwall fan.

6. 'The average English footballer could not tell the difference between an attractive woman and a corner flag.'
– Walter Zenga, Italian goalkeeper.

5. 'I'd like to sign Rio Ferdinand – but for £10 million less.'
– Arsène Wenger thinks United paid too much for him.

4. 'I'm finding it difficult to find a girlfriend in Barnsley, or indeed settle into a decent way of life. Local girls are far uglier than the ones back in Belgrade or Skopje, the capital of Macedonia, where I come from. Our women are much prettier. Besides, they don't drink as much beer as the Barnsley girls which is something I don't like at all. England is a strange country, and I found it hard to adapt to living here. To be honest, I expected more of Barnsley as a town and a club.'
– Georgi Hristov upsets the locals at Barnsley.

3. 'Stone me! We've had cocaine, bribery and Arsenal scoring two goals at home. But just when you thought there were no surprises left in football, Vinnie Jones turns out to be an international player.'

– Jimmy Greaves, when the Wimbledon hard man is selected for Wales.

2. 'He cannot kick with his left foot, he cannot head a ball, he cannot tackle and he doesn't score many goals. Apart from that, he's all right.'

– George Best on David Beckham.

1. 'Everyone thinks they have the prettiest wife at home.'

– Arsène Wenger's reply to Sir Alex Ferguson in 2002 when the United manager claimed his side were the best team in the League.

Press conference moments

Every week, the manager is faced by a pack of hungry wolves, microphones and digital Dictaphones in hand, ready to pounce on any verbal slip-ups or admissions. And every week, a manager somewhere cracks up. Here are ten of our faves.

10. Sir Alex Ferguson
Ahead of the Champions League final against Barcelona, Sir Alex Ferguson demanded that a reporter be banned because he asked a question about Ryan Giggs, which the journalists had been told was off-limits that day.

AF: 'The guy that asked the question about Giggsy... at the press conference...'

KS: 'Which one?'

AF: 'Him that asked the question... Who?'

KS: 'Oh yeah, I'll tell you later.'

(A few minutes later) AF: 'Is he coming on Friday?'

KS: 'The guy with the laptop?'

AF: 'Aye. Then we'll get him. Ban him on Friday.'

9. Liam Gallagher
Liam Gallagher gatecrashed Manchester City's post-match press conference, slipping into manager Roberto Mancini's seat and started proceedings by saying, 'What do you want to know, lads? Top of the League. Well done, City.'

8. Harry Redknapp
This press conference was held after Spurs gave away an injury-time penalty in the FA Cup third round against Leeds United, which Jermaine Beckford calmly scored to make it 2-2, thus forcing a replay at Elland Road.

Without thinking it through, a journalist asked Harry, 'Is a replay something that you really didn't want, either way?'

Much to the amusement of the other journalists, Redknapp sarcastically replied, 'No, I was really looking forward to it, I thought it'd be a good idea with a minute to go. I thought we'd give them a goal because I'd like to go to Elland Road on a Tuesday night. I haven't been up there for a few years.'

7. Gordon Strachan
Reporter: 'Welcome to Southampton Football Club. Do you think you are the right man to turn things around?'

Strachan: 'No. I was asked if I thought I was the right man for the job and I said, "No, I think they should have got George Graham because I'm useless."'

6. Mario Balotelli

After Balotelli gatecrashed an Inter Milan press conference, Inter chief executive Ernesto Paolillo said, 'He came to say hello to everybody at the training centre then left. We did not know he was coming, but it's not the first time. It's typical of Mario. I see him sometimes when he comes to Milan. I did not see the Ferrari as I was inside the press conference unveiling our new coach Andrea. We kissed hello, and he left. We had no time to speak. I've known him at Inter since he was a young boy.'

5. Harry Redknapp

Reporter Robb Palmer: 'So, Harry, you made your name as a wheeler-dealer, there's not been much wheeling and dealing...'
Harry Redknapp: 'I'm not a wheeler and dealer – F*** off... I'm a f****** football manager.'

4. Arsène Wenger, 1996–present

'I did not see it, I did not see it, I did not see it, I did not see it, I did not see it, I did not see it, I did not see it, I did not see it, I did not see it, I did not see it, I did not see it, I did not see it, I did not see it, I did not see it, I did not see it, I did not see it, I did not see it, I did not see it, I did not see it, I did not see it...'

3. Roy Keane (Friday 20 November 2009)

RING RING
Keane: 'Who's phone is that? That's the second time it's gone off.'
Reporter: 'I think that's my phone, sorry.'
RING RING
Keane: 'Why don't you turn it off? You're sitting there, that's the second time it's gone off. Why don't you put it on silent?'
Reporter: 'It's not the second time.'
Keane: 'But why don't you turn it off??'
RING RING
Reporter: 'I'll turn it off in a minute.'
Keane: 'So you're just gonna let it ring?'
Reporter: 'No, I'll try and let it ring out.'
RING RING
Keane: 'Oh right... that's good manners.'

2. Ian Holloway

Back in 2006, Ian Holloway had just taken over at Plymouth Argyle. In his first press conference he was told the club had just arranged a pre-season game against Real Madrid in Austria. When Holloway was asked for his reaction to the tie, he said: 'What do you want me to say? Yeah, we're playing Real Madrid, I'm sure they're worried about us,' before succumbing to fits of laughter. It wasn't a joke when it came to the actual game, as Argyle only lost 1-0, and that was a penalty!

1. Jimmy Armfield

In a Manchester United press conference, Alex Ferguson asked the assembled reporters, 'How many f****** caps have youse lot got?'

'Forty-three,' came the prompt reply from Jimmy Armfield at the back of the room. Jimmy had spent his whole career at Blackpool, playing over 600 games, captained England on 15 occasions and was voted 'Best Right Back in the World' at the 1962 World Cup. He only missed out on a place in the 1966 squad due to injury.

Most excitable pundits

Their job is to inform, to illuminate, to explain what precisely is happening out there on the pitch. For a large part of the time, that is what many pundits do. But once in a while the occasion gets the better of them and suddenly they are reduced to screaming and shouting and generally acting, well, like us, really.

10. Phil Thompson
Being a pundit on *Soccer Saturday*, Phil Thompson has to be loud. But he's probably the loudest. He gets very excited whenever a big goal in a big game goes in, and his excitement shines through.

9. Gary Birtles
A regular on Sky's Football League coverage and co-commentator at matches, he throws out all the superlatives after a wonder goal.

8. Jason Roberts
As part of the **606** team Jason has brought excitement and passion to big topics and talking points. He's also held his own with some of the big guns in the 5 live commentary team, commentating on numerous games. 'Jumpers for goalposts', anyone?!

7. Andy Gray
Andy Gray was known for his excitable nature when sitting in the commentary seat, and sayings like 'Take a bow, son'. He would also speak about how he wouldn't want to be anywhere else in the world than at the specific game he was commentating on. His excitement when a great goal went in was legendary. He would often pause and then shout 'What a hit' and then get even more excited as he watched the replay.

6. Paul Merson
The ex-Arsenal midfielder is something of a comedy character on Sky Sport's *Soccer Saturday*. He often gets names wrong while wrapped up in the all the excitement. During the end of the 2011 season, Blackpool had to get a result against Manchester United to stay up. When Charlie Adam equalised, Merson went crazy. Unfortunately, Blackpool did end up going down.

5. Matt Le Tissier

Another of the *Soccer Saturday* lads, the ex-Southampton man gets very excited during games, especially when his old club is involved. One example was in 2012 when Southampton scored against Portsmouth, and Le Tissier cheered, then the goal was disallowed. Only for the goal to be given again.

4. Gary Neville

Despite not being in the commentating game for long, Neville showed real excitement during Chelsea's successful 2012 Champions League campaign. Firstly, when Torres scored the winner against Barcelona to seal Chelsea's place in the Champions League final, he made a very odd noise. He revisited this rather strange sound, when Drogba scored late on to take the Champions League final to extra time.

3. Ray Hudson

Pundit for NBC in the USA, Ray has been known to get a little excited while commentating on Spanish Football. A notable occasion was an Iker Casillas penalty save against Atlético Madrid – the Geordie went absolutely crazy as he broke into a scream and then began to talk like the late, great Sid Waddell at the darts. He made 40 appearances for Newcastle between 1973 and 1977.

2. Ian Wright

Watching Ian Wright commentate on England is sometimes more interesting than watching England play. He often makes the half-time/full-time highlight reels, just for his reaction in the studio. He also showed his passion when a pundit for *Match of the Day*. But we feel the live environment is where Wrighty is best – he just can't control himself.

1. Chris Kamara

His work on *Soccer Saturday* alongside Jeff Stelling has transformed him into a YouTube sensation. He has been known to get a little carried away, particularly in a match between Fulham and Middlesbrough when the referee disallowed a goal but Kamara wasn't sure what was happening. The chaotic, excitable commentating is a classic.

Most divisive pundits

We love them, we hate them, we hang on their every word, we disagree with their every other word. The Pundit – the footballer or football manager turned broadcaster. It's hard to put your football bias aside when welcoming these ex-pros to your TV or radio but if it's hard for us, think how hard it is for them. Some, of course, hide their allegiance better than others. Here's our top ten.

10. David Pleat

David Pleat has had a long career as a player, manager and pundit and, usually, with experience comes skill. David is often more informative and tactically aware than some of his counterparts but has found himself on more than one occasion tripping and stumbling over his words leaving viewers and listeners praying he'll get to his point. Some of his memorable moments include 'Short Shirt Shorts' featured on *Fantasy Football League* and coming out with quotes like 'For such a small man, Maradona gets great elevation on his balls.'

9. Stan Collymore

Stanley Victor Collymore, known in media circles as the loudest man in the press box. You can guarantee that come Call Collymore time on TalkSport other journalists in the press box dive for cover, and those unable to dive for cover leave the press box bleeding from their ears. Stan signed for Liverpool from Nottingham Forest in 1995, and the rest is history. And it wouldn't be right to not mention those horrific white suits before the 1996 FA Cup final. Horrific. You can hear Stan after every Premier League game that TalkSport broadcasts. Alternatively, if you stick your head out of the car window at full time, you should be able to hear him as you drive away from the game.

8. Alan Hansen

'You can't win anything with kids.' It doesn't matter how good your analysis of the game is or how well you understand football, fans will always home in on the one mistake you make. As it happened, this turned out to be an absolute howler. Talking about the Manchester United side in 1995, Hansen was forced to eat his words as those 'kids' went on to win a League and FA Cup double. As much a part of the furniture on the *Match of the Day* sofa as the sofa itself, Hansen can usually be relied upon for calm and measured analysis with an occasional 'colourful' flourish. Some highlights include 'I don't think anyone enjoyed it. Apart from the people who watched it' and 'The Argentine defender warrants shooting for a mistake like that.'

7. Rodney Marsh

Controversial is probably the best way to describe Rodney Marsh. He was sacked as a pundit on Sky Sports for joking that David Beckham had turned down a move to Newcastle United because of trouble with the 'Toon Army in Asia' back in 2005. But the ex-Manchester City striker had been a divisive character before the ill-judged tsunami joke. Marsh ridiculed Bradford City's chances of staying in the Premier League in 1999/2000. He was so confident he told the Bradford fans he'd shave his hair off if they stayed up. It was a bet which he was forced to honour after City avoided relegation. Marsh subsequently had his hair removed in the centre circle at Valley Parade.

6. Ron Atkinson

'Big Ron,' as he's now universally known, is another of those pundits that controversy seems to follow around. A stellar managerial career that started at Kettering town and included West Bromwich Albion, Manchester United and Atlético Madrid gave Big Ron a good insight into football. However, his common sense and taste may have been called into question when he made a racially offensive remark about Marcel Desailly. Although the UK transmission had finished, it was still broadcast to several Middle Eastern countries. He tendered his resignation. Big Ron is still working in the media; you can hear him occasionally on BBC Radio 5 live and as a regular pundit on 'The Punt' podcast.

5. Andy Townsend

Two words. Tactics Truck. *The Premiership* was ITV1's answer to *Match of the Day,* and part of that show was Andy Townsend's Tactics Truck. Some fans wish said truck was sent round the M25 on a Friday evening, never to return. The former Irish international is ITV's number one pundit and can often be found giving tactical analysis from the touchline of various European stadiums. In fairness, his analysis is usually insightful and those captaining instincts often shine through when dealing with Adrian Chiles and Roy Keane.

4. Jamie Redknapp

Has one man ever misused one word quite as much as Jamie Redknapp overuses the word 'literally'? 'These balls now – they literally explode off your feet.' We're not sure.

Jamie's footballing career was more than enough to ensure him a career in the media, but when you factor in his marriage to Louise Nurding and the fact his dad is Harry Redknapp and you 'literally' have the perfect mix of football knowledge and celebrity status to keep him on our screens for the forseeable.

3. Gary Neville

Just the mention of the former Manchester United captain's name is enough to set some fans on edge. When it was announced that he would be joining the Sky team, there was panic amongst fans that the 20-year Manchester United man would bring nothing but Manchester United bias. Even the 'Nevgasm' in the game between Barcelona and Chelsea in the Champions League semi-final in 2012 did nothing to put out the fires of divisiveness, with public opinion split between those saying it showed 'passion' and 'lunacy'. We'll let you make your own mind up about Gary, but we love what he brings to our screens.

2. Ian Wright

There are reasons why the nation loves Ian Wright. Equally, there are reasons the nation hates him. That's OK, though, because this is a list of divisive pundits and Ian Wright fits the bill perfectly. We love his complete and unashamed bias towards the England set up. We love that he jumps around the studio, hugging his fellow presenters when England score, and we love that he thinks his son Shaun Wright-Phillips should be a permanent fixture on England's right wing. The very reason we love him is why he is no longer on our screens. He told the BBC that he thought he was 'just there as a comedy jester to break the ice with Alan Shearer and Alan Hansen' and quit in 2008.

1. Robbie Savage

The blond Welshman was a footballer that was despised by everyone apart from the team that he played for, and that includes his current side, **606**. And that's not really changed since he retired from football. He's not frightened to make his point and, equally, he's not frightened to shout people down if he thinks they're wrong. Savage has endeared himself to millions through his antics, including offering to buy a Newcastle fan a taxi if they finished in the Champions League places and telling John Toshack, 'There's more chance of me flying Concorde to the moon blindfolded than there is of you taking Wales to the World Cup.' He's also come out with crackers such as 'I look at myself and read what people say on the Internet and some fans say the club should get rid of me – which shows how fickle some people can be.' Our very own Robbie Savage, who himself admitted, 'I am not Pelé or Maradona.'

TV blunders

We've got a lovely bunch of blunders. Here they are, standing in a row. Big ones, small ones, some as big as your head. Some, in fact, so big that they do not even make it onto the list. Remember when ITV took over the highlights package of the Premiership? Where are you going? Come back! It's OK, it's that nice Mr Lineker and his friends Mark and Alan for the next few years, you can rest easy. We give you a clangers convention, a selection of SNAFUs, a gang of gaffes.

10. Alan Hansen's phone goes off
Broadcasting 101. Turn your phone off. TURN IT OFF. Hansen's surprisingly cheap-sounding ringtone interrupts an innovative and thought-provoking rant about terrible defending.

9. Kamara rodent confusion
'Their football, Arsenal, is on another level, but Spurs are fighting like
beavers. Defending for their football lives. It's a terrific game.'
Yes, 'like beavers'. What did he mean? What's *like* a beaver but isn't a beaver? We have no idea, and we suspect Chris Kamara doesn't either.

8. Martin Keown hit on the head
Not only did the former Arsenal defender have to stand next to 606's very own Robbie Savage, but to add injury to insult (so to speak) he also got a ball in the head during the live pre-game build-up between Arsenal and Leeds pitch-side at the Emirates. [DAD JOKE ALERT] Luckily, it didn't hit anything important.

7. German Sky Sports presenter Jessica Kastrop
During the warm-up, she was hit on the head by a shot from Chelsea player Khalid Boulahrouz. He was aiming for the opposite touchline.

6. England v United States – ITV
Another goal missed, another ITV mistake. This time, viewers who chose the commercial channel's HD missed England's only goal against the United States in the 2010 World Cup group stages. You win some, you lose some.

5. Sky Sports News 'finger error'
During one of the rolling bulletins in April 2010, the news feed read, '45 MINS: SH*T BY DEMPSEY INSIDE AREA, GOES WIDE'. He should have stayed off the dodgy prawns.

4. Geographical nightmare
When covering the 2011 World Cup finals in South Africa, the Chicago-based WGN TV network showed a graphic of South *America* with the World Cup imaging over the top of it. At least they got the hemisphere right.

3. Real Madrid v Bayern Munich – ITV, April 2012
And again! Real Madrid were beating Bayern Munich in the Champions League semi-final when – shock, horror – the network prematurely cut away from the game. This time, though, instead of adverts, the network threw to the ITV newsreader Mark Austin playing with his jacket buttons. That's not a double entendre, thank god.

2. Chris Kamara – *Soccer Saturday* reporting fail
It's an end-of-season crunch game between Portsmouth and Blackburn on 3 April 2012, and the dynamic Sky Sports *Soccer Saturday* team throw over to excitable pitch-side reporter and children's clown Chris Kamara to update viewers about a red card given to Pompey's Anthony Vanden Borre. The former footballer had no idea what was going on. His excuse? 'I saw him go off, but I thought they were bringing a sub on, Jeff!'

1. Everton v Liverpool – ITV
It is the 28th minute – *the 28th minute, mind* – of added time in the 2009 FA Cup semi-final replay. Somewhere in an ITV gallery, an automated system accidentally turns on the 'GO TO ADVERTS' button just as Everton's Danny Gosling scores the winner.

MONEY

Best-value tickets

In the crazy world of football, where a man can be fined a quarter of a million pounds and pay it off with just two weeks' wages, ticket prices have shot up considerably. We all remember the time we had five pounds pocket money on a Saturday and came back with change after buying our ticket, a programme and a can of cola. Times have changed, and football isn't a cheap hobby – but there is value to be had in the market.

With the country lurching in and out of recession and the wider global economy acting crazier than Joey Barton on a good day, it is nice to know that there are some places where you can still get real value for your hard-earned moolah. Here are **606**'s top ten football Poundshops.

10. Blackburn Rovers

In the 2011/12 season, Blackburn Rovers offered the cheapest tickets in the Premier League. It's just £10 for the cheapest seats at Ewood Park. Couple that with £3 for a programme, £2.30 for a pie and £2.20 for a cup of tea, and a day out at the Lancashire side would set you back just £17.50. Comfortably the cheapest in the Premier League.

9. Manchester United

If you'd rather be watching the action at the other end of the Premier League, the cheapest of the top five is Manchester United. The cheapest ticket at Old Trafford, if you can get one, is £28. When you add in a pie, a cup of tea and a programme, a day out to see the 19-time Premier League champions would cost you £35.60, meaning a family of four can take a trip to the Theatre of Dreams for £142.40.

8. Rochdale

The cheapest day out to watch any of the 92 Football League sides comes at Spotland, though. It's just £16.20 for a ticket, programme, pie and a cup of tea at Rochdale. When you consider that the tea costs just £1 at the Lancashire club, you could stretch the budget to one per half!

7. AC Milan

The picture is pretty rosy in Italy, too. You can head to one of the most famous grounds in the world, the San Siro, and, as long as you don't mind sitting in the seats up in the gods, you can do it for €10. That's pretty good value when you think the most expensive non-executive seats will set you back about €180.

6. Schalke 04

If European football is more your thing, Schalke 04's ticket prices start at just €15 for a standing seat. When you factor in that your match ticket gets you from the centre of Gelsenkirchen to the stadium on public transport, your entrance to the game, where you're allowed to stand, and back to the centre again, that's pretty good value. You also get free transport to the stadium from towns and train stations within a 50km radius with a season ticket that costs just €300.

5. Annan Athletic

If you're watching football in Scotland, you've got four Leagues to take your pick from. Just 14 miles away from Carlisle, where you'll pay £23 to watch League 1 football, you can flirt with Annan Athletic which is just £9 to watch Scottish League 3 football. That means you'll have £14 to spend on whatever you like! Bargain.

4. Euro 2012

The European Championships 2012 held in Poland and Ukraine had a ticketing system with a top end of €600. If, however, you were fortunate enough to get a seat behind the goal in the group games, you'd only be paying €30. Having to pay £500 a night for a two-star hotel in Krakow has nothing to do with the value of the ticket, so we won't even mention it.

3. Borussia Mönchengladbach

Unbelievably, Schalke isn't the cheapest in the Bundesliga. That honour goes to Borussia Mönchengladbach. It costs just €9.50 to stand in certain sections at Borussia Park. That means for the same price as the most expensive ticket at the Emirates, you and 12 mates could get a ticket each to watch Borussia Mönchengladbach.

2. Barcelona

Barcelona are widely regarded as the side that plays the best club football in the world. Iniesta, Xavi, Puyol and Messi may command stratospheric wages, but going to watch the Catalonians isn't expensive. At all. The cheapest ticket at the Nou Camp for a member of the general public is €19. However, that is for a 'Band D' game and in the 2011/12 season there were just a couple of those, such as versus Rayo Vallecano and Levante.

1. World Cup Final, Wembley 1966

Cast your minds back to 1966, England were facing West Germany in the World Cup final and the nation was holding its collective breath. A ticket for the Old Wembley would have set you back... wait for it... 10 shillings and 6 pence. That's

52.5p. If you convert 52.5p into today's money, the ticket to the World Cup Final in 1966 would set you back £3.45. And, while we're at it, if you were to buy the most expensive ticket at Stamford Bridge, the equivalent price in 1966 would have been £13, the average wage for three weeks' work.

Readers should also note that a 2012 Premier League table of the best value for money clubs, sitting right at the top were none other than... Manchester City. Quite remarkable. As someone used to say.

Most expensive players

Some are born to greatness, others have it thrust upon them. Either way, such players usually command huge fees in the transfer market. Their skill is not in question. The real question is: can they handle the pressure placed on them by the club and the fans? Here are ten who varied in their role as one of the world's most expensive players.

10. Gianluigi Buffon (Parma to Juventus in 2001) – £32.6 million

The most expensive ever goalkeeper, Buffon will be remembered most at Juventus not for his price tag, but for sticking with the team when they were relegated to Serie B as punishment for match fixing.

9. David Villa (Valencia to Barcelona, 2010) – £34.2 million

He was banging in the goals for fun for Valencia, before he eventually made a big move to Barcelona. He'd been linked with a number of big European Clubs including Chelsea and Real Madrid, but Barca got their man, making up a scary frontline of Messi and Villa.

8. Andy Carroll (Newcastle to Liverpool, 2011) – £35 million

We don't know which is worse, £50 million on Fernando Torres, or £35 million for Andy Carroll. Both have been massive flops. It was on the deadline of the January transfer window 2011 that Liverpool sold Torres to Chelsea, and they had to quickly find a replacement so decided to splash £35 million on the striker. He won over a few fans during Euro 2012 with a powerful header against Sweden in the group stages. However, he will need to replicate the header a few times over to justify the price tag.

7. Hernan Crespo (Parma to Lazio, 2000) – £35.5 million

President Sergio Cragnotti was known for splashing the cash in his time as Lazio president. He signed Christian Vieri, Juan Sebastien Veron, and Marcelo Salas before persuading goal-scoring machine Hernan Crespo to join. He sent Matias Almeyda and Sergio Conceicao the other way as part of the deal but certainly got his money back when Crespo later moved on to Inter Milan and Chelsea.

6. Luis Figo (Barcelona to Real Madrid, 2000) – £37 million

One of the most controversial transfers in football history, Luis Figo joined Real

Madrid from Barcelona. People just don't do that, but he did. He was named World Player of the Year in 2001, and if there was ever £37 million well spent, it was on Figo. He wowed the Bernabeu faithful with his pinpoint crossing and elegant touch and trickery.

5. Zinedine Zidane (Juventus to Real Madrid, 2001) – £46.5 million

Real Madrid smashed their record transfer fee of £37 million for Luis Figo, when they signed Zinedine Zidane in 2001. It paid dividends, though, as Zidane popped up with the winning goal in the 2002 Champions League final against Bayer Leverkusen.

4. Fernando Torres (Liverpool to Chelsea, 2011) – £50 million

Torres was getting restless at Anfield, having not won a trophy in his time at the club, although he declared that he 'loved Liverpool'. He joined Chelsea on deadline day of the January transfer window in 2011, and it's fair to say his time there hasn't exactly been memorable. Until recently, he had more yellow cards than goals. Money well spent!

3. Kaka (AC Milan to Real Madrid, 2009) – £56 million

Manchester City almost signed Kaka prior to this, which resulted in Milan fans protesting outside the San Siro. He joined Real Madrid in the summer of 2009, becoming one of president Florentino Perez's 'Galacticos', alongside Christian Ronaldo (see below). Expensive summer at the Bernabeu.

2. Zlatan Ibrahimovic (Inter Milan to Barcelona, 2009) – £56.5 million

This deal included Samuel Eto'o going the other way, to Inter Milan. It was a great deal for Inter, as Ibrahimovic turned out to be a flop at the Nou Camp, scoring 16 goals and accused of being lazy.

1. Cristiano Ronaldo (Manchester United to Real Madrid, 2009) – £80 million

The Portuguese step-over king is the most expensive player in world football. He'd been looking for a move away from Old Trafford for a while, but Fergie played it brilliantly and waited for the right bid. And boy did they get a good offer. The deal was completed in the summer of 2009.

Most expensive boots

The last three boots in this list were specially sourced and organised for auction by Rio Ferdinand to raise money for his charity, the Live the Dream Foundation. Those, and the rest on this list, are either there to marvel and drool over, or to make you slightly sad at what the game has become. If you think that spending £300 on a pair of boots will make you a better player, and you're not already a professional player, then please make your way to the **606** offices, as we have a pair of our patented Clima-Cool Pro 3000 XL Crotchmaster Laser Superfly Total Pants on offer for £299.99.

10. A 'normal' pair of Nike Mercurial Vapour VIII iD Boots – £185
Perfect for the Hackney Marshes or other such salubrious playing fields, custom built and tailored to suit all weathers, the workman cannot blame his tools wearing these beauties.

9. Adidas miF50 adizero – £210.00 (plus more for customisation)
These super-smart boots actually record data and 'measure key performance metrics such as speed and distance'. It is not yet known whether it records who gets the first round in at the pub after your Sunday game.

8. A pair from Ryan Giggs – £249.99
Giggs has worn Reebok all his career, and to celebrate his 800th appearance for Manchester United the company made a specially designed boot of which only 800 signed pairs appeared.

7. Nike Tiempo Legend IV Elite FG – £274.99
The boot of choice for the likes of Carlos Puyol, Gerard Pique and Andrea Pirlo, this white and green marvel will only set you back just under three hundred smackers. Some clubs' season tickets cost less.

6. Lionel Messi Signed Football Boot – £349.99
A personally signed pair of boots by football's current reigning hero could actually turn out to be an investment. Messi looks like becoming the G.O.A.T. (Greatest Of All Time), if he's not already.

5. Nike Mercurial Vapor Superfly II's – £1,500 (estimated)
Orravan Design in Paris has customised these stunning boots to include 5,000

coloured Swarovski crystals for PSG defender Mamadou Sakho. I bet he thought he was quite the world leader in boot customisation, but he clearly should have waited for this **606** book to come out, because now he just looks like a cheapskate (see 1, 2, and 3 below).

4. Sir Stanley Matthews' 1952/3 season – £38,400 (at auction)

This is the pair of boots the football legend wore in the FA Cup final in 1953, the aptly named 'Matthews final'. These were sold at auction for £38,400. It is not known what Sir Stanley would have thought of footballers attaching diamonds and rubies to their boots...

3. Rio Ferdinand's Nike Total 90 Laser II's – valued at £125,000

From the sublime to the ridiculous. These have been customised by *Blue Peter*'s famous golden retriever, Goldie, who has retired from broadcasting and entered a second career as a football boot ruiner. Oh no, silly us, we mean these boots have been ruined by none other than famous conductor and part-time 'graf' artist Goldie. Apparently Rio plays at Number 5, who knew, and said numeral has pointlessly been fashioned in rose gold, with GOLD-TIPPED LACES, I ask you, while the boots are covered in 120 more stones than John Terry's (see below).

2. Nike Total 90 Laser II's as worn by Wayne Rooney – valued at £125,000

A perfectly good pair of boots ruined by 2,576 gems and more than 40 carats of diamonds, these glorified hobnails have a number 10 moulded out of rose gold. (What is it with the rose gold?) Which is currently looking a bit thin, and might need a gold transplant soon.

1. John Terry's bejewelled Umbro Specials – valued at £135,000

The boots he wore after parking in a disabled bay, sorry, we mean a 3-0 win over Belarus for England. 2,374 separate jewels, including 84 black diamonds set in white gold on the tips of the studs, have been used on these monstrosities. 27 carats of white diamonds, 11 carats of sapphires. Not quite sure who the market for these is. Perhaps there's a banker with a total lack of taste with a boot-shaped hole on the wall of his Docklands apartment.

Most expensive season tickets (2012/13)

Football is a game of highs and lows, but unfortunately the only way season ticket prices seem to go these days is up. Some of these prices, though, are way up, especially in comparison to other European clubs of the same ilk – a Bayern Munich season ticket costs just under £100, and if you want to watch all of AC Milan's game, it'll set you back a paltry £116.90. That's only £16.90 more than the most expensive ticket to ONE Arsenal home game.

10. Manchester City – £745

8.= Southampton – £780

8.= Liverpool – £780

7. West Ham United – £850

6. Fulham – £909

5. QPR – £949

4. Manchester United – £950

3 Chelsea – £1,250

2. Tottenham Hotspur – £1,845

1. Arsenal – £1,955

Special mention for Peterborough United – £15,000

No, we haven't accidentally added an extra zero. For the 2011/12 season, Championship side Peterborough United were offering eight posh (geddit?) seats at an eye-watering £15,000 a pop. That's roughly £640 per League home game. True love for your team can only take you so far, but a winning lottery ticket might help your cause a little more.